COMMENTS ON THE BOOK

THIS BOOK MAY CHANGE YOUR LIFE. . .

"Divine Rest for Human Restlessness encourages us, who have largely lost our appreciation for the Sabbath, to rethink its origins, its purpose, and its significance, and to experience anew its symbolism and its power for contemporary life. A thoughtful reading of this book may change your life. . . your life for the better."

Robert T. Fauth, President, Eden Theological Seminary

A MESSAGE ACUTELY DESIGNED TO SERVE OUR REAL NEEDS. . .

"Today's frenetic search for peace and contentment can find no better guide than the scholarly but person-centered appeal in Dr. Bacchiocchi's **Divine Rest for Human Restlessness.** His mass of authorities and his patient Biblical scholarship are a message acutely designed to serve our real needs."

A. T. DeGroot, Ph.D., D.D. Formerly, **Dean of the Graduate School, Texas Christian University.** Currently, **Director, Ecumenism Research Agency.**

A WEALTH OF RESOURCES. . .

"I am grateful to Dr. Samuele Bacchiocchi for his book **Divine Rest For Human Restlessness,** which shows how the basic human hunger for respite in the storm is really one manifestation of God's purpose in giving us the Sabbath. Dr. Bacchiocchi has given the church a wealth of resources to speak to the confusion of harried contemporary humanity."

Dr. James L. Merrell, Editor, **The Disciple** (Journal of the Christian Church).

A RICH AND STIRRING THEOLOGICAL INTERPRETATION. . .

"Divine Rest for Human Restlessness offers a rich and stirring theological interpretation of the Good News of the Sabbath. The study focuses, as a theological work should do, upon God's creation, revelation, redemption, and providential care. ... Most strongly manifest is the warm and affirmative tone throughout the book. ... This book may righly be expected to have a wide and appreciative audience."

John E. Steely, **Professor of Historical Theology, Southeastern Baptist Theological Seminary,** Wake Forest, North Carolina.

SHOWS HOW CHRISTIANS CAN ENHANCE THEIR OWN FAITH EXPRESSION. . .

"In this volume Professor Bacchiocchi has shown how Christians can enhance their own faith expression, which after all is deeply rooted in Judaism, through appreciation of this [Sabbath] central tenet of Hebraic belief. As a social ethicist as well as an ecumenist, I am also pleased by his interesting attempt to relate the Sabbath tradition to the contemporary concern for ecological integrity."

John T. Pawlikowski, OSM, Ph.D. **Chairman,** Department of Historical and Studies, Catholic Theological Union (Chicago).

GOOD FOR THE SERIOUS SCHOLAR AND INTERESTING FOR THE CASUAL READER. . .

"Divine Rest for Human Restlessness should be good for the serious scholar and also interesting to the casual reader as it brings new meaning to the completeness of the Sabbath. As the author points out, the Sabbath truly expresses God's best news for humanity."

Ellsworth S. Reile, President, **Mid-America Headquarters of Seventh-Day Adventist**

MAKES THE GOSPEL COME ALIVE IN TERMS OF THE SABBATH. . .

"**Divine Rest for Human Restlessness** makes the Gospel come alive in terms of the Sabbath.   Here the Sabbath comes forth as a gracious gift of God and not a legalistic demand to burden man.   So often, especially in Lutheran theology, Law and Grace have been solidified into two separate categories that stand over against each other. ... This study can be a helpful beginning to a restoration of the Sabbath apart from its legalistic ramifications in the life of the total body of Christ, the Church."

Ernest A. Bergeson, **Pastor of First Lutheran Church** (Waltham, Massachussetts).

COMPELLING SCHOLARSHIP AND URGENT RELEVANCE. . .

"The compelling scholarship and urgent relevance of this straightforward yet nonpolemical study immediately commend **Divine Rest for Human Restlessness** to the attention of thoughtful readers everywhere."

Donald N. Bowdle, Ph.d., Th. D.   **Dean and Professor of History and Religion, Lee College** (A Church of God Institution).

A DELIGHTFUL RARITY. . .

"Dr. Bacchiocchi has produced a delightful rarity in theological studies—an insightful, penetrating, scholarly work written in a go-ahead-with-dinner-dear-I-can't-put-this-book-down style.   **Divine rest for Human Restlessness** is a must for layman and preacher alike. ... The book should set off much-needed discussion on the Sabbath in today's world."

Dr. D. W. Holbrook, **Director, Home and Family Services.**

DESTINED TO STIMULATE THE THINKING, REVIVE THE SPIRIT. . .

"**Divine Rest for Human Restlessness** is destined to stimulate the thinking, revive the spirit and feed the soul of thousands today who are willing to lift their hearts heavenward."

H. Ward Hill, **Chairman, Division of Humanities, Union College**

THE MOST PROVOCATIVE BOOK. . .

"**Divine Rest for Human Restlessness** is the most provocative book on the meaning of the Sabbath since the publication 30 years ago of Abraham Heschel's **The Sabbath, Its Meaning for Modern Man.**   This new book, which dialogs with virtually all the literature on the subject, is a must for those who are tired of dissertations on **which** day is the Sabbath and **when** to keep it but wish to move on to the **why** and **how** of satisfying Sabbath observance."

Dr. Lawrence T. Geraty, **Professor, Archaeology and History of Antiquity, Andrews University.**

A PRICELESS CONTRIBUTION. . .

"**Divine Rest for Human Restlessness** is a priceless contribution to Sabbath literature.   Having already, in his book **From Sabbath to Sunday,** dealt with the question of "which day", he now deals with the "which way" aspect of the Sabbath.   But he goes much further than this as he majors on the "why" of the Sabbath, drawing out the mind to comprehend, in the light of the Scripture, God's reasons for His seventh-day gift to man.   The book commends itself to every Christian reader but it is a must for the minister of the Gospel."

A. N. Duffy, **Ministerial Association Secretary, Australasian Division of SDA**

BY THE SAME AUTHOR

From Sabbath to Sunday examines political, social, pagan and Christian factors which contributed to the abandonment of the Biblical Sabbath and to the adoption of Sunday observance in early Christianity. The study shows that such a change was encouraged by external pressures rather than Biblical precepts.

The outcome of the change in the day of rest and worship was not merely a different name or number of the weekday, but a different authority, meaning and experience. It has been the difference between a man-made **holiday** and God's established **holy day**.

The study closes urging to recover those permanent values of the Sabbath rest, worship, fellowship and service which are relevant for the present restless life.

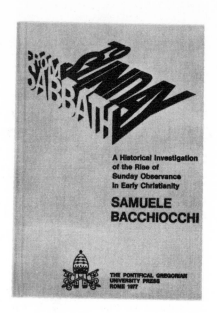

A Historical Investigation of the Rise of Sunday Observance in Early Christianity

SAMUELE BACCHIOCCHI

THE PONTIFICAL GREGORIAN UNIVERSITY PRESS ROME 1977

COMMENTS ON THE BOOK

"It is a thorough and painstaking piece of research . . ."
Bruce M. Metzger, *Professor, Princeton Theological Seminary*

"Here is a remarkable ecumenical portent . . ."
Review, *Expository Times*

"The scholarship of *From Sabbath to Sunday* is not just impeccable, it is truly a marvel . . ."
Review, *The Catholic Historical Review*

"A most impressive, helpful work of first rank scholarship . . ."
Vernon C. Grounds, *President, Denver Conservative Baptist Theological Seminary*

"The book will, I am sure, stimulate a reexamination of long established attitudes . . ."
Norman Vincent Peale, Author of *The Power of Positive Thinking*

"A scholarly and fascinating study of the transition *From Sabbath to Sunday* . . ."
Robert T. Fauth, *President, Eden Theological Seminary*

"An invaluable contribution to the Sabbath literature of our world . . ."
Dr. James P. Wesberry, *Executive Director, The Lord's Day Alliance USA*

"Altogether a stimulating and luminous study . . ."
Review, *The Banner*

"His findings are significant and deserve one's careful consideration . . ."
Thomas A. Krosnicki, *Executive Director, Catholic Bishops' Committee on Liturgy*

"A superb theological interpretation of the Sabbath . . ."
Walter Brueggeman, *Professor, Eden Theological Seminary*

"A most important contribution to the study of the origins of Sunday observance . . ."
Richard Bauckman, *Lecturer, University of Manchester*, England

The book is distributed by the author. To purchase a copy mail your order (US $9.95, postage paid) to:
        Dr. Samuele Bacchiocchi
        230 Lisa Lane
        Berrien Springs
        Michigan 49103, USA

DIVINE REST
FOR
HUMAN RESTLESSNESS

A THEOLOGICAL STUDY OF THE GOOD NEWS
OF THE SABBATH FOR TODAY

SAMUELE BACCHIOCCHI

The book is distributed by the author. To purchase
a copy mail your order (US $8.95, postage paid) to:
Dr. Samuele Bacchiocchi
230 Lisa Lane
Berrien Springs
Michigan 49103, USA

Foreword by **DR. JAMES P. WESBERRY**
Executive Director
THE LORD'S DAY ALLIANCE OF THE UNITED STATES

ROME 1980

To my wife, Anna,
without whose love, patience and encouragement
I would never have finished this book.

Cover design and art work by Franco Payne

First reprint by TESAR PRINTING COMPANY, August 1980

Offset reproduction of original edition printed by
THE PONTIFICAL GREGORIAN UNIVERSITY PRESS, June 1980

Printed by Tipografia P. U. G. - Rome

FOREWORD

Divine Rest for Human Restlessness is the precious life blood of a truly great author. He has poured heart, mind and soul into it. It is tremendous in scope, greatness and influence. Dr. Bacchiocchi is without doubt one of the most outstanding Sabbath scholars in today's world.

A Seventh-day Adventist, he was graduated from the Gregorian University in Rome, the first non-Catholic to do so and with *summa cum laude*. For his brilliant academic achievement he was awarded a gold medal donated by Pope Paul VI. His ecumenical spirit matches his vast academic attainments. His magnanimity transcends uncompromising differences and he is an eminent example of one who practices real *"agape"* love. This is evidenced by the invitation so graciously extended to the Executive Director of the Lord's Day Alliance and editor of *Sunday* magazine, a Southern Baptist, to write this foreword. This is truly a high honor for anyone and especially for me. I acknowledge it with deepest gratitude. I have great admiration, affection and appreciation for Dr. Bacchiocchi and cherish his friendship, one that has greatly enriched my life.

Except for a few paragraphs in the book which I would have written from a slightly different perspective the book is another great masterpiece of Sabbath literature. Except for these spots, which are understandable, the average reader might consider the book written for faithful observers of the Lord's Day. The book is not polemical. It is a practical presentation of how the Sabbath day of rest, worship and service can provide a divine remedy to some of the pressing human problems of today. It deals with the meaning and message of the Sabbath for Christians in today's world. The author's aim is to show how the various meanings of the Sabbath so thoroughly examined, ultimately enable Christ to bring rest, joy and peace into our lives. The attractiveness of the book is greatly enhanced by many works of art by a distinguished Italian artist.

The theme of "GOOD NEWS" like a golden thread runs through the book from beginning to end. Each chapter bears a "Good News" title. The Sabbath celebrates the good news of human roots. "Adam's first full day of life was the seventh day" . . . which he spent "not working but celebrating with his Maker the inauguration of the completed creation." A strong case is made for the Creation-Sabbath. Chapter Two tells us that God invites his people week after week to hear and celebrate the glad news of *His* perfect creation. No chapter is more beautiful than the one under the heading, "The Good News of God's Care." The Sabbath proclaims God's care for all mankind and expresses God's concern for all of his creatures. The Sabbath provides a weekly opportunity to celebrate the good news of God's loving care.

The book is chocked full of wonderful sermonic material. What a chapter the one is which sets forth "The Good News of Belonging!" The Sabbath assures us of God's constant availability. It is a symbol of belonging to God. It results in physical, social, and spiritual renewal. The Sabbath not only tells us that we are greatly loved but that we are wanted and that we belong to God who loves us. In Chapter Five we come to "Good News From the Cross"—or "The Good News of Redemption." The Sabbath tells us that God has liberated His people from their sins and death through the saving mission of his Son Jesus Christ. What thrilling good news we receive as we kneel at the foot of the cross in worship!

Nowhere will one find a more meaningful treatment of the Sabbath than in Chapter Six which deals with "The Good News of Service." The joyful celebration of the Sabbath of God's creation, sanctification, redemption and restoration of all the natural order, teaches the Christian to act not as a predator but as curator of the land. The solution of today's problems is to be found in the recovery of the Biblical values of the Sabbath.

All seven chapters are like priceless gems. They shine with peerless beauty and purpose. They hold the reader's interest. They follow in succession like an architect drawing a seven-story building—each fitting in and each closely related to the other. Each chapter seems to be the best and so it is with the last as it unfolds practical implications of Sabbathkeeping for Christian life today—good news for keeping the Sabbath in a way that honors Jesus Christ.

The last chapter very appropriately bears the title of the book, "Divine Rest for Human Restlessness." It is a summary of all six preceding chapters. It presents seven ways the Sabbath enables our Lord to bring rest, joy and peace into our lives. It is a powerful sermon in itself. This sevenfold blessing belongs to all who keep their chosen Sabbath in spirit and truth. The Sabbath is revelant. It is vital for God's people today. It brings divine rest to our human restlessness. God's great challenge to us today is not merely to prove what day the Sabbath is but "to proclaim and demonstrate by word and example to believers and unbelievers how God's gift of the Sabbath can bring permanent peace and rest to our anguished, compressed and tension-filled lives."

This is a truly great book on GOOD NEWS. The author has dealt well with his subject. He has built a gold mine of Sabbath material and made an invaluable contribution to the strengthening of the Sabbath throughout the world! No one, no matter of what faith or denomination he or she may be, can read this book without finding Divine rest for his or her restlessness. While Sundaykeeping Christians will have some difference of opinions, the principles Dr. Bacchiocchi enunciates so eloquently, scholarly, Scripturally, and scientifically, and so well illustrated, are a challenge to us all. We cannot help but wish that Dr. Bacchiocchi might have added another chapter entitled "The Good News of the Resurrection."

We rejoice and pray God's blessings upon this monumental work as it will be translated into several languages and read by those of all faiths throughout the world. May this book be used of God to call us all back to the basic principle of the Sabbath without which no individual or nation can rise to the moral level God requires of humanity.

Dr. James P. Wesberry
Editor of *Sunday*
Executive Director, *The Lord's Day Alliance of the United States*

INTRODUCTION

The story behind a book may sometimes be as interesting as the content of the book itself. My interest for a deeper understanding of the history and theology of the Sabbath goes back to my early youth. My parents taught me from childhood to celebrate the Sabbath as the memorial of God's creation and redemption. The importance my parents attached to the proper observance of the seventh-day Sabbath was largely due to the unique way in which my father discovered this significant Biblical institution.

In 1935 at the age of twenty, father, a devout Catholic at that time, was introduced for the first time to the study of the Bible by a fellow carpenter who belonged to the Waldensian Church. In his earnest desire to become better acquainted with the teachings of the Scriptures, father joined the Waldensian Church, attending with keen interest the mid-week Bible study conducted by the Waldensian School of Theology in Rome. Not long afterwards, a theology student presented a study on the origin and significance of Sunday worship. The presentation resulted in a lively debate between those students who defended the Biblical genesis of Sunday observance and those who refuted such a view, arguing instead for a later ecclesiastical origin of the day. Father regards that animated discussion, which left him astonished and perplexed, as the experience that sparked his interest for the study of the Biblical basis and historical genesis of the Lord's day.

Months of intense study led father to the conclusion that the seventh-day Sabbath had not been nullified but rather clarified and magnified by Christ's teaching and example. In fact, he became convinced that the Sabbath is a divine institution that enables the believer to express and experience commitment to the Savior. Unable to find a Christian Church that observed the seventh-day Sabbath, for several months father chose to worship privately, thus disconnecting his affiliation with the Waldensian Church. An invitation to attend a Bible study held in the home of a friend first introduced father and mother to a pastor of the Seventh-day Adventist Church, which they soon joined.

Resting and worshiping the Savior on His Sabbath day was not easy during my youth. Those were the days when the shortened workweek did not yet exist and thus Saturday was a working day for most people, including teachers and students. My classmates called me a "Jew" for missing school on Saturday. Relatives and priests frequently urged me to abandon the beliefs and practices of my Seventh-day Adventist Church, especially Sabbathkeeping. Such frequent confrontations instilled within me the desire someday to investigate the history, theology and relevancy of the Sabbath day. As a teenager, however, I could have never imagined that one day I would be allowed to conduct such an investigation at the prestigious Pontifical Gregorian University. It was unthinkable in those days for a non-Catholic to be accepted for a regular doctoral program at a Pontifical University in Rome.

My acceptance at the Gregoriana in the Fall of 1969 marked the admission of the first "separated brother" into a regular study program in over 400 years of history of the University. I hasten to acknowledge that I was treated not as a "separated brother" but as a genuine Christian brother. The climate of cordiality and respect was exemplified especially in the freedom and guidance I received while conducting my doctoral research into the controversial question of the genesis of Sunday observance in early Christianity.

The publication of my abridged dissertation *From Sabbath to Sunday*, by the Pontifical Gregorian University Press in 1977, represented for me not only a dream come true but also an unprecedented opportunity to share my findings with scholars and Christans of all persuasions. In fact, the scores of generally positive reviews that have appeared in leading journals and magazines, as well as the hundreds of favorable comments that the book has elicited from scholars of different confessions, have contributed to already six reprints of the book for a total of over 70,000 copies.

The many responses and evaluations I have received suggest the existence of significant trends. There seems to be, for example, a genuine interest to re-examine the historical process that led many Christians to abandon a millenerian institution such as the observance of the seventh-day Sabbath and to adopt Sunday instead. Such an interest is apparently reflective of the renewed effort being made to understand the relation between the Old and New Testaments and the concomitant relation between Judaism and Christianity. At a time of increasing dialogue between the two faiths, it is especially helpful to appreciate more fully the fact that Christianity sprang up out of the roots and trunk of Judaism.

It has been most gratifying to note the willingness on the part of numerous scholars to acknowledge the necessity of reconsidering the origin and the assumptions underlying Sunday observance, in the light of my study *From Sabbath to Sunday*. Willy Rordorf, for example, in the preface to the Italian edition of his book *Sabato e domenica nella Chiesa antica* (May 1979), graciously writes: "It is evident that Bacchiocchi does not share the view of the historical evolution [of Sunday observance] which is presented in the introduction to our collection of documents. Yet he refers to the same texts. It will be necessary therefore to take up the very same texts and study them more carefully, if we are to arrive at a better ecumenical understanding among Christians of different confessional origin" (p. viii). In reviewing my book in *The Expository Times* (1978) Marcus Ward remarks: "After reading this, any reasonable man must question the general easy, uncritical acceptance of Sunday as the Lord's day" (p. 349). Similarly Clayton K. Harrop, New Testament Professor at Golden Gate Baptist Theological Seminary, in his appraisal of *From Sabbath to Sunday*, acknowledges that the book "should cause those of us who still believe that Sunday is the day for Christian worship to look more carefully at our reasons for such practice and be less harsh toward those who choose to differ from us."[1] In a similar vein Norman Vincent Peale comments: "The book will, I am sure, stimulate a re-examination of long established attitudes."[2]

The willingness on the part of some to re-examine historical and theological assumptions underlying the origin and nature of Sunday observance is apparently reflective of another significant trend, namely, the recognition that, as stated by Norman Vincent Peale, "Christians everywhere stand in need of the spiritual values inherent in the Sabbath."[3] Upon his election as Executive Director of the Lord's Day Alliance of the USA, Dr. James P. Wesberry stated in his inaugural address: "One of our nation's greatest needs as we come to our bicentennial is to get back to the Fourth Commandment and once again 'Remember the Sabbath day, to keep it holy.' Where will we be 200 years from now if the present trend regarding this Day keeps up? I want to promise you today that I will give every ounce of my strength and the very best I have by way of leadership to promoting this noble and thrilling cause for the glory of God. It challenges all that is within me."[4]

In keeping with such a noble commitment Dr. Wesberry, a distinguished Southern Baptist, has graciously offered to write the foreword for this book. Words fail to express my gratitude to him for commending my book so generously to the public. Though we disagree on the day on which to rest and worship, we mutually agree on its vital function for the survival of Christianity. At a time when secular concerns often obscure sacred commitments, when gadgets have become for many more important than God, when the tyranny of things enslaves many lives, the Sabbath provides a vital divine lifeline to rescue us from the bondage of materialism by elevating our thoughts for one day above the world of matter, thus enabling us to rediscover the peace of God for which we were created.

To acknowledge my indebtedness to all those who directly or indirectly have contributed to the realization of this book is a most difficult task. Indirectly, I have received encouragement and inspiration to write this book from scores of scholars and lay-persons of all confessions, who, after reading *From Sabbath to Sunday,* have written to me expressing their common concern for the need to recover the values and experience of genuine Sabbathkeeping. Directly, I am endebted to Dr. E. K. Vande Vere, Dr. Emil Leffler and Mrs. V. H. Campbell, for reading the manuscript and suggesting stylistic improvements. Special thanks go to Dr. Beverly B. Beach for taking time not only to improve the text but also to make valuable suggestions. Words are inadequate to express my indebtedness to Dr. Leona Glidden Running, Professor of Biblical Languages at Andrews University, for having unstintingly given of her time and skill to correct first the manuscript and then the galley proof.

Franco Payne, an Italian artist, is to be credited for all the illustrations contained in the book, including the design of the cover. His ability to portray abstract ideas visually will undoubtedly be appreciated by many readers. Recognition must also be given to the Pontifical Gregorian University Press for typesetting and printing the book in a record time of about two months.

Special thanks go to Donald A. Carson, Associate Professor of New Testament at Trinity Evangelical Divinity School, for making available to me the "unified" symposium (about 700 pages) which was sponsored by the Tyndale Fellowship for Biblical Research in Cambridge, England. Carson has edited and contributed chapters to this monumental study, which is soon to be published under the title *From Sabbath to the Lord's Day: A Biblical Historical and Theological Investigation.* Though I do not concur with all the conclusions of this work, yet it does represent in my view the most objective and realistic attempt made by Sundaykeeping scholars to establish the historical genesis of Sunday observance. The privilege offered to me to read this yet unpublished manuscript has made it possible for me to react to it in a few places in the course of the present study.

I am under no illusion that this book will convince everyone to observe the day God made for the physical and spiritual well-being of mankind (Mark 2:27). The most I can hope is that these theological reflections on the relevance of the message and experience of the Sabbath to some of the pressing contemporary human needs will aid some persons to discover a largely forgotten treasure, the Sabbath. These pages have been written with the earnest desire to share with others the blessing the Sabbath has brought to my life. My fervent hope is now that this book will help those persons who struggle to find meaning in their existence, who seek for rest in their restless lives, who live among personal and social contradictions and tensions, to find through the Sabbath *Divine Rest for their Human Restlessness.*

The Sabbath reminds us that our ancestral roots are good because they are rooted in God Himself. It reassures us that not only our origin but also our destiny is rooted in God. Thus it provides us with a sense of continuity with the past and a hope for the future.

CHAPTER
I

the Sabbath
GOOD NEWS
of human roots

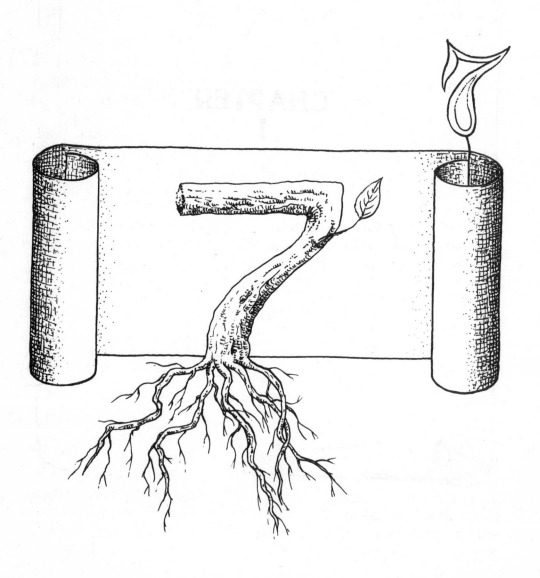

The recent book and film *Roots* by Alex Haley have captivated millions of readers and viewers. Probably Haley never dreamed that his novel would spur so many Americans to search for their ancestral roots in archives and libraries throughout the United States and across the ocean.

The eager search for ancestral roots is perhaps symptomatic of a deeper search, namely, the search for life's meaning. The urge to trace back one's family tree may well reflect the desire to discover not only one's roots, but also the very meaning of one's life. What many thinking persons fear most today is not total destruction, but total meaninglessness. Modern science and technology have given us plenteous research, abundance of goods, instant communication and a mass of facts! What gives meaning to life, however, is not plenteous research but profound beliefs, it is not abundance of goods but abiding goals, it is not instant communication but individual commitment, it is not mass of facts but a mastering faith.

The sense of disillusionment, emptiness, alienation and meaninglessness experienced by many modern thinking individuals cannot be overcome by tracing ancestral roots, nor through skillfully developed economic, scientific or political systems, but only through a faith that reaches higher than mankind. Such faith must have a three-dimensional scope, that is to say, it must embrace the belief in a divine origin, a present purpose and an ultimate destiny for human life.

PART I

RELEVANCE OF THE SABBATH

1. *A Basis For a Cosmic Faith*

The Sabbath is relevant for modern persons because it nourishes such a three-dimensional faith. The themes of the Sabbath, as we shall study them, encompass creation, redemption and final restoration; the past, the present and the future; man, nature and God. If, as aptly expressed by Paul Tillich, a "symbol participates in the reality for which it stands," [1] then the cosmic symbology of the Sabbath provides modern believers with a basis for a cosmic faith: a faith that reaches out to past, present and future realities. [2]

The only logical place to start our inquiry into the cosmic message of the Sabbath and its relevancy for today is at the Biblical account of its origin. Generally, the origin of an institution affects its relevancy. Moreover, the very first words found in the Biblical record on any subject can be regarded as the keystone of all later developments. Even a minimal acquaintance with the Bible recognizes that the origin of the Sabbath is explicitly connected with the creation event. In fact, a study of the structure of the first creation story (Gen. 1:1-2:3) reveals, as will be shown in the following chapter, that the seventh day represents the majestic culmination and completion of creation. According to the Biblical record, in six days God first created spaces (heaven, earth and sea) and second, inhabitants for those spaces (fish, fowl, land animals and man); then, "On the seventh day God finished his work which he had done, and he rested on the seventh day from all his work which he had done. So God blessed the seventh day and hallowed it, because on it God rested from all his work which he had done in creation" (Gen. 2:2-3).

2. Celebration of Human Beginnings

Our immediate concern is not to reflect on the profound theological implications of what God did and said on the seventh day, but rather to evaluate the significance of the seventh day in the chronological setting of the story. It is noteworthy that the account of the seventh day is located at the dividing point between the end of the first story of creation (Gen. 1:1-2:3) and the beginning of the second story of the creation which deals with man and his garden home (Gen. 2:4-25). This collocation of the seventh day at this dividing point implies the significant role of the seventh day: the celebration and inauguration of human history.

In the first creation story the seventh day is closely connected with human origins. This is indicated by the fact that it follows immediately after the creation and blessing of mankind—the crown of creation (Gen. 1:26-31). In fact, the story of man and that of the Sabbath are not only given in sequence but also receive greater coverage than all other creation events. This reflects both their interdependency and their importance.[3] Adam's first full day of life was the seventh day which, one can legitimately assume, he spent not working but celebrating with his Maker the inauguration of the completed and perfect creation. This assumption rests on the fact that man was created to live in accordance with the "image" and example of his

Creator (Gen. 1:26). In fact, in the Fourth Commandment, the injunction to work and to rest is based upon man's responsibility to imitate the pattern established by God at the creation week (Ex. 20:8-11). Moreover, the Lord Himself declared emphatically that "the Sabbath was made for man" (Mark 2:27). The Hebrew word for man is *"Adam,"* a name used to designate both a specific person—Adam—and mankind as a whole (cf. Gen. 5:2). In the first creation story, then, the seventh day marks the celebration of the creation of this world in general and of man in particular. For this reason Philo, the great Jewish philosopher, delights to call the day "the birthday of the world"[4] and Ralph Waldo Emerson names it "the jubilee of the world."[5] For the same reason we have chosen in this chapter to designate the seventh day as the *Good News of Human Roots* since the day celebrates human beginnings.

3. *Inauguration of Human History*

The second creation story (Gen. 2:4-25),[6] which describes in greater detail the genesis and early history of human life, is also closely linked to the seventh day, since it is placed in the context of its institution. The story, in fact, begins immediately after the account of the celebration of the first seventh day (Gen. 2:2-3) with the words: "These are the generations of the heavens and the earth" (Gen. 2:4a—RSV). A more accurate translation of *toledoth*—"generations" is "history," "story," "account." The last rendering is adopted by the New International Version which reads: "This is the account of the heavens and the earth when they were created."

Why does the story of the foundation of human life take the institution of the seventh day as its point of departure? Various scholars recognize in this the author's intention to link the history of salvation directly to the institution of the seventh day.[7] Ten times in Genesis the history of God's people is linked together by means of the *toledoth*—"history, generations" and the first link in this chain is placed in conjunction with the seventh day.[8] Why? Undoubtedly because the day celebrates the inauguration of human history. A second possible reason is suggested by the fact that the creation week, with its culmination of the seventh day, provides the time-unit for measuring the chronological development of history which finds expression in the genealogical sequence. We shall later see that the Sabbath measures history not only *quantitatively* but also *qualitatively*, by focusing on God's saving activities manifested in and through His people. This brief analysis has shown that according to the Biblical witness, the origin of the seventh-day Sabbath is rooted in the creation event. Its function within that event is to celebrate the completion of creation and the inauguration of human history, or we might say, to celebrate the *Good News of Human Roots.*

PART II

THEORIES OF THE ORIGIN OF THE SABBATH

Before considering the far-reaching implications of the Biblical account of the Edenic origin of the Sabbath, attention must in all fairness be given to other explanations of its origin which have been vigorously advocated over the last century. Without denying the relevance of the Biblical record, in many cases historians have preferred to trace the Sabbath back as far as possible in the extrabiblical sources, or we might say, to "the things the historian can see," rather than to the "things that are not seen." The results of these endeavors are far from being unanimous. The various hypotheses which have been proposed, as we shall see, not only fail to convince but implicitly point to the Biblical explanation as deserving greater recognition.

The leading theories date the origin of the Sabbath respectively (1) before or at the time of Moses, (2) after the settlement in Canaan, (3) during or after the exile. The main reasons adduced for these origins can be labelled as (1) astrological-astronomic, (2) socio-economic, (3) magical-symbolic.

1. *Pre-Mosaic/Mosaic Origin*

Saturn. The theory of the Mosaic origin of the Sabbath rests primarily on the supposed influence of Saturn or of lunar phases or of a Mesopotamian seven-day period. An old and still common theory derives the OT Sabbath from the Saturn day of the Kenites, a tribe with whom Moses came in close contact by marriage when he fled to Midian (Judg. 4:11, 17).[9] It is speculated that the day of Saturn was a tabu-day on which the Kenites, who were metal workers, would not light their smelting ovens. The Israelites would have adopted this Kenite tabu-day and extended its regulations to normal household chores. Support for this hypothesis is sought in the prohibition of firemaking on the Sabbath (Ex. 35:3; Num. 15:32-36) which is made dependent upon the supposed ancestral worship of Sakkuth and Kaiwan (Am. 5:26), alleged names for Saturn.[10]

The primary weakness of such an hypothesis is that it rests on the assumption that the Kenites had a seven-day week in which its respective days were dedicated to the planetary gods. To the best of our knowledge, however, the introduction of the planetarian week occurred much later, approximately at the time of the origin of Christianity.[11] Moreover, there is no indication in the OT or in the ancient Jewish literature that the Sabbath was ever regarded as sacred to Saturn.[12] For these and other reasons the Kenite hypothesis is now discredited by practically all scholars.[13]

Lunar phases. The lunar theory which links the origin of the Sabbath with the days associated with the four phases of the moon and/or with the day of the full moon has enjoyed greater popularity. These days apparently had some religious significance in ancient Mesopotamia, the homeland of Abraham. The evidence for the existence of such days is provided primarily by an Assyrian calendar which was found among the cuneiform tablets in the British Museum in 1869 by the Assyriologist George Smith.[14] This calendar, which appears to be a transcript of a much older Babylonian original,[15] lists the thirty days of the thirteenth or intercalary month and marks the 7th, 14th, 19th,[16] 21st, and 28th days of the month as *ûmê lemnûti*, that is, evil or unfavorable days (*dies nefasti*). On these days the king, the priest and the physician were to abstain from certain activities, in order not to offend the gods.[17] The origin of these evil days is attributed by some to the four phases of the moon which recur approximately every seven days.[18] The Hebrews would thus have derived their Sabbath from an ancient Mesopotamian lunar-phases cycle.[19] The mention in the OT of the Sabbath in conjunction with the new moon is presented as a lingering trace of this lunar origin of the Sabbath.[20]

This theory, though seemingly persuasive, reveals under close examination at least three weaknesses. First, since the duration of a lunar month (lunation) is not 28 days (4×7) but just over 29 days (a period which cannot be subdivided into four exact weeks of seven days each),[21] any association of the seventh day with the phases of the moon must be viewed not as an original but as a secondary development. Second, if the Babylonians employed the evil days in a civil "weekly" cycle (which apparently they never did),[22] then the cycle would be interrupted at the beginning of every month, since its first evil day (*ûmu lemnu*—7th day) occurred after eight or nine days from the last evil day (28th day) of the previous month. The difference in the number of days depended on whether the last lunar month had 29 or 30 days. Such an irregular cycle tied to the beginning of the lunar month could hardly have given origin to the Hebrew week which was a constant seven-day week, running unfettered by lunar or solar cycles. Third, nothing in the cuneiform texts indicates that the Babylonians ever employed the recurring evil days as a "weekly" division of time for civil purposes. The rules for such days affected the king and priests but not the people as a whole.[23] Moreover, this was not the only "weekly" cycle known to the Babylonians, since there are also frequent instances of the "division of the month into six parts, involving a five-day week."[24] In contrast, the Hebrew holy (not evil) Sabbath was employed as the *only* religious and civil weekly division of time and was observed as a festival by the entire community.

Šabattu. In several Akkadian documents of ancient Mesopotamia occurs the term *šabattu,* which is strikingly similar to the Hebrew word for Sabbath (*šabbat*). The term apparently designated the fifteenth day of the month, that is, the day of the full moon. An example from about the time of Abraham is found in the famous Babylonian creation epic called *Enuma elish* (5:18), where Marduk addresses the moon saying, "At the month's very start, rising over the land, thou shalt have luminous horns to signify six days. On the seventh day be thou a [half-] crown. At *šabbatu,* stand in opposition [to the sun] in mid-month."[25] What significance was attached to such a day? Apparently, the day of the full moon—*šabbatu*—was sacred to Sin, the moon-god who occupied a significant place in the Babylonian pantheon.[26] In several tablets *šabattu* is defined as *ûm nûh libbi,* usually translated as "day of rest of the heart" or "day of appeasement."[27] *Šabattu,* then, was the day of the full moon, when presumably the gods were propitiated or appeased.[28] The similarity of look and sound between the Akkadian *šabattu* and the Hebrew *šabbat* (Sabbath), as well as the association in the OT between the Sabbath and the new moon, has led some scholars to conclude confidently that the Sabbath was originally not weekly but a monthly festival connected with the day of the full moon. The transformation of the Sabbath from a monthly to a weekly festival would have occurred much later, under Ezekiel in response to a demand for rest.[29]

The remarkable ingenuity of such a theory has astonished several scholars. Karl Budde, for example, registers his regret for such an unfounded theory, by pointing out that there is not "a single word in Ezekiel which prescribes a new mode of celebration for the Sabbath. On the contrary Ezekiel complains constantly (20:12ff; 22:8, 26; 23:38; 44:24) that for long years . . . Israel has failed to observe the Sabbath *in the old*

sense." [30] The champions of the full moon theory ignore also
such older passages as 2 Kings 4:23 and 2 Kings 11:4-12 which
speak of the Sabbath over two centuries before Ezekiel's time.[31]
Furthermore, these scholars fail to explain how an alleged
"monthly Sabbath" came to be observed as a weekly day of
rest and worship, irrespective of the day of the full moon. If
the Israelites had observed the day of the full moon for centuries, why is it that no memory of it can be found in later
times? For example, the day of the full moon in Hebrew is
called not *"šabbat"* but *kese* (Ps. 81:4), a term which has no
word-form association with or derivation from the Akkadian
šabattu. It would seem therefore that the Babylonian lunar
month (with its evil days and *šabattu*) had no direct influence
on the origin of the Hebrew Sabbath and calendar. This is
also borne out by the fact that the Jewish month-names show
no similarity to the Babylonian ones.[32] Any ideological or etymological, that is, word-form similarity between the Babylonian
šabattu/evil days and the Hebrew Sabbath must then be explained on the basis of a common Semitic heritage. The
Babylonians were related to the Hebrews both linguistically
and culturally, thus both could readily have learned about the
creation Sabbath from a common source. However, as in the
case of the story of Creation (*Enuma elish*) and of the story
of the Flood (*Gilgamesh Epic*), the Sabbath too could have been
corrupted and transformed from a holy day to evil days associated with lunar phases. Such a development, however, suggests not derivation but deterioration of the primeval Sabbath.
In fact, no trace can be found in the Babylonian *šabattu* or
evil days of the lofty purposes and human values expressed by
the Biblical Sabbath.

Seven-day period. Several ancient Mesopotamian documents mention celebrations or events lasting a period of seven
days. For example, two inscriptions attributed to King Gudea
of Lagash (a Mesopotamian city state), who ruled in the twenty-
first century B.C., speak of a celebration of the dedication of
a temple which lasted seven days and of the installation of
certain steles which took seven days.[33] In the Mesopotamian
stories of the Flood, the duration of the storm was seven days
and the first bird was sent out seven days after the ship came
to rest upon a mountain.[34] On the basis of these and a few
other similar references,[35] some scholars have confidently asserted that beyond "the shadow of a doubt" the OT Sabbath
derives from an ancient Mesopotamian seven-day week.[36] Such
a bold claim, however, rests more on fantasies than facts. The
evidence for an early Babylonian week, as Siegfried H. Horn,

a seasoned and knowledgeable archeologist, rightly underscores, "is meager indeed, especially in view of the hundreds of thousands of cuneiform records recovered in the Mesopotamian valley. If the ancient Sumerians, Babylonians, or Assyrians possessed a week like that of the Hebrews in Biblical times, or gave to the seventh day of such a week special sanctity, they would certainly have left us a clearer record of it." [37]

The reference to a dedicatory celebration lasting seven days can hardly be construed as proof for the existence of a seven-day week, since "records exist of many temples dedicated at other times, by other kings, in shorter or longer periods of time." [38] Similarly the seven-day periods mentioned in the Mesopotamian Flood stories may represent a vague recollection of the existence of a seven-day week at the time of the Biblical Flood but not necessarily a reflection of its common usage at the time of the composition of these stories. The Biblical account of the Flood contains repeated references to seven-day periods (Gen. 8:8-12), thus suggesting, as commentators generally recognize, the existence of the seven-day week. [39] The cuneiform Flood stories, in spite of distortions and legendary embellishments, do come closer to the Biblical story than the Flood stories from other parts of the world. [40] The similarity suggests the perpetration of the Biblical notion of a seven-day week in literary works, even though its civil usage apparently fell into desuetude as indicated by the existence of shorter "weeks." [41] "The logical conclusion is", as aptly stated by Horn, "that there had once been a seven-day week, but that it had been lost before historical records were kept, and that only an indistinct memory of it remained."

2. Settlement

Social institution. The failure of extra-Biblical sources to provide a satisfactory explanation for the origin of the Sabbath has driven scholars to search for its roots within OT texts. Such a study has led some to conclude that the Sabbath was first introduced after the occupation of Canaan. [42] The reasons given for its introduction are based primarily on social and economic considerations. The need to give a day of rest to laborers and the necessity of a market day in which to sell and buy produce would have induced the introduction of the Sabbath as a "day off." [43] In time, it is argued, the Sabbath underwent an evolution from a social to a religious institution, that is, from a day for the sake of slaves and of marketing, to a day for the sake of Yahweh. Credit for such a transformation is given to the prophets and priests who by the time of the exile developed a theology of the Sabbath to promote its religious observance.[44]

Support for such a theory is sought in those texts which present the Sabbath primarily in social terms. Of these, Exodus 23:12 and 34:21 are viewed as particularly important. The former enjoins to rest on the seventh day so "that your ox and your ass may have rest, and the son of your bondmaid, and the alien, may be refreshed." The latter text stresses the need to observe the seventh day even in peak agricultural seasons: "in plowing time and in harvest you shall rest." The importance of these texts is seen in the fact that they contain no explicit theological motivation, and thus they are regarded as the "earliest version of the Sabbath commandment."[45] Moreover, since these texts speak of agricultural activities which demanded the use of cattle, slaves and day laborers—conditions supposedly unknown during the wilderness wandering—the Sabbath must then have been introduced after the settlement in Canaan to meet new social needs.

The logic of such arguments cannot be denied, but, in our opinion, it rests on unwarranted presuppositions. It is assumed, for instance, that humanitarian concerns preceded theological reflections and formulations, and consequently those texts of the Pentateuch which speak of the Sabbath strictly in social terms must reflect the original form of Sabbathkeeping, while those texts that spell out religious or theological aspects must apply to a later period.[46] What motivated humanitarian considerations and regulations at a time when human life had such little value? Superstitious and cultic understanding of land and people could hardly have provided such motivation, since we find no traces of them in the OT. Moreover, have mythical superstitions ever promoted the cause of human rights? This was hardly the case among the contemporaries of the ancient Israelites, who, for instance, saw no evil in the institution of slavery and used their legal systems to protect it.[47] On the contrary, among the Israelites the sabbatical institutions provided for a day of rest for all, including slaves, for the cancelation of debts (a major cause of slavery) and the emancipation of slaves.[48]

Does not the humanitarian function of the Sabbath presuppose theological reasons and motivations? Theological motives, however, need not always be explicitly expressed, especially when the Sabbath is inserted among basic civil and cultic laws (cf. Ex. 23:12; 34:21). Civil codes in most cases provide no rational explanation for the laws. Nevertheless, even in Exodus 23—a chapter that contains a variety of civil and cultic legislation—the Sabbath is not devoid of theological justification. In fact, the very so-called "earliest version of the sabbath commandment" (Ex. 23:12) is placed in the context of an admonition to be considerate toward the underprivileged: "You shall not oppress a stranger; you know the heart of a stranger, for you were strangers in the land of Egypt" (Ex. 23:9). Is not the appeal to the bitter Egyptian servitude from which Yahweh delivered the Israelites a strong theological motivation to induce them to show kindness toward others?[49] Were not the weekly Sabbaths and the sabbatical year helpful vehicles to express appreciation for divine mercy received by showing compassion toward others? "To keep the Sabbath for men's sake," as Abram Herbert Lewis writes, "is to keep it for God's sake."[50] Is it not true even today that the recognition of divine mercies received constitutes the strongest theological motivation for humanitarian considerations?

What about the reference to cattle, slaves and laborers that were to be allowed to rest on the Sabbath even at the peak of agricultural seasons? Does this imply that the Sabbath was first introduced after the occupation of Canaan, when the Israelites were settled in the land and employed dependent workers?[51] Such a conclusion fails to consider two significant factors. First, recent investigations into the preconquest period suggest that the Israelites lived not as wandering nomads but as semisettled nomads on the fringes of the desert (possibly Negeb).[52] This condition could explain the introduction of agriculturally oriented laws before the actual settlement in Canaan. Second, even granting that the Israelites lived in the desert as wandering nomads and did not own oxen, asses, or slaves or cultivate land, could not a prophetic gifted leader such as Moses have foreseen beyond the immediate situation of the people and thus promulgate laws to meet future conditions? Did not the Pilgrim Fathers, before disembarking on Cape Cod, sign the *Mayflower Compact* which became for many years the principal governmental charter of the Plymouth Colony?[53] Why should a similar foresight be denied to Moses?

Market days—Number seven. To explain how the Israelites after the occupation came to choose the seventh day, appeal is sometimes made to the alleged influence of the Canaanites, market days or the number seven. Did the Israelites adopt the Sabbath from the Canaanites, as some suggest?[54] The proposal may appear plausible, especially since the Canaanites exerted an influence not indifferent upon the Israelites. The fact remains, however, that no trace of the Sabbath has ever been found among the Canaanites or among their kinsmen, the

Phoenicians.[55] Did the Israelites develop the Sabbath out of an original seven-day market week?[56] Market days recurring regularly every five, six, eight or ten days were common among many peoples. What militates against this theory is the fact that no trace has been found of regular market weeks in Palestine, much less at seven-day intervals. Moreover the prophetic denunciation of the trading done by some on the Sabbath suggests that the day at times deteriorated into a market day rather than originated from it (Neh. 13:14-22; Jer. 17:19-27; Amos 8:5).

Did the Israelites derive their Sabbath from the great symbolic importance attached to the number seven by many ancient Near Eastern people?[57] Some have suggested that the number seven because of its prestige was first used to fix the duration of spring and fall festivals (the feast of Unleavened Bread and Booths, each of which lasted seven days) and that later these seven-day festival units were used to measure time throughout the year.[58] This hypothesis sounds interesting but does not explain how the number seven became prestigious in the first place. Moreover, it would seem more plausible that the existence of a continuous seven-day week would influence the duration of an annual seven-day festival rather than vice versa.[59] Obviously, a connection exists among the seven-day week, the seven-day annual festivals and the number seven. But, since the number seven runs contrary to every known astronomical measurement of time, the best explanation for its importance and its usage still remains the Biblical account of the divine blessing and sanctification of the seventh day at the completion of creation.

This sketchy survey should serve to illustrate some of the weaknesses present in the criteria used to defend the settlement-origin of the Sabbath as a social institution. We have shown that this theory provides no convincing alternative explanation for the origin of the Sabbath because it rests on an arbitrary selection of texts, unwarranted assumptions and unfounded claims regarding the alleged influence of market days or of the number seven.

3. Exile

Innovation or consolidation? The period of the Jewish exile in Babylon (605-539 B.C.) is generally regarded as crucial for the history of the Sabbath. For some scholars, as was noted earlier,[60] the exile represents the very time of the origin of the Sabbath. For others, the exilic and postexilic periods are the turning point

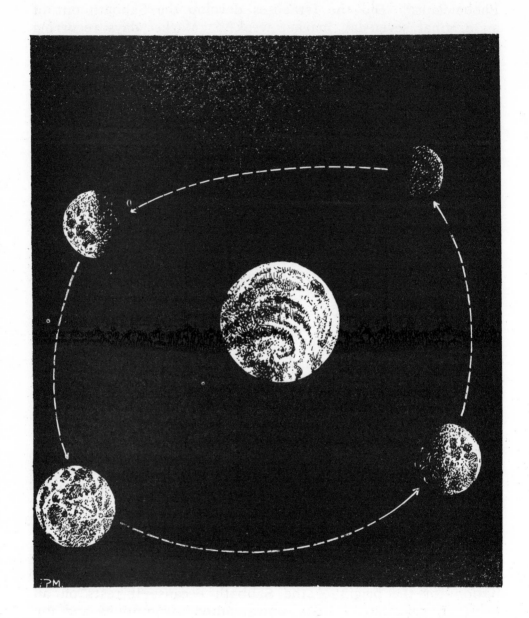

Since the number seven runs contrary to every known astronomical measurement of time, the best explanation for its importance and its usage still remains the Biblical account of the divine blessing and sanctification of the seventh day at the completion of creation.

in the theological and cultic development of the Sabbath.[61]   We
need not be detained further by the first view, since we found it
to be openly contradicted by OT preexilic references to the Sabbath.   The second view, however, deserves some consideration.
The exile, it is claimed, contributed in at least two ways to transform the Sabbath from a social institution (a day for the sake
of slaves and cattle) to a religious festival (a day for God's
sake).   First, the loss of the homeland and of dependent workers
would have eliminated the social reasons for the Sabbath and
at the same time induced the search for theological justifica-
tions.   Second, it is argued that the loss of a *holy place* (Jerusalem temple in 586 B.C.) made *holy time* (the Sabbath) of utmost importance, especially since it could be celebrated even
in exile.[62]

The information provided by the OT for this period lends
no support to this Sabbath transformation theory.   The exilic
prophets do not present an innovative theology and practice
of the Sabbath.   Ezekiel, for example, prescribes no new manner or motivation for the celebration of the Sabbath.[63]   On the
contrary, the prophet goes as far as viewing the past profanation of the Sabbath as a major cause for the calamities which
had befallen Israel (Ezek. 20:15-16, 21, 36; 22:26, 31).   To promote a return to proper Sabbathkeeping, Ezekiel appeals not
to a *new* theological rational but to the *old* historical meaning
of the Sabbath, namely, its being a "sign" or pledge of Israel's
covenantal relationship with God (Ezek. 20:12, 20).   This covenantal function of the Sabbath was most relevant during the
exile experience, for the threat of national disintegration or even
disappearance was an ever-present reality.   Ezekiel, however,
presents the covenantal meaning and function of the Sabbath,
not as a new concept arising out of the exilic experience, but
as a traditional belief rooted in the historical genesis of Israel,
the Exodus experience.   In other words, the strength of the
prophet's argument rests on his application of a long-estab-
lished meaning of the Sabbath to the new critical exile situation.[64]

Did the Sabbath develop into holy time as a result of the
loss of a holy place (the Jerusalem temple)?   Again, this is
hardly suggested by Ezekiel, who frequently associates the Sabbath with holy things (Ezek. 22:26; 23:38) and with service
in the future temple (Ezek. 45:17; 46:1-4, 12).[65]   The exilic period
with its deportation and cultic deprivation seems to have contributed not to radical ideological or practical *innovations*, but
rather to the *consolidation* of institutions such as the Sabbath.
This is suggested also by the messages given and measures

adopted by Jeremiah during the exile and by Nehemiah after the exile, to stop trading activities in Jerusalem on the Sabbath (Jer. 17:19-27; Neh. 10:31, 33; 13:15-22). Their efforts were aimed not at transforming the Sabbath institution, but at reforming its abuses.

These observations are not intended to deny that later (during the intertestamental period) the Sabbath underwent radical transformations. In fact, the Sabbath came to be regarded as a gift given by God exclusively to Israel.[66] Such an exclusivistic view encouraged both rabbinical and sectarian Judaism to develop comprehensive guidelines to insure proper Sabbath-keeping.[67] Unfortunately, those guidelines, as emphatically reported in the Gospels, became a legalistic burden rather than a spiritual guide to genuine Sabbathkeeping.[68] This development, however, occurred after the period of the Old Testament.

What conclusions can be drawn from this sketch of the leading hypotheses regarding the origin of the Sabbath? We have found that all the conjectures regarding the *time* (Mosaic, settlement, exilic) and the *manner* (astronomical, sociological, magical) complicate rather than clarify the origin of the Sabbath and of the seven-day week. No proof can be brought forward for the hypotheses that the Sabbath derives from the planet Saturn, from the phases of the moon, from market days, from the prestige of the number seven or from the exile. One wonders if all these conjectures that reduce the Sabbath to a mythical or sociological phenomenon may not reflect a hidden or overt desire of some to relieve themselves from the necessity of understanding and observing it. It is hoped that the unsuccessful attempts to base the origin of the Sabbath in extra-Biblical sources will provoke a fresh appreciation for the Biblical account of the Sabbath origin and meaning.

PART III

THE CREATION SABBATH

1. *Objections and Objectors to Creation Sabbath*

The theories of the origin of the Sabbath, just surveyed, represent the conclusions drawn by critical scholars over the past century. But, puzzling as it may seem, the creation-origin of the Sabbath was challenged long before our time and by such "conservative" people as the Palestinian Jews, the early Fathers, radical groups of the Reformation, and more recently, modern dispensationalists. Why, one wonders, have so many

over the centuries rejected the matter-of-fact account of the
Edenic origin of the Sabbath given several times in the Pen-
tateuch (Gen. 2:1-3; Ex. 20:11; Ex. 31:17)? The reasons differ.
Brief consideration will now be given to the principal ones.

Identity crisis. The strong desire to preserve a Jewish
identity, at a time when Hellenistic forces were pressing for the
abandonment of the Jewish religion, apparently led Palestinian
Rabbis to reduce the Sabbath from a creation ordinance established for mankind to a Mosaic ordinance given exclusively to
Israel. Such a development was encouraged especially by the
determined efforts of the Syrian king Antiochus Epiphanes to
implement a program of radical Hellenization of the Jews
through the prohibition of sacrifices and Sabbathkeeping (175
B.C.). The result was that many Jews fell away, "sacrificed
to the gods and desecrated the Sabbath" (1 Macc. 1:43). Pious
Jews resisted passionately against such Hellenization, preferring
to be slaughtered rather than desecrating the Sabbath (1 Macc.
2:32-38). The need to preserve a Jewish identity at that critical
time inspired an exclusivistic and nationalistic view of the Sabbath. Some Rabbis taught that the privilege of Sabbathkeeping was denied to the Gentiles and reserved exclusively to Israel.
As stated in the book of *Jubilees*, "He [God] allowed no other
people or peoples to keep the Sabbath on this day, except Israel
only; to it alone he granted to eat and drink and keep the Sabbath on it" (2:31).[69] If the patriarchs are sometimes mentioned
as keeping the Sabbath, this is regarded as an exception "before
it [the Sabbath] was given" to Israel.[70]

The notion of the Sabbath as an exclusively Jewish institution, established not at creation for all mankind but by Moses
for Israel alone, makes God guilty, to say the least, of favoritism
and discriminatory practices. It must be said, however, that
such a view represents a late secondary development rather
than an original tradition. This is borne out by the fact that
in Hellenistic (Greek) Judaism the Sabbath was viewed as a
creation ordinance for mankind.[71] Moreover, even in Palestinian
literature (both apocalyptic and rabbinic) frequent mention is
made of God, Adam, Seth, Abraham, Jacob, and Joseph as scrupulously observing the Sabbath.[72]

Apologetic need. The notion of the Mosaic origin and exclusive Jewish nature of the Sabbath was adopted by some of
the early Fathers to challenge those Christians who defended
the binding obligations of the Sabbath commandment in the
Christian dispensation. The standard and frequent argument
is that the patriarchs and righteous men before Moses did not
observe the Sabbath, and thus the day must be regarded as a

temporary ordinance, deriving from Moses, and enjoined exclusively on the Jews on account of their unfaithfulness.[73] The reduction of a creation ordinance to an infamous sign of Jewish disobedience may reflect the need for short-term apologetic arguments, but it lacks a comprehension of the permanent and lofty values placed upon the Sabbath by the Scripture.

Absence of "Sabbath." In Genesis 2:2-3 there is a three-fold reference to the "seventh day" but no mention is made of the Sabbath. To some, this absence indicates that the Sabbath as an institution originated not at creation but later at the time of Moses.[74] It is true that the name "Sabbath" does not occur in the passage, but the cognate verbal form *šabat* (to cease, to stop, to rest) is used and the latter, as noted by U. Cassuto, "contains an allusion to the name 'the Sabbath day.'"[75] Moreover, as the same author sagaciously remarks, the use of the name *seventh day* rather than *Sabbath* may well reflect the writer's concern to underline the *perpetual order* of the day, independent and free from any association with astrological "sabbaths" of the heathen nations.[76] By pointing to a *perpetual order*, the seventh day strengthens the cosmological message of the creation story, precisely that God is both Creator and constant controller of this cosmos. In Exodus, however, where the seventh day is given in the context of the genesis not of this cosmos but of the nation of Israel, the day is explicitly designated "sabbath," apparently to express its new historical and soteriological function. This new dimension of the Sabbath will be considered in chapters III and V.

Absence of a command. The absence in Genesis 2:2-3 of any explicit command to observe the seventh day is also interpreted as added indication that the Sabbath is not a creation ordinance, a moral law binding on all mankind, but a temporary institution which Moses introduced for Israel alone and justified by grounding it on the creation week.[77] This argument makes Moses guilty of distortion of truth or, at least, a victim of gross misunderstanding. He would have traced back the Sabbath to creation when in reality it was his own new creation. Such a charge, if true, would cast serious doubts on the integrity and/or reliability of anything else Moses or anyone else wrote in the Bible.

What is it that makes any divine precept moral and universal? Do we not regard a law moral when it reflects God's nature? Could God have given any stronger revelation of the moral nature of the Sabbath than by making it a rule of His divine conduct? Is a principle established by divine *example* less binding than one enunciated by a divine *command*? Do

not actions speak louder than words? "God's mode of operation," as noted by John Murray, "is the exemplar on the basis
of which the sequence for man is patterned. There can be little
doubt that in Genesis 2:3 there is at least an allusion to the
blessing of the seventh day in man's week." [78] The fact that the
Sabbath is presented in the creation story as a divine example
rather than a commandment for mankind could well reflect
what God intended the Sabbath to be in a sinless world, namely,
not an alienating imposition but a free response to a gracious
Creator. By freely choosing to make himself available to his
Creator on the Sabbath, man was to experience physical, mental
and spiritual renewal and enrichment. Since these needs have
not been eliminated but heightened by the fall, the moral, universal and perpetual functions of the Sabbath precept were
repeated later in the form of a commandment.[79]

Absence of example. The oldest and perhaps the strongest
argument against the Edenic antiquity of the Sabbath is the
absence of explicit reference to Sabbathkeeping after Genesis 2
for the whole patriarchal period, that is until Exodus 16.[80] The
sources outside the Bible, as we noticed earlier, provide us (for
the pre-Mosaic period) only faint and inconclusive indications
of a primeval type of "Sabbath" among the Semitic people of
ancient Mesopotamia. However, considering the nature of the
Sabbath, one could hardly expect to find clear evidences of its
observance among heathen nations, but one would anticipate
finding such evidence among the faithful patriarchs. How can
we account for this apparent silence? Could it be that between
Adam and Moses, for some unexplainable reason, the Sabbath,
though instituted, was not observed? The non-observance of
the feast of the booths between Joshua and Nehemiah, a period
of almost a thousand years, would provide a parallel situation
(Neh. 8:17). Or could it rather be that the custom of Sabbathkeeping is not mentioned because it was simply taken for granted? The latter explanation seems more plausible for a number
of reasons.

First, we have a similar example of silence regarding the
Sabbath between the books of Deuteronomy and 2 Kings. Such
silence can hardly be interpreted as non-observance of the Sabbath, since when the first incidental reference occurs in 2 Kings
4:23, it describes the custom of visiting a prophet on the Sabbath. Second, Genesis does not contain laws like Exodus, but
rather a brief sketch of origins. Since then no mention is made
of any of the other commandments, the silence regarding the
Sabbath is not exceptional.[81] Third, there are throughout the
book of Genesis and the early chapters of Exodus [82] circum-

stantial evidences for the use of the seven-day week, which would imply the existence of the Sabbath as well. The period of seven days is mentioned four times in the account of the Flood (Gen. 7:4, 10; 8:10, 12). The "week" is also apparently used in a technical way to describe the duration of the nuptial festivities of Jacob (Gen. 29:27) as well as the duration of mourning at his death (Gen. 50:10). A like period was observed by the friends of Job to express their condolences to the patriarch (Job. 2:12). Probably all the mentioned ceremonials were terminated by the arrival of the Sabbath.

Lastly, the Sabbath is presented in Exodus 16 and 20 as an already existing institution. The instructions for the gathering of the double portion of the manna on the sixth day presuppose a knowledge of the significance of the Sabbath: "On the sixth day, when they prepare what they bring in, it will be twice as much as they gather daily" (Ex. 16:5). The omission of any reason for gathering a double portion on the sixth day would be quite unaccountable, if the Israelites had no previous knowledge of the Sabbath. Similarly in Exodus 20, the Sabbath is presupposed as something already familiar. The commandment does not say "know the Sabbath day" but "Remember the Sabbath day" (Ex. 20:8), thus implying that it was already known. Furthermore, the commandment by presenting the Sabbath as rooted in creation (Ex. 20:11) hardly allows a late Exodus introduction of the festival.[83]

To speculate on how the patriarchs kept the Sabbath would be a fruitless endeavor since it would rest more on imagination than on available information. Considering, however, that the essence of the Sabbath is not *a place to go* to fulfill rituals, but a set *time to be* with God, ourselves and others,[84] it seems entirely possible that the patriarchs spent the Sabbath holy hours within their household, engaged in some of the acts of worship described in Genesis, such as prayer (Gen. 12:8; 26:25), sacrifice (Gen. 12:8; 13:18; 26:25; 33:20), and teaching (Gen. 18:19).

Legalistic tendencies. The objections against the creation Sabbath which we have briefly considered are generally raised by Christians who rightly react against the excessively legalistic and literalistic manner in which the Sabbath has often been observed by those who defend it as a creation ordinance.[85] Such a reaction is indeed justifiable but it does not also justify the doing away with a *precept* because some *pervert* it. Legalists unfortunately tend to forget that by His actions and words, the Savior made the Sabbath a day of "mercy" rather than of "sacrifice" (Matt. 12:8), a time to love God and one's fellow beings

By His actions and words the Savior made the Sabbath a day
of "mercy" rather than of "sacrifice" (Matt.12:8), a time to
love God and one's fellow beings rather than to parade one's
righteousness by fulfilling rituals.

rather than to parade one's righteousness by fulfilling rituals. A correct understanding and experience of the Sabbath can prove to be powerful antidotes against legalism. Why? Because the Sabbath teaches us not to work for our salvation (legalism), but to cease from all our works, in order, as Calvin so well expressed it, "to allow God to work in us."[86]

Conflict with modern science. In concluding this survey of objections against the creation-Sabbath, mention should be made of those who reject this Biblical teaching because they are unable to reconcile it with modern scientific theories of origin. The current prevailing theory assumes that it took millions of years for the surface layers of the earth to be formed and that life originated "spontaneously," evolving from simple, one-celled "ancestors." To reconcile such a theory with the creation account, some well-intentioned theologians have interpreted the creation week as meaning not six literal days, but rather six ages of geologic time.[87] Others prefer to view the creation week primarily as a time during which God's creative activities and goodness were revealed to man. Obviously these interpretations do away with the creation-Sabbath, simply because they imply that God did not actually rest and sanctify a literal seventh-day.

The problem with scientific logic, as wisely stated by Herold Weiss, is that it "refuses to allow theology to inform it."[88] When a person insists on believing only what can be demonstrated in a laboratory, he chooses to trace his roots *downward* from biological specimens rather than *upward* from the image of God. Ultimately, this leads a person to believe in nothing else but himself. The tragic consequence of such a philosophy is that it empties life and human history of ultimate meaning, leaving both life and history with no divine beginning or destiny. Life is reduced to a biological cycle which by chance alone determines its own beginning and end. Thus the ultimate reality is not God but matter, which historically has been viewed as eternal or as evil. The creation story with its Sabbath-memorial challenges this nihilism, urging each generation, whether burdened with scientific facts or with mythological fantasies, to acknowledge that this world is a creation and a gift of God entrusted to man, whose life is meaningful because it is rooted in God.

Is it really necessary to be able to explain the creation week in the light of modern scientific theories in order to accept the Sabbath as a creation ordinance? Has modern science the know-how and the instruments to test and explain how long it takes to "create" a solar system such as ours with its multiform

When a person insists on believing only what can be demonstrated in a laboratory, he chooses to trace his roots downward
from biological specimens rather than upward from the image of
God. Ultimately, this leads a person to believe in nothing else
but himself.

life? We seem to forget that science can observe and measure only the ongoing processes of *conservation* and *disintegration*. In fact, modern science by assuming that these ongoing processes have always functioned in the past essentially as in the present (uniformitarianism) excludes the possibility of a divine *fiat* (spoken-into-existence) process. Thus, ultimately the problem is not how to reconcile the creation-week with modern theories of origin, but how to conciliate the Biblical teaching of a *Divine creation* with the prevailing scientific view of *spontaneous generation*. Is it possible to harmonize the two? Obviously not, since the two views rest on entirely different premises. The latter accepts only natural causes while the former acknowledges God as the Supernatural Cause: "By faith we understand that the world was created by the word of God, so that what is seen was made out of things which do not appear" (Heb. 11:3).

If we accept by faith that God created this world, then why should we disbelieve what He has revealed to us about the time He took to accomplish it? Someone could object that the notion of God creating and resting according to the limitations of a seven-day human week militates against His very eternal and omnipotent nature. It is evident that Almighty God did not need geological ages nor literal days to create our world but only the will to call it into existence (Ps. 33:6). But does not the fact that in His revelation God tells us that He chose a human rather than a divine time-schedule to create our world point to another equally important quality of His divine nature: love? Is not God's willingness to enter into the limitations of human time at creation a reflection of His concern to give a divine example or perspective to the work-and-rest week of His creatures? Is not this also a prefiguration of God's willingness to enter, if the need should arise, into human flesh in order to become "Emmanuel," "God with us"? This dimension of the Sabbath will be the subject of later considerations.[89] For the present, we conclude that to question the creation-origin of the Sabbath, in order to harmonize the creation-week with modern theories of origins, means to reject not only the message of Genesis 1:1-2:3, but also its commentary given in the Fourth Commandment, which speaks of six literal days of creation and one literal day of rest, sanctified by God when this world was created (Ex. 20:11).

2. *Creation-Sabbath in Scripture*

This brief survey of objections against the creation-Sabbath has dealt primarily with references found in the first two books of the Bible, Genesis and Exodus. This could leave the impression that the rest of the Scripture and history are silent on the subject. But this is hardly accurate, since support for the Edenic origin of the Sabbath is found both in history and in other parts of Scripture. To these indications we shall now refer succinctly, to enable the reader to view the issue in its Biblical and historical perspective.

Mark 2:27. Two significant sayings of Jesus, reported in Mark 2:27 and John 5:17, allude to the creation Sabbath. According to Mark, Christ said: "The Sabbath was made for man, not man for the Sabbath" (2:27). The context of this pronouncement is a charge of Sabbathbreaking leveled against the disciples because they relieved their hunger by eating raw ears of grain plucked along the hedge of a field. To refute such a charge and to assert the fundamental human function of the Sabbath as a protector and not a depriver of physical and spiritual well-being, Christ appealed to the original purpose of the day, saying: "The Sabbath was made on account of [90] man and not man on account of the Sabbath" (Mark 2:27).[91]

Our Lord's choice of words is significant. The verb "made"—*ginomai* alludes to the original "making" of the Sabbath [92] and the word "man"—*anthropos* suggests its human function. Thus to establish the human and universal value of the Sabbath Christ reverts to its very origin, right after the creation of man. Why? Because for the Lord the law of the beginning stands supreme. This is exemplified in another instance, when in reproving the corruption of the institution of marriage which had occurred under the Mosaic code, He reverted to the Edenic law, saying: "From the beginning it was not so" (Matt. 19:8).[93] Christ then traces both marriage and the Sabbath to their creation origin in order to clarify their fundamental value and function for mankind.

John 5:17. The Fourth Gospel reports another significant Sabbath pronouncement of Jesus. Charged with healing on the Sabbath, He defended Himself, saying: "My Father is working until now and I am working" (John 5:17). Two earlier studies of this passage have shown how God's "working" has been traditionally interpreted as constant care (*cura continua*) or continuous creation (*creatio continua*) and the adverb "until now" has been understood as "continually, always." [94] The unwarranted conclusion resulting from such an interpretation has generally been that the *continuous* working of God, whether in creation or preservation, overrides and rescinds the Sabbath law.

Such a conclusion is without sanction on at least two

counts. First, because in the Gospel of John the working and the works of God are repeatedly and explicitly identified not with creation or preservation, but with the redemptive mission of Christ (cf. John 4:34; 6:29; 10:37-38; 14:11; 15:24; 9:3). Second, the adverb "until now" emphasizes not the *constancy*, but the *inauguration* and *culmination* of God's working. In other words, God is working *until this very hour* since the first Sabbath and until the conclusion of His work—the final Sabbath. The adverb "until now" presupposes a "beginning" and an "end." The beginning is the creation Sabbath when God completed creation and the end is the final Sabbath when redemption will be concluded. The Sabbaths in between the first and the final Sabbath are for God and His creatures (John 9:4) not a time of listless resting but of concerned "working" for the salvation of human beings. We conclude, therefore, that Christ, by alluding to the creation Sabbath to justify the legitimacy of His redemptive ministry performed on that day, provides in John 5:17 an implicit endorsement of its Edenic origin.

Hebrews 4:1-11. The creation origin of the Sabbath is also accepted by the writer of Hebrews.[95] In the fourth chapter of the book, the author establishes the universal and spiritual nature of the Sabbath rest by welding together two OT texts, namely Genesis 2:2 and Psalm 95:11. Through the former, he traces the origin of the Sabbath rest back to creation when "God rested on the seventh day from all His works" (Heb. 4:4; cf. Gen. 2:2-3). By the latter (Ps. 95:11), he explains that the scope of this divine rest includes the blessings of salvation to be found by entering personally into "God's rest" (Heb. 4:3, 5, 10). Our immediate concern is not to understand the various meanings of the rest mentioned in the passage,[96] but rather to note that the author traces its origin not to Joshua's day, at time of the settlement (Heb. 4:8), but back to the time of creation, when "God rested on the seventh day from all his works" (Heb. 4:4). The context clearly indicates that the author is thinking of the "works" of creation, since he explains that God's "works were finished from the foundations of the world" (Heb. 4:3). Thus in Hebrews 4, the creation Sabbath rest is not only accepted, but it is also presented as the basis for understanding God's ultimate purpose for His people.

3. Creation-Sabbath in History

Jewish tradition. Passing now from Biblical to extra-biblical sources, one finds a widespread recognition of the creation origin of the Sabbath in both Jewish and Christian history. The Jews developed two differing views regarding the origin of the Sabbath. Broadly speaking the two views can be distinguished linguistically and geographically. Palestinian (Hebrew) Judaism, as noted earlier, reduced the Sabbath to an exclusive Jewish ordinance linked to the origin of Israel as a nation at the time of Moses. This view represents not an original tradition but a secondary development which was encouraged by the necessity to preserve a Jewish identity in the face of Hellenistic pressures (especially at the time of Antiochus Epiphanes, 175 B.C.) to abandon Jewish religion. This is indicated by the fact that even in Palestinian literature there are references to the creation origin of the Sabbath. For example, the *Book of Jubilees* (about 140-100 B.C.), while on the one hand it says that God allowed "Israel only" to keep the Sabbath (Jub. 2:31), on the other holds that God "kept Sabbath on the seventh day and hallowed it for all ages, and appointed it as a sign for all His works" (Jub. 2:1).

In Hellenistic (Greek) Jewish literature the Sabbath is unmistakably viewed as a creation ordinance designed for all people. Aristobulus, Philo's predecessor, for example, writes in the second century B.C. that "God the creator of the whole world has also given us the seventh day as rest because life is full of trouble for all men." [97] Two centuries later Philo gave a much fuller treatment to the Sabbath. He not only traces the origin of the Sabbath to creation, but also delights to call it "the birthday of the world." [98] Referring to the creation story, Philo explains: "We are told that the world was made in six days and that on the seventh God ceased from his works and began to contemplate what had been so well created, and therefore he bade those who should live as citizens under this world-order to follow God in this as in other matters." [99] Because the Sabbath exists from creation, Philo emphasizes that it is "the festival not of a single city or country but of the universe, and it alone strictly deserves to be called public, as belonging to all people." [100]

Early Church. The recognition of the creation origin of the Sabbath is also found in the documents of the early Church, even though in some instances its importance is either challenged or applied to Sunday. In the *Syriac Didascalia* (about 250), for example, the Sabbath/Sunday controversy centers on the priority of the two days with respect to creation. Sunday is presented as "greater" than the Sabbath because it preceded the latter in the creation week. As the first day of creation, Sunday represents "the beginning of world." [101] In the treatise

On the Sabbath and Circumcision, found among the works of Athanasius (about 296-373), the superiority of Sunday over the Sabbath is argued on the basis of creation versus re-creation: "The Sabbath was the end of the first creation, the Lord's day was the beginning of the second in which He renewed and restored the old." [102] The fact that both Sabbath and Sunday keepers would defend the legitimacy and superiority of their respective days by appealing to their roles with reference to creation, shows how important the latter was in their view.

In the so-called *Constitutions of the Holy Apostles* (about 380), Christians are admonished to "keep the Sabbath and the Lord's day festival; because the former is the memorial of the creation, and the latter of the resurrection." [103] Several other references to the creation Sabbath are found in the same document. For example, a prayer commemorating Christ's incarnation begins with the words, "O Lord Almighty, Thou hast created the world by Christ and hast appointed the Sabbath in memory thereof, because that on that day Thou hast made us rest from our works for the meditation upon Thy laws." [104] The theme of the creation Sabbath, as noted by Jean Daniélou, is also "at the center of Augustinian thought." [105] The culmination of the creation week in the Sabbath rest, provides for Augustine (354-430) the basis to develop two significant concepts. The first is the notion of the progress of the history of this world toward a final rest and peace with God. In other words, the realization of the eternal rest represents for Augustine the fulfilment of "the Sabbath that the Lord approved at the beginning of creation, where it says, 'God rested on the seventh day from all his works.' " [106]

The second Augustinian interpretation of the creation Sabbath may be defined as the mystical progress of the human soul from restlessness into rest in God. A fitting example is found in one of the most sublime chapters of his *Confessions*, where Augustine prays: "O Lord God, Thou who hast given us all, grant us Thy peace, the peace of rest, the peace of the Sabbath, the peace without an 'evening'.[107] For this very beautiful order of things will pass away when they have accomplished their appointed purpose. They all were made with a 'morning' and an 'evening'. But the seventh day is without an 'evening' and it has no setting, because Thou hast sanctified it so that it may last eternally. Thy resting on the seventh day after the completion of Thy works, foretells us through the voice of Thy Book, that we also after completing our works through Thy generosity, in the Sabbath of eternal life shall rest in Thee." [108] This mystical and eschatological interpretation of the creation Sabbath shows what a profound appreciation Augustine had for its significance, in spite of the fact that he failed to accept the literal observance of the Fourth Commandment.[109]

Middle Ages. The Augustinian spiritual interpretation of the creation Sabbath continued with some degrees of approximation during the Middle Ages.[110] But a new development occurred following the Constantinian Sunday law of 321. In order to give a theological sanction to the imperial legislation demanding rest from work on Sunday, church leaders often appealed to the Sabbath commandment, interpreting it as a creation ordinance applicable to Sunday observance. Chrysostom (about 347-407) anticipates this development in his exposition of Genesis 2:2, "God blessed the seventh day and hallowed it." He asks "What do the words 'He hallowed it' actually mean? . . . [God] is teaching us that among the days of the week one must be singled out and wholly devoted to the service of spiritual things." [111] This reduction of the creation Sabbath from the specific observance of the *seventh day* to the principle of resting *one day in seven* in order to worship God made it possible to apply the Sabbath commandment to the observance of Sunday. Peter Comestor, for example (died about 1179), defends this application, arguing on the basis of Genesis 2:2 that "the Sabbath has been always observed by some nations even before the Law." [112] This recognition of the Sabbath as a creation and thus universal ordinance was motivated, however, not by the desire to promote the observance of the seventh day, but by the necessity to sanction and regulate Sunday keeping.

In late mediaeval theology the literal application of the Sabbath commandment to Sunday keeping was justified on the basis of a new interpretation which consisted in distinguishing between a moral and a ceremonial aspect within the Fourth Commandment.[113] Thomas Aquinas (about 1225-1247) offers the most articulated exposition of this artificial and unwarranted distinction in his *Summa theologica.* He argues that "the precept of the Sabbath observance is moral . . . in so far as it commands man to give some time to the things of God . . . but it is a ceremonial precept . . . as to the fixing of the time." [114] How can the Fourth Commandment be *ceremonial* for specifying the *seventh day* but *moral* for enjoining to set apart *a day* of rest for worship? Basically because for Aquinas the moral aspect of the Sabbath is grounded on Natural Law, that is to say, the principle of a regularly stated time for worship and rest is in accordance with natural reason.[115] The ceremonial aspect of the Sabbath, on the other hand, is determined by the symbolism of the seventh day: commemoration of "Creation" and pre-figuration of the "repose of the mind in God, either, in the present life, by grace, or, in the future life, by glory." [116]

One wonders, How can the Sabbath be ceremonial (transitory) for symbolizing God's perfect creation and the rest to be found in Him both in the present and future life? Is it not this reassurance that provides the basis for setting aside *any time* to worship God? To reject as *ceremonial* the original message of the seventh day Sabbath, namely that God is the perfect Creator Who offers rest, peace and fellowship to His creatures, means to destroy also the very *moral* basis for devoting any time to the worship of God. The belief in God as perfect Creator, as will be brought out in the following chapter, constitutes the cornerstone of the Christian faith and worship. Apparently Aquinas himself recognized the inadequacy of his reasoning since he makes a distinction between the Sabbath and other symbolic OT festivals such as Passover, "a sign of the future Passion of Christ." The latter, Aquinas explains, were "temporal and transitory . . . consequently, the Sabbath alone, and none of the other solemnities and sacrifices, is mentioned in the precepts of the decalogue." [117] Aquinas' uncertainty as to the ceremonial aspect of the Sabbath is also reflected in his comment that Christ annulled not the precept of the Sabbath but "the superstitious interpretation of the Pharisees, who thought that man ought to abstain from doing even works of kindness on the sabbath; which was contrary to the intention of the Law." [118] Aquinas' uncertainty, however, was largely forgotten and his moral-ceremonial distinction of the Sabbath became the standard rationale for defending the Church's right to introduce and regulate the observance of Sunday and holy days. This resulted in an elaborate legalistic system of Sunday keeping akin to that of the rabbinical Sabbath. [119]

Lutheranism. The sixteenth-century reformers expressed differing views regarding the origin and nature of the Sabbath. Their position was influenced by their understanding of the relationship between the Old and the New Testaments as well as by their reaction against the legalistic and superstitious observance not only of Sunday but of a host of holy days as, well. Luther and some radicals, in their concern to combat legalistic Sabbatarianism promoted not only by the Catholic Church but also by left-wing reformers such as Andreas Karlstadt, [120] attacked the Sabbath as a Mosaic institution "specifically given to the Jewish people." [121] This position was largely determined by a radical distinction between the Old and New Testaments. In the *Large Catechism* (1529) Luther explains that

the Sabbath "is altogether an external matter, like other ordinances of the Old Testament, which were attached to particular customs, persons, and places, and now have been made
free through Christ."[122] This view is stated even more emphatically in article 28 of the *Augsburg Confession* (1530): "Scripture
has abrogated the Sabbath-day; for it teaches that, since the
Gospel has been revealed, all the ceremonies of Moses can be
omitted."[123]

The above statements may give the impression that Luther
rejected the creation origin of the Sabbath, reducing it exclusively to a Mosaic institution. Such a conclusion, however, is
not correct, since Luther affirms, for example, in the same *Large
Catechism*, "The day [Sabbath] needs no sanctification for itself,
for in itself it has been created holy. From the beginning of
the creation it was sanctified by its Creator."[124] Likewise, in
his comments on Genesis 2:3, Luther says: "Since the Scriptures
mention the Sabbath much sooner than Adam fell in sin, was
it not appointed at that time that he should work six days and
rest on the seventh? This is so without doubt."[125] The same
view is expressed by Melanchthon, Luther's associate and suc-
cessor. In the 1555 edition of his *Loci Communes*, Melanchthon
unequivocally states that "from the time of Adam the first
fathers kept it [Sabbath] as a day on which they put aside the
work of their hands and met publicly for preaching, prayer,
thanksgiving and sacrifice, as God ordered."[126] Melanchthon
distinguishes between the function of the Sabbath before and
after the Fall. Before the Fall the Sabbath was designed to
allow God to "have His rest, habitation, joy and delight" in His
creatures. "After the Fall," Melanchthon writes, "the Sabbath
was re-established when the gracious promise was given that
there would be a second peace of God, that the Son of God
would die and would rest in death until the Resurrection. So
now in us our Sabbath should be such a dying and resurrection
with the Son of God, so that God may again have His place
of habitation, peace and joy in us."[127]

What a profound insight into the Biblical meaning of the
Sabbath! A day to enable the believer to die and to be resurrected with Christ.[128] A day to allow God to have "His place
of habitation, peace and joy in us."[129] It is to the study of
Sabbath themes such as these that the pages of this book are
dedicated. But, one wonders, how could Luther and Melanchthon on the one hand view the Sabbath as a creation ordinance,
and on the other hand regard the day as a Mosaic institution?
Primarily by adopting and developing Aquinas' distinction between natural and Mosaic law, or, as often called, moral and

ceremonial law. This distinction is articulated more clearly by Melanchthon than by Luther, though even the latter says that "Moses' legislation about the Sabbath . . . is null and void" because "it is not supported by the natural law." [130]   It is Melanchthon, however who in responding to those who carried Luther's unguarded statements to an extreme by denying the observance of any day, clearly explains: "In this commandment there are two parts, one general, which is always necessary for the Church, and one specific, which refers to a special day that pertains only to the government of Israel. . . . For the *general* in this commandment pertains to that which is moral and natural and permanent, namely the keeping of the Church's worship; and the *specific*, which points to *the* seventh day, pertains to ceremony . . . it is not binding on us; therefore, we have gatherings on the first day, namely on Sunday." [131]

It is hard to understand the logic behind such reasoning. How can the principle of setting aside *one day* or some time of the week "to maintain the office of preaching and public worship be considered as *moral*, while the actual specification of the *seventh day* be treated as *ceremonial*, that is, pertaining "only to the government of Israel"? To argue that the seventh day is ceremonial because it cannot be discovered by unaided human reason (Natural Law), is to fail to recognize that neither can human reason alone discover the principle that some time must be set aside for maintaining "the office of preaching and public worship." [132]   The latter principle, in fact, cannot even be explicitly derived from the Fourth Commandment, where mention is made not of attending public preaching services on the Sabbath but only of resting unto the Lord (Ex. 20:10).[133]   The notion of the Decalogue as based on or supported by Natural Law is a fabrication of scholasticism (influenced by classical moral philosophy).[134]   In the Scriptures the Sabbath and the rest of the Ten Commandments are rooted not on human reason but on a special divine revelation. The fact that unaided human reason can discover some of the ethical values of the Decalogue may show their rationality but not their origin.

The Lutheran distinction between moral and ceremonial or natural (creation) and Mosaic aspects of the Sabbath can be viewed as an honest but inadequate effort to save some of the values of the Sabbath in the face of two opposite threats: on the one side, there were radical antinomians who denied the need for observing any day; [135] on the other side there were Catholic and Reformed legalists who defended the observance of holy days as things "necessary to salvation." [136]   The *Augsburg Confession* refers to these "monstrous disputations" and ex-

plains that "these errors crept into the Church when righteousness of faith was not taught clearly enough." [137]   Luther is to
be commended for his efforts to steer clear of the Scylla of
legalism and the Charybdis of antinomianism.   It is only regrettable that to charter such a course, he rejected as Mosaic
and ceremonial those vital meanings and functions of the
seventh-day Sabbath which, as we shall see, enable believers to
understand and experience "righteousness of faith." [138]   Instead,
Luther chose to retain Sunday, as a convenient day "ordained
by the church for the sake of the imperfect laity and the working
class," [139] who need "at least one day in the week . . . to rest
and . . . to attend divine service." [140]   Luther's radical distinction
between natural law and Mosaic law and between Law and
Gospel, was adopted and developed to extremes by radicals such
as Anabaptists, leftist Puritans, Quakers, Mennonites, Hutterites
and many modern antinomian denominations.[141]   These have
generally claimed that the Sabbath is not a creation ordinance
but a Mosaic institution which Christ fulfilled and abolished.
Consequently, believers in the Christian dispensation are free
from the observance of any special day.

Catholicism.   The Catholic view of the Sabbath in the sixteenth century reflects basically Aquinas' distinction between
Mosaic and Natural Law.   This can be seen, for example, in
the *Catechism of the Council of Trent* (1566), the so-called
"Roman Catechism."   The fourth chapter of part III explains
the difference between the Sabbath and the rest of the commandments, saying: "The other precepts of the Decalogue belong to the natural law, and are perpetual and unalterable . . .
because they agree with the law of nature, by the force of
which men are impelled to their observance; whereas this commandment, touching the sanctification of the Sabbath, if considered as to the time appointed (for its observance), is not
fixed and unalterable, but susceptible of change, nor does it
belong to the moral but ceremonial law, neither is it a principle of the natural law . . . but from the time the people of
Israel were liberated from the bondage of Pharaoh, they observed the Sabbath day." [142]   The conclusion that follows is that
"the time when the observance of the Sabbath [as the seventh
day] was to be removed, is that the same time when the other
Hebrew rites and ceremonies were to be abrogated, namely, at
the death of Christ." [143]

The irrationality of viewing only the specification of the
seventh day within the Fourth Commandment, as a Mosaic or
ceremonial law, was exposed earlier.   As a further comment,
it should be pointed out that on the basis of Natural Law, even

Luther is to be commended for his efforts to steer clear of the Scylla of legalism and the Charybdis of antinomianism. It is only regrettable that to charter such a course, he rejected as Mosaic and ceremonial those vital meanings and functions of the seventh-day Sabbath which enable believers to understand and experience righteousness by faith.

the second commandment which forbids the worshiping of iconographic (pictorial) representation of the Deity (Ex. 20:3-6) should be treated as ceremonial, since it can hardly be defended on the basis of human reason alone. This may be a reason for the Catholic deletion of the second commandment (Ex. 20:3-6) from their Decalogue.[144] But, is human reason the legitimate criterion for accepting or rejecting precepts of the Decalogue? Apparently the Catholic Church has taken this position to defend her right to introduce the observance not only of Sunday but of other days as well. Examples of such a claim abound, especially in Catholic documents of the sixteenth century.[145] Johann Eck (1486-1543) for instance, in his *Enchiridion* directed against some of the Reformers, argues that "If the church has had power to change the Sabbath of the Bible into Sunday and to command Sunday keeping, why should it not have also this power concerning other days? . . . If you omit the latter, and turn from the church to the Scripture alone, then you must keep the Sabbath with the Jews, which has been kept from the beginning of the world." [146]

It is noteworthy that Eck, though claiming the authority of the Catholic Church for the change of the Biblical Sabbath into Sunday, still acknowledges the creation origin of the Sabbath, when saying that it "has been kept from the beginning of the world." [147] The same view is expressed in a more official Catholic document, the *Catechism of the Council of Trent* (1566). "The Sabbath," the *Catechism* explains, "is so called by the Lord in Exodus (Ex. 20:8-11; Gen. 2:2), because having finished and completed the creation of the world, 'God rested from all his work which he had done (Gen. 2:2-3).' " [148] A little later the Sabbath is declared to be "a sign, and as it were, a memorial of the creation of this admirable world." [149] This frank recognition of the Sabbath as an institution and memorial of creation contradicts and challenges the Catholic right asserted in the same document to alter it: "It pleased the Church of God, that the religious celebration of the Sabbath day should be transferred to the Lord's day." [150] This unresolved contradiction, as we shall soon see, reappears in a different and yet similar form in the Reformed tradition.

Sabbatarians. Radical reformers promoted two opposing views regarding the Sabbath. One group, mentioned earlier, pressed to its logical conclusion the Lutheran distinction between the Old and New Testaments, rejecting the observance of the Sabbath or of any day, as part of the Mosaic dispensation which Christ had fulfilled and replaced with the dispensation of Grace. Another group, however, pursued the logical implications of the Calvinistic unity between the two Testaments, accepting and promoting the observance of the seventh day Sabbath as a creation ordinance meant for all time and people. We shall call the latter "Sabbatarians," a name frequently given to them by their opponents.[151] Recent studies have shown that Sabbatarians constituted a respectable group at the time of the Reformation, especially in such places as Moravia, Bohemia, Austria and Silesia.[152] In fact, in some Catholic catalogues of sects, they are listed immediately after the Lutherans and Calvinists.[153] Erasmus (1466-1536) mentions the existence of Sabbatarians in Bohemia: "Now I hear that among the Bohemians a new kind of Jews are springing up, whom they call Sabbatarii, who serve the Sabbath with great superstition."[154] Similarly, Luther reports on the existence of Sabbatarian groups in Moravia and Austria.[155] In fact, in 1538 Luther wrote a *Letter Against the Sabbatarians* (*Brief wider die Sabbathers*), arguing from the Bible against their observance of the seventh-day Sabbath.[156]

Oswald Glait, a former Catholic priest who became first a Lutheran and then an Anabaptist minister, began in 1527 or 1528 successfully to propagate his Sabbatarian views among Anabaptists in Moravia, Silesia and Bohemia.[157] He was supported by the learned Andreas Fisher, also a former priest and Anabaptist.[158] Glait wrote a *Booklet on the Sabbath* (*Buchlenn vom Sabbath*—about 1530) which is not extant. From a refutation of Glait's book by Caspar Schwenckfeld[159] we learn that Glait maintained the unity of the Old and New Testaments, accepting the validity and relevance of the Decalogue for the Christian dispensation. Glait rejected the contention of his critics that the Sabbath commandment is a ceremonial law like circumcision. He held instead that the "Sabbath is commanded and kept from the beginning of creation."[160] God enjoined "Adam in paradise to celebrate the Sabbath."[161] Therefore "the Sabbath . . . is an eternal sign of hope and a memorial of creation, . . . an eternal covenant to be kept as long as the world stands."[162] On account of this teaching, Glait faced expulsions, persecutions and finally death by drowning in the Danube (1546).[163]

The death of Glait, perhaps the most prominent leader of the Sabbatarian Anabaptists, did not stop the propagation of the Sabbath doctrine. This is indicated by the existence of seventh-day Sabbathkeepers at the time of the Reformation in several European countries such as Poland, Holland, Germany, France, Hungary, Russia, Turkey, Finland and Sweden.[164] In the seventeenth century their presence became particularly felt in

England. This is indicated by the fact that, as noted by R. J. Bauckham, "an impressive succession of Puritan and Anglican spokesmen addressed themselves to combatting the seventh day . . . Their efforts are a tacit admission of the attraction which the doctrine exercised in the seventeenth century, and seventh day observers . . . were harshly treated by Puritan and Anglican authorities." [165] The Seventh Day Baptists became the leading Sabbatarian church in England.[166] Their first church in America was founded at Newport, Rhode Island, in December 1671.[167] Seventh-day Adventists gratefully acknowledge their indebtedness to Seventh Day Baptists for bringing to them knowledge of the Sabbath in 1845.[168] A few years later (1860) the Sabbath was accepted as a creation ordinance by what became known as the Church of God Seventh Day.[169] In more recent times this teaching has been adopted by the Worldwide Church of God and by scores of smaller denominations.[170]

Reformed tradition. Churches in the Reformed tradition, such as English Puritans, Presbyterians, Congregationalists, Methodists, and Baptists, adopted what might be called a "compromise position," on the one hand acknowledging the Sabbath as a creation ordinance, while on the other hand defending Sunday as a legitimate substitution of the Sabbath accomplished by the Church. They generally distinguished between the temporal and the spiritual observance of Sunday. Calvin can rightly be regarded as the pioneer and promoter of this view which exerted far-reaching influence, especially in Anglo-American Puritan Sabbatarianism. The basis of Calvin's teaching regarding the Sabbath is to be found in his rejection of Luther's antithesis between Law and Gospel. In his effort to maintain the basic unity of the Old and New Testaments, Calvin Christianized the Law, spiritualizing, at least in part, the Sabbath commandment.[171]

Calvin explicitly acknowledges the Sabbath as a divine ordinance established at creation. In his *Commentary on Genesis* 2:3, written in 1554, he affirms: "First, therefore, God rested; then he blessed this rest, that in all ages it might be held sacred among men: or he dedicated every seventh day to rest, that his own example might be a perpetual rule." [172] He reiterated the same conviction one year before his death (1564) in his *Harmony of the Pentateuch,* saying: "Certainly God took the seventh day for His own and hallowed it, when the creation of the world was finished, that He might keep His servants altogether free from every care, for the consideration of the beauty, excellence and fitness of His works." [173] A few paragraphs later, Calvin explains that "the hallowing of the Sabbath, was prior to the law." [174]   God reiterated the precept at the time of Moses, because in the meantime it had become "altogether extinct among heathen nations, and almost obsolete with the race of Abraham." [175]

How did Calvin reconcile his acceptance of the Sabbath as a creation ordinance for mankind with his view "there can be no doubt, that, on the advent of our Lord Jesus Christ, the ceremonial part of the commandment was abolished"? [176]   In other words, how can the Sabbath be at the same time both a creation ordinance for all and a Jewish ceremonial (Mosaic) law abolished by Christ? Calvin attempted to resolve this tension by re-proposing with new qualifications Aquinas' distinction between the moral and ceremonial aspects of the Sabbath. At creation the Sabbath was given as a perpetual ordinance but "afterwards in the Law, a new precept concerning the Sabbath was given, which should be peculiar to the Jews, and but for a season." [177]   What is the difference between the Jewish (Mosaic) Sabbath and the Christian (creation) Sabbath? The difference is not easy to detect, especially for someone not trained to distinguish theological nuances. Calvin describes the Jewish Sabbath as being "typical" (symbolic), that is, "a legal ceremony shadowing forth a spiritual rest, the truth of which was manifested in Christ." [178]   The Christian Sabbath [Sunday] on the other hand is "without figure." [179]   By this he apparently means that it is a more pragmatic institution, designed to accomplish three basic objectives: first, to allow God to work in us; second, to provide time for meditation and church services; third, to protect dependent workers. [180]

An unresolved contradiction. Calvin's attempt to resolve the tension between the Sabbath as "a creation perpetual ordinance" and as "a ceremonial temporal law" can hardly be considered successful. Did not the Sabbath fulfill the same pragmatic functions for the Jews as it does for the Christians? Moreover, by teaching that for Christians the Sabbath represents "self-renunciation" and the "true rest" of the Gospel, [181] did not Calvin also attribute to the day a "typological-symbolic" significance, much like the type he assigned to the Jewish Sabbath? This unresolved tension can be followed in the teaching of Calvin's successors and has been the cause of endless controversies. For example, Zacharias Ursinus, the compiler of that important Reformed confession known as *Heidelberg Catechism* (1563), teaches that "the Sabbath of the seventh day was appointed of God from the very beginning of the world, to declare that men, after His example, should rest from their labours," and "although the ceremonial Sabbath has been abolished in the New Testament, yet the moral still continues and pertains to us as well as to others." [182] This position was later defended tenaciously in the monumental work, *The Doctrine of the Sabbath*, written in 1595 by the famous English Puritan Nicolas Bownde,[183] as well as in other confessional documents such as the Synod of Dort of 1619 [184] and the *Westminster Confession of Faith* of 1647.[185]

These and similar documents fail to offer a rational explanation for the artificial and arbitrary distinction between the so-called *moral* (constant, perpetual, natural) aspect of the Sabbath applied to Sunday and its *ceremonial* (contingent, temporary, Mosaic) aspect supposedly annulled by Christ. To contend that the specification of the *seventh day* is a ceremonial element of the Sabbath, because it was designed to aid the Jews in commemorating creation and in experiencing spiritual rest, means to be blind to the fact that Christians need such an aid just as much as the Jews; it means to leave Christians confused as to the reasons for devoting one day to the worship of God. R. J. Bauckham acknowledges the existence of such a confusion when he notes that most "Protestants in the mid-sixteenth century had as imprecise ideas about the basis of Sunday observance as most Christians at most times have had." [186]

The unresolved contradiction between the moral and ceremonial aspects of the Fourth Commandment has aroused recurrent controversies over the relationship between Sunday and the Sabbath commandment. Truly the Sabbath has had no rest. The moral/ceremonial distinction of the Sabbath has led to two major opposing views of Sunday. In the Netherlands, for example, the two views were hotly debated during more than a decade after Synod of Dort (1619). On the one side, Dutch theologians such as Willem Teellinck, William Ames, and Antonius Walaeus wrote major treatises defending the creation origin of the Sabbath and thus the legitimate application of the Fourth Commandment to the observance of Sunday.[187] On the other side, a leading professor, Franciscus Gomarus, produced a major response entitled *Enquiry into the Meaning and Origin of the Sabbath and Consideration of the Institution of the Lord's Day* (1628), in which he argues for a Mosaic origin of the Sabbath and consequently for an independent ecclesiastical origin of Sunday.[188]

The debate over these two conflicting positions has flared up time and again in different countries [189] and no reconciliation appears yet to be in sight. A fitting example is provided by the publication of two recent studies, one by Willy Rordorf (1968) [190] and the other by Roger T. Beckwith and Wilfrid Stott

(1978).[191]   Rordorf espouses the thesis that the Sabbath is not a creation ordinance binding upon Christians, but a "social institution" introduced after the occupation of Canaan and annulled by Christ. He thus divorces Sunday completely from the Fourth Commandment, viewing the day as an exclusively Christian creation, introduced to celebrate Christ's resurrection through the Lord's Supper celebration.[192]   By severing all links with the Sabbath commandment, Rordorf reduces Sunday to an *hour of worship* which could be scheduled in accordance with the demands of modern life. The practical implications of this position are obvious. If fully carried out, it could prove to be "the death certificate of Sunday," [193] since in time even the hour of worship could readily be squeezed out of the hectic schedule of modern life.

Beckwith and Stott, in their book *This is the Day: The Biblical Doctrine of the Christian Sunday* (1978), challenge Rordorf's thesis, by arguing that the Sabbath is a creation ordinance, which Christ did not reject but accepted and clarified and which the Apostles used to frame the Lord's Day.[194]   Consequently they conclude that, "when viewed in the light of the New Testament as a whole, the Lord's Day can clearly be seen to be a Christian sabbath—a New Testament fulfillment to which the Old Testament sabbath points forward." [195]   The practical implication of their conclusions is that Sunday is not merely an hour of worship, as argued by Rordorf, but "a whole day, set apart to be a holy festival . . . for worship, rest and works of mercy." [196]   Our immediate concern is not to respond to the respective positions of Rordorf and Beckwith/Stott, which, as I have shown in my published dissertation, contain several gratuitous assumptions.[197] Rather, the reader is requested to take notice at this point that the controversy over the origin and nature of the Sabbath is far from over. What is at stake is not merely an academic dispute, but the question of the very meaning and relevance of the Sabbath for the Christian life.

Conclusions

Three main conclusions seem to stand out from the sketch we have traced of the Biblical and historical witness to the origin of the Sabbath. First, there is in the Scriptures an unmistakable consensus supporting the creation origin of the Sabbath. Second, a major and the oldest Jewish tradition traces the origin of the Sabbath back to the culmination of creation. Third, we have found in the history of Christianity considerable support for the Edenic origin of the Sabbath, not only among seventh-day Sabbath keepers but also among many Sunday keepers. The latter have defended the Sabbath as a creation ordinance in order to justify Sunday as the Christian Sabbath. The challenge to the Creation Sabbath has come chiefly from two fronts: on one side, from Christians who resent and react against legalistic Sabbatarianism; on the other side, from critical scholars who reject the historicity of the Pentateuch and especially of the creation story.

To argue at this point on the basis of a presumable preponderant historical support for the validity of the Sabbath as a creation ordinance would make historical outworking the criterion for accepting or rejecting any Biblical doctrine. Majority vote, however, is not an accepted principle of Biblical interpretation (hermeneutics). Our survey is merely designed to show that belief in creation Sabbath is deeply rooted in both Scripture and history. To reject such a teaching by labeling it as "superstitious, legalistic or inconsistent with modern science" may lead to self-deception, for such labeling does not in honesty explain away a Biblical precept nor relieve the Christian from its obligation.

Our present quest has shown that, according to the unanimous testimony of the Scriptures, the origin of the Sabbath is rooted in the creation event and marks the inauguration of human history. What are some of the practical implications of this Biblical teaching for the Christian faith? In the first place, it means that Sabbathkeeping is not a temporary Jewish ceremonial law, but a permanent precept pertaining to all creatures.[198] Second, it means, as so well stated by Elizabeth E. Platt, that "we have our roots in the Sabbath; we belong in it from Genesis on into Eternity in God's plan." [199] Third, it means that our ancestral roots are indeed good, because they are rooted in God Himself. Last, it means that our world and our existence have value because they are not a product of chance but a personal creation of a loving God.[200]

We no longer live in the *perfect beginning* but in an *imperfect middle*: an age characterized by injustice, greed, violence, corruption, suffering and death. In the midst of the chaos and disorder of our age, we seek for certainty, meaning and hope. The Sabbath brings us weekly reassurance and hope. It reassures us that our origin and destiny are rooted in God. It provides us with a sense of continuity with the past and a hope for the future. It invites us to rest in God while living in a restless *middle* and waiting for that end (yet endless) rest and peace of God (Heb. 4:9) for which we were created. This is then the message of the creation Sabbath: *Good News of Human Roots.*

Skepticism can be an outgrowth of forgetfulness. A person who neglects the Sabbath, the memorial of creation, is liable to forget and become skeptical about the God of creation.

CHAPTER
II

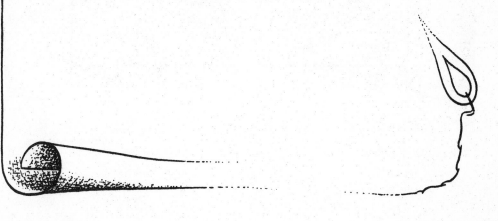

the Sabbath

GOOD NEWS
of perfect creation

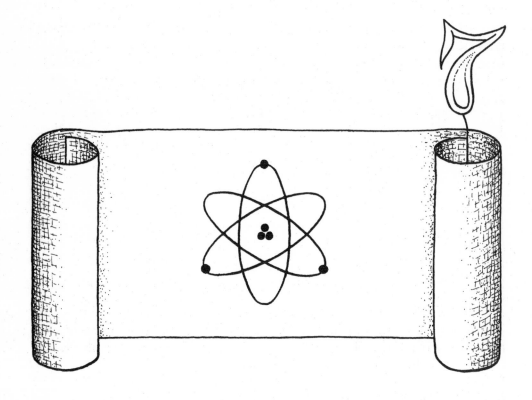

The value of an object is often determined by its origin. The original Last Supper of Leonardo da Vinci in Milan is valued far more than the thousands of similar productions, even though they usually show fewer cracks and more color. Why? Because da Vinci's original, in spite of its poor state of preservation, represents unsurpassed artistry. Similarly the value of our world and of our lives is to be found not merely in their present state of disorder and decay but rather in their original perfection and in their ultimate restoration. The Sabbath serves to remind us of both. This chapter focuses on the former: *The Sabbath, Good News of Perfect Creation.*

In the preceding chapter we found that the Sabbath is rooted in the creation event, marking its completion and inaugurating human history. But, what does the creation Sabbath tell us about the character of the Creator, the quality of His creation, and the relationship between the Creator and His creatures? These questions will be examined in this and subsequent chapters.

PART I

THE GOOD NEWS OF THE CREATION SABBATH

1. *The Scope of the Creation Sabbath*

Before considering the glad tidings of the creation Sabbath, it may be helpful to take a quick preliminary look at some of its roles within the Scriptures. In four different places the Sabbath is explicitly related to creation. The first occurrence is found in Genesis 2:2-3 where the seventh day is presented as the majestic conclusion of the creation event: "And the seventh day God finished his work which he had done, and he rested on the seventh day from all his work which he had done. So God blessed the seventh day and hallowed it, because on it God rested from all his work which he had done in creation."

The other three references (Ex. 20:11; Ex. 31:17; Heb. 4:4) depend upon this first account of the creation Sabbath, but fulfill different functions. In Exodus 20:11 the creation Sabbath is presented as the theological basis for the Sabbath commandment which ordains work during six days and rest on the seventh: "For in six days the Lord made heaven and earth, the sea, and all that is in them, and rested the seventh day, therefore the Lord blessed the sabbath day and hallowed it."

In Exodus 31:17 the creation Sabbath is given as the ground not only of its unceasing obligation ("throughout your generations"—vv. 13-15) but also of a "perpetual covenant" relationship: "It is a sign for ever between me and the people of Israel that in six days the Lord made heaven and earth, and on the seventh day he rested and was refreshed" (v. 17). Finally, in Hebrews 4:4, part of Genesis 2:2 is quoted ("And God rested on the seventh day from all his works") to establish the universality of the Sabbath rest which includes all the blessings of salvation to be found by entering personally into "God's rest" (Heb. 4:1, 3, 5).[1] The fact that an appeal is made to the creation Sabbath to justify the importance of the work-rest commandment, the seriousness of the covenant, and the universality of the blessing of salvation, all of these indicate what vast significance the Bible attributes to the creation Sabbath. Why has the creation Sabbath played such a vital role in the course of salvation-history? To begin answering this question consideration will first be given to the meaning of the Sabbath in the story of creation, and to its implications for a divine-human relationship.

2. Good News of Perfect Creation

An obvious function of the seventh day in the creation account is to conclude God's creation by proclaiming it absolutely complete and perfect. This meaning is expressed especially through the septenary structure of the narrative, the terms used and the function of God's rest. Let us therefore examine each of these three elements in the order mentioned.

Septenary structure. The story of creation (Gen. 1:1 to 2:3) reveals an amazing symmetry built around the number seven (and multiples) which is used both to structure the narrative and to relate many of its details. For example, in Hebrew Genesis 1:1 has *seven* words, and the second verse fourteen— twice *seven*. The three nouns that occur in the first verse, namely *God* (*'Elohim*), *heavens* (*šamayim*), *earth* (*'ereṣ*) are repeated in the story as follows: *God* thirty-five times, that is, five times *seven*; *earth* twenty-one times, that is, three times *seven*; similarly *heavens* (or *firmament—raqia^c^*), twenty-one times, that is, three times *seven*. There are also *seven* references to *light* (*'or*) in the account of the fourth day (Gen. 1:14-18) and *seven* times the expression *it was good* occurs (note the seventh time is *very good*—[Gen. 1:31]).[2] It is particularly significant that the seventh and last section (Gen. 2:2-3) which deals with the *seventh day* has in Hebrew "three consecutive sentences (three for emphasis), each of which consists of *seven* words and contains in the middle the expression *the seventh day*":[3]

1. And on the *seventh day* God finished His work which He had done (v. 2a—*seven* words in Hebrew).
2. And he rested on the *seventh day* from all his work which he had done. (v. 2b—*seven* words in Hebrew).
3. So God blessed the *seventh day* and hallowed it (v. 3a—*seven* words in Hebrew).

It is noteworthy that the number seven not only is a recurring motif in the story of creation, but it also provides the actual frame for the structure of the whole narrative. After the introductory statement (Gen. 1:1), the story is arranged in seven sections, each corresponding to one of the seven days of creation. The recurring sentence "and there was evening and there was morning, one day . . . a second day . . . a third day . . . etc.," marks the logical division of the story that reaches its climatic moment in the seventh day. The latter is repeated three times, undoubtedly to emphasize its function as the goal, conclusion and perfection of the whole creation. The following diagram may help one to appreciate the function of the septenary structure:

Literary Structure of the Creation Story — Genesis 1:1-2:3

And there was evening
and there was morning . . . . *one day* (1:5)

And there was evening
and there was morning . . . . *a second day* (1:8)

And there was evening
and there was morning . . . . *a third day* (1:13)

And there was evening
and there was morning . . . . *a fourth day* (1:19)

And there was evening
and there was morning . . . . *a fifth day* (1:23)

And there was evening
and there was morning . . . . *a sixth day* (1:31)

And God finished his work . . . . *on the seventh day* (2:2a)
and He rested . . . . *on the seventh day* (2:2b)
So God blessed . . . . *the seventh day* (2:3a)

This organization of the story in six days which reach their culmination in the seventh day (which is repeated thrice for added emphasis) shows, as Nicola Negretti persuasively demonstrates in his comprehensive structural analysis of this section, that the purpose of the septenary structure is to finalize into the seventh day the accomplishments of the six intermediate days.[4] The seventh day, as Negretti points out, "concludes, brings to perfection and overcomes the preceding six days."[5]

Why are the structure and many of the details of the creation story based upon the number *seven*? The reason is to be found in the symbolic meaning which this number had both for the Israelites and for the Gentiles. Recent studies on the usage of the number seven reveal that this number was used both in Biblical and ancient Near Eastern literature to express the meaning of *completion* and *perfection*.[6] How did the number seven come to acquire such a meaning? Most probably as a result of its association with the seventh day of creation.[7] In other words, the completion and perfection denoted by the seventh day of creation could easily have been extended to the general use of the number seven.

Various examples have been found in the Sumero-Akkadian and Ugaritic epic literature where the number seven is used in different schematic arrangements to bring any given action to its climax and completion.[8] An Ugaritic tablet, for instance, provides an example of an antithetic structure (sequence of six days contrasted with the final, resolutive action of the seventh day) somewhat similar to the story of creation: "March a day and a second: A third, a fourth day; A fifth, a sixth day—Lo! At the sunrise on the seventh: Thou arrivest at Udum the Great, Even at Udum the Grand."[9]

This passage reminds us of the story of the taking of Jericho, when armed men followed by *seven* priests with *seven* trumpets marched around the city for *seven* days. "On the *seventh* day they rose early at the dawn of day, and marched around the city in the same manner *seven* times: it was only on that day that they marched around the city *seven* times. And at the *seventh* time, . . . the people shouted, and the trumpets were blown. . . . and the wall fell down flat" (Jos. 6:15, 16, 20; emphasis supplied). The conclusive function of the septenary structure is obvious. Walking around the city walls on the first six days serves as prelude to the dramatic conclusion experienced on the seventh day. The completion of the operation is emphasized not only by means of contrast between the action of the six days and that of the seventh, but also by the sevenfold circuiting of the city walls on the seventh day. The act is repeated seven times on the seventh day, undoubtedly to summarize and conclude the activity of the previous six days. This is indicated by the fact that it is "at the *seventh* time . . . [that] the people shouted, the trumpets were blown. . . . and the wall fell down" (Jos. 6:16, 20).

Numerous other Biblical examples could be cited where the number seven is used to express totality, completion and perfection.[10] Peter, for instance, expected to be commended by Christ for proposing to extend forgiveness to his brother up to seven times, that is, as far as the number of perfection. Christ replied utilizing the same number, but admonishing Peter to multiply it "seventy times" (Matt. 18:21-23). The lesson is obvious: perfect forgiveness knows no numerical limitations.

This brief excursus into the symbology of the number seven should suffice to explain why this number forms the recurring motif and the frame of the story of creation. Being the symbol of completion and perfection, its frequent recurrence is designed to heighten the function of the seventh day as the herald of the perfection of God's original creation.

Words. This message of the Sabbath is further enhanced by the terms employed to describe the celebration of the first Sabbath (Gen. 2:2-3). For the sake of clarity, the frequency of the words used will be listed in the following diagram.

Words in Genesis 2:2-3 — Frequency	
God (*'Elohim*)	three times
Seventh day (*yom haššebi'i*)	three times
His work (*mela'kto*)	three times
Done (*'asah*)	three times
Rested (*yišbot*)	two times
Finished (*yekal*)	one time
Blessed (*yebarek*)	one time
Hallowed (*yeqaddeš*)	one time
Created (*bara'*)	one time

The diagram shows that the first four words, namely *God, seventh day, work,* and *done,* have the highest frequency, each occurring three times. Why did the writer repeat these four terms thrice? Obviously because they are central to the message of the passage. Threefold repetition is used in the Bible to emphasize the importance of an action. The Aaronic benediction, for instance, contains threefold blessings to emphasize their fullness (Num. 6:23-26). In this case the threefold emphasis is on "God" and on what He did on "the seventh day" with reference to "his work" of the previous six days. What is said about God's view of "his work" on the seventh day? Three verbs characterize God's assessment of His creation on the seventh day as being fully "done" (repeated thrice), "finished," "created." Another three verbs describe how God celebrated His magnificent accomplishments: "He rested . . . blessed . . . and hallowed" the seventh day. The significance of these latter verbs will be considered subsequently. For the present, notice that the verbs emphasize that on and through the seventh day God proclaimed the good news that His creation was "finished" and fully "done."

The rest of God. To dramatize the importance of such glad tidings, the passage tells us that God did something special on the seventh day. What did He do? Twice it says in Genesis 2:2-3 that God "rested." In the Near Eastern creation myths, the divine rest (technically called *otiositas*), which usually implies the establishment of a secure world order, is generally achieved either by eliminating noisy, disturbing gods or by creating mankind.[11] For example, in the Babylonian creation epic *Enuma elish* the god Marduk says, "Verily, savage-man I will create. He shall be charged with the service of the gods, that they might be at ease!"[12] In the creation Sabbath, however, the divine rest is secured not by subordinating or destroying competitors, nor by exploiting the labor of mankind, but rather by the *completion of a perfect creation.* God rested on the seventh day, not to conclude His work of creation, but rather because His work was "finished . . . done" (Gen. 2:2-3). As stated by Niels-Erik Andreasen, "it is not the rest (cessation from work) which concludes creation, but it is the concluded creation which occasions both rest and the Sabbath."[13]

Any responsible craftsman works on his product until he has brought it up to his ideal and then he stops working on it. In an infinitely higher sense, God, having completed the creation of this world with all its creatures, desisted from creating on the seventh day. This is essentially the meaning of the Hebrew verb *šabat* which is twice translated "rested." Its more accurate rendering is "to stop, to desist, to cease from doing." In fact, to express rest from physical exhaustion the Hebrew employs a different verb, namely *nuah*, which is also generally translated in English "to rest." The latter, in fact, occurs in Exodus 20:11 where God's pattern of work-rest in creation is given as the basis for the commandment to work six days and to rest on the seventh. In Genesis 2, however, the verb *šabat* is used because the function of God's rest is different. It fulfills

a cosmological rather than an anthropological function. In
other words, it serves to explain not why man should rest but
rather how God felt about His creation: He regarded it as complete and perfect, and to acknowledge it—God stopped.

This function of God's rest has been recognized by numerous scholars. Karl Barth, for example, remarks: "We read in
Genesis 2:2 that on the seventh day God, the Creator, completed
His work by 'resting.' This simply means that He did not go
on with the work of creation as such. He set both Himself and
His creation a limit. He was content to be the Creator of this
particular creation, to glory, as the Creator, in this particular
work. He had no occasion to proceed to further creations. He
needed no further creations. And He had found what he created
'very good' (Gen. 1:31)." [14] "When creation ended with man,
having found its climax and meaning in the actualization of man,
God rested on the seventh day from all the work that He had
done. It was to this that He looked in the recognition that
everything was very good and therefore did not need to be
extended or supplemented." [15]

Dietrich Bonhoeffer similarly explains that "in the Bible
'rest' really means more than 'having a rest.' It means rest
after the work is accomplished, it means completion, it means
the perfection and peace in which the world rests." [16] We might
say that by confronting His creation with His cessation-rest, God
proclaimed the Good News that there was no need to put additional finishing touches on what He had created, since He
regarded all of it "very good" (Gen. 1:31).

Did God spend the seventh day merely standing motionless
before His marvelous and active creation? It is hard to believe
that a dynamic God would spend a day in a static posture. The
next chapter will show that God's cessation from *doing* expresses
His desire for *being* with His creation, for giving to His creatures not only *things* but *Himself*. Our immediate concern, however, is to note the glad tidings that the Sabbath proclaims in
the creation narrative by the use of the number seven, emphatic
terms and the imagery of God's rest. It is the reassuring Good
News that this world and all its creatures came into existence,
not in a deformed state by chance, but in a perfect way by a
personal act of God.

PART II

CELEBRATING THE GOOD NEWS OF CREATION

How are we to celebrate on the Sabbath the Good News of God's perfect creation? What is the significance of this celebration as far as our personal life and our relationship with God, with nature and with others is concerned? Various responses will be given to these questions in subsequent chapters. At this junction three suggestions will be made.

1. *Resting as if All Work Were Done*

A first way to celebrate the completion and perfection of God's original creation is by resting on the Sabbath as if all our work were done. This may sound like an unrealistic suggestion, since we often find ourselves at the end of a working week frustrated over unfinished tasks. Does it not frequently happen that, in spite of our best efforts, we accomplish in the six days only part of what we set out to do? How then can we celebrate the Good News of the Sabbath by resting as if all our work were done? The answer is to be found in the very function of the Sabbath, which is to give a sense of "completeness" to our incomplete work and life. A rabbinical comment on Exodus 20:9 ("Six days you shall labor, and do all your work"), hints at this function of the Sabbath: "Is it possible for a human being to do all his work in six days? Does not our work always remain incomplete? What the verse means

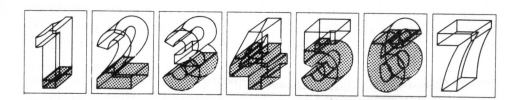

By enabling us to detach ourselves from our daily tasks, the Sabbath gives a sense of completion to the work of the previous six days and to life itself. Whether our best efforts have produced much or little, during each Sabbath God invites us to celebrate His creative and redemptive accomplishments on our behalf, by entering into His Sabbath rest.

to convey is : Rest on the Sabbath as if all your work were done. Another interpretation : *Rest even from the thought of labor.*" [17]

True, the Sabbath often seems to arrive earlier than expected. We may feel disappointed with ourselves because of unfinished tasks. Is this not a forceful reminder of our human finiteness and limitations? The Sabbath, however, by enabling us to detach ourselves from our daily tasks, gives a sense of completion to the work of the previous six days and to life itself. In some weeks the result of our labor seems greater than in others, but it is a fact that whether our best efforts have produced much or little, during each Sabbath God invites us to celebrate His creative and redemptive accomplishments on our behalf, by entering into His Sabbath rest. He invites us to interrupt our daily routine and rest as if all our work were done, in order that we may enter into the joys of His "finished" creation and salvation (Gen. 2:2; John 19:30). This emphasis is found in the Fourth Commandment where God's completion of His six days' creation work and His rest on the seventh are given as the basis for human beings to share in the same experience (Ex. 20:8-11).

It would be impossible on the Sabbath to praise God for His marvelous accomplishments while living under a deep sense of personal failure and frustration because of work that remains undone. Thus on and through the Sabbath, God invites us to view our work in the light of His accomplishments. He tells us, "whether your hard work has produced little or much, rest on the Sabbath as if all your work were done, because My grace is sufficient for you." The sense of completeness that the celebration of the Sabbath brings to our life gives meaning and direction to what otherwise would be continuous, meaningless, and linear existence. Human beings cannot endure life as an unending stretch without breaks of some kind. As the student needs tests and examinations at regular intervals to discover where he stands, so the Christian needs the weekly Sabbath, to discover the joys, the direction and significance of his own existence.

Pacifico Massi acutely observes that "after man has detached himself from the things of life by ceasing to work, man can really assume the attitude of a priest of the creation, and the sacred day has been specifically made for this, so that man might be able to exercise this priesthood in expressing his praise and elevating it to God with intellectual light full of love." [18] What a challenging thought! The Sabbath not only provides a sense of completeness to our imperfect and unfinished work, but it raises us also to the level where we can function as ministers who celebrate the Good News of the Sabbath by offering to God admiration and praise for what He has done for us, in us and through us. This experience of offering to God on the Sabbath not only our praise, but also the accomplishments of our work, gives a sabbatic quality to the preceding work days.

2. Renewing Faith in a Perfect Creator

A basis for true worship. A second way to celebrate the perfection of God's original creation is by renewing our faith in God as our perfect Creator. Faith in God as Creator is the cornerstone of the Christian faith. The first article of the "Apostles' Creed" which most Christians recite and/or accept, states: "I believe in God the Father, Almighty, Creator of heaven and earth—*creatorem caeli et terrae.*" [19] Such a belief is implied in the opening declaration of the Bible: "In the beginning God created the heavens and the earth" (Gen. 1:1). To celebrate the Sabbath means to subscribe to this fundamental Biblical teaching by confessing, not merely with words but also with corresponding actions, belief in God as the perfect Creator. It means to recognize that the existence of this world itself is an absolute gift from God. George Elliott eloquently writes that "Against atheism, which denies the existence of a personal God; against materialism, which denies that this visible universe has its roots in the unseen; and against secularism, which denies the need to worship, the Sabbath is an eternal witness. It symbolically commemorates that creative power which spoke all things into being, the wisdom which ordered their adaptations and harmony, and the love which made, as well as pronounced, all 'very good.' It is set as the perpetual guardian of man against that spiritual infirmity which has everywhere led him to a denial of the God who made him, or to the degradation of that God into a creature made with his own hands." [20]

Why is the belief in God as perfect Creator vital for a meaningful relationship with Him? Why does such a belief constitute the first article of the Creed and the first statement of the Scripture? Basically it is because no one can truly worship God unless he first accepts Him as his perfect Creator. To worship means to acknowledge and praise the worthiness of God. Would God be worthy of praise if He had not originally created this world and all its creatures perfectly? Could a person find reasons to praise the company that produced and sold him a car full of mechanical defects? In the same way it would be hard to find reasons to praise God if His original workmanship had not been perfect or if He had not been directly responsible

Could a person find reasons to praise the company that produced and sold him a car full of mechanical defects? In the same way it would be impossible to find reasons to praise God if His original workmanship had not been perfect. The Sabbath proclaims that this world and all its creatures came into existence, not in a deformed state by chance, but in a perfect way by a personal act of God.

for our existence. Moreover, as well stated by Barth, "if the confession of the work of creation is false and impotent and impossible, so too is that of reconciliation and redemption." [21]

Renewing faith in the Creator. Why has the belief in God as our perfect Creator been challenged in so many different ways during much of mankind's history? The reasons differ. Ancient polytheistic peoples, as some who are living today, preferred to worship that which can be seen or touched. Thus the sun, the moon, the wind and the lightning were viewed not as God's creations but as gods in themselves. The question for them was not, "Is there a God?"—but rather, "Who is your God?" The struggle for supremacy among the many gods obscured the belief in the true Creator-God. In our time the reasons for disbelief in God as the Creator of an originally perfect world are largely of a different nature. The triumph of scientific and rational thinking has resulted in the tendency to discard the whole concept of the existence of a supernatural God. A major contributory factor to this shift in human thinking from polytheism and/or monotheism to agnosticism and atheism has been the theory of evolution, and its influence on the natural sciences. The attempt to explain the origin of life and of this world on a natural and rational basis has led not only secular thinkers but also many professing Christians to reject the Biblical teaching of a Divine *fiat* (spoken) creation. The prominent contemporary question is no longer, Who is your God? but rather, Is there a God? For many "God is dead" or, if He is alive, He has no direct involvement in the origin or subsistence of this world.

Why is there such a prevailing skepticism about God being the Creator of an originally perfect world? Why do many persons today have greater faith in the theory of spontaneous generation than in an original divine and perfect creation? Is it possible that the widespread abandonment of the seventh-day Sabbath—the reminder of God's perfect creation—has facilitated such prevailing skepticism? Ellen White provides an affirmative answer to this question when she writes: "Had the Sabbath been universally kept, . . . there would never have been an idolater, an atheist, or an infidel." [22] The statement needs some qualifications, since the mechanical observance of creation's memorial day does not guarantee per se the acceptance of God as Creator. It is possible to go through the motions of the observance of a day without understanding of or commitment to what is being celebrated. Yet the fact remains that skepticism can be an outgrowth of forgetfulness. A person who neglects the Sabbath, the memorial of creation, is liable to forget and become skeptical about the God of creation. Is this not similarly true in human relationships? I was engaged to be married for four years, which to me seemed like an eternity, because much of the time my fiancée and I were separated by an ocean. During the prolonged separation I was tempted to forget and to doubt who my fiancée was and how much she loved me. How did I overcome my incipient skepticism? I would take time to read and reread her letters and to look at her pictures. That helped me to overcome any doubt and to renew my commitment to my fiancée. In a similar fashion the Sabbath provides a weekly opportunity to overcome any incipient skepticism by inviting us to "remember" and thus to renew our faith in our perfect Creator.

During the week as we use and admire the many sophisticated man-made machines, we are tempted to place our trust in human achievements and resources. God was well aware of this very real danger that human beings may lose sight of their Creator and worship instead human creations. Therefore, in His divine concern and wisdom, He established the seventh-day Sabbath to safeguard His creatures from the disaster of self-worship. Through the Sabbath, God invites His people week after week to hear and to celebrate the Good News of His perfect creation, by contemplating His handiwork and thus renewing their faith in the perfect Creator. Because this vital function of the Sabbath meets a continuing human need—greater today than ever before—no Sabbath discontinuance can ever be sanctioned nor ever be legitimately contemplated. Thus any human attempt to invest another day of the week with the symbolic-memorial function of the creation-Sabbath would mean to disregard the event for which the day stands.

3. Delighting in God's Creation

A weekly interlude. A renewed faith in the Creator makes it possible to celebrate the Sabbath in a third way, namely, by taking delight in the beauty and perfection of God to be found in the worship experience, in our lives, in the lives of others and in the world around us. The Sabbath invites us not to prostitute the world but to delight in its beauty. It invites us to look above and beyond the cloud of sin and suffering that darkens our world and recapture in thought the astonishment, the joy and admiration, experienced by the first human pair.

Harvey Cox maintains that thousands of Westerners are today turning to Eastern meditation because "it provides a modern equivalent of what the observance of Sabbath once did but does no more." [23] Why turn to Eastern meditation, which is based on strange and un-Biblical world views, when the Sabbath affords both the setting and valid reasons for meditating, contemplating and rejoicing in the goodness of God's creation? Oriental meditation often encourages a total way of life based on escaping the sad realities of this world. The Sabbath, on the other hand, encourages not a permanent escape from this troubled world, but only a one-day weekly interlude in order to catch a glimpse of the divine realm of order, purity and love. Such a renewed vision equips the believer with hope and faith to live in this present world, while looking forward by faith to the world to come, or we might say, to live in time while preparing for eternity.

A window of eternity. The Sabbath affords the means of recapturing some measure of Edenic delight. It offers the opportunity to look at the world through the window of eternity. In the Judeo-Christian tradition the Sabbath has been regarded as a day of joy and jubilation. Isaiah calls the Sabbath "a delight," and a day to "take delight in the Lord" (58:13-14). To ensure the festive atmosphere of the Sabbath, the Jews prepared themselves for the event with special clothing, meals, and proper frame of mind. No fasting was permitted and even the seven-day mourning period was to be interrupted.[24] Similarly many Christians have experienced the Sabbath delight.[25] Luke tells us that all the people who were blessed by the Sabbath ministry of Christ *"rejoiced* at all the glorious things that were done by him" (Luke 13:17). Ellen White urges parents to do all in their power to "make the Sabbath, . . . the most joyful day of the week. . . . [to] lead their children to regard it as a delight, the day of days, the holy of the Lord, honorable." [26]

How difficult it is for the members of one church to understand the joys, the intimacies and paradoxes experienced by those of another! The sense of release, peace and tranquility that the Sabbath brings cannot be understood, unless one experiences them. Abraham Joshua Heschel perceptively interprets such an experience, when he says: "The seventh day is like a palace in time with a kingdom for all. It is not a date but an atmosphere. It is not a different state of consciousness but a different climate; it is as if the appearance of all things somehow changed. The primary awareness is one of our being *within* the Sabbath rather than of the Sabbath being within us. We may not know whether our understanding is correct, or whether our sentiments are noble, but the air of the day surrounds us like spring which spreads over the land without our aid or notice." [27]

The Sabbath affords the means of recapturing some measure
of Edenic delight. It offers the opportunity to look at the world
through the window of eternity.

Why is everything more beautiful and delightful on the Sabbath? Why does it seem, to use the words of Maltbie D. Babcock, that "all nature sings, and round me rings the music of the spheres"? Why do the divine services seem richer, the people friendlier, the food more delicious, ladies, gentlemen and children more beautiful internally and externally? Basically, because the Sabbath offers not only the time but also the spiritual resources to perceptibly enjoy God, people and things. By renewing faith in a perfect Creator and Redeemer, the Sabbath enables the believer to view things not merely as they are, but as they must have been originally and as they will again be ultimately. It is like putting on for 24 hours a pair of spectacles that make flat pictures look three-dimensional. Those who do not find the Sabbath delightful but depressing are those who casually accept the Sabbath time but not its Good News. They fail to renew their faith in a perfect Creator and do not allow their Savior to bring His rest into their restless lives. Consequently they find the Sabbath a burden rather than a blessing, a day of gloom rather than of gladness, bad news of things that cannot be done rather than Good News of things to be enjoyed. But to the Christian who loves the Lord of the Sabbath and who accepts its Good News, the Sabbath is a day of joyful celebration. It is a day to celebrate God's marvelous accomplishments in the world and in his personal life. When Friday evening comes, he gratefully says: "Thank God it is Sabbath!" He rejoices at the thought that another Sabbath has come; a day to taste and know that the Lord is good; a day to thank God for the accomplishments of a week that is past; a day to renew one's faith in and commitment to the perfect Creator and Savior; a day to sing the Psalmist's Sabbath song, "Thou, O Lord, hast made me glad by thy work; at the works of thy hands I sing for joy. How great are thy works, O Lord!" (Ps. 92:4-5—A Song for the Sabbath); a day to celebrate the *Good News of God's Perfect Creation.*

CHAPTER
III

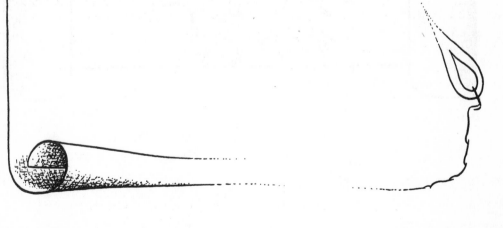

the Sabbath

GOOD NEWS
of God's care

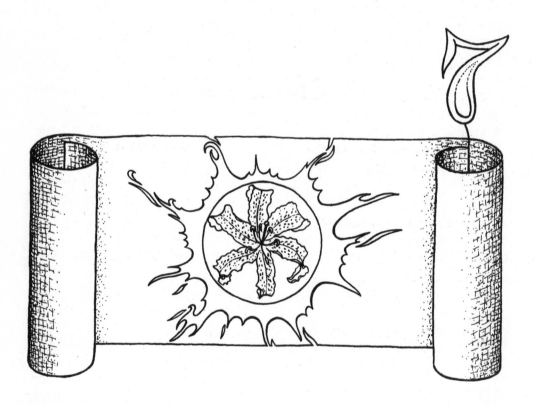

"You don't really care for me! If you did, you would show it by taking time to be with me and to remember me with a card or some flowers." Such a complaint, often expressed among lovers, reflects the human need to be constantly reassured that others care. Reassurance is sought not only from relatives but also from employer, teacher, doctor, government and manufacturer. Is it not true that even goods bought without a warranty are valued less? Manufacturers, well aware of this human need, market their products with various types of warranties. "What I like about my auto," a person will often remark, "is the excellent service my dealer provides."

The search for reassurance of personal interest and care is not limited to the horizontal level of human relations, but extends also to the vertical human-divine relationship. A basic human concern is, "Does God really care for me?" "How can I know that God is really interested in me?" The general loss of reassurance that God really cares for this world and for individual lives may be viewed as a fundamental crisis in modern Christianity. The slogan "God is dead," which has found resonance in some Christian circles, exemplifies the sense of disillusionment experienced by many. Their feeling is that if God really exists, He is at best an "absentee landlord."

The untold suffering and the loss of millions of lives which mankind has experienced in our century as a result of two world wars, countless local conflicts, the holocaust, and many natural disasters, represent some of the reasons for the prevailing skepticism concerning the existence of a benevolent God. In addition, the ability of modern science to solve what past generations regarded as unsolvable problems has led many to put their faith in human resources rather than in divine providence. Any attempt to examine these and other significant reasons for the prevailing disbelief in God's concern for human affairs, would lead far beyond the limits of this study.[1] Our attention will be focused on what role the Sabbath can play in restoring confidence in God's concern for humanity.

The previous chapter showed that the Sabbath reassures the believer that God is his perfect Creator. This reassurance represents per se a revelation of the Creator's concern for His creatures. What greater satisfaction than to know one is a

creation of a perfect Creator! However, the knowledge alone
of being the product of a divine creation does not necessarily
satisfy the immediate concern for the assurance of God's care
for me *now*. Why? Mainly because creation is a divine act
accomplished in the remote *past*, and consequently it does not
necessarily speak to the *present*—to the immediate need for assurance of divine concern. But, the message of a perfect creation, hardly exhausts the scope of the Sabbath. Further glad
tidings are proclaimed by the Sabbath which, if accepted, contribute more directly to overcome the sense of God's absence
from the world and from human lives. Three of these messages
will be considered in this chapter under the following headings:
(1) the blessing of the Sabbath; (2) the sanctification of the
Sabbath; (3) the pattern of work and rest. Other aspects of
God's care signified by the Sabbath will be considered in later
chapters.

PART I

THE BLESSING OF THE SABBATH

The divine act of blessing and hallowing the Sabbath
exemplifies God's love and concern for humanity. Seven times
in the creation story God proclaimed His creation "good" (Gen.
1:3, 10, 12, 17, 20, 25, 31) and three times He "blessed" it. The
threefold blessing is given in an ascending order. First, the
creatures of the water and the air are blessed with physical
fertility (Gen. 1:22). Second, the man and the woman are
blessed with physical fecundity and dominion (Gen. 1:28-30).
Lastly, the seventh day is blessed and imbued with sanctity
(Gen. 2:3; Ex. 20:11). Being the final recipient of God's blessing,
the Sabbath expresses and guarantees God's ultimate and total
blessing over all His creation and creatures.

1. *The Meaning of the Sabbath Blessing*

What is the significance of the blessings bestowed by God
upon the Sabbath and how do they express divine concern for
mankind? Are they just a good wish like human blessings?
In the Scripture God's blessings represent not merely a good
wish, but rather a concrete assurance of fertility, prosperity,
happiness—in sum, a full and abundant life. For example, God
blessed the first couple saying, "Be fruitful and multiply" (Gen.

1:28; cf. 9:1; 49:22-26). Similarly we read in the Aaronic benediction: "The Lord bless you and keep you" (Num. 6:24). The blessing of God results, then, in the preservation and assurance of abundant life. This meaning is expressed explicitly by the Psalmist when he writes: "...the Lord has commanded the blessing, life for evermore" (Ps. 133:3). Applying this meaning to the Sabbath, it would mean that God by blessing the day was not doing wishful thinking, but gave to mankind a permanent assurance of full and abundant life.[2]

It must be said, however, that the meaning of both the blessing and sanctification of the Sabbath is not spelled out in Genesis 2:3. This is puzzling because in most instances God's benediction is accompanied by an explanation of its content. For example, "God blessed them [animals], saying, 'Be fruitful and multiply and fill the water in the seas, and let the birds multiply on the earth" (Gen. 1:22). Similarly, God said to Abraham regarding his wife, Sarah: "I will bless her, and she shall be a mother of nations; kings of peoples shall come from her" (Gen. 17:16; cf. 9:1; 17:20). Yet with regard to the blessing of the Sabbath, nothing is said as to what such a blessing entails. One wonders why. Nicola Negretti offers an explanation which appears very convincing. He explains that the inner sense of the holiness and blessing of the Sabbath "remains sealed" in Genesis. When are the seals removed? In the unfolding of the history of salvation.[3]

2. *The Blessing of the Sabbath in the Manna Experience*

The mystery of the blessedness and sanctity of the Sabbath begins to be unveiled in Exodus with the establishment of Israel as God's covenant people. The day becomes now linked not merely to a finished creation, but to the new nation which God has miraculously brought into existence: "See! The Lord has given you the Sabbath" (Ex. 16:29). From being cosmological, a symbol of a perfect world, the Sabbath has now become a soteriological-historical symbol of God's redemptive plan for His people. Thus the Sabbath becomes now more intimately connected with the ups and downs of the life of God's people. Some of the redemptive features and function of the Sabbath will be studied in chapter V.

Physical nourishment. The manna story offers a starting point to understand the nature of the original blessing of the Sabbath. Notice first of all certain parallelisms between the creation and the manna narrative. Both are divine acts accomplished according to the seven-day structure. Both testify to the perfection of God's activities: the daily creation was "good" and the daily portion of the manna was satisfying (Ex. 16:18). In both instances the creative activity ceases on the Sabbath: creation is "finished" (Gen. 2:2) and the manna ceased to fall (Ex. 16:25). In both cases God's blessings are bestowed upon the Sabbath: by proclamation at creation (Gen. 2:3) and by preservation in the manna (Ex. 16:24). In the context of the aridity of the desert and of the murmuring of the people caused by their inability to secure food, the miracle of the preservation of the manna throughout Sabbath stands as a most conspicuous revelation of the nature of the Sabbath blessings, namely, God's reassuring gift of physical nourishment and life.

The literary structure of the manna narrative focuses on the blessedness of the Sabbath. A crescendo is noticeable from the opening announcement of the gift of the manna (Ex. 16:4) to the closing divine proclamation of the Sabbath (Ex. 16:29). The initial announcement is silent over the Sabbath. But the silence is gradually broken first by means of the prescription of the exact "omer" measure (Ex. 16:16-17) and then by the account of the spoiling and preservation of the manna (Ex. 16:20-24). These actions set the stage for the official proclamation of the Sabbath first by Moses (Ex. 16:23, 25-26) and then by God (Ex. 16:28-29). Some of the details are especially significant. For example, what was the reason for the specification of an omer per person per day? Was it not to ensure the precise measurement of the double portion to be gathered on the sixth day? Such precision was necessary to guarantee the genuineness of the miracle of the seventh day, when, contrary to the preceding days, left-over portions would not spoil (Ex. 16:24). The miracle in turn was to predispose the people to accept and experience the blessing and the holiness of the Sabbath. Such blessing consisted of the miraculous provision on the Sabbath of the physical nourishment of the corruptible manna and the spiritual enrichment of the incorruptible heavenly manna, the Word of God.

The Word of God. What is the significance of the absence of any manna on the ground on the Sabbath? Apparently it was designed to predispose the people to look upward and receive a greater blessing from above, that is, not only nourishment for physical life but also enrichment for the spiritual life. This important lesson is brought out in Deuteronomy 8:3 where the Israelites are admonished not to forget the blessings received through the manna experience: "And he humbled you and let you hunger and fed you with manna, ... that he might make you know that man does not live by bread alone, but that man lives by everything that proceeds out of the mouth of the Lord."

During six days God's blessings reached the Israelites through the visible manna, but on the seventh day the blessings were received through God's invisible voice. The Israelites were asked not to go out on the Sabbath to seek more material blessings, but to rest content within the confinements of those already received, in order to hear without interference the Word of God. Such an invitation acquired special significance in view of the fact that at that historical juncture the Israelites had their ears still more attuned to the sounds of Egypt than to the voice of God. In His deep concern to restore broken relationships, God through the Sabbath taught the Israelites to make themselves available to receive the blessing of His word and presence. One might say that ultimately the blessing of the Sabbath is the presence of Christ Himself, "the living bread which came down from heaven; if anyone eats of this bread, he will live for ever" (John 6:51). By the blessings of the Sabbath, as Gerhard von Rad remarks, "the way is prepared for an exalted good, actually the final saving good." [4] Chapter V will trace further the relationship between the blessings of the Sabbath and God's saving acts which culminate in Christ's redemptive ministry. These preliminary observations may suffice to illustrate how the blessing of the Sabbath expresses God's loving concern for humankind and gives assurance of an enriching life.

PART II

THE SANCTIFICATION OF THE SABBATH

The divine blessing of the Sabbath is followed by another extraordinary act, equally expressive of God's concern for His creatures, namely, the sanctification of the Sabbath: "God blessed the seventh day and *hallowed* it" (Gen. 2:3). Other possible renderings of the Hebrew verb (*yeqaddeš*) are "made it holy" or "sanctified it." The verbal form used (Piel) has both a causative and a declarative sense. This means that God declared the seventh day holy and caused it to be a means of holiness for mankind.[5] It is noteworthy that the word "holy" is used here for the first time in the Bible with reference, not to an object such as an altar, a tabernacle or a person, but with regard to time, the seventh day.

1. *The Meaning of Sabbath Holiness*

What is the meaning of the "holiness" that God placed upon the Sabbath? It does not refer to the structure of the day, since the Sabbath follows the same cycle and length of all the other six days. How can such an impersonal element as time be imbued with sanctity? In Genesis no explanation is given. As in the case of the blessing, so the sanctification of the Sabbath hides a certain mystery, which is gradually unveiled in the unfolding of the history of salvation. However, in Exodus, where the holiness of the Sabbath is reiterated several times, its meaning is elucidated by means of its explicit association with the manifestation of God's glorious presence. In the manna narrative the holiness of the Sabbath is announced but not yet explained (Ex. 16:23). Why? Apparently because at that moment the revelation of God's glory was partial and preparatory to the fuller manifestation to occur at Sinai. The Israelites were invited to "come near before the Lord" (Ex. 16:9), but they were given only a glimpse of "the glory of the Lord" in the form of "the cloud" which they saw in the distance as "they looked toward the wilderness" (Ex. 16:10).

Sabbath holiness as God's presence. At Sinai the manifestation of God's glorious presence occurs repeatedly and most impressively, assuming in some cases cataclysmic proportions. The proclamation of the Decalogue, for instance, occurs in the midst of a fiery and thundering manifestation of God's power and presence (Ex. 19:16-19; 20:18-19). From the Mount made holy by the glorious presence of God, the Sabbath is explicitly proclaimed as God's holy day: "Remember the Sabbath day, to keep it holy" (Ex. 20:8). The commandment, it should be noticed, not only *opens* with the invitation to remember and keep holy the Sabbath (cf. Deut. 5:15), but also *closes* reiterating that its holiness is grounded in God's sanctification of the day at creation (Ex. 20:11). In Hebrew the identical verb is used in both instances.

The experience of God's glorious presence on Mount Sinai served to educate the Israelites to acknowledge the holiness of God manifested in time (the Sabbath) and later in a place of worship (the Tabernacle). The motif of God's glory, as shown below, is found in all of these (Sinai, Sabbath and Tabernacle) and ties them together. The Israelites were instructed to prepare themselves for the encounter with God's holy presence (Ex. 19:10, 11), when the Lord would "come down upon Mount Sinai in the sight of all the people" (Ex. 19:11). The preparation included personal cleansing (Ex. 19:10, 14) and the setting of a boundary around the mountain (Ex. 19:12, 23) which was to be invested with God's glory. The nexus with the holiness of the Sabbath can hardly be missed. Indeed, personal preparation and the setting of a boundary between common and holy time are the basic ingredients necessary for the sanctification of the Sabbath. Can one enter into the experience of God's holy presence on the Sabbath without making necessary preparation? Or is it possible to honor God's presence on His holy seventh day without setting a boundary in time that fences off personal profits and pleasures?

An experience of God's presence. The meaning of the holiness of God is further clarified at Sinai by the invitation God extended to Moses "on the seventh day" to enter into the cloud and thus experience the intimacy of His presence. "Then Moses went up on the mountain, and the cloud covered the mountain. The glory of the Lord settled on Mount Sinai, and the cloud covered it six days; and on the *seventh day* he called to Moses out of the midst of the cloud. Now the appearance of the glory of the Lord was like a devouring fire on the top of the mountain in the sight of the people. And Moses entered the cloud, and went up on the mountain" (Ex. 24:15-18; emphasis supplied). It is generally recognized that the seventh day here designates the Sabbath. Nicola Negretti, for instance, in his literary analysis of the passage, shows how the "sabbatical structure . . . provides a stylistic and chronological link between the manifestation of the glory and the beginning of the divine revelation." [6] Similarly, Ellen White comments, "upon the seventh day, which was the Sabbath, Moses was called up into the cloud." [7] God's invitation to Moses to enter on the seventh day into His glorious presence unveils the cryptic meaning of God's sanctification of the Sabbath at creation. The holiness of the Sabbath is now explained to be not a magic quality infused by God into this day, but this holiness is rather His mysterious and majestic presence manifested on and through the Sabbath in the lives of His people.

This meaning of the holiness of the Sabbath is brought out even more forcefully a few chapters later, when, at the end of the revelation of the tabernacle, God says to the people of Israel, "You shall keep my sabbaths, for this is a sign between me and you throughout your generations, that you may know that I, the Lord, sanctify you" (Ex. 31:13). The sanctity of the Sabbath is now clearly equated with the sanctifying presence of God with His people. The mystery of the sanctification of the creation-Sabbath is now unveiled. It consists precisely of the presence of God bestowed upon the world in His very last creative act: the sanctification of the seventh day. For six days God filled this planet with good things and living beings, but on the seventh He filled it with His presence. God's presence is the source of the very blessings of life and happiness promised through the Sabbath. Separated from God's presence, human life is but a fleeting shadow. David was well aware of this truth when, under the weight of the separation from God caused by his sin, he prayed, "Cast me not away from thy presence, and take not away thy holy Spirit from me" (Ps. 51:11). As the symbol and assurance of God's presence in this world and in human lives, the Sabbath represents a most sublime expression of God's loving care.

2. Sabbath Holiness as a Link

The definition of the holiness of the Sabbath as the special manifestation of God's presence points to its function as a link between God and human beings. To use a popular theological concept, this link could be described as a divine-human encounter. In an attempt to grasp more fully the implications of this function of the Sabbath, consideration will now be given to the linkage the day provides in Exodus between law and grace and between the Tabernacle and the people of Israel.

A link between law and grace. The promulgation of the Decalogue and of the various civil and cultic laws (Ex. 21 to 23) is followed in Exodus by the revelation of the blueprint for the construction of the Tabernacle (Ex. 25 to 31). The latter is viewed as the symbol of God's dwelling among the people (Ex. 25:8; 29:45) and of His provision for the forgiveness of their sins (Ex. 29:36, 38; 30:10). How is the Sabbath related to these two, that is, to law and grace? In the narrative the seventh day functions as the link between the two, since it is on this day that Moses "entered into the cloud" (Ex. 24:18) of God's glorious presence to receive both "the tables of stone, with the law and the commandment" (Ex. 24:12) and "the pattern of the tabernacle" (Ex. 25:9). In this context the Sabbath functions as the day when God's care is manifested through His revelation of principles of conduct on the one hand and provisions for atonement and worship on the other hand. A vital principle is implied here: The Sabbath is the day when God both communicates a knowledge of His will and grants His grace to implement it. The latter is suggested also by the fact that the revelation of the tabernacle closes with the reiteration of the Sabbath as the sign that "I, the Lord, sanctify you" (Ex. 31:13).

For six days God filled this planet with good things and living beings, but on the seventh He filled it with His presence. God's presence is the source of the very blessings of life and happiness promised through the Sabbath.

In Exodus the Sabbath is linked also to the Tabernacle by means of the theme of God's glory. The divine glory manifested at first on Mount Sinai in the form of a cloud (Ex. 24:15-16) is later transferred to the Tabernacle. When "Moses finished the work" (Ex. 40:33) of constructing the Tabernacle, "then the cloud covered the tent of meeting, and the glory of the Lord filled the tabernacle. And Moses was not able to enter the tent of meeting, because the cloud abode upon it, and the glory of the Lord filled the tabernacle" (Ex. 40:34-35). The manifestation of God's glory in the form of a cloud, first experienced by Moses "on the seventh day" on Mount Sinai (Ex. 24:16) and later transferred upon the Tabernacle, provides a link between the sanctification of the Sabbath at creation and of the Tabernacle in the wilderness. It suggests that as the cosmic creation was concluded with its sanctification on the seventh day by God's personal presence, so the creation of a place of worship is completed and inaugurated by the divine presence resting upon it (Ex. 40:34-35).

A link between the tabernacle and the Israelites. The holiness of the Sabbath as the experience of God's presence provides a further link between the Tabernacle and the people. The Tabernacle served as a visible reassurance that the Lord dwelt "among the people of Israel" (Ex. 25:8; cf. 29:45). Similarly, the Sabbath was to reassure the Israelites throughout their generations that "I, the Lord, sanctify you" (Ex. 31:13). Sanctification by virtue of God's presence is the element shared in common by both the Sabbath and the Tabernacle. The presence of God manifested upon and within the tabernacle through the Sabbath was to become a personal experience of each believer. "The uniqueness of the holy place," writes Samuel Terrien, "through the Sabbath, became an interior and universal reality." [8] As God's sanctuary in time, the Sabbath offers to every believer the opportunity to experience in a special way the presence of God, irrespective of circumstances. In fact, for many faithful ones who through the centuries have been prevented by sickness or by unfavorable circumstances from worshiping in a sanctuary with fellow believers, the Sabbath has truly been a portable sanctuary—a day when even prison bars have not barred the presence of God from lighting the soul of the believer. This helps us understand why, after the exile and dispersion, the Jews who had been deprived of their Temple organized meeting places (synagogues), sometimes even in the open air (Acts 16:13), where they would resort on the Sabbath to study the Scripture and to pray.[9] The awareness that God's holy presence manifested in a sacred place (Temple, church) through the Sabbath could

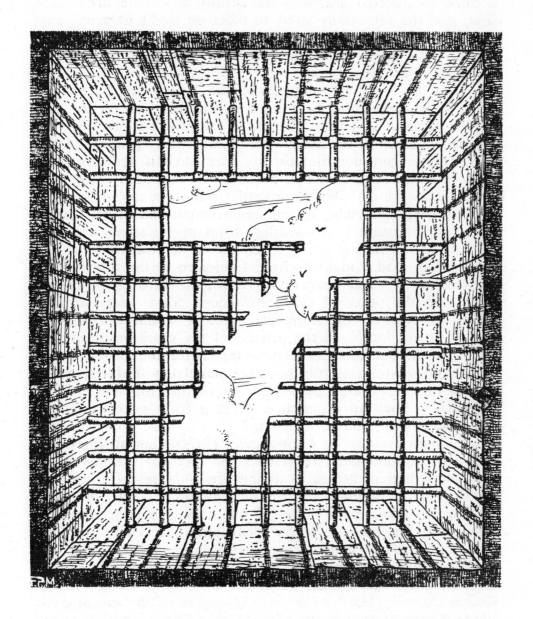

For many faithful ones who through the centuries have been prevented by sickness or by unfavorable circumstances from worshiping in a sanctuary with fellow believers, the Sabbath has truly been a portable sanctuary—a day when even prison bars have not barred the presence of God from lighting the soul of the believer.

become an internal and personal reality has enabled the Jews first, and the Christians later, to meet on God's holy day even though few in number, assured by the promise that "where two or three are gathered in my name, there am I in the midst of them" (Matt. 18:20).

I vividly recall the many Sabbaths I spent in the town of Fano, Italy, worshiping God alone in the seclusion of my room or out in nature. I was a teenager selling Christian literature during the summer to earn a scholarship. During the weekdays I had to face considerable hostility from various quarters: from the local religious and civil authorities who constantly threatened to punish me for distributing unauthorized literature; from superstitious customers who feared being contaminated by the unendorsed literature I was selling; from my relatives who gave me a roof but viewed me as a heretic to be rescued from hellfire. When Friday night arrived, I rejoiced at the thought that for one day I could forget the hostile world around me and enter into the peace of God's presence. Since there were no fellow believers in the immediate area, I would worship God alone but not lonely, in the privacy of my room or in an open field. So the Sabbath has been for me, as for countless believers throughout history, a truly portable sanctuary—a day to forget human misery through the experience of the closeness of God's presence.[10] Such an experience offers a fresh reminder of the Good News that God cares for us.

Sabbath holiness as Emmanuel. The coming of Christ into this world undoubtedly represents *the link par excellence* that reconnects human beings to divine life and presence. Can the holiness of the Sabbath and the incarnation of Christ be placed in a logical relationship? Yes, if one considers their respective functions. The purpose of the incarnation is perhaps best epitomized in the two names given to the Lord at His birth: "you shall call his name *Jesus*, for he will save his people from their sins. . . . His name shall be called *Emmanuel* (which means, God with us)" (Matt. 1:21, 23). Associating the meanings of the two names together, we may say that Christ came to restore life to His people by reuniting them to the presence of God.

How is this purpose of the incarnation related to the purpose of God's creation as expressed through the blessing and sanctification of the Sabbath? The latter expresses, as was shown earlier, God's assurance to His creature of abundant life through God's presence. Then, do not the purpose of God's creation and that of Christ's incarnation coincide to a large extent? One might say that what God promised to His creation by blessing and sanctifying the Sabbath, He fulfilled by sending

Christ into this world to become "Emmanuel—God with us."
"How often have we heard," writes Herbert W. Richardson, "that
Jesus Christ abolished the Sabbath so that men may be truly
free! But this suggestion is sheer theological nonsense. The
work of Jesus Christ cannot contradict the purpose for which
God created the world. To assert such a contradiction, by
explicitly or implicitly opposing the Sabbath, is to reiterate the
old Gnostic claim that the god of the Old Testament and the
God of the New Testament are two different 'Gods.' " [11] Richardson continues by rightly asserting that "the Sabbath Day was
created by God, so that He Himself might enter into the world
and sanctify it by His personal presence." [12] God's sanctification of the Sabbath represents a most telling revelation of God's
concern for this world. It tells that God revealed His love
toward mankind, not only by entering into the limitation of
human time on the seventh day of creation to bless this world
with His holy presence, but also by entering, after the estrangement caused by sin, into the limitations of *human flesh* to
become again "Emmanuel—God with us." Chapter V will trace
this Messianic-Redemptive meaning and message of the Sabbath
in the OT and NT, as well as in Jewish literature. Such a study
can lead to a fuller appreciation of the good news of God's
care which the Sabbath proclaims.

PART III

THE PATTERN OF WORK AND REST

1. *Work as God's Care*

In the Fourth Commandment the pattern of six days of work
and the seventh for rest is based upon the creation week (Ex.
20:11). It should be noticed that the commandment encompas-
ses both the six days' work and the seventh day's rest experience.
In fact, the command to rest on the seventh day is preceded
by the injunction, "six days you shall labor and do all your
work" (Ex. 20:9; Deut. 5:13). This means that the work of
the six days is viewed as a prelude or a necessary pilgrimage
to reach the "rest" experience of the seventh day.

It is divine concern for human well-being which led God
to ordain the pattern of six days for work and the seventh for
rest. Experience teaches us that work and rest are two genuine
and significant human needs. A person who is workless is one
who feels worthless. Work is needed to experience self-worth,

to develop one's creative abilities and reflect the image of the ever-active Creator. If work was needed before the fall to enhance human life with rewarding activities, how much more needed it is today when idleness lures people into all sorts of vices and crimes!

It must be said, however, that the many mechanical and monotonous jobs which people have to perform nowdays to earn a livelihood contribute little to personal growth and fulfillment. On the contrary they tend to dehumanize. Fortunately, however, shorter work-weeks today provide increasing opportunities to work at personal projects that give greater enrichment, satisfaction and pleasure.

2. Rest as God's Care

All work, whether it be compulsory or voluntary, if it is not balanced by rest, can become an oppressive and unrelenting master. Unrelenting work patterns can degrade human personality, can destroy the equilibrium between body and spirit and turn a person into a brute. This was true in the ancient agricultural societies where dependent workers were often oppressed and exploited by unscrupulous masters, but it also applies to today's technological society where machines often tend to annihilate personal individuality. In some instances it is insatiable greediness that drives people to work uninterruptedly, thus becoming slaves of greater gain.

God was well aware of human vulnerability to lucrative ambitions. Hence, in His concern to protect both employers and employees from the senselessness of uninterrupted work, through the Sabbath commandment, God ordained not only work but rest also. Subsequent chapters will consider various vital functions of the Sabbath rest. Presently attention will be given to the liberation the Sabbath provides to human beings.

Rest as freedom from work. The Sabbath rest spells freedom from work for the master, the servants and the animals (Ex. 20:10; 23:12; Deut. 5:14). Why are even "dumb beasts" included in the Sabbath rest? Because God's compassion extends also to unintelligent and defenseless creatures. Could this all-inclusiveness of the Sabbath rest reveal God's concern for the restoration of total harmony between man and nature? Moreover, why are "the son of your bondmaid, and the alien" (Ex. 23:12) specifically singled out? Obviously, because these had no recourse or protection against the commands and exploitation of others. The Sabbath rest then reveals God's concern especially for the human rights of the defenseless of our society.

What about the "workaholics" of our society? Is not the Sabbath rest a divine remedy to aid those who seek to find ultimate fulfillment in their work? The Sabbath rest teaches that the chief end of life is not, as advocated by Marxism, to work to transform nature, but to rest to enjoy God's presence and creation. The Sabbath rest teaches also freedom from things. One of the most difficult lessons to learn is how to have things without becoming addicted to them; how to live with people without losing one's independence. On the Sabbath, by abstaining from the production or purchase of goods, one learns detachment and independence from matter and attachment to and dependence on the Spirit.

The Sabbath rest promotes freedom from greed. In order to keep up with the Joneses, some Christians today, like the Israelites of old, choose to moonlight on the Sabbath (Ex. 16:27), hoping to secure added income and goods. But the Scripture points to the senselessness of such an effort, when it pointedly says "they found none" (Ex. 16:27). That is to say, one misses obtaining both the material and the spiritual manna and consequently finds oneself restless and dissatisfied. The Sabbath teaches the greedy heart to be grateful—to stop for one day looking for more, and start instead gratefully to acknowledge the blessings received. A person who learns gratitude experiences inner peace, inasmuch as a grateful heart is the abiding place of Christ and of His peace.

Rest as freedom for God. The Sabbath rest signifies freedom for God. By making Himself totally available to His creatures on the seventh day, God manifested the greatness of His love toward them. In a similar way, human beings are invited to respond to God's love by making themselves available to Him. This is why the Commandment enjoins to do all the work in six days in order to be free to devote the seventh day "to the Lord your God" (Ex. 20:10). The purpose of the Sabbath rest is not merely humanitarian, that is, to provide needed physical refreshment. If this were its only function, its value for modern persons would be dubious and questionable, since most people today already have at their disposal two or three weekly days for leisure. Moreover, is there anything more depressing than having nothing to do, waiting for the Sabbath hours to pass away in order to resume some meaningful activity? If this were the sole purpose of the Sabbath rest, then other rational plans could readily be devised to achieve such an objective. Perhaps it is this misconception of the Sabbath rest that leads so many to seek "refreshment" on this day through motorized or unmotorized flights to distant scenes, sporting events, alcohol and flirtation. Such activities relieve human beings of none of their burdens, but only lay new ones upon them.

In the Scripture, however, the Sabbath rest is qualified. It is not a frivolous good time but "solemn rest, holy to the Lord" (Ex. 31:15; 16:23-25; 20:10; Lev. 23:3). While the Sabbath is given to mankind (Ex. 16:29; Mark 2:27), yet it belongs to Yahweh (Ex. 16:23, 25; Is. 56:4; 58:13; Mark 2:28). Therefore, human rest on the Sabbath is not a *self-centered* (anthropocentric) relaxation when all wishes and desires can be fulfilled without restraint, but rather a *divine-centered* (theocentric) rest when, freed from the care of work, a person becomes free for God Himself. In this new freedom he finds genuine refreshment. As emphatically stated by Karl Barth, "to observe the holy day means also to keep oneself free for participation in the praise and worship and witness and proclamation of God in His congregation, in common thanksgiving and intercession. And the blessing and profit of the holy day definitely depends also on the positive use of this freedom." [13]

God summons His people on the Sabbath to be free from work in order to be free before Him and to listen to His voice. The Sabbath rest, to use Aquinas' happy expression, is an invitation to have "a day of vacation with God"—*ad vacandum divinis.*[14] How sour the weekdays would be without the Sabbath vacation with God and fellow beings! The weeks would be as tasteless as spaghetti without sauce or as food without salt. As a spicy sauce gives gusto to spaghetti, so a joyful Sabbath radiates a festive gleam to the work-days. A happy rhyme expresses this truth, saying:

> A Sabbath well spent
> Brings a week of content
> With joy for the toils of tomorrow.
> A Sabbath profaned
> Whatever is gained
> Is a sure forerunner of sorrow.

What an amazing divine concern the Sabbath rest reveals! It epitomizes God's care and plan for human freedom: freedom from the tyranny of work; freedom from pitiless human exploitation; freedom from over-attachment to things and people; freedom from insatiable greediness; freedom to enjoy God's blessings on the Sabbath in order to be sent forth into a new week with renewed zest and strength.

Divine perspective. Another aspect of God's care signified by the pattern of work and rest is seen in the divine perspective

How sour the weekdays would be without the Sabbath vacation with God and fellow beings! The weeks would be as tasteless as spaghetti without sauce or as food without salt. As a spicy sauce gives gusto to spaghetti, so a joyful Sabbath radiates a festive gleam to the work-days.

that such a pattern provides for human work and rest. The concept and experience of work and rest are human, yet the Scripture applies them to God first. Why? Is it not astonishing that the Almighty God, who in one moment could have spoken this world into existence, should have chosen to accomplish this creation in six days and then rest on the seventh? Why did God use the very time cycle established for His creatures? Does this not indicate His concern to give a divine perspective to all human work and rest?

One of the greatest satisfactions that comes to human beings is that of imitating a great master, whether such a master be a musician, a painter, a scientist, a teacher, a businessman, a statesman, or a spiritual leader. It is amusing sometimes to watch young fans imitating their "idol" in their hairdo, clothing, gestures, singing, or even in their choice of a perfume scent. This lesson was brought home to me some time ago when I built a wall-to-wall bookshelf in my study. Gianluca, my seven-year-old boy, offered to help but ended up helping himself to the pieces of redwood I sawed off. What did he do with them? He nailed them together and then asked with a sense of pride, "Dad, do you like my shelf?" It looked like anything but a shelf, but he was proud of it. Why? Because he was doing on a small scale what his father had done on a larger scale. Similarly, a Sabbathkeeper can find satisfaction and fulfillment in his work and rest, because the Sabbath assures him that he is doing on a small scale what God has done and is doing on an infinitely larger scale.

Does this mean that a Sabbathkeeper should view all his work as a divine calling or vocation? It is easy for a minister who binds broken hearts to answer "yes," but what about a mechanic who repairs burnt-out clutches? Can he be equally sure that his profession is a divine calling? Paul was a tentmaker by profession, but he never says that God called him to make or to patch up tents. On the contrary he states unequivocally that he was "called to be an apostle" (Rom. 1:1). Many of the jobs people must do hardly reflect what they regard as their calling. But the Sabbath commandment enjoins to "do all your work" (Ex. 20:9; Deut. 5:13). Obviously this includes the pleasant and the unpleasant, the glamorous and the menial, the sacred and the secular tasks.

The Sabbath summons the believer to view all his work, not necessarily as a specific divine calling, but as a reflection of the work and rest of God; as a participation in the divine restoration of this world (John 9:4). This divine perspective provides the spiritual resources needed to perform even menial

"Dad, do you like my shelf?" It looked like anything but a shelf, but he was proud of it. Why? Because he was doing on a small scale what his father had done on a larger scale. Similarly, a Sabbathkeeper can find satisfaction and fulfillment in his work and rest, because the Sabbath assures him that he is doing on a small scale what God has done and is doing on an infinitely larger scale.

tasks not grudgingly but joyfully. It gives validity and meaning both to the work of the six days and to the rest of the seventh day. The believer who, through the Sabbath, views his work and rest as a holy partnership with God will find fulfilment not by escaping from the realities and obligations of life, but by gladly assuming his responsibilities in the likeness of His Creator.[15] The conclusion, then, that emerges from these reflections is that the pattern of six days for work and the seventh for rest, which God established at creation through His personal participation, constitutes a sublime revelation and reminder of His concern for man's physical, social and spiritual well-being.

PART IV

CELEBRATING THE GOOD NEWS OF THE SABBATH

What an amazing divine concern this institution expresses for human well-being! The day effectively epitomizes the promise of God's blessings through His divine presence. What should be the human response to this divine manifestation of concern? How is a believer to celebrate and experience on the Sabbath the blessings of God's sanctifying presence? The Fourth Commandment offers two significant proposals: (1) Remember the Sabbath day, (2) Work six days and rest on the seventh.

1. *Remember the Seventh Day*

In its opening directive the Fourth Commandment says, "Remember the sabbath day, to keep it holy" (Ex. 20:8). What does the act of remembering the Sabbath mean? Are the "remembering" and the "keeping holy" of the Sabbath related? Is the "remembering," perhaps, a necessary prerequisite to experiencing the holiness of the Sabbath? Dates play an important role in personal and national life. People celebrate birthdays, wedding anniversaries, Mother's and Father's days, national independence day, and the like. The significance of any date is determined by the events associated with it. On Mother's Day, for example, you take time to remember not merely the day mother brought you into this world, but especially her incessant care. Similarly the Sabbath is a time to remember God not only for His original perfect creation, but also for His constant care for this world and all its human beings. It means to remember God's saving acts, such as creation, manna, Exodus, redemption, and final restoration.

Taking time to remember historical and personal divine interventions is not merely a memory drill, but rather a vital exercise in maintaining a meaningful relationship with God. Experience teaches that relationships are built on mutual remembrance. "Did you remember me while you were away?" is a question a wife will ask her husband. Forgetting a person means removing him or her from one's life. God is cognizant of the fact that human beings can only maintain a living and loving relationship with Him to the extent that they are able to preserve a fresh memory and awareness of His past, present and future doing for them. Thus on and through the Sabbath the Lord invites us to remember the Good News that He originally created us perfectly; that He cares for us constantly; that He redeemed us completely, and that He will restore us ultimately.

To remember and to keep the Sabbath holy means to take time to acknowledge and praise God for all His mercies. It means to say "no" to the false pretensions of human self-sufficiency and to say "yes" to the Lord of the Sabbath by making oneself available for Him. It means to acknowledge God's doing rather than trusting one's own achievements. It means to stop worrying about one's own wants and start thinking about the needs of others, whether they be "sons" or "servants" (Ex. 20:10). It means forgetting self and selfish interests in order like Mary to honor Christ as the special guest, acknowledging Him in all one does. By remembering and cultivating the presence of Christ in all his activities (whether these be worshiping, talking, eating, walking, reading, listening to music, visiting, etc.), the believer experiences and celebrates the holiness of the Sabbath, that is, the manifestation of God's personal presence in his life. The consciousness of the nearness of God quickens and brings into life all that is purest and best.

2. Work and Rest

Work six days. The Commandment also proposes a work-rest program as a means to celebrate and to experience on the Sabbath God's sanctifying presence. Why is a clear line of demarcation drawn between the *"all your work"* to be done in six days and the *"no work"* to be done on the seventh (Ex. 20:9-10)? Does the work of the six days constitute an antithesis to the rest of the Sabbath? No, because, as noticed earlier, both work and rest are contemplated in the Commandment. The work of the six days is conceived as a natural prelude or prerequisite to enter into the rest experience of the Sabbath. Being the preparatory experience for the Sabbath rest, the work of the

The Sabbath is the day when God both communicates a knowledge
of His will and grants His grace to implement it.

six days shares in the celebration of the Sabbath. One could say that as the doing of all work during the week predisposes the believer to enter more freely and more fully on the Sabbath into communion with God, so the Sabbath experience of God's presence enables the Christian to maintain an awareness of God's presence during the week. Thus the work-rest program of the Sabbath commandment makes it possible to extend to all the weekdays God's sanctifying presence experienced in a special way on the Sabbath.

Rest on the seventh day. Why does the Fourth Commandment make abstention from weekdays' work absolutely necessary for experiencing the holiness of the Sabbath? Why does it take such great pains to spell out so explicitly all the classes of persons to whom rest is to be granted (Ex. 20:10; Deut. 5:14)? Why does God make "rest" such a categorical imperative for the sanctification of the Sabbath? Does He find more pleasure in seeing His creatures inactive rather than engaged in some meaningful activity? How does the Sabbath rest enable the believer to keep the day holy? What is involved in resting on the Sabbath? The answer to these questions is provided to a large extent by the very function of the Sabbath rest, precisely to act as a dividing line between the six working days and the seventh holy day. How can one distinguish holy time, if there is no common time from which to distinguish it? "Can we really understand the holy day," asks Karl Barth, "before we have understood the working day? . . . Can man view and tackle his own work under the command of God without first . . . pausing, resting and keeping holy-day in the sight of God, rejoicing in freedom? Can he value and do justice to his work except in the light of its boundary, its solemn interruption? Is not this interruption the true time from which alone he can have other time?" [16]

The Sabbath rest gives wisdom to distinguish between the lesser and the greater, between the common and the holy. As God by resting on the seventh day separated this day from the previous six days, making it the day of His holy presence, so the believer by resting on the Sabbath draws a clear-cut boundary line between this day and his working days. The drawing of this dividing line between work and rest, between working time and holy time, is the basis of the sanctification of the Sabbath. God has drawn the dividing line between the first six days of the week and the seventh, choosing the latter as the special time to bless human beings with His presence. The believer who accepts God as his Creator must accept also what God has created and not change it into something else. Such an acceptance expresses reverence for God. It is in deference to God that the believer interrupts his work program ("the seventh day is a sabbath *to the Lord your God*"—Ex. 20:10). Yet this pause is for man's own salvation, since it is in God's presence that he finds rest, peace and eternal life.

Pan-Sabbatism. Some Christians reject the distinctive life-style of the Sabbath day, because they maintain that it has a divisive rather than a unifying effect on the Christian life. Hiley H. Ward, for example, in his book *Space-Age Sunday*, argues that the notion of a "Lord's Day" is outdated in today's space-age and consequently should be substituted by "a Lord's Week" observance.[17] Basically, Ward proposes that the Sunday "one-day religion" should be replaced with a *daily* (pan-Sabbatism) "prayer-consciousness," daily gathering with "Christian friends . . . before breakfast, or at a later hour of the evening," and daily church-sponsored programs of "evangelism and educa-tion." [18]

Such a proposal may appear praiseworthy, but in reality it is unrealistic and destructive of the very quality of spiritual life it intends to foster. It is impractical because it expects persons who hardly take time to worship God on what they regard as their Lord's Day to engage in daily worship gatherings, whether with few or with many. How can such a daily program be implemented in view of modern life's pressing demands for time? It is destructive because it represents the substitution rather than the extension of the total worship experience of God's holy day. Like praying "without ceasing" (I Thess. 5:17), is meaningful only if it represents not a substitution but a reflec-tion of the praying done at specific set times. So daily worship exercises, whether private or public, are valuable only if they represent not the substitution but the reflection of the total worship experience of the Sabbath.[19]

Worship in its fullest sense is a total and orderly response to God. Is such a total response really possible during the weekdays when so much attention must be given to the pressing demands of one's work? The *subconscious* awareness of God that a person may experience while engaged in the Sunday through Friday work can hardly be viewed as a total or adequate response to God. The claim that everything a believer does is an act of worship is as absurd as the belief that everything is God (pantheism). The end result in both instances is that no real worship is offered to God, because nothing really matters. Are not these views deceptive devices designed to do away with both the belief in and the worship of God? The theory that every day is Sabbath ultimately results in no Sabbath at all. This truth is brought out perceptively and cuttingly in the following poem:

> Shrewd men, indeed, these new reformers are!
> Each week-day is a Sabbath, they declare:
> A Christian theory! The unchristian fact is
> Each Sabbath is a week-day in their practice.[20]

It cannot be denied that some Christians live a *one-day* religion, or perhaps more accurately, a *one-hour* weekly religion. As soon as their churchgoing clothes are put away in the closet, they seem to turn off God from their minds and live for another week as though God did not exist. The solution to such a *perversion,* widespread though it may be, is to be found not in substituting the Sabbath *precept* with generic attitudes or programs, but in helping Christians to rediscover its intended meaning and function. The prevailing impatience to do away with the Biblical plan for a whole seventh-day Sabbath rest may well explain the widespread neglect for both daily and weekly worship.[21]

The work-rest program spelled out in the Sabbath Commandment represents not only an astonishing revelation of God's concern for human well-being, but also an indispensable condition for experiencing in an orderly way God's sanctifying presence. It represents an orderly response to a Holy God, because it is not a momentary spiritual elation, nor a carefree abandonment to an unconventional life-style (religious communes) whose ideal is to experience passively the moving of the Spirit, but a planned encounter. The planning involves the completing of the goals set for the week, or at least the best efforts put forth to complete them, in order to be available on the Sabbath to experience in a fuller measure God's holy presence.

God's holiness cannot be extracted from objects but it can be experienced in time. The Sabbath rest provides the setting for experiencing God's holy presence. It invites the believer to rest in the holy presence of his Maker, in order to understand the meaning of all His doing and making; in order to bring order into an often disorderly life. This means that resting on the Sabbath is not simply a one-day celebration of God's holiness, but is the extending of the divine holy presence to all the other working days. With the assurance of God's presence, the Sabbath sends us forth into the other days of the week, making them all by reflex "little Sabbaths." Since, then, the six working days find their meaning in the seventh day of rest, and the seventh day finds its meaning in God's presence among His people, the meaning of all human time is found in communion with God.

How should the Sabbath rest (free time) be used in order to experience an enriching communion with God? This question will be examined especially in chapter VI, *The Sabbath: Good News of Service*, where an attempt will be made to formulate some Biblical guidelines for the use of Sabbath time.

The Sabbath indeed proclaims glad tidings of God's care for mankind. The study of the Sabbath work-rest program and its divine blessings and sanctification has shown that the day expresses God's profound concern for His creatures. The Sabbath signifies God's assurance of a present and future abundant life, blessed by His holy presence. It offers God's gift of freedom to mankind: freedom to love and to serve both God and fellow-beings. The seventh day provides a welcome weekly opportunity to celebrate the *Good News of God's Care.*

CHAPTER
IV

the Sabbath

GOOD NEWS
of belonging

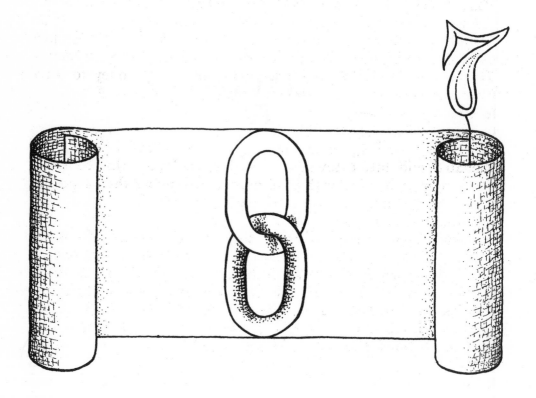

The desire to belong to someone is a fundamental human urge. In my native country until recently, children born out of wedlock were often deprived of a paternity. On their birth certificate, as well as in their identification documents, in place of the father's name (surname) there would be the two letters "N.N.," which stands for *nescio nomen* that is, "name unknown." Frequently newspapers reported the touching story of such an "anonymous-nameless" person's success in finding his or her natural father, after years of tireless and often expensive search. The fact that people will spend much time and money to trace their ancestry illustrates how deep-rooted is the need to know to whom one belongs.

Experience teaches that a person who does not belong to anyone or anything is in most cases unmotivated, rebellious, alienated and bitter toward all and everything. On the other hand, it is in a relationship of mutual belonging that a person experiences love, identity and security, which are essential ingredients for healthy growth and adequate motivation. How do people express mutual belonging? Basically, through words, attitudes and actions. Sometimes gifts are given or exchanged as a token-symbol of mutual devotion and belonging. A young lady remarked to a friend, "What a gorgeous engagement watch your fiancé has given you!" Obviously, that watch served not only to tell the time of day, but also to remind the young lady that she belonged to someone who loved her.

Part I

THE COVENANT AS DIVINE-HUMAN BELONGING

The need to express mutual belonging exists both at the human and at the divine-human level. God, in fact, has revealed Himself not as an abstract entity or ideal, but as a personal Being, vitally interested in the well-being and commitment of His creatures.

1. Biblical Models

Various human models have been used during the history of salvation to help human beings conceptualize and experience a meaningful relationship with the invisible God. Some of the significant human models found in the NT are: "forgiveness" which derives from the cancellation of debts; "reconciliation" and "adoption" which are drawn from personal and familial relationship; "redemption" which derives from the emancipation (manumission) of slaves; "justification" which is based on the declaration of guiltlessness by a law court; "sanctification" which derives especially from the sanctuary model, the symbol of God's sanctifying presence.

A prominent human analogy used in the OT, and to a lesser extent in the NT, is the concept of the covenant, a means widely used in the ancient world to regulate social and political relationships beyond natural blood kinship. Basically the covenant was a treaty or a contract between two parties who freely and willingly bound themselves to accept certain mutual obligations.[1]

2. The Covenant Model

The covenant concept was adopted with radical modifications to express the mutual belonging relationship existing between God and His people. One striking characteristic of the Biblical covenant, not found in the ancient political covenants, is God's emotional appeal to His people. The Lord says, for example: "You have seen what I did to the Egyptians, and how I bore you on eagles' wings and brought you to myself. Now therefore, if you will obey my voice and keep my covenant, you shall be my own possession among all peoples" (Ex. 19:4-5). Though the covenant was based on God's revealed commandments which the people were expected to observe (Ex. 24:7; Deut. 27:1), its ultimate function was to reveal God's saving grace in and through His people: "You shall be to me a kingdom of priests and a holy nation" (Ex. 19:6; cf. Deut. 14:1-2; 26:19).

Law and grace in the covenant. The dichotomy often made between law and grace is not present in the OT covenant. Recent studies have shown that "it is with the demands of the commandments that God's grace becomes known. That is, it is not possible to equate the covenant with grace and then the commandments with law. The discrepancy between covenant and commandments [i.e., grace and law] in the way in which it has been understood in Protestantism does not exist in the Old Testament."[2] This will soon become clearer when considering the role of the Sabbath in the covenant relationship. For the present it is sufficient to note that the covenant analogy is used effectively in the Scriptures to aid in conceptualizing and experiencing a mutual belonging relationship between God and His people ("You shall be my own possession among all peoples" Ex. 19:5).

Covenant signs and symbols. In the Bible several covenant signs or symbols are given to remind human beings of God's concern for them and of their commitment to God. The rainbow is given to Noah as a covenant sign (Gen. 9:8-17). Circumcision is offered as a covenant sign to Abraham and his descendants (Gen. 17:1-4). Bread and wine are chosen by Christ as the emblems "of the covenant" ratified through His blood (Mark 16:24; Matt. 26:28). These and similar signs [3] have been given during the history of salvation to reassure human beings of God's concern to save them and to restore them to fellowship with Him. One might say that the covenant concept, which is introduced in the OT and renewed and ratified by Christ in the NT, represents God's everlasting promise and plan to save a people who in turn will extend salvation to others. This concept is expressed incisively by Peter when he writes, "You are a chosen race, a royal priesthood, a holy nation, God's own people, that you may declare the wonderful deeds of him who called you out of darkness into his marvelous light" (I Peter 2:9; cf. Deut. 20:10; Gen. 12:2-3).

3. *The Sabbath as Symbol of Belonging*

Unique symbol. It is noteworthy that among the various God-given convenant signs or symbols, the Sabbath occupies a unique place. It is unique because it is not an object or a place accessible only to a few, but a day (time) available to all. It is unique also because it has functioned as the symbol *par excellence* of the divine election and mission of God's people. Five times in the Scripture the Sabbath is designated as "a perpetual covenant" or as a "sign" between Yahweh and His people (Ex. 31:13, 16, 17; Ezek. 20:12, 20).[4] De Quervain brings out lucidly this role of the Sabbath when he writes: "It is the observance of this commandment that decides in the old covenant whether Israel fears and loves God and knows that it is the people of God. For this day is the sign of the covenant set up in Israel. He who does not join in the rejoicing, who does not rest from his work in this joy, despises God's goodness and faithfulness and puts his hope, not in God's election, but in his own work. Hence the Sabbath is in a special way *the* sign of *good tidings* in the Old Testament." [5]

Unique origin. The Sabbath is a unique covenant sign, first of all because it is the first sign given by God to reveal His desire to fellowship with His creatures. The day tells us that God created human beings to live not in mystical solitude but in the joy of His fellowship. As explained in Hebrews, "God rested on the seventh day" that He might invite His people "to enter it [God's rest]" (Heb. 4:4-6). Karl Barth rightly calls God's rest at the conclusion of creation "the covenant of the grace of God," because it invites "man to rest with Him . . . to participate in God's rest."[6] By resting, Barth explains, God "seriously accepted the world and man when He had created them, associating Himself with them in the fullest sense . . . Hence the history of the covenant was really established in the event of the seventh day."[7] The covenant is God's "yes" to His creatures and the Sabbath is the time to listen again to this "yes." As the symbol of God's initial invitation to mankind to fellowship with Him, the Sabbath provides the starting point and the basis for all subsequent manifestations of divine grace. When the harmonious fellowship was interrupted by human disobedience, the immediate result was loneliness and separation from God. "The Lord God sent him forth from the garden" (Gen. 3:23), and Adam and Eve found themselves exiled from the direct fellowship with God. When Eden was lost, the Sabbath remained as the weekly reminder and the symbol of God's desire and plan to restore the broken relationship of fellowship and mutual belonging with His fallen creatures.

Unique survival. The Sabbath is unique also because it has survived not only the Fall, but also the Flood, the Egyptian slavery, the Babylonian exile, the Roman persecution,[8] the French and Russian temporary introduction of the ten—day week,[9] blank—day calendar proposals (interrupting the weekly-cycle), antinomianism, and modern secularism. The day still stands for God's people as the symbol of God's gracious provision of salvation and belonging to God. The ancient prophets recognized the value of Sabbathkeeping in maintaining allegiance to God. Ezekiel, for example, when he saw the danger of the total extinction of God's people as a result of the exile, appealed to them to remember their divine election by means of the distinguishing function of the Sabbath (Ezek. 20:12-21). Similarly Isaiah presents the Sabbath as the symbol of belonging to the covenant not only for the Jews (Is. 58:13-14), but also for "the foreigners who join themselves to the Lord" (Is. 56:6, 7, 2, 4).

Unique function. The Sabbath is, furthermore, a unique covenant symbol because it has helped believers throughout the ages to maintain their faith—their belonging relationship with

God. The regular observance of the Sabbath, as noted by Dennis J. McCarthy, "was a medium which handed on knowledge of the covenant as a relationship and a doctrine." [10] Achad Haam underlines this vital function of the Sabbath in the history of Judaism, stating: "We can affirm without any exaggeration that the Sabbath has preserved the Jews more than the Jews have preserved the Sabbath. If the Sabbath had not restored to them the soul, renewing every week their spiritual life, they would have become so degraded by the depressing experiences of the work-days, that they would have descended to the last step of materialism and of moral and intellectual decadence." [11]

Sabbathkeeping has contributed to the survival not only of Judaism but of Christianity as well. The essence of a Christian life is a relationship with God. Such a relationship grows and becomes more meaningful, especially through the time and opportunities for worship, service, meditation, and fellowship provided by the Sabbath day. Consequently a proper observance of God's holy day reflects a healthy relationship with God, while disregard for it bespeaks spiritual decline. This was true in ancient Israel; it is also true in modern Christianity.

In a country like Italy, for example, where less than 10 % of the Christian population attend church services on what they regard as their Lord's day (Saturday evening or Sunday) there is today the largest Communist party of Western Europe (about 35 % of the electorate vote for it). The relationship between the two can hardly be viewed as being merely a coincidence. In other Western European nations where church attendance is even lower than in Italy, secularism, atheism, anticlericalism, immorality, and religious skepticism are rampant. It would be naïve to attribute all the social and religious evils to the prevailing disregard for God's holy day, but by the same token it would be blindness to fail to see the tragic consequences resulting from the profanation of the Sabbath in society.

In a speech delivered on November 13, 1862, President Abraham Lincoln emphasized this vital function of the Sabbath, saying: "As we keep or break the Sabbath day, we nobly save or meanly lose the last and best hope by which man arises." [12] Obviously for Abraham Lincoln the Sabbath day meant Sunday. Puritans applied the name and the precept of the Sabbath to Sunday. This does not detract from the fact that one of America's outstanding presidents recognized in the Sabbath precept the last best hope that can renew and elevate human beings. If this were true in Lincoln's day, is it not truer in our time, when so many "isms" (materialism, secularism, hedonism, atheism, capitalism, communism, evolutionism, liberalism) are com-

peting for human allegiance? When the tyranny of things enslaves many lives? Today therefore more than ever before, the
Sabbath is needed to liberate human beings from the bondage
to the many isms, and to enable them to rediscover the peace
of fellowship and belonging to God for which they were created.

PART II

REASONS FOR THE DIVINE CHOICE OF THE SABBATH AS COVENANT SYMBOL

The preceding considerations suggest three basic reasons
why the Sabbath is a unique symbol of human-divine belonging,
namely, because of its origin, its survival, and its function. To
comprehend more fully its uniqueness, it may help at this point
to inquire why God has chosen the Sabbath (a day rather than
an object) to aid human beings to experience and express a
belonging relationship with Him. What characteristics does the
seventh day possess that enable it to function as a meaningful
symbol of a covenant relationship? The Scripture suggests at
least seven reasons.

1. *Ownership*

A first reason for the divine choice of the Sabbath to sym-
bolize a mutual belonging relationship is suggested by the fact
that the day is, to use M. G. Kline's words, the Creator's "seal
of ownership and authority." [13] As a seal of divine ownership,
the Sabbath provides the legitimate basis for a covenant relationship. This meaning of ownership is explicitly expressed
both in the Fourth Commandment and in its sister institutions,
the sabbatical and the jubilee years. In the Commandment the
believer is invited to "remember" on the Sabbath that "in six
days the Lord made heaven and earth, the sea and all that is
in them (Ex. 20:11; 31:17). As Creator, God is the only legitimate Owner of this world. In the sabbatical and jubilee years
the Israelites were enjoined to relinquish the use of the land
and to liberate their fellow beings from poverty and bondage
(Lev. 25; Deut. 15:1-18), in order to acknowledge that Yahweh
is the only rightful owner of the land ("The land is mine and
you are but aliens and my tenants"—Lev. 25:23—NIV).

As the symbol of divine ownership, the Sabbath enables
the believer to realize constantly and effectively that this world
and his very life belong to God. This recognition of God's

As the symbold of divine ownership, the Sabbath enables the believer to realize constantly and effectively that this world and his very life belong to God. This recognition of God's ownership of one's life is indispensable for a total commitment and belonging to God.

ownership of one's life is indispensable for a total commitment and belonging to God. Is this not true also at the human level? Can husband and wife truly say they belong to each other, unless they are willing to say to each other, "I am yours and you are mine"? One of the pitfalls of a lifestyle characterized by husbands, wives and children working to earn separate incomes (often irrespective of need) is the false sense of independence and separate ownership it fosters. It often leads a member of the family to say: "This is my money, or my car or my house. I have worked for it, so I am free to do with it whatever I wish."

This deceptive sense of ownership, which sometimes strains or even destroys human relationships, can weaken also the very connection between a person and his God. The wealth and abundance of goods which a person may acquire as a result of diligent work can easily induce a false sense of autonomy and independence from God. Are not autonomy and independence —living one's own life without any regard to God—the essence of a sinful life? The Sabbath, symbol of divine creatorship and ownership, is designed to aid the believer to overcome any incipient feeling of self-sufficiency. As the first couple observed their Sabbath on their first full day of life, standing before their Creator empty-handed, acknowledging their indebtedness for all, so the believer who on the Sabbath ceases from his own work, acknowledges his indebtedness and dependency upon the working of God.

To observe the Sabbath means to confess God as Creator and Owner of all life and wealth. It means to recognize that God's total claim over one's life is expressed by consecrating the Sabbath time to God. Ownership implies boundaries; there is to be no transpassing. God has chosen to set in time the boundaries of His dominion. The believer who accepts God's claim over the last day of the week—the Sabbath—accepts God's claim over his whole life and world.[14] The believer who accepts this particular sign of God's ownership, stopping his work on the Sabbath in order to allow God to work in him,[15] demonstrates and experiences a total belonging to God.

2. Holiness

A second reason for the divine choice of the Sabbath to express a covenant relationship is suggested by the holiness of the Sabbath. As a holy day, the Sabbath effectively exemplifies not only the divine choice of time but of people as well. The holiness of the Sabbath is frequently affirmed in the Scripture.

God Himself "made it holy" (Gen. 2:3; Ex. 20:11) and repeatedly calls it "holy" (Ex. 16:22; 31:14; Is. 58:13). The fundamental meaning of the word "holy" appears to be "separation, setting apart" for divine manifestation.[16] When applied to the Sabbath, it expresses, as we have seen, the distinctiveness of the day resulting from the special manifestation of God's presence in the life of His people. Isaiah, for example, pictures God as refusing to be present at the Sabbath assembly of His people, because of their "iniquity" (Is. 1:13-14). God's absence makes their worship experience not holy but rather an "abomination" or a "trampling of my courts" (vs. 12-13).

As the symbol of God's free choice of His special time to manifest His presence, the Sabbath can constantly and effectively remind the believer who keeps it of his special divine election and mission in this world. In other words, as the Sabbath stands as the "Holy Day" among the weekly days, so the believer who keeps it is constantly invited to stand as God's chosen "Holy person" among a perverse generation. Holiness in time points to holiness of being. The link between the holiness of God's people and that of the Sabbath can be seen in the divine choice of both.[17] As God chose the seventh day to enter with His presence into the experience of His people, so He chose a people to bring His holiness to the world. "You are a chosen race, a royal priesthood, a holy nation, God's own people, that you may declare the wonderful deeds of him who called you out of darkness into his marvelous light" (I Pet. 2:9; cf. Deut. 7:6). As God's holiness in time, the Sabbath fittingly expresses God's plan for a holy people. In other words, Sabbathkeeping serves constantly to remind God's people "that I the Lord, sanctify you" (Ex. 31:13; Ezek. 20:12).

As a reminder of God's "sanctification-election" of a people, the Sabbath signifies *mission* rather than *merit*. It means to fulfil the mission entrusted by God, namely, to "declare the wonderful deeds of him who called you out of darkness into his marvelous light" (I Pet. 2:9). In an attempt to convert the world, Christians often adapt themselves to its standard and become part of it. This trend, as A. Martin points out, "results more and more in the dissolution of the Church."[18] The Sabbath challenges the believer to resist this pressure of conformism. It reminds him to be in the world without becoming a part of it. Being God's chosen day from among the weekdays, the Sabbath can forcefully remind the believer who keeps it to be God's chosen messenger to his secularly minded fellow beings.

It is noteworthy that the expression "to sanctify" or "to keep holy" translates the Hebrew word *le-kadesh*, a term which is commonly used in the Talmud to describe the engagement of a woman to a man.[19] As a woman who declared her belonging to a man was "sanctified, made holy," so a person who consecrates his or her life to the Lord is "holy," belonging exclusively to God. The Sabbath was chosen by God as the emblem of this mutual belonging relationship, because it expresses both divine initiative and human response. On the one hand it signifies that God has chosen to sanctify His people and, on the other hand, that the latter accepts God's partnership—His sanctifying presence. Such an acceptance is expressed in a practical way, namely, by making oneself totally available to God on the Sabbath. The Lord does not force His presence upon anyone, but stands at the heart's door and knocks (Rev. 3:20). The Sabbath provides the opportunity to open one's door in order to welcome the Savior as the guest of honor. The person who makes himself available on the Sabbath for Christ, allowing Him to work within his life, is made different— he is sanctified.[20]

Human nature generally is not inclined to desist from work at regular intervals. One prefers to choose one's own time for resting according to one's work program, humor or social exigencies. The Sabbath, however, is God's chosen time that recurs with clock-like regularity, without being conditioned by human likes or dislikes. A person can either accept or reject its obligations. The believer who accepts them, taking leave for 24 hours from his daily work and worries in order to enter into the presence and peace of God, reconfirms his covenant with God. "Such a man," writes M. L. Andreasen, "has used the Sabbath for its intended purpose; it has accomplished for him what God had in mind; it has become the sign and seal of sanctification, and God owns him as His." [21]

3. Incorruptible and Universal

Incorruptible. A third reason for God's choice of the Sabbath to signify mutual commitment is found in the incorruptible and universal nature of time. Being time, the Sabbath is a symbol which is always fresh in meaning, and readily accessible to every human being. The Sabbath is *incorruptible* because it is not a material sign like the Tabernacle, or the Temple; it is immaterial since it is time rather than space or matter. The ideas which are attached to material objects in the course of time tend to deteriorate and disintegrate like the objects them-

F.P.M.

Monuments are regarded with devotion but are gradually deprived of meaning and life. If one were to ask one hundred Romans who built the Colosseum and when, chances are ninety per cent would reply, "Don't ask me! I haven't a clue." The Sabbath, however, is not a relic of antiquity which has lost its meaning, since being time and not matter it is beyond human ability to manipulate and destroy. Its meaning is always fresh and relevant.

selves. My native city of Rome is filled with glorious monuments of antiquity. Most Romans view them with a sense of pride, as symbols of past greatness. Yet if one were to ask one hundred Romans who built the Colosseum (the very symbol of the eternity of Rome) and when, chances are ninety per cent would reply, "Don't ask me! I haven't a clue."

Monuments are regarded with devotion but are gradually deprived of meaning and life. The Sabbath, however, is not a relic of antiquity which has lost its meaning, since being time and not matter it is beyond human ability to manipulate and destroy. The Sabbath of Adam, that of Jesus, as well as yours and mine, is still the same 24-hour day. Its meaning is always fresh and relevant. In fact, it is more relevant today than when it was originally given, because its meaning and function have grown in the unfolding history of salvation. In Eden, where in a sense every day was a Sabbath (that is to say, a paradise in the presence of God), the Sabbath served to heighten the consciousness and the experience of God's presence. But today, when the week-days are spent in a difficult and hectic world, the Sabbath can be truly an island of tranquility, where one can safely harbor to regain the peace of God's presence.

Universal. Being *time*, the Sabbath is not only incorruptible but also *universal*, that is, accessible to all. Since time can be shared, God through the Sabbath can reach every human being without crowding out anyone. Thus there is no need to make a pilgrimage to Rome or to Jerusalem or to Salt Lake City, to observe the Sabbath, because the day reaches every human being weekly, whether one lives in a splendid palace or in a squalid prison. Moreover, no special objects are needed to celebrate the Sabbath. To celebrate the Passover, for example, lambs, unleavened bread and bitter herbs were needed. Similarly, to celebrate the Lord's Supper, bread and wine (as well as basins and water for Christians who practice footwashing) are required. These elements are not readily available to all in every circumstance. With the Sabbath celebration, such a problem does not exist, because the only thing really needed for its celebration is a heart that loves the Lord.

In the offering of money there is no equality. A wealthy person is able to give a larger offering than someone who is poor. It is not so with the offering of time, because every person has an equal measure of it. This means that through the Sabbath God gives an equal opportunity to all to express belonging to Him. One may have less money to offer God than others, but not less time since each person has an equal measure of it. Human life is a measure of time. What a person does with it is indicative of his system of values and priorities. There is no time for those toward whom one feels indifferent, but one makes time for those whom one loves. To be able on the seventh day to withdraw from the world of things to meet the invisible God in the quiet of one's soul means to love God totally; it means to express inwardly and outwardly one's total love and belonging to God.

4. *Renewal of Baptismal Covenant*

A fourth reason for God's choice of the Sabbath as a sign of a mutual belonging relationship is suggested by the fact that the day provides a weekly renewal of the baptismal covenant (vow). In the NT baptism is not described in covenantal language, though it fulfils the very function of marking the entrance of the believer into the church, the new-covenant community, which is the body of Christ ("we were all baptized into one body"—1 Cor. 12:13). A reason for the limited use of the OT covenant model in the NT to describe the relation of the early Christians to one another and to Christ is suggested by the Roman prohibition of secret societies.[22] For the Romans a covenant meant an illegal society. Christians, for reasons of prudence, may have avoided a terminology that raised suspicion of political treason.[23]

Though the distinctive OT covenant terminology is absent in the NT description of baptism, its basic concept is present. This is indicated by the association of baptism with the Exodus event (I Cor. 10:1-2) and with circumcision (Col. 2:11-13), both of which are clear covenant experiences. In fact, as well stated by Louis Tamminga, much of "Bible history is covenant history . . . The fundamentalist-evangelical world has, by and large, failed to grasp the fact that it is the covenantal relationship between God and His people that binds the Scriptures together." [24] How is the Sabbath related to the covenant experience of baptism? Basically in its meaning and function. Baptism is a symbolic reenactment of Christ's death, burial, and resurrection in the life of the believer who enters into covenant with Christ by dying to sin and rising into a new moral life (Rom. 6:3-4). Does the Sabbath share this baptismal meaning and experience of death and resurrection? Is the Sabbath, like baptism, a form of renouncement and renewal? Philip Melanchthon (1496-1560) acknowledges these two meanings of the Sabbath in his *Loci Communes* (1555), saying: "After the Fall the Sabbath was re-established when the gracious promise was given that there would be a second peace with God, that the Son of

God would die and would rest in death until the Resurrection. So now in us our Sabbath should be such a *dying* and *resurrection* with the Son of God, so that God may again have his place of habitation, peace and joy in us, so that he may impart to us his wisdom, righteousness, and joy, so that through us God may again be praised eternally. Let this meaning of the Sabbath be further pondered by God-fearing men." [25] In compliance with Melanchthon's exhortation, let us ponder this meaning of the Sabbath.

Renouncement. Like baptism, the Sabbath does signify renouncement. No two persons can become one, without renouncing certain rights in order to gain greater privileges. Through the Sabbath God invites human beings to renounce several things in order for them to receive His greater gifts. In the first place they are to renounce the security of the weekly work (Ex. 20:10), even when circumstances seem unfavorable: "in plowing time and in harvest you shall rest" (Ex. 34:21). A. Martin rightly notes that in the context of Jewish life, the interruption of work especially at plowing and harvest time, was a genuine form of renouncement which could easily result "in less food available." [26] Even today, however, Sabbathkeeping for some persons entails real sacrifice and renouncement. This is particularly true in countries where the right to be free from work in order to observe the seventh-day as God's holy day does not exist. Many books of *Acts* could be written to recount the heroic witness of past and present believers who have chosen and do choose to renounce better jobs, promotion or pay (sometimes even their very livelihood and freedom), rather than to disown their commitment to God.

Like baptism, the Sabbath also means renouncement of that greediness and selfishness which, though symbolically buried under the baptismal waters, continually tends to reappear and thus needs to be overcome. Some persons have been made slaves but many more have chosen to become slaves of their grasping greediness. The latter work and would wish others to work for them all seven days out of seven, in order to gain more and more and be satisfied with less and less. The Sabbath is designed to cure such insatiable greediness by enjoining to rest, that is, to stop being greedy and start being grateful. It commands to take time not to seek more material goods but to gratefully acknowledge the bounties received. A grateful heart is indispensable for maintaining a meaningful, mutual, belonging relationship, and for experiencing inner rest and peace.

Like baptism, the Sabbath means also renouncement of self-sufficiency. Through the Sabbath, the confession of surrender to Christ, which the believer makes at baptism, is renewed every week. The success a Christian achieves in his work may make him feel secure and self-sufficient, thus forgetful of his dependency upon God: "lest I be full, and deny thee, and say, 'who is the Lord?' " (Prov. 30:9). The Sabbath, by enjoining cessation from work, invites the believer to glance away from his own achievements and to look instead to God's work and working in him. During the week a Christian may feel worthy of salvation because of all that he does. But on the Sabbath as he ceases from his works, he becomes conscious of his human dependency upon God, recognizing that it is not his doing but God's doing that saves. The Sabbath forbids a Christian, as forcefully stated by Karl Barth, to have "faith in his own plans and wishes, in a justification and deliverance which he can make for himself, in his own ability and achievement. What it really forbids him is not work, but trust in his work." [27]

The Sabbath, then, provides a weekly opportunity to renew the baptismal confession of self-renouncement, in order to "allow the omnipotent grace of God to have the first and the last word at every point." [28] In two senses Sabbath-keeping may be a more significant confession of commitment than circumcision was in the OT or than baptism is in the Christian dispensation. First, because circumcision and baptism are covenant signs received generally at a tender age, when infants or teenagers do not fully understand their implications. Second, because both of them are a *one-time* commitment rite. On the contrary, Sabbathkeeping represents not a *one-time* but a weekly *life-time* renewal of the commitment made to God in one's youth.[29] What this means then is that the person who habitually disregards the Sabbath, choosing rather to do his own "pleasure" (Is. 58:13), reveals not a sudden or a momentary weakness, but rather a deep-rooted and wilful rejection of his baptismal commitment to God. This is why the prophets equate Sabbath-breaking with "apostasy" or "rebellion" (Ezek. 20:13, 21; Neh. 13:18; Jer. 17:23), because it is not a passing inordinate desire, but a permanent attitude of disobedience. The Christian life could be described as a "love affair" with the Lord which is sealed through baptism and cultivated through the Sabbath. Or one might say that the Sabbath strengthens the sacred vow of faithfulness made to God at baptism.

Renewal. Even as the water in baptism has the dual meaning of death and a new life, so the *rest* of the Sabbath signifies both renouncement and *renewal.* If baptism be regarded as the point of entrance into the new Christian life, the Sabbath is the weekly renewal of that initial commitment. This weekly renewal is made possible through the time the Sabbath affords to take stock and ascertain where one stands. The opportunity the Sabbath provides to have a special rendezvous with oneself, with others, and with God, results in *physical, social* and *spiritual* renewal.

The *physical renewal* (recreation) the Sabbath rest provides differs from the rest experience of the week-days. During the week one can at best rest from work but not from the thought of it. The business man goes home with his work in his brief-case or in his mind; the student must prepare for the next day's assignments or tests; the housekeeper must plan for tomorrow's meals and cleaning. The anxiety over tasks that remain to be done occupies the mind even while the body rests. As a result, a person sometimes feels more tired in the morning than before he went to bed. On the Sabbath, however, a Christian should and can rest not only from work, but also from the thought of it, knowing that on that day he need not worry about time-clocks, deadlines, tests, production or competition. On the Sabbath the body can rest because the mind is at rest, and the mind is at rest because it rests in God.

The Sabbath contributes also to *social renewal*, by strengthening those relationships established through baptism. The daily work scatters the immediate family members as well as the church members in different directions, leaving little time to cultivate marital, parental and fraternal relationships. During a busy working week, it is easy to forget the needs of the members of the body of Christ into whom "we were all baptized" (I Cor. 12:13). Sometimes even the members of one's own family are neglected. On the Sabbath, as the believer experiences afresh the assurance of God's presence and love, he is motivated and challenged to strengthen neglected relationships; to alleviate the suffering of others; to share with all, friends and foes, his friendship, fellowship and concern. This service which is rendered on and through the Sabbath renews and strengthens that covenant relationship with God and His people established at baptism.

Most important of all, the Sabbath is a time of *spiritual renewal*. It is a time when the believer renews his baptismal commitment by taking time to remember and appreciate God's saving activities. In a sense, the believer on each Sabbath is baptized anew into Christ's death through the renouncement experience described earlier, and into Christ's resurrection through the spiritual renewal the day provides.[30] The latter takes place on the Sabbath especially through the private and communal worship experience, which differs substantially from that of the week-days. Sabbath worship is not a moment of meditation squeezed into a busy work-day program, but rather it is a whole day when earthly concerns are laid aside, when the many distracting voices are silenced, in order to acknowledge God's "worth-ship," to experience His presence and to hear more distinctly His voice. Through this special encounter with God, the believer receives fresh forgiveness; he brings order into his fragmented daily life; he reestablishes his moral consciousness; he gains a new set of divine goals for his life; he receives fresh inspiration and grace to do the will of God. This spiritual renewal that the Sabbath provides to the new life begun at baptism serves to strengthen and enrich the covenant relationship between God and the believer.

5. *Spiritual*

A fifth reason for God's choice of the Sabbath to symbolize His covenant relationship with His people is suggested by the fact that the seventh day provides a fitting reminder of the spiritual nature of this relationship. Perhaps Jesus came closest to defining God's nature when He told the Samaritan woman, "God is spirit, and those who worship him must worship in spirit and truth" (John 4:24). The context suggests that Christ described God as "Spirit" to counteract the misconception that God is to be worshiped in a special holy place. For the Samaritan woman the right *place* was fundamental to worship: "Our fathers worshiped on this mountain; and you say that in Jerusalem is the *place* where men ought to worship" (John 4:20). Jesus responded by offering a most profound insight into the nature of true worship. He explained that human beings communicate with God not through holy places, objects, or things, but "in spirit and truth," that is, in a spiritual and truthful way. Genuine worship is offered to God not by going to special shrines or by performing elaborate rituals, as such, but by speaking and listening to God with heart, soul and mind (Mark 12:30).

The Sabbath and God's nature. Can the Sabbath contribute to preventing the deadening objectification of God and thus aid in maintaining a living relationship between God and His people? A look into the nature of the Sabbath suggests several reasons for a positive answer. In the first place the Sabbath as a *temporal* symbol aptly characterizes *God's nature,* since the latter is as mysterious as the nature of time. Like God, time cannot be defined or controlled. As a person can relate to time but cannot control it, so he can relate to God but cannot control Him. In other words, both God and time transcend human outreach. They cannot be manipulated and changed into something else. Abraham Joshua Heschel characterizes time as "*otherness,*" a mystery transcending human experience, and "*togetherness,*" an occasion to experience fellowship.[31] Are not *otherness* and *togetherness* basic characteristics of God's nature? Being a measure of time and not an object, the Sabbath can effectively remind the believer that he belongs to the God who cannot be objectified, circumscribed or incapsulated, to the God who is "beyond," "wholly other," transcending human analogies ("To whom then will you liken God?"—Is. 40:18) and controls. At the same time, as a moment of togetherness, the Sabbath reminds the believer that his God is not only "beyond" but also very "close," so close that he can rest in Him (Heb. 4:10).

An antidote against idolatry. The Sabbath helps maintain a spiritual relationship with God not only, as just seen, by reminding the believer of God's nature, but also by protecting him from idolatry. Fritz Guy aptly states that "worship by means of a holy day is removed as far as possible from idolatry. It is quite impossible to cut, carve or construct the image of a day."[32] Some might challenge this statement by pointing to the Hebrews, who apparently succeeded, especially in the days of Jesus, in objectifying the Sabbath by tying its observance to minute regulations. The reduction of the Sabbath from an occasion to meet with God, to a "thing" to be kept with utmost precision, can turn the day from a means of worship into an object of worship.[33] This adulteration of the Sabbath does not detract, however, from its unique quality, but only serves to show that even the most "fireproof" God-given symbol can be prostituted into an object of legalistic and even idolatrous worship.

Of all symbols, the Sabbath as time still remains the one that best resists objectification. It provides the surest protection from worshiping "*it*" rather than worshiping "*Him.*" It is noteworthy that both at creation and in the Ten Commandments, mankind is given not a "holy object" but a "holy day" in which to experience the holiness of God. The first Four Commandments spell out the three "don'ts" and the one "do" that should regulate the relationship between God and His people. First, don't give to God a divided loyalty by worshiping Him as One among many gods. Second, don't worship God by means of material representations. Third, don't use thoughtlessly the name of God. Then comes the Fourth Commandment which is a "do" rather than a "don't." It invites mankind to "remember" God not through a holy object but through a holy day. The first three commandments seem designed to remove the obstacles to

a true spiritual relationship with God, namely, the worship of
false gods or of their images and disrespect for the true God.
With the way to God's presence cleared, the Fourth Commandment invites the believer to experience divine fellowship, not
through the recitation of magic charms, but in time shared together. Obviously God sees time as a most fitting symbol of
the spiritual relationship that should exist between Himself and
His people. The importance of this divine choice is under-
scored by the repeated attempts human beings have made to
reduce a living and spiritual relationship with God to the veneration of dead objects: shrines, icons, tombs, creeds, and relics
(such as the bones of saints, pieces of wood from a cross, or
pieces of garments).

The small chapel of St. Laurence in Rome is called *Sancta
Sanctorum*—"The Most Holy." Above its altar, a Latin inscription reads: *Non est in toto sanctior orbe locus,* which means,
"there is no holier place in the world." On what ground is such
an astonishing claim made? Primarily on the basis of the great
number of relics—dead objects—the chapel contains. The most
venerated object is an image of the Redeemer claimed to have
been produced by a divine agency. Can God be blamed for
these human attempts to seek "holiness" through things rather
than through an I-Thou spiritual relationship? Certainly not,
for God took utmost precaution to prevent human beings from
materializing and objectifying His spiritual nature. This is
evidenced, for example, by the fact that when the second Person
of the Godhead became a Human Being for about thirty-three
years, He refrained from leaving a single material mark that
can be authenticated as His own. Christ did not build or own
a house; He did not write books or own a library; He did not
leave the exact date of His birth or of His death; He did not
leave descendants. He left an empty tomb, but even this place
is still disputed. He left no "thing" of Himself, but only the
assurance of His spiritual presence: "Lo, I am with you always,
to the close of the age" (Matt. 28:20).

Why did Christ pass through this world in this mysterious
fashion, leaving no physical footprints or material traces of
Himself? Why did the Godhead miss the golden opportunity
provided by the incarnation to leave a permanent material
evidence and reminder of the Savior's stay on this planet? Is
this not clear evidence of God's concern to protect mankind
from the constant temptation of reducing a spiritual relationship into a "thing-worship"? It was because of this same concern that God chose the Sabbath—a day rather than an object—
as the symbol of a divine-human belonging relationship. Being

time, a mystery that defies human attempts to define it, the Sabbath provides a constant protection against the worship of objects and a fitting reminder of the spiritual nature of the covenant relationship between God and His people.

6. *Commitment*

A sixth reason for God's choice of the Sabbath as a covenant symbol is that this day expresses effectively the mutual commitment that binds God and His people. A mutual belonging relationship can endure only if both parties remember and honor their respective obligations. How does the Sabbath express divine and human commitment?

Divine commitment. The Sabbath stands first of all for divine commitment. God's last creative act was not the fashioning of Adam and Eve, but the creation of *His rest* for mankind (Gen. 2:2-3). Such a divine rest has a message for the creation as a whole as well as for humanity in particular. With regard to creation, as noted in chapter two, God's rest signifies His satisfaction over the completion and perfection of His creation. With regard to humanity, God's rest symbolizes His availability to His creatures. By taking "time out" on the first Sabbath to bless the first couple with His holy presence, God through this day provides a constant reassurance to His creatures of His availability and concern. As eloquently expressed by A. Martin, "The promise to which God commits Himself through the Sabbath is to have time for mankind. God is not an idea but a Person who assures all creation of His presence. The Sabbath is the sign of this promise. However, this is not limited solely to the Sabbath time. In the same way as Christ's presence is not limited to the space occupied by the bread, so the Sabbath reminds mankind of the permanence of God's [presence]." [34]

This divine commitment becomes explicit in the covenant relationship, where the Sabbath is presented as God's assurance of His sanctifying presence among His people (Ex. 31:13; Ezek. 20:12). Human disobedience did not alter God's original commitment. On the contrary, when the estrangement caused by sin occurred, God through the Sabbath guaranteed His total commitment to restore the broken covenant relationship. This commitment led God to give "his only Son, that whoever believes in him should not perish but have eternal life" (John 3:16). The Sabbath, as Karl Barth correctly explains, "reminds man of God's plan for him, of the fact that He has already carried it out, and that in His revelation He will execute both His will with him and His work for and toward him. It points him to the Yes which the Creator has spoken to him, His creature, and which He has made true and proved true once and for all in Jesus Christ." [35]

The availability of God which the Sabbath guarantees makes prayer possible. How distressing to be unable to talk to an important person because he is booked up and unavailable perhaps for a month or more! The Sabbath is God's assurance of His constant availability. It tells us that God is listening and responding, that He wants to dialogue and fellowship with His creatures. It tells us that God is available and thus can be approached in prayer not only on the Sabbath but every day. As the father who, by making himself especially available for his family on the Sabbath, reveals not a weekly but rather a permanent devotion to his family, so God, by pledging to be especially close to His creatures on the Sabbath, reassures them of His constant interest and availability. The weekly regularity of the Sabbath serves as a continual reminder that God "is mindful of his covenant for ever" (Ps. 105:8).

Human commitment. The Sabbath stands not only for divine but also for human commitment. It signifies not only "that *I*, the Lord, sanctify you" but also that "*you* shall keep my sabbaths" (Ex. 31:13). By reassuring human beings that God is available and "working until now" (John 5:17) to accomplish the ultimate restoration of this world to His eternal fellowship, the Sabbath invites the believer to assume his responsibility, by making himself available for God. By accepting God's invitation to keep the Sabbath with Him, the believer enters into a special relationship with God. This relationship is not, as Karl Barth points out, "an indirect but a direct connection, not only a relationship but genuine intercourse." [36] It is by assuming this obligation that a person becomes free: free for God, for self, for the immediate family and for others. The free offering of time to God is a supreme act of worship, because it means acknowledging God with the very essence of human life: time. Life is time. When "time is up" life ceases to be. The offering of the Sabbath time to God enables the believer to acknowledge that his whole life, not just one seventh, belongs to God. It represents the Christian's response to God's claim on his life. By bringing all routine work to a halt for one day, he acts out his commitment to the Lord of his life.[37] A similar objective is accomplished through the return of the tithe to God, as a recognition of His ultimate ownership.

What is involved in the offering of the Sabbath time to God will be considered in chapter six. Our immediate concern has been to understand how the Sabbath meaningfully expresses

The Sabbath is God's assurance of His constant availability.
It tells us that God is listening and responding, that He wants
to dialogue and fellowship with His creatures. It tells us that
God is available and thus can be approached in prayer not only
on the Sabbath but every day.

both divine and human commitment. We have found that the Sabbath, on the one hand, symbolizes God's commitment to be available for and to save humanity. On the other hand, Sabbath keeping expresses the believer's acceptance of the Creator and Redeemer's claim upon his life.

7. Redemption

A seventh reason for God's choice of the Sabbath to sym-bolize His covenantal relationship with His people is its redemp-tive function. As a symbol of God's saving activities, the Sab-bath provides the basis for experiencing meaningful belonging. The degree of one's commitment to a person is related to what such a person has done to deserve loyalty and devotion. A mother who gives up her son for adoption soon after his birth in order to be free to pursue her professional career can hardly expect that the boy later in life will feel filial attachment to her. The Sabbath reassures the believer that God never gives him up but has given His very life in order to restore to him life and divine fellowship. This redemptive function of the Sabbath will be examined in the following chapter, which is devoted specifically to *The Sabbath: Good News of Redemption.* The study will show how both in the OT and NT the physical Sab-bath rest points to the greater spiritual rest of salvation to be found in Christ. The believer who on the Sabbath stops his *doing* to experience his *being* saved by divine grace renounces human efforts to work out his own salvation and acknowledges his belonging to God, the author and finisher of his salvation.

Conclusion

We asked at the outset, What intrinsic characteristics does the Sabbath possess to enable it to function as a meaningful symbol of a divine-human covenant relationship? Seven signifi-cant aspects have been considered in this chapter. First, as the sign of divine ownership, the Sabbath constantly reminds the believer of his belonging to God. Second, as God's holiness in time, the Sabbath reassures the believer who keeps it of his divine election and mission in this world. Third, as an incor-ruptible and universal symbol, the Sabbath is always fresh in its meaning and enables every human being to express commit-ment to God. Fourth, as a type of baptism, the Sabbath provides a weekly opportunity to renew the baptismal covenant, by ex-periencing anew self-renouncement as well as physical, social and spiritual renewal. Fifth, as a temporal symbol, the Sabbath protects the believer from idolatry, reminding him of the spiritual nature of his covenant relationship with God. Sixth, as a fitting symbol of mutual commitment, the Sabbath reassures humanity of God's availability and invites the believer to express his belonging to God by offering Him a specific measure of time—the seventh day—as a token expression of his total life. Lastly, as a reminder of God's saving activities, the Sabbath enables the believer to experience and celebrate the assurance of God's love and the *Good News of Belonging* to God and His people.

CHAPTER
V

the Sabbath

GOOD NEWS
of redemption

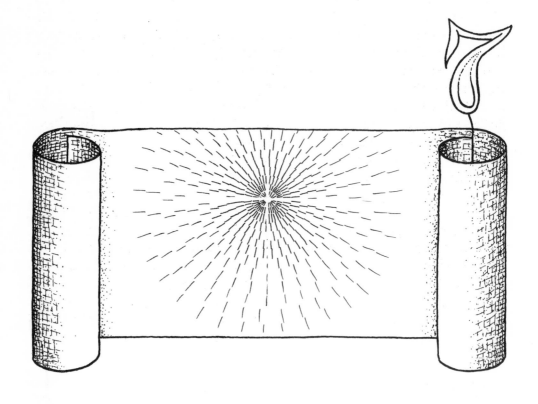

The struggle to become and to remain free from external and internal restraints has engaged humanity ever since the Fall. Much blood has been shed, countless lives have been sacrificed during mankind's history, to gain freedom from external oppression and exploitation! Perhaps an even greater investment of human resources has been made and is presently being put forth to liberate human beings from the internal tyranny of sickness, sorrow and death. God's Good News to mankind is that this struggle for human liberation from both external and internal bondage has been won. It has been won, however, not through human efforts but through divine intervention. The history of salvation is the story of God's intrusion into human time and life, to liberate His people not only from the physical bondage of Egypt or of Babylon, but also from the spiritual captivity of disobedience and death (I Cor. 15:54-56). To accomplish this redemptive mission Christ came into this world. He came "to proclaim release to the captives . . . to set at liberty those who are oppressed" (Luke 4:18).

The Christian mandate is to proclaim the Good News of how God has wonderfully delivered humanity from the bondage of darkness and death and led them into His marvelous light and life (I Pet. 2:9). This Good News is to be proclaimed verbally and accepted personally. Symbols such as baptism, the Lord's Supper and the Sabbath provide vital means to appropriate and experience the Good News of God's redemption in one's personal life. This chapter will examine how the last of these sacred symbols, the Sabbath, has been used by God both in the OT and the NT to give to His people the assurance and experience of a present and future divine redemption.[1]

PART I

REDEMPTIVE SABBATH THEMES
IN THE OLD TESTAMENT

1. *The Blessing and Sanctification of the Sabbath*

The story of creation is in a sense a redemption story: redemption from disorder into order, from chaos into cosmos.[2] Within the creation event the Sabbath reveals the purpose of God's first redemptive act. It tells us that God created this world not merely for the enjoyment of making something new and beautiful out of formless matter (Gen. 1:2), but especially for the pleasure of sharing Himself with His creatures. Our earlier study of the divine blessings and sanctification of the Sabbath has already shown that these divine acts represent God's assurance to His creatures of abundant life through His holy presence.

A promise of Emmanuel. When the prospect of a joyous life at the presence of God was shattered by sin, the Sabbath became the symbol of divine commitment to restore broken relationships. From being the symbol of God's initial *cosmological* accomplishments (that is, the bringing into existence of a perfect cosmos out of chaos), the Sabbath became the symbol of God's future *soteriological* activities (that is, the redemption of His people from bondage into His freedom).[3] From serving as a symbol of God's *initial entrance into human time* to bless and sanctify a perfect world with His divine presence, the Sabbath became a symbol of God's *future entrance into human flesh* to become "Emmanuel—God with us." The first as well as the second coming of Christ represent the fulfillment of God's purpose for this world, expressed initially through the blessings and sanctification of the Sabbath.[4]

To trace how the Sabbath has fulfilled this redemptive function both in the OT and in the NT is not an easy task. Why? In the first place, because the Sabbath has provided the basis for constant new reflections. Various strands of sabbatical concepts such as the "rest" theme, the cosmic week and the liberation experience of the Sabbath years, have all been used to express future (eschatological) expectations of divine deliverance. Second, the liberation message of the Sabbath has been applied, as we shall see, both to immediate national concerns for political restoration and to future expectations of divine redemption. This dual application to the same theme readily creates confusion in the mind of an unwarned reader. Third, the Biblical and extrabiblical sources provide us with fragmented information rather than systematic explanation of the various levels of meanings attributed to the Sabbath. We shall find that certain allusions to sabbatical themes in the OT become clearer in the light of their NT interpretation. To comply with the brevity required by the non-technical nature of the present study, attention will be given only to two additional redemptive themes of the Sabbath, namely, the Sabbath rest and the Sabbath liberation.

2. *The Sabbath Rest*

The Sabbath Rest in Hebrews. It might be helpful to trace the theme of the Sabbath rest from the NT back into the OT, rather than vice versa. This procedure is suggested by the fact that it is the NT that clarifies the Messianic implications of the Sabbath rest. The logical place to start is the fourth chapter of the book of Hebrews, where the writer on one hand reassures the Christian community that "there remains a sabbath rest for the people of God" (4:9), while on the other hand he exhorts them "to strive to enter that rest" (4:11). The tension between *permanence* and *perseverance*, the *already* and the *not-yet*, recurs several times in Hebrews.[5] Our immediate concern, however, is not to explore the significance of this tension, but rather to ascertain the meaning and usage of the term "sabbath rest"—*sabbatismos* which occurs in this form only here (4:9) in the NT. Does it refer to the rest of the seventh-day Sabbath and if so, what meanings are attributed to such a rest?

The context and the linguistic usage of *sabbatismos*—"Sabbath rest" indicate that the reference is indeed to the rest of the seventh day. The theme of the rest to be found in God by His people is introduced in chapter 3:7 with no apparent connection with the Sabbath rest. But as the author develops the theme of rest, he traces its origin back to God's rest on the seventh day of creation, by quoting from Genesis 2:2, "And God rested on the seventh day from all his works" (Heb. 4:4). Having identified the promise of God's rest to His people with the seventh-day creation rest in verse 4, the author feels free in verse 9 to substitute the common term "rest"—*katapausis*,[6] with the more specific term "Sabbath rest or Sabbathkeeping"—*sabbatismos*. That the latter denotes specifically the observance of the seventh-day Sabbath is further indicated by the usage of the term with such an explicit meaning in the writings of Plutarch, Justin Martyr, Epiphanius and others.[7] Moreover, the cognate verb *sabbatizo*—"to rest" is also used several times in the Septuagint in clear reference to Sabbath observance (cf. Ex. 16:30; Lev. 23:32; 2 Chron. 36:21). These factors strongly suggest that the "Sabbath rest"—*sabbatismos* that remains for the people of God (4:9) is indeed related to the rest experience of the seventh day.

Three levels of meaning. What meaning does the writer of Hebrews attribute to the Sabbath rest? By welding together two texts, namely Psalm 95:11 and Genesis 2:2, the writer presents what one might call three different levels of meaning of the Sabbath rest. At a first level, the Sabbath rest points to God's creation rest, when "his works were finished from the foundation of the world" (4:3). This meaning is established by quoting Genesis 2:2. At a second level, the Sabbath rest symbolizes the promise of entry into the land of Canaan, which the wilderness generation "failed to enter" (4:6; cf. 3:16-19), and which was realized later when the Israelites under Joshua did enter the land of rest (4:8). At a third and most important level, the Sabbath rest prefigures the rest of redemption which has dawned and is made available to God's people through Christ.

How does the author establish this last meaning? By drawing a remarkable conclusion from Psalm 95:7, 11, which he quotes several times (Heb. 4:3, 5, 7). In Psalm 95, God invites the Israelites to enter into His rest which was denied to the rebellious wilderness generation (vv. 7-11). The fact that God should renew "again" the promise of His rest long after the actual entrance into the earthly Canaan, namely at the time of David by saying "today" (Heb. 4:7), is interpreted by the author of Hebrews to mean two things: first, that God's "Sabbath rest" was not exhausted when the Israelites under Joshua found a resting place in the land, but that it still "remains for the people of God" (4:9). Second, that such rest has dawned with the coming of Christ (4:3, 7). The phrase "Today, when you hear his voice" (4:7) has a clear reference to Christ.[8] The readers had heard God's voice in the "last days" (1:2) as it spoke through Christ and had received the promise of the Sabbath rest. In the light of the Christ event, then, ceasing from one's labor on the Sabbath (4:10) signifies both a present experience of redemption (4:3) and a hope of future fellowship with God (4:11). For the author of Hebrews, as Gerhard von Rad correctly points out, "the whole purpose of creation and the whole purpose of redemption are reunited" in the fulfillment of God's original Sabbath rest.[9]

The Sabbath rest in the Old Testament. One wonders, on what basis does the author of Hebrews interpret the Sabbath as the consummation of God's purpose for creation, accomplished through Christ's redemption? Is this to be regarded entirely as his own innovative interpretation or is he giving a fresh approach to existing eschatological notions of the Sabbath rest? A study of the theme of the Sabbath rest in the OT and in contemporary Jewish literature indicates the latter to be the case. The concept of the Sabbath *rest—menûhah—*"to the biblical mind," as Abraham Joshua Heschel explains, "is the same as happiness and stillness, as peace and harmony." [10] The notion was utilized in the OT to describe not only the weekly Sabbath rest experience, but also the national aspiration for a peaceful life in a land at rest (Deut. 12:9; 25:19; Is. 14:3), where the king would give to the people "rest from all enemies" (2 Sam. 7:1; cf. 1 Kings 8:5), and where God would find His "resting place" among His people and especially in His sanctuary at Zion (2 Chron. 6:41; 1 Chron. 23:25; Ps. 132:8, 13, 14; Is. 66:1).

The rest and peace of the Sabbath, which as a political aspiration remained largely unfulfilled, became the symbol of the Messianic age, often known as the "end of days" or the "world to come." [11] Theodore Friedman notes, for example, that "two of the three passages in which Isaiah refers to the Sabbath are linked by the prophet with the end of days (Is. 56:4-7; 58:13, 14; 66:22-24) . . . It is no mere coincidence that Isaiah employs the words 'delight' (*oneg*) and 'honor' (*kavod*) in his descriptions of both the Sabbath and the end of days (58:13—'And you shall call the Sabbath delight . . . and honor it'; 66:11—'And you shall delight in the glow of its honor'). The implication is clear. The delight and joy that will mark the end of days is made available here and now by the Sabbath." [12]

The Sabbath rest in Jewish literature. Later rabbinic and apocalyptic literature provide more explicit examples where the Sabbath is understood as the anticipation and foretaste of the world-to-come.[13] For example, *Pirke Rabbi Eliezer* 18 describes the structure of history as follows: "Seven aeons has God created, and of them all He has chosen only the seventh aeon. Six are for the coming and going [of men] and one [the seventh] is wholly sabbath and *rest* in eternal life." This seventh sabbatical age is frequently associated with the coming of the Messiah. "Our Rabbis taught," says the Babylonian Talmud, "at the conclusion of the septennate the son of David will come. R. Joseph demurred: But so many sevenths have passed, yet has he not come!" [14]

In the apocalyptic work known as *The Book of Adam and Eve* (about first century A.D.), the archangel Michael admonishes Seth, saying: "Man of God, mourn not for thy dead more than six days, for on the seventh day is a sign of the resurrection and the *rest* of the age to come." [15]   How did the Sabbath come to be regarded as the symbol of the resurrection and rest in the world to come? Apparently the harsh experiences of the desert wandering first, and of the exile later, encouraged the viewing of the Edenic Sabbath as the paradigm of the future new age. In fact, the new age which is generally equated with the Messianic age [16] is characterized by material abundance (Amos 9:13-14; Joel 4:19; Is. 30:23-25; Jer. 31:12), social justice (Is. 61:1-9), harmony between persons and animals (Hos 2:20; Is. 65:25; 11:6), extraordinary longevity (Is. 65:20; Zech 8:4), refulgent light (Is. 30:26; Zech 14:6, 7) and absence of death and sorrow (Is. 25:8). These various characteristics of the Messianic age are grouped together in 2 Baruch, another Jewish apocalyptic work of the latter half of the first century A.D. Its author describes "the time of My Messiah," saying: "And it shall come to pass, when He has brought low everything that is in the world, and has sat down in peace for the age on the throne of His kingdom, that joy shall then be revealed, and *rest* shall appear." [17]   The description of the Messianic age continues and includes the familiar themes of the absence of death and sorrow, of social justice, of harmony in nature, etc.

This brief survey indicates that after the Fall the Sabbath rest was understood, both in the OT and in later Jewish literature, as the consummation of God's purpose for His creation. The weekly experience of the Sabbath rest epitomized the national aspirations for a resting place in the land of Canaan and in the sanctuary of Jerusalem. But all of this in turn pointed forward to the future order of peace and rest to be established by the Messiah. "The time of salvation" came to be viewed as "wholly sabbath and rest." [18]   The existence of this Messianic/eschatological interpretation of the Sabbath rest provides the basis for understanding why the author of Hebrews identifies Christ's redemption with the Sabbath rest. With the coming of Christ "the good news" of the Sabbath rest has been realized and is being experienced by all those "who have believed" (Heb. 4:2, 3, 7). This redemptive understanding of the Sabbath rest is not a unique conception of the author of Hebrews. Christ Himself, as will be shown later in this chapter, viewed His redemptive mission as the realization of that rest promised by the Sabbath (Matt. 11:28; 12:7; Luke 4:18-21; John 5:17; 9:4). For the present it suffices to notice that in the OT, the experience of the Sabbath rest both at a personal and national level served to nourish the hope of a future Messianic redemption. [19]

3. *The Sabbath Liberation*

The Sabbath and redemption. The theme of Sabbath freedom or liberation is another significant redemptive motif which appears in various forms both in the OT and in later Jewish literature. Being a day of rest, the Sabbath is uniquely equipped to function as a symbol and agent of both physical and spiritual liberation. The release from the pressure of work provided by the Sabbath could effectively epitomize both past and future divine deliverance. This may explain the reason for the frequent association of the Sabbath with the theme of redemption. Both in the Exodus and in the Deuteronomic version of the Decalogue, God introduces Himself as the merciful Redeemer: "I am the Lord your God, who brought you out of the land of Egypt, out of the house of bondage (Ex. 20:2; Deut. 5:6). To guarantee this newly given freedom to every member of the Hebrew society, God enjoins through the Fourth Commandment that freedom from work must be granted to "you, or your son, or your daughter, your manservant, or your maidservant, or your cattle, or the sojourner who is within your gates" (Ex. 20:10; cf. Deut. 5:14).

The link between the Exodus liberation and the Sabbath is *implicitly* suggested in the Exodus version of the Fourth Commandment by the preface where God introduces Himself as Israel's Liberator (Ex. 20:2). However, in the Deuteronomic version, the link between the Sabbath and the Exodus liberation is established *explicitly* by means of the "remembrance clause": "You shall remember that you were a servant in the land of Egypt, and the Lord your God brought you out thence with a mighty hand and an outstretched arm; therefore the Lord your God commanded you to keep the sabbath day" (Deut. 5:15).[20] "Here," writes Hans Walter Wolff, "the reason for observing the day of rest is that affirmation which was absolutely fundamental for Israel, namely, that Yahweh had liberated Israel from Egypt. On every sabbath Israel is to remember that her God is a liberator." [21] This motif of redemption constitutes an addition to that of creation given in Exodus 20:11. The fact that the theological scope of the Sabbath is enlarged in Deuteronomy to include the remembrance of the Exodus indicates that this institution is not static but dynamic. Its meaning and function increase with the unfolding of salvation history.

Remembering deliverance. Why is Israel called upon to remember on and through the Sabbath her past liberation from Egypt? A first reason is that by recalling vividly the divine benefits received, a person can meaningfully experience and

7

SABBATH

The blessings of redemption evoked by the Sabbath are to be enjoyed not at the expense or neglect of others, but rather by manifesting a genuine concern for the human rights and needs of others. This essential principle was clarified and emphasized by the Savior's Sabbath teaching and ministry.

express indebtedness and commitment to God. To remember God as one's Creator means to acknowledge the ground for one's existence. Nevertheless, creation remains a distant past act that does not easily touch the immediate concerns and needs of a person. Redemption, on the other hand, is God's constant intervention in history and thus speaks more directly to immediate human needs. In a sense there is a deliverance from Egyptian bondage which is not limited to a particular country or century, but which may recur in every country, in every age and in every soul.

A second reason for the summons to remember the Exodus deliverance was to motivate the Israelites to be compassionate toward dependent workers. Niels-Erik Andreasen emphasizes that "the real purpose of this 'remembrance clause' in Deuteronomy 5:15 is to provide a strong motive for all Israelites who remember their own deliverance from servitude, to extend such a deliverance from servitude on the Sabbath to those in their midst who are not free to observe it."[22] In other words, as the same author explains, "every seventh day the heads of the households in Israel are called upon to provide the dependents in a small but real way with the kind of freedom which they received from God at the exodus."[23] Thus the call to remember the Exodus deliverance through the Sabbath was for the Israelites a concrete experience which involved showing consideration toward the less fortunate. This implies a fundamental principle, namely that the blessings of redemption evoked by the Sabbath are to be enjoyed not at the expense or neglect of others, but rather by manifesting a genuine concern for the human rights and needs of others. We shall find that this essential principle, which unfortunately in the course of time was largely ignored, was clarified and emphasized by the Savior's Sabbath teaching and ministry.

Sabbath years. The temporary weekly release from the hardship of life and social inequalities assumed a heightened and more permanent nature at the time of the sabbatical year (every seventh year—Lev. 25:8) and in the jubilee year (every "seven sabbaths of years"—Lev. 25:8). Both of these annual institutions were closely linked to the weekly Sabbath. This is indicated not only by their dependency upon the cycle of seven (reflective of the week ending in a Sabbath), but also by the fact that they were to be kept as "a sabbath to the Lord . . . a sabbath of solemn rest for the land, a sabbath to the Lord" (Lev. 25:2, 4).[24] At these annual institutions, the Sabbath truly became the liberator of the oppressed in Hebrew society. The land was to lie fallow, to provide free produce for the disposses-

sed and animals. The slaves were emancipated if they so desired
and debts owed by fellow citizens were remitted. The jubilee
year also required the restoration of property to the original
owner. If no kinsman (*goel*) offered to redeem his fellow Jew
who on account of financial distress had sold himself to servitude, God Himself became his Redeemer (*goel*) from bondage
by means of the sabbatical legislation (Lev. 25:54-55).

Though seldom observed, these annual Sabbath institutions
by promising a national restoration to the people and to the
land became the symbol of the future restoration to be accomplished by the Messiah.[25] As the *rest* of the Sabbath served to
epitomize the future rest, harmony and peace of the Messianic
age, so the *restoration* of these annual Sabbaths served to announce the future restoration and liberation to be brought about
by the Messiah. Before mentioning specific examples of Messianic usages of the Sabbath-years themes, it may be helpful to
note why the latter were uniquely well-suited for such a purpose.

Redemptive features of Sabbath years. Several features of
the Sabbath years had a clear eschatological import. First, the
theme of *release* of debts, slaves and property provided an effective imagery to illustrate the expected Messianic liberation.
It is noteworthy that the sabbatical years are technically referred
to as "the release, the Lord's release, the year of release" (Deut.
15:1, 2, 9; 31:10; Lev. 25:10). The term "release"—*aphesis* is
commonly used in the Septuagint (Greek translation of the OT)
to translate the Hebrew designations for the sabbatical and
jubilee year (*shamat, shemittah, yobel, deror*).[26] The same term
"*aphesis*" is used in the NT almost always with the meaning of
"forgiveness." [27] This suggests that the vision of the sabbatical
release from social injustices functioned as the prefiguration of
the future Savior's release from the bondage of sin. Such a
Messianic typological usage of the Sabbath release is clarified
and corroborated, as we shall soon see, by the redemptive meaning attributed to the Sabbath in the NT.

A second eschatological feature can be seen in the trumpet
blast by means of a ram's horn (*yobel*—from which the term
"jubilee" derives) which ushered in the jubilee year. The imagery of this trumpet blast was apparently used by Isaiah to
describe the inauguration of the Messianic age (Is. 27:13).[28] Possibly, it is to the same imagery of the jubilee that the NT refers
when it speaks of the trumpet announcing the return of Christ
(1 Cor. 15:52; 1 Thess. 4:16; Matt. 24:31). Related to the
trumpet blast there is a third eschatological motif, namely, the
date of the tenth day of the seventh month—Atonement Day—on
which the ram's horn was blown to inaugurate the year of jubilee

(Lev. 25:9). Is it not significant that the sabbatical restoration of the year of jubilee was inaugurated by the cleansing (Lev. 16:18-19) and new moral beginning offered by God to the people on the Day of Atonement? [29]

The significance of this fact is noticed, for example, by Rousas John Rushdoony, who writes: "Because the jubilee began on the evening of the Day of Atonement, it made clear the foundation of the new creation, atonement through the blood of the Lamb of the Covenant. Creation and recreation were thus basic to the Sabbath: man *rests* in God's finished work of redemption proclaimed before time. By faith, man, anticipating the final victory and rejoicing in the present deliverance, lives by faith in the sufficiency of God." [30] The jubilee year, then, by pointing to the covenant God who restores the land and the people to new beginnings, could encourage faith in the future deliverance of the Messiah. The infrequency of these Sabbath years may well have contributed to heighten the expectancy and hope for the Messiah's future deliverance.

Sabbath years and the Messiah in the Old Testament. The vision of the sabbatical and jubilee years was actually utilized to represent the expectation of the Messianic redemption. A few examples will suffice to substantiate this statement. Daniel 9 provides an interesting instance of the double use of the sabbatical and jubilee year time periods. The chapter opens describing Daniel seeking to understand the time of the end of the captivity in the light of Jeremiah's prophecy of 70 years (Jer. 29:10). This prophetic period is explicitly explained in 2 Chronicles 36:21 as representing a prolonged "Sabbath" (ten sabbatical cycles) of desolation that the land would experience as a result of Israel's disobedience (cf. Lev. 26:34-35).

In the light of this prophecy, Daniel prays to understand the time when the predicted repatriation would occur (9:3-19). In response, the angel Gabriel appears to make known to him God's plan for a greater Messianic restoration to take place not after seventy years but after "seventy weeks of years" (9:24).[31] As the 70 years of Jeremiah, which predicted the end of *national captivity*, consisted of *10 sabbatical years* (10×7), so the 490 years (70×7) of Daniel, which predict the end of *spiritual bondage*, contain *10 jubilee years* (10×49). That this jubilary division of time points directly to the coming of the Messiah is indicated both by the specific reference to "Messiah Prince"— *mašiaḥ nagîd* (v. 25) and by the description of His mission ("to finish the transgression, to put an end to sin, and to atone for iniquity . . ."—v. 24). As the theme of the Sabbath rest is used to epitomize both political and Messianic expectations, so the vision of the release of the Sabbath years is here utilized to announce the time of both the national and Messianic restoration.[32]

Isaiah 61:1-3 provides another example where the theme of the jubilee year is applied to the mission of Yahweh's Anointed Servant (61:1). While the original identity of this figure is disputed, there is no question that at Qumran and in the NT, the personage described in this text was understood to be the Messiah who ushers in the end-time restoration. His mission is presented as being "to proclaim the year of the Lord's favor" (61:2), a clear reference to the proclamation of the year of jubilee (Lev. 25:10). The latter is indicated also by the use of the designation "release"—*deror* (v. 1), which is the technical term employed to designate the year of jubilee (Lev. 25:10; Jer. 34:8, 15, 17; Ezek. 46:17). The "good tidings" (Is. 61:1) proclaimed by Yahweh's Anointed (Messiah) by means of the delightful jubilee imagery is the promise of amnesty and release from captivity. Christ, as we shall soon see, utilized the same imagery to announce and explain the nature of His redemptive mission.

Sabbath years and the Messiah in Jewish literature. There are indications that the language and imagery of the Sabbath year found in Isaiah 61:1f. was used both in rabbinical and sectarian Judaism, to describe the work, of the expected Messiah.[33] For example, a fragmentary text discovered in 1956 in Qumran Cave 11 (known as 11Q Melchizedek) utilizes the very theme of the sabbatical restoration of Isaiah 61:1f. to explain the work of the Messianic figure known as "Melchizedek" (lines 5, 8, 9, 13).[34] He ushers in the year of jubilee (line 2), proclaiming "remission"—*shemittah* (line 3), and "release"—*deror* (line 6) to the "captives" (line 4). The reference is clearly to Isaiah 61:1, the very text quoted by Christ in His opening address in Nazareth to announce His mission (Luke 4:18-19). The seventh line, unfortunately very fragmentary, seems to refer to the "seventy weeks of years" of Daniel 9:24, since it speaks of "the year of the la[st] jubilee" as being "the [t]enth [ju]bilee" ($10 \times 49 = 490$ which is the same as Daniel's $70 \times 7 = 490$).[35] Moreover, like Daniel 9:24, this last year of jubilee involves atonement for iniquity ("to atone for all sons of [light and] men . . ."—line 8). The existence of this Messianic interpretation of the jubilee is confirmed also by rabbinical sayings. Elijah, for example, is reported to have said to Rabbi Judah, "The world has no less than 85 jubilee cycles and in the last jubilee-cycle the Son of David will come." [36]

This brief survey of sabbatical themes such as the Sabbath blessing/sanctification, the Sabbath rest and the Sabbath liberation, suffices to show that the Sabbath served in OT times not only to provide personal rest and liberation from social injustices, but also to epitomize the hopes for future political and Messianic restoration of peace and prosperity. We have found that the Sabbath has been understood as representing the very goal of human history. In fact, the sabbatical-septenary structure of time was used by some to measure the waiting time to the coming of the Messiah. Rabbi Abraham Joshua Heschel captures vividly the OT redemptive understanding of the Sabbath, when he writes: "Zion is in ruins, Jerusalem lies in the dust. All week there is only hope of redemption. But when the Sabbath is entering the world, man is touched by a moment of actual redemption; as if for a moment the spirit of the Messiah moved over the face of the earth." [37]

PART II

REDEMPTIVE MEANING OF THE SABBATH
IN THE NEW TESTAMENT

The existence of this Messianic/redemptive understanding of the Sabbath in OT times, poses important questions: How does the Sabbath in the NT fulfill such OT redemptive expectations? What is the relationship between Christ's redemptive mission and the Messianic restoration contemplated by the Sabbath in the OT? Did Christ fulfill the eschatological expectations inherent in the Sabbath, by bringing to an end its function as in the case of the Temple's services (Heb. 8:13; 9:23-28), or by enriching its meaning and function through His redemptive mission? To answer these questions it is necessary herewith to examine some significant testimonies reported in the Gospels regarding the Savior's Sabbath teaching and ministry.

1. *The Nazareth Address*

A model of Sabbathkeeping? Luke's account of the opening scene of Christ's ministry provides a suitable starting point for our inquiry into the relationship between the Savior and the Sabbath. According to Luke, it was "on a Sabbath day" that Jesus officially inaugurated His ministry in the synagogue of Nazareth, by making a programmatic speech.[38] It is noteworthy, first of all, that Luke introduces Christ as an habitual observer of the Sabbath ("as his custom was"—4:16).[39] Does he intend by this to set Christ before his readers as a model of Sabbathkeeping? M. M. B. Turner maintains that it is "Jesus' more recently acquired habit of *teaching* in the synagogues that is primarily in view," especially since Luke uses the same expression in "Acts 17:2 in respect of Paul's (Sabbath) synagogue *ministry*." [40a] Without denying the possibility that Luke may have thought also of Christ's custom of teaching on the Sabbath, it hardly seems justifiable to conclude that the phrase "provides no worthwhile evidence of any theological commitment on behalf of Jesus or Paul to Sabbath worship." [40b] Why? In the first place because Luke speaks of Christ's customary Sabbathkeeping in the immediate context of His upbringing in Nazareth ("where he had been brought up"—v. 16). This suggests that the allusion is especially to the custom of Sabbath observance during Christ's earlier life.[41] Second, even if the phrase referred exclusively to Christ's habitual Sabbath *teaching* in the synagogue, would not this also provide a theological model? Has not the Christian Church adopted the teaching model of the Sabbath (whether it be Saturday or Sunday) by reading and expounding the Scripture during the divine service? [42]

Third, the word "Sabbath" occurs in Luke's Gospel 21 times and 8 times in Acts,[43] that is, approximately twice as often as in any of the other three Gospels. This surely suggests that Luke attaches significance to the day. Fourth, Luke not only begins but also closes the account of Christ's earthly ministry on a Sabbath, by mentioning that His entombment took place on "the day of Preparation and the sabbath was beginning" (23:54).[44] Lastly, Luke expands his brief account of Christ's burial by stating positively that the women "rested on the sabbath in obedience to the commandment" (23:56b—NIV). Why does Luke present not only Christ but also His followers as habitual Sabbathkeepers These references can hardly be construed as insignificant or incidental. The many examples and situations of Sabbathkeeping reported, strongly suggest that Luke's intention indeed may well have been to set before his readers "a model of reverence for the Sabbath." [45] To understand such a "model," however, it is necessary to study how Luke and the other Evangelists relate the Sabbath to the coming of Christ.

Messianic fulfillment of Sabbath liberation. In His inaugural Nazareth address, Christ read and commented upon a passage drawn mostly from Isaiah 61:1-2 (also 58:6) which says: "The Spirit of the Lord is upon me, because he has anointed me to preach good news to the poor. He has sent me to proclaim release to the captives and recovering of sight to the blind, to set at liberty those who are oppressed, to proclaim the acceptable year of the Lord" (Luke 4:18).[46] The vital function of this passage has been noticed by many. Hans Conzelmann correctly views it as a nutshell summary of the "Messianic program." [47] The original passage of Isaiah, as noted earlier, describes by means of the imagery of the Sabbath year the liberation from captivity that the Servant of the Lord would bring to His people. The fact that the language and imagery of the Sabbath years found in Isaiah 61:1-3 (and 58:6) were utilized by sectarian and mainstream Jews to describe the work of the expected Messiah makes Christ's use of this passage all the more significant. This means that Christ presented Himself to the people as the very fulfillment of their Messianic expectations which had been nourished by the vision of the Sabbath years.[48]

This conclusion is supported by what may be regarded as a brief summary of Jesus' exposition of the Isaianic passage, which is recorded in Luke 4:21: "Today this scripture has been fulfilled in your hearing." In other words, the Messianic redemption *promised* by Isaiah through the Sabbath year, is "now" being *fulfilled*. As Paul K. Jewett aptly comments, "the great Jubilee Sabbath has become a reality for those who have been loosed from their sins by the coming of the Messiah and have found inheritance in Him." [49] The theme of *promise* and *fulfillment* is recurrent in all the Gospels. Many aspects of Christ's life and ministry are repeatedly presented as the fulfillment of OT prophecies. The risen Christ Himself, according to Luke, explained to His disciples that His teaching and mission represented the *fulfillment* of "everything written about me in the law of Moses and the prophets and the psalms" (Luke 24:44; cf. 24:26-27).[50]

How does the Sabbath fit into this theme of promise and fulfillment? What did Christ mean when He announced His mission to be the fulfillment of the sabbatical promises of liberation? Did He intend to explain, perhaps in a veiled fashion, that the institution of the Sabbath was a type which had found its fulfillment in Himself, the Antitype, and therefore its obligations had ceased? [51] (In such a case Christ would have paved the way for the replacement of the Sabbath with a new day of worship.) Or did Christ through His redemptive mission fulfill the promised sabbatical rest and release, in order to make the day a fitting vehicle to experience His blessings of salvation? To answer this question it is necessary to examine the Sabbath teaching and ministry of Christ reported in the Gospels. So far we have noticed that, according to Luke, Christ delivered His programmatic speech on a Sabbath claiming to be the fulfillment of the Messianic restoration announced by means of the Sabbath years (Is. 61:1-3; 58:6).

Annual or weekly Sabbath? Is the Messianic fulfillment of the redemption promised by the *annual* Sabbath equally applicable to the *weekly* Sabbath? M. M. B. Turner's answer is negative, basically for three reasons. First, because Isaiah 61 and 11Q Melchizedek) does not "actually mention the *weekly* Sabbath." Second, because Jesus utilizes the language of Isaiah 61 also on days other than the Sabbath. Third, because "Luke gives no editorial hint that the OT passage was particularly appropriate to a Sabbath (the 'today' of v. 21 is much broader in content than this)." [52] Are these objections really valid? Turner's first argument fails to recognize the close conceptual link that existed between the annual and the weekly Sabbaths. The former basically represented an intensification and actualization of the temporary "release" offered by the weekly Sabbath to all the members of the Hebrew society. Consequently the Sabbath years were also regarded as "a sabbath to the Lord" (Lev. 25:4; 2 Chron. 36:21). Moreover, we have found that not only the annual but also the weekly Sabbath rest was viewed as pointing forward to the Messianic rest and restoration. This suggests that mentioning of the former would not preclude, but would most probably include, the latter.

With regard to the second objection, why would Christ have to confine the use of "Messianic jubilee motifs" only to His Sabbath ministry, when such a motif represented the totality of His redemptive mission? The third objection also is hardly justifiable. Is it really true that "Luke gives no editorial hint that the OT passage chosen was particularly appropriate to a Sabbath"? [53] What about his emphatic use of "today" (v. 21)? Is this not related to His mention of the Sabbath? Such a possibility is recognized, for instance, by Howard Marshall, who points out that the *today* "refers primarily to the actual day on which Jesus spoke as being the day when prophecy began to be fulfilled." [54] This is not to deny that the "today" has also a broader scope, being part of the inbreaking of the Messianic age, "the acceptable year of the Lord" (v. 19). Moreover, does not Luke provide another noteworthy "hint" by placing Christ's initial announcement of His fulfillment of the sabbatical year (Luke 4:16-21) in the immediate context of two Sabbath healing episodes (Luke 4:31-38)? Such a sequence suggests that Christ's *proclamation* of His fulfillment of the expected sabbatical liberation is followed by a *demonstration* of how its realization was being accomplished.

Sabbath release and Savior's redemption. It has been convincingly shown that the determinative catchword that "binds Isaiah 61:1-2 and 58:6 together in Luke 4 is the small word *aphesis*," [55] which is used twice in Luke and is translated the first time as "release" for the captives and the second time as "liberty" for the oppressed (Luke 4:18). Is this promised sabbatical "release" realized through the physical and spiritual healing that Jesus provided to needy persons especially on the Sabbath? Note that both Mark and Luke place Christ's first miracle, the release of the demon-possessed man, on a Sabbath (Mark 1:21-28; Luke 4:31-37), presumably to set "the stage for the Sabbath works and healings which follow later." [56] Obviously, Christ's saving ministry was not confined to the Sabbath but continued irrespective of days. However, His daily ministry also, as we noted earlier, had a sabbatical significance since it represented the realization of the expected Sabbath liberation. But, one must not overlook the fact that a considerable coverage is given in the Gospels to His Sabbath saving ministry. No less than seven Sabbath healing episodes are reported, besides several controversies about Sabbathkeeping.[57] More important still is the redemptive significance which is often attributed to Christ's acts of healing performed on the Sabbath. A study of the latter will help to clarify how the Sabbath is related to Christ's redemptive mission.

2. Early Sabbath Healings

According to both Mark and Luke, the very first two healing episodes occurred on a Sabbath (Mark 1:21-31; Luke 4:31-39). Luke, in fact, places them immediately after the Nazareth address. The first took place in the synagogue of Capernaum during a Sabbath service and resulted in the *spiritual* healing of a demon-possessed man (Luke 4:31-37; Mark 1:21-28). The second was accomplished immediately after that service in Simon's house, and brought about the *physical* restoration of Simon's mother-in-law (Luke 4:38-39; Mark 1:29-31). The result of the latter was *rejoicing* for the whole family and *service*: "immediately she rose and *served* them" (Luke 4:39). The themes of *liberation, joy,* and *service* which are present in an embryonic form in these first healing acts are more explicitly associated with the meaning of the Sabbath in the subsequent ministry of Christ.

3. *The Crippled Woman*

Freedom on the Sabbath. The episode of the healing of the crippled woman, reported only by Luke, brings out rather clearly the relationship between the Sabbath and the Savior's saving ministry (Luke 13:10-17). It is noteworthy that in the brief narrative the verb "to free"—*luein* is used by the Lord *three* times. In the English RSV translation, the verb is rendered each time with a different synonym, namely "to free, to untie, to loose" (13:12, 15, 16). This threefold repetition suggests that the verb is used *not accidentally* but *intentionally*. The verb is employed by Christ first in addressing the woman, "you are *freed* from your infirmity" (v. 12). At the words of the Lord that woman, who for 18 years had been "bent over," "was made straight" (vv. 11, 13). The ruler of the synagogue became indignant over Christ's healing act. His reaction brings into focus the contrast between the prevailing perversion of the Sabbath on the one hand, and Christ's effort to restore to the day its true meaning on the other. For the ruler the Sabbath means rules to be obeyed, while for Christ it is a day in which to love and to save needy human beings.

To clarify the function of the Sabbath, Christ twice again uses the verb "to free." First, by referring to a customary concession: "You hypocrites! Does not each of you on the sabbath *untie* his ox or his ass from the manger, and lead it away to water it?" (Luke 13:15). Then, building upon the concept of untying an animal, again Christ uses the same verb in the form of a rhetorical question in order to draw the obvious conclusion: "And ought not this woman, a daughter of Abraham whom Satan *bound* for eighteen years, be *loosed* from this bond on the Sabbath day"? (Luke 13:16). Arguing from a minor to a major case, Christ shows how the Sabbath had been paradoxically distorted. An ox or an ass could be legitimately *untied* on the Sabbath for drinking purposes (possibly because a day without water could have resulted in loss of weight and consequently in less market value), but a suffering woman could not be released on such a day from the shackles of her physical and spiritual infirmity. It was necessary on the Sabbath, therefore, for Christ to act deliberately against prevailing misconceptions in order to restore the day to God's intended purpose. It should be noticed that in this as well as in all other instances, Christ is not questioning the binding obligations of the Sabbath commandment, but rather He argues for its true values which had been largely obscured by the accumulation of traditions and countless regulations.[58]

Sabbath release and Savior's redemption. The imagery of loosing on the Sabbath a victim bound by Satan's bonds (Luke 13:16) recalls Christ's announcement of His mission "to proclaim *release* to the captives . . . to set at *liberty* those who are oppressed" (Luke 4:18). Does not Jesus' act of freeing on the Sabbath a daughter of Abraham from physical and spiritual bonds exemplify how the liberation of the Messianic Sabbath was being fulfilled (Luke 4:21)? The connection between the two is recognized by a number of scholars. Harald Riesenfeld, for example, correctly points out that the "deeds of healing on Sabbath days must be interpreted as signs that in the person of Jesus was being realized something of what the Sabbath had pointed forward to in the eschatological expectations of the Jewish people." [59] "The work of liberating the victims of Satan's tyranny," aptly comments George Bradford Caird, "must go on seven days a week. So far from being the wrong day, the sabbath was actually the best day for such works of mercy. For the sabbath—the day which God had given to Israel as a weekly release from the bondage of labour—was also a weekly foretaste of the rest which awaited the people of God in the kingdom, the final release from all bondage. To liberate men and women from the reign of Satan and to bring them under the gracious reign of God was therefore to fulfill the purpose of the sabbath, not to profane it." [60]

Paul K. Jewett perspicaciously remarks: "We have in Jesus' healings on the Sabbath, not only acts of love, compassion and mercy, but true 'sabbatical acts,' acts which show that the Messianic Sabbath, the fulfillment of the Sabbath rest of the Old Testament, has broken into our world. Therefore the Sabbath, of all days, is the most appropriate for healing." [61] Similarly C. F. Evans points out that Christ "went out of His way to heal on the Sabbath . . . In reply to the ruler of the synagogue who states the Pharisaic ruling that healing is only permissible on the Sabbath if it is to save life, Jesus claims the Sabbath as the necessary day for that healing which is the rescue of a member of the chosen race from the bondage of Satan (Luke 13:14-16). The Sabbath, being a memorial of the peace and rest which is God's, is pre-eminently the day for the performance of those works which constitute its fulfillment, inasmuch as they are signs of the advent of the Messianic order of peace." [62]

Some scholars reject this interpretation, arguing that the comparison between the loosing on the Sabbath of oxen and donkeys from their cribs for drinking purposes and the freeing of a woman from Satan's bond suggest that the Sabbath was not a particularly appropriate day for Christ's works of mercy.

For all the people blessed by Christ's Sabbath ministry
the day became the memorial of the healing of their bodies and
souls, of the exodus from the bonds of Satan into the freedom
of the Savior.

Why? Basically because they reason that as the untying and watering of animals took place daily, irrespective of the Sabbath, so Christ's saving acts are performed, not because it is Sabbath but in spite of it.[63] Such an argument comes short on at least two counts. First, the animals are explicitly included among the beneficiaries of the Sabbath commandment ("your ox, or your ass, or any of your cattle," Deut. 5:14; cf. Ex. 20:10). Thus showing kindness even to dumb beasts was especially appropriate on the Sabbath.[64] Second, Christ challenges the contention of the ruler of the synagogue that healing ought to take place only during the "six days" rather than "on the sabbath day" (Luke 13:14), by affirming exactly the contrary, namely, that the woman ought to be loosed from her bond "on the sabbath day" (v. 16). This implies then that Christ chose to heal her not in spite of the Sabbath but rather because the day provided a most fitting occasion.[65]

The physical and spiritual freedom that the Savior offered to that sick woman on the Sabbath represents a token manifestation of Christ's proclaimed fulfillment of the Sabbath liberation (Luke 4:18-21) which had dawned with His coming. This redemptive meaning of the Sabbath is further clarified in other incidents now to be examined. But, before leaving this episode, one may ask, How did the woman and the people who witnessed Christ's saving intervention come to view the Sabbath? Luke reports that while Christ's "adversaries were put to shame . . . the people rejoiced" (13:17), and the woman "praised God" (13:13). Undoubtedly for the healed woman and for all the people blessed by Christ's Sabbath ministry the day became the memorial of the healing of their bodies and souls, of the exodus from the bonds of Satan into the freedom of the Savior.

4. *The Paralytic and the Blind Man*

Similarities. Two Sabbath miracles reported by John further exemplify the relationship between the Sabbath and Christ's work of salvation (John 5:1-18; 9:1-41). The two episodes can be examined together since they show substantial similarity. Both healed men had been chronically ill: one an invalid for 38 years (5:5) and the other blind from birth (9:2). In both instances Christ told the men to act. To the paralyzed man He said, "Rise, take up your pallet, and walk" (5:8); to the blind man, "Go, wash in the pool of Siloam" (9:7). Both of these actions represent the breaking of rabbinical Sabbath laws, and thus both are used by Pharisees to charge Christ with Sabbath-breaking (John 5:10, 16; 9:14-16). In both instances

Christ repudiated such a charge by arguing that His works of salvation are not precluded but rather contemplated by the Sabbath commandment (5:17; 7:23; 9:4). Christ's justification is expressed especially through a memorable statement: "My Father is working until now and I am working" (John 5:17; cf. 9:4).

Negation or clarification of the Sabbath? What did Christ actually mean when He formally defended Himself against the charge of Sabbath-breaking by appealing to the "working until now" of His Father? Did He use the example of His Father to rescind the obligation of Sabbath keeping both for Himself and for His followers, or to clarify its true nature and meaning? To put it bluntly, does Christ's statement represent a *negation* or a *clarification* of the Sabbath law? In a previous study we have shown that the "working until now" of the Father and of the Son has historically received three basic interpretations, namely, (1) continuous creation, (2) continuous care, (3) redemptive activities.[66] The exponents of these three views basically agree in regarding Christ's pronouncement as an implicit (for some, explicit) annulment of the Sabbath commandment. Does such a conclusion reflect the legitimate meaning of the passage, or rather arbitrary assumptions which have been read into the passage? To answer this question and, it is hoped, to understand the significance of Christ's saying, we shall briefly examine the role of the adverb "until now"—*heos arti*, the meaning of the verb "is working"—*ergazetai* and the theological implications of the passage.

The meaning of the adverb "until now." Traditionally the adverb "until now" has been interpreted as the *continuous* working of God (whether it be in creation, preservation or redemption) which allegedly overrides or rescinds the Sabbath law. But does the adverbial phrase "until now" suggest that God is *constantly* working without respect to the Sabbath? The adverb itself, especially as used in its emphatic position before the verb (in Greek), presupposes not *constancy* but *culmination*. The latter is brought out by some translators through the use of the emphatic form "even until now."[67] This adverbial phrase presupposes a beginning (*terminus a quo*) and a conclusion (*terminus ad quem*). The former is apparently the initial creation Sabbath (Gen. 2:2-3) and the latter the final Sabbath rest, which is envisaged in the similar Sabbath pronouncement as the "night . . . when no one can work" (9:4). What Jesus is saying, then, is that though God established the Sabbath at the completion of creation, because of sin He has been "working until now" to bring the promised Sabbath rest to fruition.

The meaning of the verb "working." What is the nature of the "working until now" of the Father? In the Gospel of John the working and works of God are repeatedly and explicitly identified, not with a continuous divine creation nor with a constant maintenance of the universe, but with the saving mission of Christ. For example, Jesus explicitly states: "This is the *work* of God, that you *believe* in him whom he has sent" (6:29). And again, "If I am not doing the *works* of my Father, then do not *believe* me; but if I do them, even though you do not *believe* me, *believe the works*, that you may know and understand that the Father is in me and I am in the Father" (10:37, 38; cf. 4:34; 14:11; 15:24).[68] The redemptive nature of the works of God is especially clear in the healing of the blind man since the act is explicitly described as the manifestation of "the works of God" (John 9:3). This means then that God ended on the Sabbath His *works of creation* but not His *working in general*. Because of sin, He has been engaged in the work of redemption "until now." Or to use the words of A. T. Lincoln, one might say, "As regards the work of creation God's rest was final, but as that rest was meant for humanity to enjoy, when it was disturbed by sin, God worked in history to accomplish his original purpose."[69]

Theological implications. What are the theological implications of Christ's defense? Does He appeal to the "working" of His Father to nullify or clarify the function of the Sabbath? To understand the implications of Christ's defense, one needs to remember that the Sabbath is linked both to the *cosmos* through *creation* (Gen. 2:2-3; Ex. 20:11), and to the *exodus* through *redemption* (Deut. 5:15). While by interrupting all secular activities the Israelite was remembering the Creator-God, by acting mercifully toward fellow-beings he was imitating the Redeemer-God. This was true, not only in the life of the people in general who on the Sabbath were to be compassionate toward the less fortunate, but especially in the service of the temple. There, as we shall soon see, the priests could legitimately perform on the Sabbath works forbidden to the Israelites, because such works had a redemptive function. On the basis of this theology of the Sabbath admitted by the Jews, Christ defends the legality of the "working" that He and His Father perform on the Sabbath.[70]

This is in fact the line of defense that Christ uses when He appeals to the example of circumcision, to silence the echo of the controversy over the healing of the paralytic (John 7:22-24). The Lord argues that if it is legitimate on the Sabbath for the priests to care for one small part of man's body (according to rabbinic reckoning circumcision involved one of man's 248 members) in order to extend to the newborn child the salvation of the covenant, there is no reason to be "angry" with Him for restoring on that day the *whole body* of man" (7:23). The Sabbath is for Christ the day to work for the redemption of the *whole* man.[71] This is borne out by the fact that in both healings, Christ looked for the healed men on the same day, and having found them, He ministered to their spiritual needs (5:14; 9:35-38). His opponents cannot perceive the redemptive nature of Christ's Sabbath ministry because they "judge by appearances" (7:24). For them the pallet and the clay are more important than the social reunification (5:10) and the restoration of sight (9:14) which those objects symbolized. It was therefore necessary for Christ to act against prevailing misconceptions in order to restore the Sabbath to its positive function.

In another Sabbath pronouncement recorded in John 9:4, Christ extends to His followers the invitation to become links of the same redemptive chain, saying: "We must work the works of him who sent me, while it is day; night comes, when no one can work." The "night" apparently refers to the conclusion of the history of salvation, a conclusion which we found implied in the adverbial phrase "until now." Such a conclusion of divine and human redemptive activity would usher in the final Sabbath of which the creation Sabbath was a prototype. To bring about that final Sabbath, the Godhead "is working" for our salvation (John 5:17) but also "*we* must work" to extend it to others (9:4). The foregoing considerations indicate that the two Sabbath healings reported by John substantiate the redemptive meaning of the Sabbath we found earlier in Luke, namely, a time to experience and share the blessings of salvation accomplished by Christ.

5. *The Disciples' Plucking Ears of Corn*

The episode of the disciples' plucking ears of corn on a Sabbath (Mark 2:23-28; Matt. 12:1-8; Luke 6:1-5) provides an additional indication of the relationship between the Sabbath and the redemptive ministry of Christ. Jesus and the disciples were walking along a path that went through the fields. The disciples "were hungry, and they began to pluck ears of grain and to eat" (Matt. 12:1). The Pharisees, who somehow (!) were also in the field on that day, regarded such an action as an outright desecration of the Sabbath and complained to Christ, saying: "Look, why are they doing what is not lawful on the sabbath?" (Mark 2:24). One wonders, Why were the disciples assuaging their hunger by eating raw ears of grain in the first place? The presence of the Pharisees among them suggests that possibly they all had attended together the Sabbath service at the synagogue, and, having received no dinner invitation, the disciples were picking and eating raw ears of grain as they were making their way along the fields to find a place to rest.[72] If this were the case, then Christ's reply to the Pharisees, particularly His quotation from Hosea, "I desire mercy, and not sacrifice" (Matt. 12:7), could well contain a veiled rebuke of their lack of Sabbath hospitality.

David's example. To defend the conduct of His disciples against the charge of Sabbath-breaking, Christ advanced two basic arguments. First, He reasoned that if it was right for David and his men to allay their hunger by eating the *holy bread* which was reserved exclusively for the priests (1 Sam. 21:1-7), then it was equally legitimate for the disciples to provide for their needs by plucking ears of grain during the *holy time* of the Sabbath.[73] The principle involved here is not, as some mistakenly assume, that people of authority such as David and Christ "transcend the law"[74] because of the special position they enjoy. Are God's laws binding only on ordinary creatures? To say the least, such a notion would make God guilty of governing with a double standard, one for common persons and one for privileged individuals. Such a preposterous view of God is totally unwarranted because the justification given in the text for David's action is not that he was *king* David, but rather that "he and those who were with him" were "in need and . . . hungry" (Mark 2:25). In other words, it is human *need* and not *position* that takes prior claim over the law. Do not ordinary citizens exceed the speed limit with impunity when taking a very sick person to a hospital?

Some argue that this principle is not applicable to the disciples, because their hunger was not as acute as that of David.[75] Such a rabbinical reasoning is absent in the OT and in the teachings of Jesus. The Scripture provides no graduated scale of human needs to determine when action is justified. The principle enunciated by Christ is, "the sabbath was made on account of (*dia*) man" (Mark 2:27), that is, to ensure his physical and spiritual well-being. This means that the welfare of human beings is not *restricted* but *guaranteed* by proper Sabbath observance. To require that the disciples deny their physical needs in order to keep the Sabbath would mean to pervert its intended function, namely, to be a day of delight and not one of privation.[76] This human function of the Sabbath will be considered further in the next chapter, entitled "The Sabbath: Good News of Service."

The priest's example. The second argument used by the Lord is more directly related to our immediate inquiry into the relationship between Christ's saving ministry and the Sabbath. According to Matthew, Jesus appealed not only to the prophetic section of the OT (i.e., the example of David—1 Sam. 21:1-7), but also to the *Torah* (Law) proper, by citing the example of the priests, who "in the temple profane the sabbath, and are guiltless" (Matt. 12:5; cf. Num. 28:9-10; Lev. 24:8-9). A host of activities, illegal for the ordinary person, were performed by the priests on the Sabbath. On that day the regular daily sacrifices were augmented by two additional flawless yearling male lambs, together with flour and oil (Num. 28:9-10). Though working more intensely on the Sabbath, the priests were "guiltless" (Matt. 12:5). Why? Was it perhaps because they took a day off at another time during the week? No, the OT does *not* offer or contemplate any such special provision for the priests. The absence of the latter constitutes a most direct challenge to those who uphold the *one day-in-seven* principle. Donald Carson wisely acknowledges this fact when he writes, "If the OT principle were really 'one day in seven for worship and rest,' we might have expected OT legislation to prescribe some other day off for the priests. The lack of such confirms the importance in OT thought of the *seventh* day, as opposed to the mere one-in-seven principle so greatly relied upon by those who wish to see in Sunday the precise NT equivalent of the OT Sabbath." [77]

Why, then, were the priests "guiltless"? The answer is to be found in the redemptive nature of their Sabbath work. We noted already that Christ alluded to the latter, when citing the example of circumcision which the priests could lawfully perform on the Sabbath because of the redemptive significance of the rite (John 7:22-23). Similarly in this instance Christ appeals to the various services and sacrifices which the priests legitimately offered on the Sabbath, because these represented God's provision of forgiveness and salvation for His people (Heb. 7:27, 9:12, 22). [78] We have found that a vital function of the weekly and annual Sabbaths was to provide "release"—*aphesis* to the oppressed. The intensification of the Temple services and sacrifices on the Sabbath (four lambs were sacrificed instead of the daily two—Num. 28:8-9) points to the special release from the burden of sin and guilt that God offered to the people on that day. The Sabbath is the time to experience in a special way the rest of God's forgiveness—and a fresh new beginning. [79]

Christ and the temple. Christ finds in this redemptive work performed by the priests on the Sabbath a valid basis to justify His own Sabbath ministry as well as that of His disciples. Why? Because He rightly views His own ministry as "something greater than the temple" (Matt. 12:6). In other words, the redemption offered *typologically* by the temple through its serving priests is now being provided *realistically* through Christ's saving mission. Therefore, just as the priests could legitimately "profane" the Sabbath in order to perform their redemptive service in the temple, so could Jesus' disciples in order to serve the One who is greater than the temple. Being the fulfillment of the redemption promised through the temple's services and sacrifices, Christ's ministry must continue on the Sabbath, even preferably on that day. What He does His followers, the new priesthood, must likewise do. "The priests," aptly writes Ellen White, "were performing those rites that pointed to the redeeming power of Christ, and their labor was in harmony with the object of the Sabbath. But now Christ Himself had come. The disciples, in doing the work of Christ, were engaged in God's service, and that which was necessary for the accomplishment of this work it was right to do on the Sabbath day." [80]

Some object to this parallelism between the priests and the disciples because in their view, the latter were not engaged in a religious activity while plucking grain.[81] What is it that makes an act religious? Is it not when its intended function is directly to serve God? Baking bread, for example, was a common work which no Israelite was to do on the Sabbath at home (Ex. 16:23). Yet in the Temple baking was a religious activity, which the priests lawfully performed on the Sabbath because it was part of their service to God (1 Sam. 21:3-6; Lev. 24:8). Had not the disciples left all to serve the One greater than the temple? Was not then the caring for their personal needs on the Sabbath while serving their Lord in His itinerant ministry a religious activity? To reduce religious activities only to rituals performed within the confines of a sacred place, thus neglecting the aspect of service to human needs, means, as pointed out by Christ, to fail to understand Hosea's statement, "I desire mercy, and not sacrifice" (Matt. 12:7; Hos. 6:6).

Authority or legality? Does Christ's use of the example of David and of the priests suggest that He justified the conduct of His disciples by asserting His *authority* to transcend the Sabbath law, or by proving the *legality* of their action within that law? A number of scholars argue for the former view. For them "it is a question of authority rather than legality" that is at stake.[82] The comparison between David and the priests on the one hand, and Christ on the other hand, is allegedly supposed to show that "persons with authority" can override the Sabbath. Consequently it is Christ's "authority which shields the disciples from guilt." [83] The ultimate conclusion drawn from such reasoning is that Christ's authoritative teaching supposedly anticipates the change in the day of worship which however did not actually occur until after the resurrection.[84] What can be said of such reasoning? Obviously, it reveals a genuine desire to find a ground for Sunday observance in Christ's teaching. But, can such a conclusion be drawn legitimately from Jesus' arguments? I think not.

Did Christ appeal to the example of David and of the priests to show that persons of *authority* have the right to *supersede* the Sabbath law? Can human authority per se be regarded as a valid criterion to transcend God's law? If this were true, there would be a constant conflict between human authority and divine precepts. Such a conflict, however, does not exist in Jesus' reasoning. What He tells the Pharisees is not that the law does not apply to important persons such as David or the priests, but on the contrary that their exceptional conduct, like that of the disciples, is contemplated by the law. This is clearly indicated by the counter-question that Christ asks twice, "Have you not read in the law . . .?" (Matt. 12:5; cf. v. 3). Note that it is *within the law* (not outside of it) that Jesus finds precedents to defend the legality of the disciples' conduct. The disciples were "guiltless" then, not because their authority (or that of Christ) transcended the law, but because their action fell *within the intention of the law itself.*[85]

Christ, the Interpreter of the law. All laws must be interpreted. The case of the priests provides a fitting example. The law ordered them to work on the Sabbath (Num. 28:9; Lev. 24:8), thus causing them to break another law—that of the Sabbath rest (Ex. 20:8-10). What does this mean? Simply that the letter of the law cannot be applied indiscriminately, but must be interpreted discriminately when applied to specific cases. In American society the Supreme Court acts as the final interpreter of the intent of the laws of the land. This is the authority that Christ claims by proclaiming Himself "Lord of the Sabbath" (Matt. 12:8; Mark 2:28). It is not the authority to abrogate or substitute the Sabbath commandment but rather to reveal its *true divine intention.*[86]

Christ demonstrates this authority as Interpreter of the true meaning of the fourth commandment by presenting five significant arguments in defending the innocence of His disciples.

First, the Lord refers to David to validate the general principle that law admits exceptions (Matt. 12:3; Mark 2:25). Second, Christ provides a specific example of exceptional use of the Sabbath by the priests, to prove that the commandment does not preclude but contemplates ministering to the spiritual needs of people (Matt. 12:5). Third, Christ claims for Himself and His disciples the same Sabbath privileges of the priests, because as the superior Antitype of the Temple and its priesthood (Matt. 12:6), He and His followers also, like the priests, must provide a ministry of salvation to needy sinners. Fourth, by citing Hosea's statement, "I desire mercy, and not sacrifice" (Matt. 12:7), Jesus explains that the order of priorities in the observance of the Sabbath is first a loving service to needy persons and then the fulfillment of ritual prescriptions. Lastly, Jesus asserts His lordship over the Sabbath, that is, His prerogative to interpret its meaning, by reaffirming the fundamental principle that the Sabbath was instituted to insure human well-being (Mark 2:28). Consequently, to deny human needs on account of the Sabbath commandment is a perversion of its original purpose.

6. *The Savior's Rest*

The Savior's rest and the Sabbath. In the light of this authoritative interpretation of the meaning of the Sabbath, it is well to consider the meaning of Christ's summons which Matthew placed just prior to the episode we have just examined. The Savior says, "Come to me, all who labor and are heavy laden, and I will give you *rest*. Take my yoke upon you, and learn from me; for I am meek and lowly in heart, and you will find *rest* for your souls. For my yoke is easy, and my burden is light" (Matt. 11:28-30). Twice in this invitation Christ promises *rest* to those who come to Him and learn from Him. Is the *rest* that Christ offers related to the *Sabbath rest*? The possible connection between the two has been noted by several commentators.[87] Such a link is suggested by Matthew's setting of Christ's invitation to receive His rest (Matt. 11:28-30), in the immediate context of two Sabbath episodes (Matt. 12:1-14).

In addition to this *structural* link, Matthew suggests also a *temporal* connection by carefully noting that the two Sabbath conflicts occurred "at that time" (Matt. 12:1), "presumably at or near the time when Jesus had spoken of His rest."[88] The possibility exists, therefore, that the rest promised by Christ is that of the true Sabbath. Earlier in this chapter we noted that the Sabbath rest in OT times was viewed as typifying the future Messianic rest. By offering rest, then, Christ could well have claimed to fulfill the expected Sabbath rest. As Christ in Luke 4:18-21 proclaims to be the Messianic fulfillment of the expected sabbatical liberation, so in Matthew 11:28-29 He claims to realize the expected Messianic Sabbath rest.[89]

The Nature of Christ's rest. What is the nature of the "Sabbath rest" that Christ offers to those "heavy-laden"? How is such a "rest" to be experienced? To a modern reader, the formula offered by Christ sounds most paradoxical. Said He, "Take my yoke upon you, and learn from me . . . and you will find rest for your souls" (Matt. 11:29). How can rest be found by taking a yoke upon oneself? Such a formula sounds like a clear contradiction of terms. The contradiction, however, is resolved when the significance of the imagery of the "yoke" is understood. The term "yoke" was used both by the Jews and by the early Christians to designate the law.[90] A few examples will suffice to bear this out. Jeremiah speaks of the leaders of the people who though "they know . . . the law of their God . . . they . . . had broken the yoke, they had burst the bonds" (Jer. 5:5). In the following chapter the same prophet says to the people, "find rest for your souls" by learning anew obedience to God's law (Jer. 6:16; cf. Num. 25:3). The invitation to take upon oneself the yoke of the law occurs frequently also in rabbinical literature. Rabbi Nehunya b. Kanah (c. A.D. 100), supposedly said, "He that takes upon himself the yoke of the law, from him shall be taken away the yoke of the kingdom and the yoke of worldly care."[91] This notion of the law as a yoke was familiar to the early Christians. The Jerusalem Council, for example, decided not to put "a yoke upon the neck" (Acts 15:10) of the Gentiles by requiring them to fulfill the law of circumcision.[92]

This imagery of the law as a yoke could deceive us into thinking that the law was viewed as a burdensome straitjacket. The truth of the matter is much different. To the devout believer the law expressed not slavery but the basis of a special covenant relationship with God. It expressed, as M. Maher aptly explains, "the desire to place oneself under the direct rule of God and to devote oneself entirely to performing his revealed will."[93] Thus the Psalmist declares "blessed" the person whose "delight is in the law of the Lord, and on his law he meditates day and night" (Ps. 1:1, 2; cf. 112:1; 119:18, 105). The conflict between Judaism and early Christianity has unfortunately obscured the fact that there were indeed noble Jews who gave attention not merely to external legal piety but also to the internal intention of God's precepts. These persons genuinely loved God and their fellow beings and later accepted the Messiah as their personal Savior by the "thousands" (Acts. 21:20; cf. 2:41; 4:4).[94] The fact remains, however, that there were also Scribes and Pharisees who expounded the law in terms of minute legal requirements which weighed as a heavy yoke upon the people. "They bind heavy burdens, hard to bear" (Matt. 23:4). Such a teaching encouraged a form of petty legalism that offered *not rest* but *restlessness* to burdened souls.

Christ, as the new Moses, claims the authority to refute such a misleading understanding and practice of the will of God, and to reveal through His teaching and ministry the true meaning of God's precepts. "Take my yoke upon you, and learn from me" (Matt. 11:29). The "yoke" of Christ's teaching is not "heavy" as that of the Pharisees but "easy" and "light" (Matt. 11:30). Why? Basically because the Savior invites His followers to commit themselves not to a new set of rules, but to Himself, the true Interpreter and Fulfiller of God's law ("Come to *me* . . . learn from *me*"—Matt. 11:28-29). Since the Law and the prophets pointed to Christ (Luke 23:27; John 5:39), it is in relationship to His mission that He interprets their meaning and function. The "yoke" of Christ's teaching brings rest because it leads a person to experience the rest of His salvation.

New rules or new rest? Does this mean that Christ supersedes and annuls the Sabbath commandment by offering His own rest instead? No. Rather Christ explains the meaning of the Sabbath rest in the light of His redemptive rest. The various Sabbath episodes analyzed so far support this view. We have found that Jesus on a Sabbath announced His mission to be the fulfillment of the expected sabbatical redemption (Luke 4:16-21). During His ministry Christ made good such a claim by intentionally working on the Sabbath for the salvation of needy sinners (John 5:17; 9:4), so that souls whom "Satan bound" would experience and remember the Sabbath as the day of their liberation (Luke 13:16). Moreover, it was on a Friday afternoon that Christ completed His earthly redemptive mission, saying "it is finished" (John 19:30), and then resting on the Sabbath in the tomb (Mark 15:42, 46; Luke 23:53-54). Like the completion of creation, so now that of redemption is marked by the Sabbath rest.[95]

This meaning of the Sabbath is supported also by the two Sabbath episodes (Matt. 12:1-14) that Matthew links with Christ's offer of His rest (Matt. 11:28-29).[96] The question raised in both episodes is, "What is lawful on the Sabbath?" (Matt. 12:2, 10). The two stories show that the Pharisees had reduced the Sabbath rest to an oppressive burden. Christ, as Lord of the Sabbath (12:8), interprets the commandment in terms of "mercy" rather than legalistic religiosity (12:7). In the first episode (plucking off ears of corn), we found that Christ identifies His ministry as well as that of His disciples with the redemptive service performed by the priests on the Sabbath in the Temple (12:6). In the second incident (man with a withered hand), to be examined in the next chapter, Christ clarifies the "value" of the Sabbath as a day "to do good" (12:12-13) and "to save" (Mark 3:4). In a sense, these two episodes bring out two related dimensions of Christ's view of the Sabbath: the first, that the Sabbath is a time to *experience* His gracious salvation; second, that it is a time *to share* blessings received by responding to human needs. The "Sabbath rest" that Christ offers to those who labor in vain to procure rest for themselves by fulfilling demanding regulations, is not a newer or simpler set of rules on how to keep the day, but an experience of the peace and rest of salvation on and through His Holy Day.

7. *The Sabbath in Hebrews*

The redemptive meaning of the Sabbath which we have found in the Gospels is reflected in the book of Hebrews. We noted earlier that the author of this book, drawing upon existing eschatological understandings of the Sabbath rest, relates God's rest on the seventh day of creation (Heb. 4:4) to all the rest and peace God intends to confer on His people. By linking together two passages,[97] namely Genesis 2:2 and Psalm 95:7, 11, the author explains that the divine rest promised at creation was not exhausted when the Israelites under Joshua found a resting place in Canaan, since God again offered His rest "long afterwards" through David (Heb. 4:7; cf. Ps. 95:7). Consequently, God's promised Sabbath rest still awaited a fuller realization which has dawned with the coming of Christ (Heb. 4:9). It is by believing in Jesus Christ that God's people can at last experience ("enter"—4:3, 10, 11) the "good news" of God's rest promised on the "seventh day" of creation (4:4).

Literal or figurative Sabbathkeeping? What inference can be legitimately drawn from this passage regarding the actual observance and understanding of the Sabbath among the recipients of Hebrews? The position of the majority of commentators is that this passage provides no indication that these Christian "Hebrews" actually observed the Sabbath or that the author intended to give a Christian interpretation to such an observance. What are the reasons advanced for such a position?

Basically three. First, it is argued that since the author discusses not the actual observance of the Sabbath but the permanence and the fulfillment of its rest through the Christ-event, no inference can be drawn regarding its literal observance. Second, it is pointed out that since "the Sabbath rest that remains for the people of God" (4:9) is a future realization,[98] the exhortation to enter God's rest (4:10, 11) has no implication for the present observance of the day. Thirdly, it is assumed that since the author in a number of places indicates that with the coming of Christ, certain old covenant institutions were made "obsolete" (8:13; 7:11-9:28), the Sabbath also was presumably viewed as belonging to the past.[99]

In our view these reasons come short on several counts. The first argument fails to recognize that the recipients of the Epistle (whether Gentiles or Jewish-Christians)[100] were so attracted to Jewish liturgy[101] (of which the Sabbath was fundamental) that it was unnecessary for the author to discuss or encourage its actual observance. What those Christians actually needed, tempted as they were to turn back to Judaism, was to understand the meaning of its observance in the light of Christ's coming. It is this meaning that the author endeavors to bring out. George Wesley Buchanan finds the passage so steeped in the OT concept of the "sabbath and jubilees releases," understood as quiet and peaceful existence in the promised land, that he claims both the author and the recipients of the Hebrews possibly still hoped to see in their own day the fulfillment of the promised Sabbath rest in terms of a concrete national independence from the Romans.[102] Though such a view is hardly defensible in the light of the writer's exhortation to enter God's rest (4:9-10) and not that of the land, it still serves to illustrate that some scholars recognize what an important role the Sabbath theology played in the thinking of the community. Moreover, the fact that the author is not engaged in a *polemical* defense of the validity of Sabbath observance but rather in an *exhortation* to experience its blessings which are still outstanding for the people of God (4:9), makes his testimony all the more valuable, since it takes its observance for granted. Additional indications will soon be offered.

Present or future? With regard to the second argument, it can hardly be said that in Hebrews the Sabbath rest is viewed primarily as a future benefit, unrelated to the present observance of the day. Some scholars have identified in Hebrews the model of the church as a company of wanderers, journeying to a future heavenly resting place.[103] Without denying the presence of the pilgrimage motif in Hebrews, it must be pointed out that the "sabbath rest" that "remains for the people of God" (4:9) is presented primarily not as a future but as a present experience into which those "who have believed *are entering*" (4:3). The latter verb is in the present tense, and in Greek is placed first in the sentence to stress the present reality of this "rest" experience.[104] The same is true of the verb "remains" (4:9), which if taken out of context could imply a future prospect, but in its context the verb refers back to the time of Joshua (4:8), in order to emphasize the present permanence of the Sabbath rest for God's people. What the author of Hebrews is saying, as well stated by A. T. Lincoln, is "that since the time of Joshua an observance of the Sabbath has been outstanding."[105] The use of both verbs in the present tense emphasizes the present permanence of the Sabbath rest rather than its future consummation. It must be said, nonetheless, that the future dimension of this rest is also contemplated in the passage, as we shall soon see.

Obsolete or remaining? This leads us to the third argument which maintains that the Sabbath is an OT shadow or type of that final rest which Christ has made available to His people and consequently its function terminated with His coming.[106] Is this what Hebrews or the rest of the NT teaches? Did the Sabbath, like the temple and its services, live out its function with the coming of Christ? Or did the Sabbath acquire fresh meaning and function with His coming? Our study of the Sabbath material of the Gospels has shown that Christ fulfilled the typological and eschatological Messianic Sabbath rest and release, not by annulling the actual observance of the day but by making it a time to experience and share with others His accomplished salvation.

Let us look now at what Hebrews has to say on this point. There is no question that the author of this book clearly teaches that Christ's coming has brought about "a decisive discontinuity" with the sacrifical system of the Old Covenant. In chapters 7 to 10, the writer explains at great length how Christ's atoning sacrifice and subsequent heavenly ministry have replaced completely the typological ("copy and shadow"—8:5) function of the levitical priesthood and its Temple. These services Christ "abolished" (10:9) and thus they are "obsolete" and "ready to vanish away" (8:13). But, does he place the Sabbath in the same category, viewing it as one of the "obsolete" old-covenant institutions? This is indeed the conclusion that some have drawn,[107] but, in our view, it is based on gratuitous assumptions rather than on what the document actually says.

The "Sabbath rest" is explicitly and emphatically presented not as being "*obsolete*" like the temple and its services, but as a divine benefit that still "*remains*" (4:9). The verb "remains—*apoleipetai,*" literally means "to leave behind" and is used here in the present passive tense. If literally translated verse 9 reads: "So then a Sabbath rest is left behind for the people of God." The contrast between the Sabbath and the sanctuary services is obvious. While the latter are "obsolete," the former is "left behind," and therefore still relevant. A similar contrast is found in the Gospel of Matthew. There the rending of the Temple's curtain in conjunction with Christ's death (Matt. 27:51) indicates the termination of the Temple's services. On the other hand, Christ's warning about the possibility that the future flight out of the city might occur on a Sabbath (Matt. 24:20) takes for granted the permanence of its observance.

The exhortation given in verse 11 to "strive to enter that rest" provides an additional indication of the permanence of the Sabbath. The fact that one must make efforts "to enter that rest" implies that the "rest" experience of the Sabbath is not exhausted in the present but has a future realization also. This Christian view of the Sabbath rest as representing not only a *present* but also a *future* "rest" experience reflects to a large extent what we have already found in the OT and in later Jewish literature. There we saw that the Sabbath was understood not only as a *present* experience of personal rest and liberation from social injustices, but also as the anticipation of the *future* rest and peace to be realized by the Messiah. Thus in his own way the author of Hebrews reaffirms the OT understanding of the Sabbath in a fresh Christian setting, namely, a day to experience the present rest of salvation while looking forward to the future and final rest in the heavenly Canaan.

An unresolved contradiction. It is unfortunate that the happy tension between the two dimensions—present and future—of the Sabbath which we have found in Hebrews (and in the Gospels) was soon overlooked and even rejected by many Christians. For what reasons? We have shown in *From Sabbath to Sunday* that as a result of an interplay of social, political, pagan-religious and Christian factors, it became expedient to change the day of worship from Sabbath to Sunday. Those who adopted this change found it necessary to empty the Sabbath of all its validity and meaning for the present life and to reduce it exclusively to a symbol of the future eternal rest. Such a view has enjoyed general support throughout Christian history. It appears for the first time in the so-called *Epistle of Barnabas* (ca. 135), where the author argues that "it is not the present sabbaths that are acceptable to me [God]" (15:8) but the future Sabbath that God will establish in the seventh millennium (15:4-

5). At that time the Lord will bring everything to rest and "then we shall be able to treat it [the Sabbath] as holy" (15:7).[108] This millenarian (chiliastic) view of the Sabbath has been held by such early Christian writers as Irenaeus, Justin Martyr, Tertullian, Hippolytus, Cyprian, Augustine (for a time), Victorinus and Lactantius.[109]

Others such as Origen, Eusebius of Caesarea, Jerome, Augustine, Chrysostom, Bede, Rabanus Maurus, Peter Lombard, Calvin and some contemporary scholars, however, choosing to retain the notion of the Sabbath rest as a symbol of the end-time rest,[110] have rejected all millenarian connotations. The historical survival of these eschatological interpretations of the Sabbath raises some very crucial theological questions: How can the typological-symbolic function of the Sabbath have terminated with the coming of Christ, when the final rest, to which the present weekly Sabbath points, still lies in the future? To retain the Sabbath as the symbol of the *future* and final rest that awaits God's people, while denying the basis of such a symbol, namely, the *present* Sabbath rest experience, is a clear contradiction of terms. How can the Sabbath nourish in the believer the hope of the future rest, when its present celebration, which is a foretaste and anticipation of that future rest, is renounced or even denounced? Moreover, this unilateral interpretation of the Sabbath as an exclusively future reality destroys the organic unity that we have found in both the OT and NT between the temporal and eschatological functions of the Sabbath. These unresolved contradictions illustrate what happens when the permanency of a divine percept such as the Fourth Commandment is tampered with.

The nature of the Sabbath rest. This brief digression has taken us some distance away from Hebrews 4. We now return to it in order to ascertain the nature of the Sabbath rest that Christians must observe. The author explains the Christian understanding of the "Sabbath rest" that is still outstanding for God's NT people (4:9), by referring to its basic characteristic, namely, cessation from work: "for whoever enters God's rest also ceases from his labors as God did from his" (4:10). Is the author thinking here of cessation from work in a literal or a figurative sense? Historically, the majority of Christian writers have interpreted this figuratively, as "abstention from servile work," that is, evil deeds, sinful activities. According to this common interpretation, which has found supporters in practically every age, Christian Sabbathkeeping means not the interruption of the daily work on the seventh day, but the abstention from sinful acts *at all times* (perpetual Sabbath).[111]

Advocates of this interpretation often appeal to the refer-

concept, however, can hardly be read back into Hebrews 4:10, where the comparison is made between the divine and the human cessation from "works"—*erga*. If by "works" were meant "sinful deeds," the analogy would require that God also has ceased from these. Such an absured concept is of course totally foreign to Hebrews (and to the rest of the Scriptures) where it is explicitly stated that God "rested" (v. 4) and "ceased" (v. 10—in Greek, the verb is identical in both instances) "on the seventh day from all his works" (4:4). The analogy then is made in terms of man's imitation of God's ceasing or resting from works of creation. In other words, as God ceased on the seventh day from His creation work so believers are to cease on the same day from their labors. This is a simple statement of the nature of the Sabbath which essentially involves cessation from work.

Is the author of Hebrews merely encouraging his readers to interrupt their secular activities on the Sabbath? Considering the concern of the writer to counteract the tendency of his readers to adopt Jewish liturgical customs as a means to gain access to God, he could hardly have emphasized solely the physical "cessation" aspect of Sabbathkeeping. This aspect yields only a negative idea of rest, one which would only serve to encourage existing Judaizing tendencies. Obviously then, the author attributes a deeper meaning to the resting on the Sabbath. This can be seen in the antithesis he makes between those who failed to enter into its rest because of "*unbelief*"—*apeitheias* (4:6, 11)—that is, faithlessness which results in disobedience—and those who enter it by "*faith*"—*pistei* (4:2, 3), that is, faithfulness that results in obedience. The act of resting on the Sabbath for the author of Hebrews is not merely a routine ritual (cf. "sacrifice"—Matt. 12:7), but rather a faith-response to God. Such a response entails not the hardening of one's heart (4:7) but the making of oneself available to "hear his voice" (4:7). It means to experience God's salvation rest not by *works* but by *faith*, not by *doing* but by *being* saved through *faith* (4:2, 3, 11). On the Sabbath, as John Calvin aptly expresses it, believers are "to cease from their work to allow God to work in them." [113]

The Sabbath rest that remains for the people of God (4:9) is for the author of Hebrews not a mere day of idleness, but rather an opportunity renewed every week to enter *God's rest*, that is, to make oneself free from the cares of work in order to experience freely by faith God's creation and redemption-rest.[114] Moreover, we noted that this Sabbath experience of the blessings of salvation is not exhausted in the present, since the author exhorts to "strive to enter that rest" (4:11). This dimension of the future Sabbath rest shows that Sabbathkeeping in

Hebrews expresses the tension between the "already" and the "not yet," between the present experience of salvation and its eschatological consummation in the heavenly Canaan. This expanded interpretation of Sabbathkeeping in the light of the Christ event was apparently designed to wean Christians away from a too materialistic understanding of its observance. To achieve this objective, the author on the one hand reassures his readers of the permanence of the blessings contemplated by the Sabbath rest and on the other hand explains that the nature of these blessings consists in experiencing both a present salvation-rest and future restoration rest which God offers to those "who have believed" (4:3).

Good news of redemption. One can hardly fail to perceive that Hebrews' interpretation of the Sabbath rest reflects to a large extent the redemptive understanding of the day we found in the Gospels. Christ's great promise to have come to offer the expected sabbatical "release" (Luke 4:18) and "rest" (Matt. 11:28) represents the core of the "Sabbath rest" available "today" to God's people (Heb. 4:7, 9). Similarly, Christ's assurance that He and His Father are "working until now" (John 5:17) to realize the final Sabbath rest is reflected in Hebrews' exhortation to "strive to enter that rest" (4:11).[115] The fact that Hebrews 4 reflects the Gospel's understanding of the Sabbath as a time to experience the blessings of salvation, which will be fully realized at the end of our earthly pilgrimage, shows that NT Christians (at least some) viewed the *Sabbath* as *Good News of Redemption*.

In an age when the forces of chaos and disorder increasingly appear to prevail, when injustice, greed, violence, corruption, crime, suffering and death seem to dominate, God through the Sabbath reassures His people that these destructive forces will not triumph, because "there remains a sabbath rest for the people of God" (4:9). Through the Sabbath God reassures us that He is in control of this world, working out His ultimate purpose. God tells us that He conquered chaos at creation, that He has liberated His people from the bonds of sin and death through the saving mission of His Son, and that He "is working until now" (John 5:17) in order to establish a New World where "from sabbath to sabbath all flesh shall come to worship before God" (Is. 66:23). In that final Sabbath, as eloquently expressed by Augustine, "we shall rest and see, see and love, love and praise."[116] How are we to celebrate on our present seventh-day Sabbath such wonderful Good News? To answer this question, the following chapter will examine various aspects of what our response should be, especially on *The Sabbath*, to *the Good News of Redemption*.

CHAPTER
VI

the Sabbath

GOOD NEWS
of service

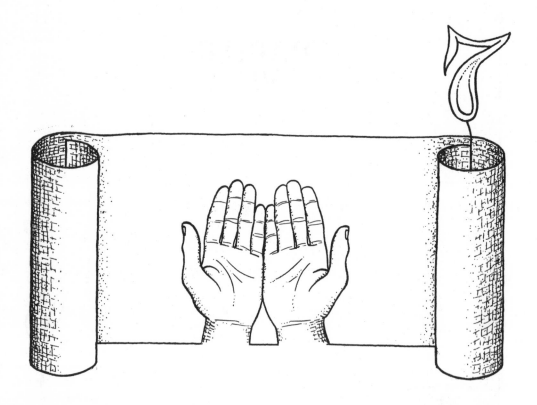

What an exciting and yet paradoxical age in which to live! We can tune our radio and TV receivers to sound and pictures coming from outer space or across the ocean, and yet we often neglect to tune our souls to God and fail to hear His voice. Scientists can explore the complexities of our solar system with sophisticated instruments mounted on rockets, and yet many are skeptical about the existence of the Designer of such a complex and magnificent system. We live and move among large crowds and yet many human beings are afflicted by a deep sense of loneliness and anonymity. Some fly to distant exotic lands to seek for excitement or rest and tranquillity, and yet boredom, restlessness and anxiety remain in their inner souls. We can feed enormous quantities of information into computers and solve most complex problems and yet most people seem unable to find answers to the fundamental question concerning the meaning and destiny of their life. We can race the sun across the sky with supersonic jets and yet we often fail to reach the needy who may live across the street. We can dial a few numbers and talk instantly with someone living in the farthest continent, and yet we often fail to communicate with our closest kin: our husband, wife, parents and children. We have learned to harness many types of natural resources in order to ensure the comforts of modern living, and yet our very existence is being threatened by resource depletion and biosphere pollution. To sum it all up, one may say that though our society has become increasingly rich in goods, it has remained poor in the good. Wealth in knowledge, possessions and creature comforts, has been matched by spiritual emptiness, economic poverty, physical exhaustion, emotional frustration and social neglect.

What contribution can a recovery of the Biblical Sabbath values make toward a solution to these pressing human problems? Can the proper observance of the Sabbath help a person overcome the sense of God's absence and experience His presence instead? Can Sabbath worship and fellowship help those afflicted by a sense of loneliness and anonymity to regain a sense of worth and belonging? Does the celebration on the Sabbath of God's creative and redemptive acts offer adequate motivation to be compassionate toward the needy? Can the admiration of nature and the limitation on its use contemplated by the Fourth

Commandment contribute to solving the ecological crisis? These are some of the basic questions dealt with in this chapter. For the sake of clarity, the study will be divided into four parts, each examining one aspect of the service the Sabbath is designed to provide: (1) Service to God; (2) Service to Self; (3) Service to Others; (4) Service to Our Habitat.

PART I

THE SABBATH AS SERVICE TO GOD

The Christian serves God every day of his life. Yet the service he renders God during the weekdays differs from that which he offers on the Sabbath. Why? Because during the week he serves God while serving an employer and meeting the many demands of life. The everyday service may be called the *Martha type*, in which the Savior is given implicit acknowledgment while pursuing one's obligations. The Sabbath service, on the other hand, is of the *Mary type*, in which explicit and undivided attention is offered to Christ. All secular pursuits are interrupted in order to acknowledge the Savior as the special guest of honor. Desisting from gainful employment in order to be available for Christ represents in itself a meaningful act of worship. It is this act of resting that makes all other Sabbath activities a worship offering to God, because they spring from a soul who has deliberately decided to honor God on His Holy Day. This means that our study of the service offered to God on the Sabbath must begin with a proper understanding of the act of resting itself and then proceed to examine the manifold activities made possible by the Sabbath rest.

1. *Rest as Divine Service*

A total response. There is a marked tendency today to divorce the "worship" from the "rest" content of the Sabbath day. It is argued that since the shorter working week provides not one but two or more days of rest, the commandment to rest on the seventh day is no longer applicable to the needs of contemporary Christians. Such a view fails to recognize that the Scripture defines the Sabbath rest, as it was pointed out in chapter III, not merely as an *anthropocentric* relaxation but primarily as a *Theocentric* rest. It is given to mankind (Mark 2:27) but it belongs to Yahweh (Ex. 20:10; Mark 2:28). If it were given to mankind only to meet physical, social and economic needs, then it would truly be a human *holiday* of dubious value today, since two or more weekly days of leisure are presently available to large segments of society. However, the focus of the Sabbath rest is not man but God: "the seventh day is a sabbath of solemn rest, holy to the Lord" (Ex. 31:15; 16:23, 25; 35:2; Lev. 23:3). In other words, the Sabbath rest is not merely a temporary recovery from simply mental or physical fatigue, but a reflection of the "rest" of God Himself (Ex. 20:11), appointed to aid human beings in regaining the Divine Image.

God does not need the "rest" of human beings. What He desires is that human beings recognize and accept His dominion over their lives and time. "In keeping with this dominion," aptly writes Franz X. Pettirsch, "the first duty of creatures endowed with reason is to acknowledge God by sacrificing possessions and property, time and space, work and business. Thus the day of worship becomes more than a socio-economic regulation; it assumes the character of a divinely inspired, profoundly religious veneration of God."[1] The deliberate consecration of the Sabbath time to God is symbolic of a total response to God. It is an act of worship which is not exhausted in an *one-hour* church service, but lasts *twenty-four hours*.[2] Such a totally conscious response is not possible during the week when the mind is occupied with pressing demands. On the Sabbath, however, by resting specifically for God, the Christian shows his commitment of the week days as well, when it is not possible in practice to offer to God the same undivided and conscious acknowledgment.

A remedy for work-worship. There is a constant risk that work may become an object of veneration. The concern for production and profit on the one hand, and the conviction that all have the right to a job, no matter of what kind, on the other hand, can easily elevate work to a high virtue, the very object of living. The merits of a deceased person are often extolled by such comments, "He was such a hard-working man. His life has been only work!" Such a view leads to the fatal error of deifying work, making it the chief value for which to live.[3] The "workoholic" lives only for his work and comes to believe that his work substitutes for God's care. Mistrusting God's providence, he constantly worries concerning the security and success of his work (Matt. 6:25-33). The Sabbath rest, by placing a limit on work, is designed to counteract this temptation to deify work. It teaches that God is the Lord of all the work that occupies human existence. It tells a person to do all his work in the best possible way (Ex. 20:10), but without putting

The Sabbath rest, by placing a limit on work, is designed
to counteract the temptation to deify work. It teaches that
God is the Lord of all the work that occupies human existence.
It tells a person to do all his work in the best possible way
(Ex.20:10), but without putting his trust in it. Why? Because
the ultimate reality is not work in itself but rest in God.

his trust in it. Why? Because the ultimate reality is not work in itself but rest in God.

Human beings were not created to produce goods for God or for themselves or for others, but rather to rejoice in the presence and service of God. The Sabbath rest stands as the symbol of this noble human destiny. "Last in creation, first in intention," the Sabbath is "the end of the creation of heaven and earth." [4] It teaches that the work of the six days finds its goal and meaning in the rest of the seventh day. This temporal rest experience is also a prefiguration and foretaste of the eternal rest awaiting God's people. Resting on the Sabbath then means to recognize the meaning of work and of life itself. It means to reject a lifestyle in which, to achieve comforts and status, one has to submit himself to the idol called work. It means to recognize that work is not a supreme value. It means to acknowledge that God has a claim on all our doing. To accept His claim, we take time out on the Sabbath to praise not the work of our hands but God's working in, for and through our lives. It means to take time to present to God as a worship offering the little or great accomplishments of our weekly work.

A remedy for leisure-worship. If some are tempted to deify work, perhaps even more are inclined to make leisure a chief aspiration. The growing availability of free time, the increased personal income coupled with the dehumanizing effects of mechanical, boring jobs, are some of the factors that have changed the attitude of many toward work. For these persons work is not an end in itself but a means to an end, a means necessary to pay for week-end leisure. They quit the hellish work on Friday, eager to take off to some near or distant place, there to fill their empty time with a new round of activities. The sad reality is that usually they return to work on Monday not fresh and blooming but faded and drooping.

Why is it that many fail to achieve the hoped-for relaxation and regeneration of their being during their free time? An important factor is the neglect of their inner spiritual needs and resources. Believing that leisure, entertainment or even physical rest per se are adequate to restore weary bodies, many seek and pay only for the rest provided by the sanctuaries of our materialistic society: the football field, the amusement park, the beach, the dance-hall, the restaurant, the ski-resort, the national park, et cetera. Such leisure or entertainment places and activities by themselves, however, provide at best a form of evasion, a temporary oblivion of oneself, but leave an internal spiritual emptiness which is at the root of much exhaustion and tension.

True regeneration occurs when the mental, physical and spiritual components of our being are brought into harmonious unity. The Sabbath is a vehicle through which Christ restores harmony to our mind, body and soul. As incisively stated by A. Martin, "The spirituality of the Sabbath restores to man the unity of his being, unity that constantly risks being shattered either by the fragmented nature of work or by the fragmented nature of leisure." [5] Such a unity is achieved on the Sabbath through the spiritual resources and opportunities the day provides to understand the meaning of our work, leisure and life itself. For the Sabbathkeeper the leisure of the seventh day is not the supreme good (*summum bonum*) to be sought after at any cost, but rather a welcome opportunity to experience a greater good, namely, the goodness of God's creation and redemption in wholesome activities. Some of the basic criteria to determine suitable Sabbath activities will be considered below.

An experience of divine rest. The profound religious nature of the Sabbath rest is indicated also by its symbolic function. Human beings need symbols which are both familiar and frequent, in order to preserve and enrich their faith. We have just seen that resting on the Sabbath symbolizes a total response to God, an acceptance of His claim over our work and leisure and an offering to Him of our total being and doing. But there is more to the symbolic meaning of the Sabbath rest that makes it truly an act of worship. There is also the opportunity the Sabbath rest provides to experience by faith God's creation, redemption and final restoration-rest. A symbol is a means of experiencing the reality for which it stands. Our earlier study has shown that the reality for which the Sabbath rest stands is the creation, redemption and final restoration-rest which God offers to His people through Christ who came to make such "rest" possible (Matt. 11:28; Luke 4:18-21). This means that the Sabbath rest is not merely a means to recover lost energies, but primarily a means to experience in this restless age the divine rest and peace of salvation already available as well as a foretaste of the greater rest and joy awaiting God's people in the kingdom of glory. "True rest," writes Alfred Barry, "is rest in the Lord, and such rest is unspoken worship." [6] Resting on the Sabbath is an unspoken but yet a most meaningful act of worship, since it enables the Christian to accept Christ's rest of salvation and to anticipate the future eternal rest of worship and of communion with God and His saints.

Many Sunday-keeping Christians find it difficult to appreciate the Sabbath rest as an act of worship. Why? Primarily because from a Biblical and historical perspective they see nothing especially sacred about their resting on Sunday. It is generally recognized, as stated by Christopher Kiesling, a leading Catholic liturgist, that "Sunday rest for Christians began only in the fourth century."[7] Since only centuries later "was the rest of Sunday invested with religious significance,"[8] producing what Kiesling describes as "a somber, severe and excessively otherworldly interpretation of Christianity,"[9] the same author proposes "the abandonment of rest on Sunday as a Christian practice."[10a] Kiesling's plan calls for the development of "new styles of Christian life which would express the joy, optimism and acceptance of creation which are characteristic of the Christian faith, hope and love."[10b]

One must appreciate the problem of trying to develop a theology and practice of Sunday *rest*, when the rest experience is foreign to the original meaning of Sunday. Yet, if the need is felt "to develop new styles of Christian life which would express the joy, optimism and acceptance of creation," why not develop such new life styles upon the institution of the seventh-day Sabbath, the day specifically established by God to express and experience the joy and optimism of creation and redemption? This proposal may sound unrealistic to many persons, especially since, to use Kiesling's words, "Sunday rest as a Christian reality is nearly dead, and Sunday worship is rapidly losing its grip on life."[11] In other words, to propose a return to the observance of the Biblical Sabbath, when many do not care about the already existing Sunday, seems absurd. But, why are Sunday rest and worship dying? Could a significant factor be the absence of a Biblical and apostolic mandate for its observance? One can hardly expect a Christian to take Sundaykeeping seriously when he is told that the day is merely a convenient time for worship chosen by the church and that in principle he is free from the observance of any special day. Would not a rediscovery and acceptance of the rich meaning and experience of the Biblical seventh-day Sabbath provide a compelling theological conviction to motivate genuine Christians to consecrate their Sabbath rest, worship and recreation to God?

Obviously not many will respond to a call to return to the observance of God's holy Sabbath day, especially since most people today want *not a holy day to* experience God's presence *but holidays* to seek personal pleasures. On the other hand, one must not overlook the fact that well over three million Seventh-day Adventists, besides hundreds of thousands of Christians of other denominations, have already responded to this call and do joyfully celebrate the seventh day Sabbath.[12] But more important than numbers is the question, should the Church abdicate her responsibility to proclaim a God-given precept, because it cuts across the prevailing materialistic concerns of our society? The mission of the Church is not to articulate the aspirations of the majority, but to interpret and proclaim God's revelation given through the Scriptures. Her function is to call people to repentance, to turn from the world back to God. This demands a change in behavior, a new understanding of one's destiny, a restored relationship with God, a new experience of worship. To achieve these objectives the Church must work through institutions of which one of the most important is the Sabbath. On this day the Christian is taught how to live and how to love God, himself and others by actually practicing this life and love for a day. He is motivated to rest, that is, to take time out to present to God as a worship offering ("living sacrifice"—Rom. 12:1), his work, his leisure, his total being—and thus find peace and rest in God. Is not this experience a learning tool that is more effective than abstract sermons? And does not this experience provide a model and a challenge for the weekdays as well?

2. *Worship as Divine Service*

Worship has been aptly defined by Walter J. Harrelson as "an ordered response to the appearance of the Holy in the life of individuals and groups." [13] *Order* and *holiness* are not only two essential ingredients of genuine worship but constitute also the very basic essence of the Sabbath. The *holiness* of the Sabbath, as noted in chapter III, consists in the special occasion the day affords for the manifestation and experience of God's presence. The *order* of the Sabbath can be seen in the way the day brings order to one's life. Human beings find little satisfaction in experiencing a confused or monotonous rhythm of time. A full and enjoyable life requires intelligent division of time: for work, for leisure, for learning, for worshop, for oneself and for others. The Sabbath teaches us to properly divide between the common and the holy in the string of days that make up our weeks, months and years. The purpose of this division is not to enhance the Sabbath day at the expense of the week days, but rather to enrich *them* with the spiritual values and experience of the Sabbath.

In a special sense the Sabbath teaches us to respond in an orderly manner to God on His Holy Day. Such a regular response requires a deliberate interruption of all secular activities. We have just seen that this act of resting to honor God represents in itself a most meaningful worship response. But how is this Sabbath time to be ordered so that the total worshop experience of the whole day will prove to be acceptable to God and enriching to the believer? Any attempt to formulate specific programs could readily lead into a legalistic observance of the Sabbath which would destroy its very spirit of freedom and joy. It is noteworthy that the Scriptures offer goals and principles rather than programs or regulations. It is wisest, therefore, to identify some of the Biblical principles relevant to our present situation rather than arbitrarily to list specific activities.

Divine service. The Sabbath commandment offers no explicit injunction to observe the seventh day of the week by attending a regular religious assembly, that is, "divine service." This speaks well for divine wisdom, since it shows awareness of the plight of those believers who throughout the centuries would be called to sanctify the Sabbath in isolation or to engage in works of mercy. Moreover, one must not forget that the synagogue, which became the public place of Sabbath worship for most Jews, developed rather late in the history of Judaism (exilic or postexilic time).[14] It is presumed that synagogue services originated as an outgrowth of Sabbath gatherings conducted in private homes (Ex. 16:29). Considering that the nucleus of the ancient Israelite home was much larger than ours, including in most cases the "in-laws" and servants (note the number of persons listed in the Fourth Commandment—Deut. 5:14), such home Sabbath gatherings could well have constituted a respectable small congregation.

Whatever may have been the origin of the Sabbath religious assembly, there is no doubt that the "holy convocation" (Lev. 23:2), became a distinctive feature of the day. This development was presumably favored, if not encouraged, both by the theological direction of the Sabbath, "to the Lord your God" (Ex. 20:10; Deut. 5:14), and by the release from work granted on the Sabbath to all persons. In other words, the fact that all were to be free to honor the Lord would readily encourage a gathering together to achieve this objective.[15] Where these convocations were initially held in OT times is not very clear. Probably, as in NT times, the services were conducted in private homes at first. 2 Kings 4:23 suggests that it was customary for some Israelites in the 9th century B.C. to visit a prophet on the Sabbath. Apparently a religious service was held at the prophet's residence. We noted in the previous chapter that religious services in the Temple were intensified on the Sabbath.

Isaiah describes worshipers assembling on the Sabbath at the temple, though unfortunately with an unrepenting attitude (Is. 1:12-15).

In postexilic times, as attested by the NT and Jewish sources, great importance was attached to the Sabbath services conducted in the synagogue. The Christian worship service was patterned to a large extent after that of the synagogue.[16] The customary attendance at the Sabbath services by Christ and the Apostles only served to endorse the validity and value of this corporate worship experience. The value of Sabbath worship, however, is dependent upon the understanding the participants have of what they are doing. Without such an understanding, the weekly church attendance becomes empty formality. It is imperative, therefore, to consider the function of the formal Sabbath worship service. We call this worship service "formal," to distinguish it from the "informal" worship activities that characterize the remainder of the day.

Celebration. The primary function of the Sabbath, as already pointed out in chapter II, is to celebrate God's marvelous accomplishments. This celebration acquires a heightened and formal aspect during the Sabbath worship service, when God's people gather together to offer God their united praise. What is it that makes communal worship on the Sabbath such a special occasion? The answer is to be found in the magnitude of God's achievements which are celebrated. To celebrate means to share the joy resulting from unusual accomplishments. Students celebrate their graduation; players and fans celebrate the winning of a game. A father celebrates the birth of his newborn child. A country torn by war joyfully celebrates the signing of a peace treaty. When a great feat is successfully achieved, it is a human desire to wish to share the joy of the occasion with others. The Sabbath worship service is the occasion when Christians assemble to celebrate and rejoice over God's memorabilia: His wonderful creation, His successful redemption of His people; and His manifold manifestations of constant love and care.

Some of these themes appear in Psalm 92, which is "A Song for the Sabbath." Here the believers are invited to celebrate the Sabbath by giving thanks, singing praises and playing the lute, the harp and the lyre (v. 3). The purpose of this joyful celebration is to declare the Good News of God's steadfast love and faithfulness (v. 2); to praise the great works of His hands (v. 4-5); to acknowledge God's care and power (v. 12-15).[17] The celebration of God's goodness and mercy constitute the basis of all true worship offered to God on any day of the week.

On the Sabbath, however, such worship reaches its fullest expression and experience. First because the day provides free time to celebrate with heart and mind. Second, because the day stands as the symbol of the past, present and future divine interventions in human history: creation, redemption, preservation and ultimate restoration. Thus, the Sabbath, by proclaiming the glad tidings that the Lord has created us perfectly, redeemed us completely, cares for us constantly and will restore us ultimately, provides not only the *time* but also the *reasons* for worshiping God. The Sabbath provides both the time and the reasons to celebrate joyfully and gratefully the goodness of life that God has given us.

Antidote to false worship. In one sense the Bible is the story of the struggle between true and false worship. God's summons to "put away the foreign gods" (Gen. 35:2), which occurs in the first book of the Bible, is reiterated in different forms in all subsequent books. In Revelation, the last book of the Bible, the summons is renewed through the imagery of three flying angels. These call upon "every nation and tribe and tongue and people" (14:6), on the one hand to renounce the perverted system of worship promoted by "Babylon," and "the beast and its image" (14:8-11) and on the other hand to "fear God and give him glory, for the hour of his judgment has come," and to *"worship* him who made heaven and earth, the sea and the fountains of water" (14:7). This solemn call to abandon false worship and to restore true worship is presented in Revelation 14 as part of the preparation for "the harvest of the earth" (14:15). Christ Himself alluded to the end-time crisis concerning true worship in His rhetorical question: "When the Son of man comes, will he find faith on earth?" (Luke 18:8).

Though the problem of worshiping man-made realities such as money (Matt. 6:24), power (Rev. 13:8; Col. 3:5), pleasure (Rom. 6:19; Titus 3:3) or even human systems of salvation (Gal. 4:9), has been present in every age,[18] it is particularly acute in our time. The triumph of modern science, technology and rationalistic thinking has led many to worship human figments rather than the Creator Himself. The mission of the Church at this time, as portrayed effectively by the three apocalytic angels, is to promote the *true worship* of "him who made heaven and earth, the sea and the fountains of water" (Rev. 14:6). The Sabbath is a most effective vehicle through which the Church can promote the restoration of true worship. By focusing on God's creative and redemptive accomplishments, the Sabbath functions as an antidote against false worship. It challenges men and women to worship not their human achievements and

The mission of the Church, as portrayed effectively by the three apocalyptic angels, is to promote the true worship of "him who made heaven and earth, the sea and the fountains of water" (Rev.14:6). The Sabbath is a most effective vehicle through which the Church can promote the restoration of true worship. By focusing on God's creative and redemptive accomplishments, the Sabbath functions as an antidote against false worship.

ambitions, but their Creator and Redeemer. The Church, by inviting individuals on the Sabbath to take time out to celebrate God's past, present and future accomplishments, challenges them to renounce their autonomy and egocentricity and accept instead God's lordship over their life and time.

Revelation. The Sabbath worship service is a time not only of celebration but also of divine revelation. The two are mutually dependent. The celebration through music, prayer and proclamation of God's goodness accomplished during the worship service contributes in varying degrees to the unfolding of the revelation of God's plan and will for human life. Such a revelation can only be experienced when all other preoccupations are set aside.[19] The Sabbath worship service is in a special sense the time when we silence the multitude of voices that entice us to adopt new moral values (which too often are old immoral values) in order to hear the revelation and proclamation of the values presented in God's Word. The revelation of God which occurs during the worship service is in a sense, as eloquently expressed by George Elliott, "a Sinai where still the Eternal speaks his awful but needed lessons of human duty; a Hermon where again Jesus in transfigured glory stands before us; an Olivet where our straining eyes catch not indistinct glimpses of the ascended Lord." [20] Elliott continues, noting that "on this mount of blessing we tabernacle not now for ever, but ever leave its radiant heights to carry something of its glory through the work-days of the week." [21]

All worship offered to God on any day has a revelatory quality, inasmuch as it lifts the soul closer to God, awakening the sense of His presence. However, the Sabbath worship provides a heightened revelation of God. Why? First, because, as noted in chapter III, on and through this day God has promised to manifest in a special sense His sanctifying presence. Second, because the Sabbath rest provides the special occasion to experience God's revelation both individually and collectively. The latter occurs when Christians move away from familiar surroundings to join in the communal worship experience of a church. In different places a person interacts and responds differently. In the communal church service, the individual is caught up in what William Hodgkins calls a "circulatory" influence, "moving from the congregation toward God, and through the Holy Spirit from God to the congregation." [22] The minister plays a vital role in this "circulatory" and revelatory experience, since it is especially through his preaching that God communicates to the waiting congregation a knowledge of His saving plan and will for their lives.

The value of the teaching and learning function of the communal worship service can hardly be overemphasized. The shocking disregard for divine and human codes of conduct, evidenced by the increasing rate of criminal and immoral acts, demands that the Church assume its responsibility in acting as a moral conscience for the nation. The Sabbath worship provides an unparalleled opportunity for the Church to reveal through its various ministries how the acceptance of the Gospel affects all levels of human behavior. The conscience that is sensitized at the moment of the worship service—the moment when a person is often most responsive to God's revelation—will be strengthened to live out God's revealed principles during the pressures and temptations of every day. Thus, the revelation received during the worship service becomes the guiding-light and inspiration of the working week.

The conclusion that emerges from the first part of this study is that both rest and worship are integral parts of the service rendered to God on the Sabbath. We have found that the act of resting on the Sabbath for God represents in itself an informal but meaningful act of worship, through which the believer expresses his commitment to God while experiencing divine rest in his life. This rest experience makes possible the formal celebration of God's goodness in the corporate worship service. Such a celebration offers in turn a fresh revelation of God's will and grace for the Christian.

PART II

THE SABBATH AS SERVICE TO ONESELF

The worship that a Christian offers to God on the Sabbath ultimately results in service to himself and to others. Why? Basically because through the Sabbath service, the believer instead of adding strength or power to God, enables God to strengthen and empower his own personal life. This is made possible especially through the time and opportunities the Sabbath provides for personal *reflection* and *renewal*.

1. *The Sabbath: A Time for Reflection*

Need for reflection. The lack of reflection is viewed by some analysts of our society as a fundamental cause of our superficial and restless culture. Human beings are born, live and die, lost in the crowd, without understanding their true selves.[23]

Many live today an intensely active, restless and noisy life, while ever sensing an inner emptiness and disillusionment. In an attempt to bring order and serenity to their inner selves, a good number of Westerners today are experimenting with Eastern meditation techniques. These are promoted and marketed as steps easy to follow, such as sitting, concentrating and chanting. It is claimed that such exercises can bring an individual in contact with divine vibrations or spiritual realities, thus producing a sense of inner harmony and serenity. Some practice these meditation exercises as a kind of psychological self-help gimmick, without committing themselves to the world view of Eastern religions from which such meditation techniques derive. Apparently, for some persons, the practice of modified Eastern, or so-called Transcendental Meditation, does appear for a time to meet the inner spiritual need for stillness, reflection and communion with a higher being or existence.

The search for inner stillness and harmony through Eastern forms of meditation points to the fundamental human need for reflection and self-analysis, in order to live a truly human life. This is especially true of the Christian life, since it presupposes a conscious and intelligent understanding of life as it relates to God, oneself, others and the world at large. But do Christians today in general take time to engage in spiritual exercises designed to increase their self-understanding through meditation upon God's revelation? According to the Gallup poll released in the December 21, 1979 issue of *Christianity Today*, only ten percent of Americans read the Bible every week. Probably in other Christian countries where evangelical movements are less influential, the percentage would be considerably lower. Moreover do those who read a few verses of Scripture, perhaps in conjunction with hurried devotions, have the time or the knowledge of how to meditate upon a text? There is a vast difference between a casual reading, a critical study and a thoughtful meditation upon a text of Scripture. It is possible that many today are turning to Eastern ("foreign") forms of meditation because their Christian churches have failed to teach them how to meditate according to the Biblical (Eastern) tradition. Could today's impatience with the Sabbath day of rest have significantly contributed also to the abandonment of the Sabbath as a time for reflection, meditation and worship?

Sabbath and meditation. The Harvard University theologian Harvey Cox, in his book *Turning East*, recounts a significant episode that occurred while he was researching on Eastern meditation at the Naropa Institute, a Buddhist study center located in Boulder, Colorado. While in Boulder, he accepted the invitation of a rabbi to celebrate with him "a genuine, old-fashioned Shabbat [Sabbath], a whole day of doing very little, enjoying the creation as it is, appreciating the world rather than fixing it up."[24]   Cox acknowledges that as he joined in the celebration of the Sabbath from Friday sundown to Saturday sundown, savoring "just being rather than doing," it occurred to him that "meditation is in essence a kind of miniature Sabbath."[25]   Both, in fact, require cessation of all activity.   He noticed, however, significant differences.   For example, while Oriental meditation is conceived as a total way of life, detached from the realities of the present world, the Sabbath is only a one-day interlude in the daily struggle for existence; an interlude that enables a person to live in this present world while looking forward to the better world to come.[26]

A second noteworthy difference between the Sabbath and Oriental meditation is to be found, according to Cox, in the universal nature of the Sabbath.   In other words, while in Oriental religions meditation is practiced by a *few* privileged persons, mostly monks, the Sabbath enjoins not a small elite, but *everyone* to stop *doing* on the seventh day in order to experience *being* with God.[27]   The Sabbath condemns the social dichotomy between the *via activa* and the *via contemplativa*, that is, a class distinction between those who work and those who meditate, whether this distinction is advocated by Eastern religions or by Christian monasticism.   The Fourth Commandment contemplates the integration in the life of every person of both work and rest, doing and being, action and reflection.   To reject this sabbatical integrated lifestyle in order to accept a foreign Eastern concept of total stillness would mean to destroy a valuable Biblical institution which has influenced Jewish and Christian ethical and religious traditions.   Our hope is that those who seek for rest, stillness, meaning and order in their life through Eastern meditation will happily discover another institution which originated in the East, the Fourth Commandment.   This institution, as noted by Cox, "may be tarnished and twisted out of shape, but it still belongs to us; and as creatures who must live amid the contradictions and dislocations of history, the mini-Sabbath of meditation can be the gift of life itself."[28]

A basis for meditation.   The Sabbath provides not only the time but also a theological basis for a meaningful meditation. As the symbol of God's originally perfect creation, of His complete redemption and of His ultimate restoration, the Sabbath invites the believer to meditate not upon an abstract higher spiritual being or power but upon a gracious God who has worked, who is working, and who will work for the eternal happiness of His children. Moreover, as a symbol of God's presence and concern, the Sabbath summons the Christian to reflect upon the fact that he is not alone. God created him to enjoy eternal fellowship with Him. On the Sabbath a special opportunity is offered to experience the sense of God's presence. The reason for living is not life itself. Such a reason only leads to despair. The Christian lives to enjoy God's immediate presence and future fellowship. This means that to meditate on the Sabbath upon its Good News is not a way to escape from the tension of the present life, but rather a way to introduce into the present restless life a sense of God's presence and the hope of a richer future fellowship.

Meditation has to do with consciousness. It could be described as an attitude of receptive awareness rather than of thoughtful investigation. To illustrate the difference between the two, let us use the example of reading a devotional book on the Sabbath. If I read it with the purpose in mind to critically examine the arguments and the texts used by the author to develop his concepts, then I am not meditating but attempting thoughtful analysis which sometimes is the hardest work. On the other hand, if I read the book leisurely and receptively, with the simple desire to let God speak to my soul through its message, then I am meditating. The spirit of freedom of the Sabbath provides the basis for such an enriching meditation, since we are enjoined to cease from work in order to freely feel, understand and enjoy the manifold manifestations of God's goodness. This means that on the Sabbath we can gaze on nature, without striving to peer into its scientific mysteries. We can listen to music without concern about the key or the number of its flats and sharps. We can take pleasure in reading poetry, without trying to discern whether all the lines are metrically balanced. We can listen receptively to the preaching of God's Word, without struggling to unravel the mystery of God's redeeming love or to harmonize apparent theological contradictions. The climate of stillness and free reception which the Sabbath provides enables us to truly meditate, that is, to discover God and ourselves; to truly experience an awareness of God's presence; to freely "taste and see that the Lord is good" (Ps. 34:8).

2. The Sabbath: A Time for Renewal

Order to life. The time and opportunities which the Sabbath provides for meditation, worship, fellowship, service and recreation, are designed to function like dynamos that recharge run-down batteries. This recharging and renewal is provided by the Sabbath in several ways. Let us consider, first of all, the order and harmony that the Sabbath restores to our fragmented life. The problem of modern living is well illustrated by a story related by Herbert Saunders about some African workers. For several days these workers were pressed relentlessly by the leader of an expedition who hired them to carry equipment on their backs to a remote post in the interior of Africa. "But one day they refused to pick up their burdens and go any further. They sat by the side of the road and turned a deaf ear to the appeals of the man in charge. Finally, in exasperation, he asked, 'Why don't you go on?' 'Because,' replied the leader of the workers, 'we are waiting for our souls to catch up with our bodies.' " [29]

Is this not a fitting description of the problem many people face today? The speed and pressure of modern living tend to destroy the equilibrium between the material and spiritual components of our being. The Scripture teaches, as Achad Haam points out, that "the two elements existing in man, the corporeal and the spiritual, can and must live in perfect unity." [30] Paul, for example, prays for the total sanctification and preservation of the "spirit and soul and body" (I Thess. 5:23). The Sabbath is designed to restore order and unity to our total being by enabling us to reorder our priorities. During the week as we work to produce, to sell, to buy and to enjoy *things*, we are tempted to view *things* as the *priority* and ultimate *reality*. We become so materially conscious and concerned that our spiritual needs are often obscured and neglected. This may even lead us to conceive of God Himself as a "nice thing." By enjoining us to refrain for one day from pursuing after more material things and to seek instead after spiritual values and relationships, the Sabbath helps us to break away from the tyranny of materialism. It helps us to recognize that the things of the spirit must have priority over those of space. This reordering of priorities restores unity and harmony to our lives. It gives our souls a chance to catch up with our bodies. If we learn on the Sabbath, as Samuel H. Dresner observes, "to mend our tattered souls and join flesh and spirit in joy and rest, in inward feeling and outward act, perhaps we shall be able to bring a portion of the spirit of this day into the other days of the week, so that even ordinary days will take on something of the Sabbath." [31]

Moral renewal. The reordering of our priorities on the Sabbath contributes to the ordering of our moral consciousness. The leaders of our political, social and religious institutions will often resort to a temporary retreat or withdrawal, in order to

In an age of changing and conflicting values, the Sabbath opens the door for moral reflection, for the development of a moral consciousness and responsibility. There is urgent need today to help people build a lifestyle based upon God's commandments.

examine themselves and their programs more objectively and thus be able to return to their tasks with fresh energies and strategies. The Sabbath offers to every ordinary human being such a retreat in time. On this day we withdraw from the rush of life in order to examine the past, present and future moral direction in our life. We take time to assess our goals, motives and attitudes toward God, people, ourselves and work. Often we may discover that our past has been a sorry mixture of achievements and failures. The Sabbath, however, as was shown in chapter V, is designed to liberate us from the failures and pains of the past. The Good News of the Sabbath is that Christ has brought us "release" (Luke 4:18) and thus we can rest and rejoice in His forgiveness. Freed by Christ's grace from the fears and guilt of our past failures, we begin to comprehend the possibilities and opportunities that God places before us. Such comprehension is enhanced especially through the experience of worship and meditation. As we take time to reflect on God's accomplishments commemorated by the Sabbath, we are challenged to achieve new goals through the assurance of His divine power and presence.

In an age of changing and conflicting values, the Sabbath opens the door for moral reflection, for the development of a moral consciousness and responsibility. There is urgent need today to help people build a lifestyle based upon God's commandments. According to a recent Gallup poll, although "a whopping 84 percent—more than eight of every ten people [Americans]—believe that the Ten Commandments are valid today . . . , fewer than half (42 percent) can name at least five" of them.[32] The Sabbath provides not only the time to better acquaint oneself with the content of the biblical principles of human conduct, but also the opportunity to internalize such principles. The very fact that the Sabbath represents the inherent expression of commitment to God inspires observers to renew their commitment not to one but to all of God's principles.

Spiritual renewal. The search for a deeper spiritual experience ranks high on the list of contemporary human needs. Experimentation with Eastern forms of meditation and hallucinatory drugs reflects the need felt by many for something beyond materialism. A more telling indication of this need is provided by the Neo-pentecostal charismatic movements which in the last few years have gained millions of adherents across denominational boundaries. A late Gallup poll reports that one American adult out of five (29.4 million persons) considers himself or herself charismatic.[33] This phenomenon is not limited to the

USA, since charismatic movements have mushroomed in many Western countries. True, some persons may experiment with new movements or drugs in order to escape the sad realities of this world; yet the fact remains they are searching for something spiritual to fill the emptiness of their lives.

The Sabbath is divinely ordained to satisfy the human need for deeper spiritual communion with God. As the symbol of God's commitment to bless His people with His presence, the Sabbath invites the believer to enter into a special spiritual relationship with Him. The prophets recognized and emphasized this vital role of the Sabbath in helping God's people experience and maintain a spiritual relationship with God. When Ezekiel saw the threat of national apostasy, he summoned the Israelites to "hallow" the Sabbath in order to "know," that is, to experience God's sanctifying presence in their lives ("that they might know that I the Lord sanctify them"—Ezek. 20:12; cf. v. 20). Similarly Isaiah urges the Israelites to "call the Sabbath a delight," that is, a day to seek the spiritual pleasure of God's communion rather than the material pleasures of selfish interests ("your pleasure"—Is. 58:13). If the people would respond to such a call, "then," the prophet assures them, "you shall take delight in the Lord" (Is. 58:14). Delighting in the Lord! This is in essence the source of the spiritual renewal offered by God to His people through the Sabbath.

In his address to the World's Parliament of Religions, A. H. Lewis eloquently expressed the spiritual function of the Sabbath when he said: "Sacred hours are God's enfolding presence, lifting the soul and holding it in heavenly converse. All that is holiest and best springs into life and develops into beauty, when men realize that God is constantly near them. The sense of personal obligation, awakened by the consciousness of God's presence, lies at the foundation of religious life and worship. God's day is a perfect symbol of His presence, of His enfolding and redeeming love." [34] Our study so far has focused on several significant opportunities for spiritual renewal provided by the Sabbath. We have considered among others the opportunity to rest, to worship, to reorder one's life, to experience God's forgiveness, to sense divine presence, to sharpen one's moral consciousness, and to renew one's commitment to God. Other opportunities for renewal offered by the Sabbath will be considered below.

PART III

THE SABBATH AS SERVICE TO OTHERS

After helping a believer to find God and himself, the Sabbath helps him to find others. After aiding a person to gain a fresh understanding and assurance of God's will and grace, the Sabbath sends him forth to reach out to others. The Christian faith is not an *egocentric* solace but rather a *heterocentric* service, that is to say, it is not centered on self but on others. The Founder of Christianity came into this world not to enrich His personal life through an exotic vacation on Planet Earth, but to bring "life" to needy human beings and to bring it "abundantly" (John 10:10). Our previous study has shown that this divine spirit of love and concern is manifested especially through the institution of the Sabbath. God "rested" not to strengthen Himself, but to share Himself with His creatures. By entering on the seventh day of creation into the limitations of *human time* to bless His creatures with abundant life, God manifested His willingness to enter into *human flesh* to restore the abundant life to His creatures. The incarnation of Christ provides both a fulfillment and a fresh revelation of divine love. By ministering, especially on the Sabbath, to physical and spiritual human needs, the Savior revealed divine love in action.

1. *Time to Share*

The celebration on the Sabbath of the blessings of God's creative and redemptive love provides both the time and the theological motivation to share with others the blessings received. The believer who on the Sabbath celebrates God's gracious deliverance from the bondage of Egypt and of sin (Deut. 5:15; Luke 4:18; 13:16) is motivated and challenged to exemplify divine love by responding to human needs. To help in remembering others, the Sabbath commandment gives quite a lengthy list of persons toward whom concern is to be shown on the Sabbath. These include son, daughter, manservant, maidservant, ox, ass, cattle, sojourner (Deut. 5:14. cf. Ex. 20:10; 23:12). This humanitarian function of the Sabbath was eventually largely forgotten. For many the observance of the day became an exercise in self-righteousness rather than an exercise in loving service for others. Throughout His Sabbath ministry, Christ took pains to clarify the true intention of the commandment. To counteract prevailing legal interpretations which restricted humanitarian service on the Sabbath to emergency situations only, Jesus intentionally ministered on this day to persons who were *not critically* but *chronically* ill.

A fitting illustration is the healing of the crippled woman which we examined in chapter V. The ruler of the synagogue objected to Christ's healing because in his view such a "work ought to be done" during the "six days . . . and not on the sabbath day" (Luke 13:14). Christ challenged such a misconception by reminding His audience of the accepted custom of watering animals on the Sabbath. If the daily needs of animals could be met on the Sabbath, how much more the needs of "a daughter of Abraham whom Satan bound for eighteen years"! Shouldn't she "be loosed from this bond on the sabbath day?" (Luke 13:16). One can hardly fail to note Christ's determined effort to press the Sabbath into the service of the Gospel, making it a day to share the blessings of salvation with others (John 9:4).

2. *Time to Do Good*

The episode of the healing of the man with the withered hand, reported by all the three Synoptics (Mark 3:1-6; Matt. 12:9-14; Luke 6:6-11), further illustrates the social function of the Sabbath. A deputation of Scribes and Pharisees, who had brought an invalid before Jesus, posed the testing question: "Is it lawful to heal on the sabbath?" (Matt. 12:10). According to both Mark and Luke, Christ replied first by asking a question of principle: "Is it lawful on the sabbath to do good or to do harm, to save life or to kill?" (Mark 3:4; Luke 6:9). Note that Christ substitutes for the verb "to heal" (*therapeuein*) the verb "to do good" (*agathopoiein*). What is the reason for such a change? Obviously because Christ wanted to include not one type but all kinds of benevolent activities within the intention of the Sabbath law. So broad an interpretation of the function of the Sabbath finds no parallel in rabbinic concessions. In fact, some scholars, misunderstanding the intended function of the Sabbath which Christ endeavored to clarify, go as far as viewing such a broad interpretation as an outright abrogation of the Fourth Commandment.[35] Such a conclusion fails to recognize that Christ enunciates rhetorically the humanitarian function of the Sabbath in reply to a specific test question concerning its proper observance. How could Christ negate the Sabbath commandment while trying to clarify it?[36]

To save or to kill? According to Matthew Christ illustrated the principle of Sabbath keeping as a time of benevolent service, by adding a second question containing a concrete example:

"What man of you, if he has one sheep and it falls into a pit on the sabbath, will not lay hold of it and lift it out? Of how much more *value* is a man than a sheep!" (Matt. 12:11-12). Both by the question of principle and by its illustration, Christ reveals the *original value* of the Sabbath, to be a day to honor God by showing concern and compassion for others. Unfortunately, with the accumulation of restrictions (Mark 7:9) the observance of the day had been reduced to a legalistic religiosity rather than an opportunity to offer loving service to the Creator-Redeemer by serving needy fellow beings. The believer who on the Sabbath experiences the blessing of salvation will automatically be moved "to save" and not "to kill" others. Christ's accusers, by failing to show concern for the physical and spiritual well-being of others on the Sabbath, revealed their defective understanding and experience of God's Holy Day. Rather than celebrating God's goodness on the Sabbath, involved in a saving ministry, they engaged in destructive efforts, *looking for faults* and thinking out methods *to kill* Christ (Mark 3:2-6).[37] Ellen White perceptively asks, "Was it better to slay upon the Sabbath, as they were planning to do, than to heal the afflicted, as He had done? Was it more righteous to have murder in the heart upon God's holy day than love to all men, which finds expression in deeds of mercy?"[38]

Understanding or misunderstanding? The fundamental humanitarian value which Christ places upon the Sabbath is expressed in Matthew with uncompromising positiveness: "So it is lawful to do good on the Sabbath" (Matt. 12:12). W. Manson aptly remarks that Christ "invalidates at one stroke the do-nothing attitude, which, under cover of the principle of not working on the Sabbath, his contemporaries mistook for obedience to the will of God."[39] Willy Rordorf, unable to accept such a positive interpretation of the Sabbath, accuses Matthew of "beginning the moralistic misunderstanding of Jesus' attitude toward the Sabbath."[40] Is it fair for a modern scholar to charge a Gospel Writer with *misunderstanding* Christ's teaching regarding the Sabbath? Even if the trustworthiness of Matthew's report could be discredited, does not his interpretation still represent the view of an Apostle and of his community? Furthermore, is not Matthew's understanding of the Sabbath as a day "to do good" (Matt. 12:12) and to show "mercy" rather than religiosity (Matt. 12:7) fully shared by the other three Gospels? In both Mark and Luke, Christ is cited as saying the same thing by means of a rhetorical question, precisely that on the Sabbath it is lawful "to do good" and "to save" (Mark 3:4; Luke 6:9). In Luke, Christ is reported as saying that the Sabbath is the day to loose human beings from physical and spiritual bonds (Luke 13:16, 12). In John, Christ invites His followers to share on the Sabbath in the divine redemptive activity (John 9:4; 5:17; 7:22-23). Therefore, the unanimous view of the Gospels is that Christ presented the Sabbath as a time to serve God especially by rendering loving service to human needs.[41]

To sanction this human value of the Sabbath, Christ affirmed, in a memorable pronouncement, His Lordship over the Sabbath (Mark 2:28; Matt. 12:8; Luke 6:5). Having established the Sabbath for the welfare of human beings (Mark 2:27), Christ claimed also "the authority to determine in what manner the Sabbath is to be kept so that God is honored and man is benefited."[42] Note that Christ's claim to be "Lord of the Sabbath" is followed in all three Synoptic Gospels by the healing of the man with the withered hand. In this healing Jesus proclaims by words and action with unquestionable positiveness the humanitarian function of the Sabbath. The collocation of this story by all the three Gospels immediately after Christ's memorable claim (Mark 2:28 and par.) provides a climactic demonstration of how Jesus exerted His Lordship over the Sabbath, not by annulling the Fourth Commandment but by revealing its true intended function—a time to celebrate God's goodness and salvation, by taking time "to do good" and "to save" others (Matt. 12:12, Mark 3:4, Luke 6:9). Who are the "others" that require our loving care and concern on the Sabbath? The answer is simple. They include the members of our immediate family as well as the needy members of the larger human family. Let us briefly consider how the celebration of the Sabbath can be shared with others.

3. *Time for the Family*

Daily work scatters the family members in different directions—husband and wife to their respective work and children to school. The pressure of work will often cause us to rob our children of our parental care, and to neglect even our relationship with our spouse. The rest of the Sabbath day brings us together by giving us time for God, for ourselves, for our families and for others. To meet the demands of his work or business, a man may have to leave home early and return late every day, thus becoming in essence a stranger to his family members. It is not uncommon to hear children say, "We hardly see daddy. He is always away." But when he rests on the Sabbath, free from the concerns of his business, then he has the opportunity to become more fully acquainted with and attuned to his

children. A most welcome moment in our home is Friday evening, when after the hustling and bustling of the week, our family
of five gathers to welcome the Lord of the Sabbath by singing,
reading, praying and leisurely listening to one another's concerns
and experiences that have been stored up during the week. The
arrival of the Sabbath serves to reknit the family bonds of
sympathy and affection.

It is noteworthy that the Scriptures link together the Sabbath and the family in several ways. Both are presented as
Edenic institutions which received a twin divine blessing (Gen.
1:28; 2:3). Both remained after the Fall as a constant reminder
of the fellowship, joy and rest of a future Paradise restored. Both
the commandment of the Sabbath and that of filial obligations
to parents are placed in sequence in the Decalogue (Ex. 20:8-12).
Both commandments are presented as being related to God's
call to a life of holiness: "You shall be holy, for I the Lord
your God am holy. Every one of you shall revere his mother
and his father, and you shall keep my sabbaths" (Lev. 19:2-3).
Why is the ideal of a life of holiness interrelated with respect
for parents and with Sabbath observance? Obviously, because
both of these precepts foster the spiritual quality of life. Parents
who use the Sabbath to promote the religious education of their
children will strengthen their moral consciousness and deepen
their children's commitment both to them as parents and
to God.

To achieve this objective parents should make the Sabbath
for their children, not an alienating imposition but a delightful
celebration. A day characterized not by *frustration* because of
the things that cannot be done on the Sabbath but by *exultation*
over the blessings that can be enjoyed on this day. Ellen White
writes in this regard, "parents can make the Sabbath, as it should
be, the most joyful day of the week. They can lead their
children to regard it as a delight, the day of days, the holy of
the Lord, honorable." [43] The difference between *gloom* and *gladness* on the Sabbath depends primarily on the motives for observing the day. Parents who teach their children to observe the
Sabbath as a law that must be kept in order to go to heaven,
will lead the children to view the day like a bitter medicine
that must be swallowed in order to become well. The children
will count the hours of the Sabbath as the astronauts count the
seconds preceding the firing of their spacecraft: 10, 9, 8, 7, 6, 5,
4, 3, 2, 1, 0, SUNSET! And they take off to some exciting activity to burn up the energy repressed during the Sabbath. On
the contrary, parents who teach their children to observe the
Sabbath as a day to joyfully celebrate God's marvelous creation,

redemption and care over their lives, will lead them to view the day not as a dreadful medicine but as a delicious cake. The hours of the Sabbath will seem too short to delight in the special food, the pleasant fellowship and the enjoyable activities. Later, we shall consider some of the criteria for Sabbath activities.

3. *Time for One's Partner*

The Sabbath provides time and opportunities to come close to one special person, namely, one's marital partner. We are helplessly witnessing an ever-increasing rate of broken marriages.[44] The rapid pace of modern life, punctuated by differing professional and social interests, contributes to the estrangement between many husbands and wives. Can the Sabbath function as a catalyst to solidify and strengthen marital relationships? It surely can, for at least two reasons: one is *theological* and the other is *practical*. *Theologically*, the sanctity of the Sabbath serves to safeguard the sacredness of marriage. Both institutions are ordained to express and experience a mutual belonging relationship: the Sabbath to God (see chapter IV) and marriage to a human partner (Gen. 2:24; Matt. 19:5-6). A Christian couple who take time on the Sabbath to renew their commitment to God will inevitably renew also their commitment to each other.

The Sabbath teaches that relationships, whether at a human or divine-human level, are sacred. The Christian commitment to God expressed especially through the consecration of the Sabbath time to the Lord stands as the basis of all other commitments. It is not difficult to see how a person who wilfully chooses to disregard God on His Holy Day will also, if the occasion arises, violate his or her marital commitment. In other words, if the symbol of one's covenant with God is intentionally ignored, there is little to stop a person from ignoring also the vows of faithfulness to the marriage partner or to anyone else. The relationship between the two is suggested in the Scripture by the connection between apostasy and adultery. As the profanation of the Sabbath is equated with *apostasy* (Ezek. 20:13, 21), so unfaithfulness to the marriage vow is condemned as *adultery* (Ex. 20:14). That the two are interrelated is indicated by the prophets' interchangeable use of them to describe Israel's unfaithfulness (Jer. 3:8, Ezek. 23-37). Therefore, *theologically*, the Sabbath can strengthen marital relationships by reminding both husbands and wives of the sacred nature of their commitment to God and to each other.[45]

Being God's chosen day among the weekly days, the Sabbath can constantly and forcefully remind the believer who keeps it to be God's chosen "Holy person" among a perverse generation.

Practically, the Sabbath contributes to solidify marital relationships by providing a relaxed atmosphere in which to experience a more intimate fellowship and interaction. The quality of a marriage relationship depends to a large extent on the degree of communication and understanding that exists between the two partners. Marriage manuals generally regard the lack of adequate communication as a major cause for the breaking down of marriages. The Sabbath provides husbands and wives with the time and the inspiration to come closer and listen to each other. The spirit of the celebration of God's goodness motivates them to give themselves unselfishly to each other. This is expressed in a variety of ways. By sharing thoughts, concerns, joys and necessary duties *together*. By walking, visiting, playing, laughing and relaxing *together*. The togetherness and closeness of body and soul that husbands and wives experience on the Sabbath enable them to overcome any estrangement caused by the tension of the week passed and thus to experience a renewed sense of unity and commitment to God and to each other.

5. *Time for the Needy*

The Sabbath is the day to serve God not only by taking time to show concern for our immediate family members but also for needy "strangers." In the various versions of the Sabbath commandment "the stranger" (*ger*), sometimes called "alien" or "sojourner," is specifically mentioned (Ex. 20:10; 23: 12; Deut. 5:14) as a beneficiary of the blessings of the Sabbath. The "stranger" initially was a foreigner who lived in the land of Israel, but in the course of time the term was used to describe a worker or laborer or a servant. When we think of the contempt the ancient world had toward work and workers, it is not surprising to note the concern of the Sabbath for the outcast of the society. Isaiah 58 provides a dramatic illustration of how true Sabbathkeeping finds expression in social concern. The prophet interrelates true fasting, interpreted as letting the oppressed go free and sharing bread with the hungry (vv. 6-7), with true Sabbathkeeping, which consists in finding "delight" not in one's own pleasures but in the Lord (vv. 13-14).[46] In the Gospels this humanitarian function of the Sabbath is clarified and emphasized by Christ's own words and actions.

To celebrate the Sabbath means to reach out and share the blessings of the day with others. In the Jewish home, an important aspect of the preparation of the Sabbath meal was the planning for possible visitors.[47] Similarly in the Christian home, the Sabbath provides the opportunity to share food and friendship with the visitor, the orphan, the lonely, the elderly, the estranged, and the discouraged who are present in our church or community. During the week we often learn that a relative, a colleague or a neighbor is physically ill or emotionally distressed. The pressures of the working week may cause us to neglect such needy persons. On the Sabbath, as we experience the presence and the love of God, we are motivated to take time to cheer the sick, to comfort the afflicted, to counsel the distressed, to share our friendship and concern with the needy. The service we render on the Sabbath to needy persons honors God and enriches our lives with a sense of satisfaction and restful achievement.

6. *Time for Recreation*

The Sabbath provides time for physical and spiritual recreation. The term *recreation* suggests activities designed to re-create, to restore energies. Earlier in this chapter we considered several significant opportunities offered by the Sabbath to experience *spiritual* renewal. Attention must also be given to the *physical* recreation of the Sabbath. Obviously, no standard formula can be offered to ensure physical renewal to each person on the Sabbath, since physical needs vary according to age and profession. The physical wants of a teen-ager overflowing with energy are likely to be quite different from those of a middle-aged bricklayer. Similarly, a farmer who works outdoors may not seek outdoor physical recreation like an office worker who spends the week shut in by four walls. Moreover, any attempt to classify or specify "legitimate" Sabbath recreational activities tends to engender legalistic attitudes and stifle the spirit of freedom and creativity of the Sabbath. We suggest, therefore, only three general criteria that may provide a handy norm for determining suitable Sabbath recreational activities.

God-centered. Sabbath recreational activities should be first of all *God-centered* and not self-centered. They should represent a celebration and rejoicing over the goodness of God's creation and redemption. Sabbath activities should be a means of expressing the words of Maltbie D. Babcock:

> This is my Father's world,
> And to my listening ears,
> All nature sings, and round me rings
> The music of the spheres.
> This is my Father's world;
> I rest me in the thought
> Of rocks and trees, of skies and seas;
> His hand the wonders wrought.

Isaiah explains that Sabbath activities should not be a means of "doing your pleasure" but rather of taking "delight in the Lord" (58:13-14). The challenge that religious leaders and parents face today is to educate both young and old to regard their Sabbath recreational activities not as an end in themselves but as a means to express delight in the Lord. We have seen that the Sabbath is the day of the special manifestation and experience of God's presence. This means that all the activities of this day should contribute to cultivating an awareness of His presence rather than detracting from it.

Freedom and Joy. A second criterion for Sabbath recreational activities is the *freedom* and *joy* they should provide. The Sabbath is a day to celebrate the redemptive freedom offered by the Savior. Such a spirit of freedom and joy, delighting in God's goodness, is to permeate all Sabbath activities. The task of a religious educator is not to name which activities are appropriate but to describe the experience of freedom a Christian should seek in his Sabbath activities. Sometimes the same activity can be either an experience of freedom or of restraint. A Sabbath picnic, for example, can be a joyful and free celebration of the goodness of God's creation and recreation in Christ, if adequate preparations for it have been made before the Sabbath and consequently everyone can freely participate in it. On the contrary, if the food has to be obtained, or if some persons have to spend hours preparing it, then the picnic can become an expression of selfishness, since it inhibits the opportunity to celebrate the Sabbath free from the pressure of work. On the basis of this principle any form of recreation which restricts the freedom to celebrate the Sabbath militates against the intended function of the commandment.

Recreative. A third criterion for Sabbath activities is their *recreative* nature. They should contribute not to the dissipation but to the restoration of mental, emotional and physical energies. The spiritual, mental and bodily renewal experienced on the Sabbath foreshadows in a sense the fuller restoration to be experienced at Christ's Second Coming. The Sabbath and the Second Coming share in common not only the restoration the Savior offers to His people but also the preparation for such an event. In other words, the weekly preparation to meet the Savior in *time* on His Holy Day is a preparation also to meet Him in *space* at His Coming. It is important, therefore, to remember that Sabbath recreation has a spiritual quality not present to the same degree in the daily recreation. It represents the restoration that God has accomplished and will yet realize in a greater degree in the lives of His people. Thus any type of recreational activity that generates an excited restlessness, or causes a "hangover" that incapacitates a person on the following day, fails to conform to God's intended use of the Sabbath. In determining which activity best recreates one's total being, each person must consider his or her personal needs. A salesman who spends his whole week talking to people may sense the need to spend some of the free Sabbath time alone reading, meditating, listening to music, putting his life together again. On the other hand, a laboratory technician who spends the week pretty much alone examining specimens and recording data may sense a special need to fellowship with people, participating perhaps in outdoor activities. A single criterion per se is inadequate for determining suitable Sabbath recreational activities. The combination of the triple criteria of God-centered activities, freedom and joy, and recreative nature, offers a safer guidance.

The Sabbath as service to others shows that a fundamental function of its celebration is to provide time, motivation and opportunities to come close to loved ones, friends, and needy persons. The ties of fellowship strengthened by the Sabbath often encourage free and joyful recreation especially amid the beauties of nature. This leads us to consider the relationship between the celebration of the Sabbath and the Christian responsibility toward the natural world.

PART IV

THE SABBATH AS SERVICE TO OUR HABITAT

1. *The Ecological Crisis*

Compulsion or conviction? The prostitution and unbridled exploitation of the natural resources are regarded by analysts of our time as a major threat to the survival of life on Planet Earth. Ecological prophets are predicting that at the very time humanity is discovering the secrets of nature, it is also risking extinction as a result of an environmental disaster. Educational programs, policies and legislation are presently being promoted by those who are concerned over the precarious ecological balance of our environment. The committed Christian shares this concern because he believes in the goodness of God's creation and cooperates with Him to restore ecological harmony in the whole created order. Such a theological conviction is indispensable for a meaningful solution to the environmental crisis.

Secular ideologies can only motivate people to respect nature and its resources out of fear: fear of punishment or of annihilation, if environmental laws are disregarded. Fear of consequences, however, can at best restrain some from exploiting, polluting or destroying the environment, but it cannot induce a genuine love and respect for all forms of life. Fear can compel but does not convince.

The fear of lung cancer has led some to quit smoking cigarettes but it has hardly shaken the determination of millions of smokers to continue smoking their health away. This illustrates that the solution to *environmental pollution* is related to the solution of *spiritual pollution*. A person who does not respect his or her own life can hardly be expected to esteem that of subhuman species. Laws per se cannot solve this problem because they clash against selfish interests. Ultimately, the solution to the ecological crisis is to found in the recovery of those spiritual values that must guide every human act. Religious convictions and ultimate concerns provide strong motivation for human behavior. Henlee H. Barnette rightly notes that "what people do to, for, and with others and their environment depends largely upon what they think of God, nature, themselves and their destiny." [48] It is only when a person understands himself and the world as the object of God's creation and redemption, that he will be both convinced and compelled to act as God's steward of his body as well as of the created order.[49] The Sabbath can play a vital role to help in recovering these spiritual values needed to solve the ecological crisis, since the day does provide the basis for both theological convictions and practical actions. These we must now consider.

2. The Goodness of God's Creation

The value of nature. The commission appointed in 1971 by the Archbishop of Canterbury "to investigate the relevance of Christian doctrine to the problems of man and his environment" concludes its findings saying: "In the report it has been argued that the recovery of belief in God the Creator is the key to mankind's future well-being." [50] It is noteworthy that leading religious thinkers regard "the recovery of belief in God the Creator" as the "key" to the solution of the environmental crisis. Science and technology, by undermining the belief in God the Creator, have reduced the desire to rejoice over the goodness of God's creation. By substituting the belief in a personal divine creation with the notion of an impersonal spontaneous generation, scientists have reduced nature and all its constituent forms to be objects that technology can use and control. Nature has been pared from being a mediator of divine revelation (a "thou"), to serving as a means of economic exploitation (an "it").[51]

The Sabbath provides an effective institution to help in recovering the "sacramental" value of nature, that is, its function as mediator or revelator of God's presence and beauty. In what way? By reminding the believer of the value and role of nature in God's creation, redemption and ultimate restoration. As the memorial of an originally perfect creation, the Sabbath reassures the Christian that despite the aberrations caused by sin, this world, both in its human and subhuman forms, still has value because God created it "very good" (Gen. 1:31). By pointing to the original goodness and perfection of this world, the Sabbath challenges the Christian to exercise a world-affirming faith, that is, a faith in God's plan for the whole natural order. As the symbol of God's blessing and sanctification of this world (Gen. 2:3), the Sabbath serves as a constant reminder that God is distinct but not separated from His world. Thus in and through nature, the Sabbath invites the Christian to experience the presence of His Creator. Offering the anticipation and foretaste of the new heaven and new earth (Is. 66:22-23), the Sabbath challenges the Christian to respect and admire this world, since God will restore it to its pristine perfection for the eternal delight of His creatures. These theological values of nature expressed by the Sabbath offer the deepest motivation for the Christian's concern for the natural world. The Christian who views himself and the world as being part and parcel of a single divine creative and redemptive purpose will be kept from exploiting or destroying the very earth with which he shares the same origin and destiny.

A dualistic misconception. The value of nature can best be seen in the light of the Biblical teaching on its redemption. It is regrettable that both Catholicism and Protestantism have emphasized to a large extent the salvation of individual souls at the expense of a *cosmic* dimension of redemption.[52] The saints are often portrayed as pilgrims who live on earth detached from the world, and whose souls at death leave their material bodies to make their pilgrimage to an abstract place called "heaven." This dualism between the material and the spiritual world, between the body and the soul reflects the influence of Platonic thought upon Christianity,[53] but it fails to represent the holistic Biblical view of man and of the world.[54] The influence of the Platonic cosmological and anthropological dualism has produced an attitude of contempt toward the natural world.

This other-worldly attitude is exemplified in such Christian hymns as "This world is not my home;" "I'm but a stranger here, Heaven is my home; Earth is a desert drear, Heaven is my home;" "Weary of the earth... I look to heaven." Such an attitude of disdain toward the earth is absent in the Psalms, the Hebrew hymnal, where the central theme is the praise of God for His wonderful works. For example, in Psalm 92, which is "A Song for the Sabbath," the psalmist urges to praise the Lord with musical instruments, because, as he says, "Thou, O Lord, hast made me glad by thy work; at the works of thy hands I sing for joy. How great are thy works, O Lord!" (vv. 4, 5).[55]

The Psalmist's rejoicing over nature is based upon his conception of the created world as being not a backdrop for the drama of God's creation and redemption, but rather an integral part of the whole drama. The Scriptures picture God as creating man to live in a garden happily, acting responsibly toward his environment (Gen. 2:15; 1:29-30).[56] When the crisis in Eden occurs, the garden gives place to the wilderness (Gen. 3:17-19), and the harmony between mankind and nature is disrupted. Nature was not involved in Adam's fall, but it does share in its consequences. The crisis in the natural order is further precipitated by the ensuing human disobedience. Human estrangement from God brings alienation from nature. Cain slays Abel (Gen. 4:8) and mankind as a whole becomes so corrupt that God finds it necessary to restore some order by means of a cataclysmic Flood (Gen. 6-8). It is noteworthy that when the human race starts anew, God establishes a covenant not only with mankind, but also "with every living creature... the birds, the cattle, and every beast of the earth" (Gen. 9:10; cf. vv. 12, 15, 16, 17). By means of this covenant God promises to preserve the regularity of nature. Despite human rebellion God promises that the chaos caused to nature by the Flood will never occur again. This divine covenant with the natural order is later presented by Jeremiah as the assurance of God's covenant with people (Jer. 33:25, 26).

Cosmic redemption. After the Flood the relationship between man and nature experiences a marked decline from God's original intention (Gen. 1:28-30). Trust gives way to fear: "The fear of you and the dread of you shall be upon every beast of the earth" (Gen. 9:2). This does not mean that human beings can no longer be trusted with the stewardship of the world.[57] It means that the natural order will now suffer from irresponsible human conduct toward God. Examples of such occurrences abound in the OT. Isaiah, for instance, writes: "The

earth lies polluted under its inhabitants; for they have trans-
gressed the laws, violated the statutes, broken the everlasting
covenant. . . . Therefore the inhabitants of the earth are scorched,
and few men are left" (24:5-6).[58] But as nature suffers the consequences of human rebellion, it also shares in mankind's reconciliation and ultimate restoration. God's redeeming purpose
is cosmic, encompassing the whole of creation, both human and
subhuman.

The vision of restored harmony between mankind and
nature is present in the OT as well as in the NT. In the OT
the end-time restoration of the earth is associated with the hope
of the Messianic age, hope which, as noted in chapter V, was
nourished by the message and experience of the Sabbath. A
most beautiful description of the end-time restoration to the
primeval paradise is found in Isaiah 11: "The wolf shall dwell
with the lamb, and the leopard shall lie down with the kid,
and the calf and the lion and the fatling together, and a little
child shall lead them. The cow and the bear shall feed; their
young shall lie down together; and the lion shall eat straw like
the ox. . . . They shall not hurt or destroy in all my holy mountain" (vv. 6, 7, 9).[59] A similar vision is found in the NT, in
which not only human beings but the whole creation share in
Christ's redemption and ultimate restoration. Paul sees that
God in and through Christ is bringing all things in heaven and
on earth to the point where they will ultimately experience unity,
harmony and reconciliation (Eph. 1:10; Col. 1:20). Thus, the
apostle explains, "We know that the whole creation has been
groaning in travail together until now waiting with eager
longing for the time when it "will be set free from its bondage
to decay and obtain the glorious liberty of the children of God"
(Rom. 8:22, 21).[60] The Seer of Revelation sees a similar vision
of the redeemed enjoying the peace and harmony of "a new
heaven and a new earth" (Rev. 21:1-4; cf. 2 Peter 3:11-13).[61]

3. The Sabbath and the Ecological Crisis

The Biblical vision of a cosmic restoration of human, animal
and plant life has vital implications now for the Christian responsibility toward nature and the environment in general. To
accept God as the Creator and Restorer of the whole created
order means to be responsive to God's goals and intentions, by
participating in His cosmic restoration program. To motivate
and actualize such a program, the Church needs symbols and
institutions that adequately interpret the human role within
God's created order. The Sabbath provides the Church with

such a needed symbol and institution, since the day offers both *theological incentives* and *practical opportunities* to develop what may be called "an ecological conscience." *Theologically*, the Sabbath inspires and encourages respect and appreciation for all of God's creation, by reminding the believer that he shares with nature in God's creation, sanctification, redemption and ultimate restoration; nature thus becomes a worthy partner. The role of scientific knowledge and technology is not to destroy but to preserve nature's balance. The Sabbath assists, in a sense, to extend to the natural world the restoration of Christ's image which is being accomplished in human life. *Practically*, the Sabbath provides valuable opportunities to translate into action these theological values of nature which the seventh day expresses. These practical opportunities will now be considered under the headings of stewardship, limitation and admiration.

Stewardship. Sabbathkeeping is an exercise in responsible stewardship of the whole earth. It means to acknowledge God's ownership of the "heaven and earth, the sea and all that is in them" (Ex. 20:11; 31:17) by relinquishing for one day the lucrative use of land and people. This involves granting freedom on the Sabbath not only to all dependent workers but also to "your ox, or your ass, or any of your cattle" (Deut. 5:14; cf. Ex. 23:12; 20:10). As aptly expressed by Samuel Raphael Hirsch, "The bird, the fish, the animal that we refrain from seizing on the Sabbath, the plant that we refrain from tearing up, the material that we refrain from fashioning or chiselling, cutting or mixing, moulding or preparing, all of this inaction is but a demonstration of homage to God, proclaiming Him Creator and Master and Lord of the world." [62]

The acknowledgement of God's ownership, expressed on the Sabbath by surrendering the right to use gainfully human and natural resources, affects the Christian's general attitude toward God and the world. It teaches a person to view himself not as a *predator* but as a *curator* of God's creation. This lesson was taught in OT times particularly through the legislation relating to the sabbatical and jubilee years. These two sister institutions of the seventh-day Sabbath were designed to teach every member of the Hebrew society to regard both land and people as God's posssssion ("The land is mine and you are but aliens and my tenants"—Lev. 25:23, NIV; cf. 25:42, 55). At these annual institutions, to acknowledge God's ownership the slaves were emancipated, debts were remitted and the land which had been sold on account of financial distress was returned to the original owner (Lev. 25; Deut. 15:1-18). Moreover, to protect the land from impoverishment caused by excessive use and to enable it to be renewed with nutrients, during the Sabbath years the land was to lie fallow ("in the seventh year there shall be a sabbath of solemn rest for the land, a sabbath to the Lord; you shall not sow your field or prune your vineyard"—Lev. 25:4). These Sabbath norms attribute to the land almost a conscious personality, granting to it a similar right ordained for human beings to rest and to be free from exploitation. Thus in its own unique way the Sabbath provided in OT times concrete instruments to deal with what today is called the "ecological problem."

Obviously, it is not possible nor necessary to apply to our modern social economic situation all of the norms of the sabbatical legislation. Slavery, for example, is no longer a major social problem. Similarly, loans generally are no longer granted by private persons but rather by public financial institutions. Yet a careful observer can hardly fail to recognize the relevance to the present ecological crisis of the principle of stewardship of God's creation implied in both the weekly and annual Sabbaths. Suppose we were to ask modern science, What benefits would accrue to human beings and their environment from observing the Sabbath according to traditional biblical guidelines? Such observance would involve shutting down for the duration of the Sabbath factories, shops and places of entertainment. It would mean stopping industrial machines as well as the millions of automobiles on the highways with the exception of those needed for social services. The result would be a cessation on the Sabbath in the flow of pollution into our atmosphere which in some of our metropolises has become a toxic smog. A scientific report on New York City's atmosphere indicates that the average person on the street of that city inhales toxic fumes equivalent to 38 cigarettes per day.[63] For the land it would mean a complete rest for the duration of one year every seven years. Obviously rational plans would have to be developed to implement such programs; economic factors could not be ignored. At a more personal level it would mean spending the day not competing but communing with nature; not stressing the body with exciting entertainments but stretching the body and the spirit within the atmosphere of peace and pleasure of the Sabbath. What would the answer of modern science be to such a sabbatical lifestyle? We believe that it would be definitively positive. Perhaps our medical and ecological scientists might even recommend the implementation of such a program to restore and safeguard the precarious balance of our personal lives and environment.

Limitation. The rest which the Sabbath is designed to provide to both people and land has been called *restitutio ad in-*

    True admiration and appreciation of nature requires a measure
of detachment. The Sabbath offers this needed detachment. On
this day the Christian must leave nature untouched. To change
it by building on it or by destroying it would be a violation
of "rest." The Sabbath is the day not to alter nature but to
admire it as an expression of the beauty and glory of God's
handiwork (Ps. 19:1).

tegrum, which means a restoration to wholeness.[64] This principle implies that when God "blessed" His creation and declared it "very good," He endowed it with the potential for regenerating its lost energies. Rest is an important factor to ensure this process of energy renewal, and time is an essential ingredient of rest. If the air and water were given time every seven days (one seventh of the year) to recover from the toxic effects of human pollution, and if the land were left fallow for one year every seven years to regain lost nutrients, would not these measures contribute to solving the ecological crisis?

What our society needs today is a "Sabbath consciousness," namely, a consciousness of responsible stewardship of the world,—human stewardship which aims not at devouring space and primary sources continuously in order to increase production but rather at limiting human greediness. The Sabbath commandment is designed to teach such a responsible stewardship. By enjoining to rest, it teaches human beings to place a limit on productivity and profit, to silence the insatiable human greediness. This important function of the Sabbath is recognized even by those who do not view themselves as Sabbath-keepers. For example, A. Martin, a Catholic scholar, affirms: "The Sabbath means to become conscious of duration. It means to become conscious of a limit.... To reflect upon the Sabbath means to address ourselves to the question of happiness. It means to remember that man must not turn upon himself, viewing himself as the center of the universe to the risk of suffocating himself. It means to denounce the myth of efficiency, profit and productivity. For a Christian to observe the Sabbath means to say no to that stupidity that prevents us from seeing further than the end of an immediate profit. To respect the Sabbath means to know that man has a limit: if he steps over it, he dies." [65]

Admiration. The limitation which the Sabbath places upon constructive or destructive uses of the physical world makes possible the admiration of nature. It is scarcely possible to appreciate the beauty of a forest while engaged in cutting down its trees or of a garden while laboring to pull up all its plants. True admiration and appreciation of nature requires a measure of detachment. The Sabbath offers this needed detachment. On this day the Christian must leave nature untouched. To change it by building on it or by destroying it would be a violation of "rest." The Sabbath is a day not to alter nature but to admire it as an expression of the beauty and glory of God's handiwork (Ps. 19:1). The recovery of an ethic of admiration of nature is indispensable to develop an ecological

conscience. "When nature ceases to be an object of contempla-
tion and admiration," notes Albert Camus, "it can then be nothing more than material for an action that aims at transforming
it." [66] The loss of an ethic of *admiration* of nature which has
been encouraged by a prevailing secular-scientific view of this
world, has resulted in an ethic of *exploitation* of nature, so that
human beings have become aliens to their habitat.

The solution to this conflict between mankind and nature
will not be found in denouncing or renouncing technological
progress, but rather, as wisely stated by Abraham Joshua
Heschel, "in attaining some degree of independence of it." [67]
"On the Sabbath we live, as it were," writes the same author,
"*independent of technical civilization*: we abstain primarily
from any activity that aims at remaking or reshaping the things
of space." [68] This movement away from the *exploitation* of
nature to its *admiration* represents in one sense a *consecration*
or offering of this creation back to God. The believer ceases
from the use of things to offer them to their Creator, and in
so doing receives them back from Him blessed and sanctified.
The recovery of this consciousness of the holiness of the world,
that is, of God's presence in the world, is essential for the
development of a genuine concern for nature. In Albert
Schweitzer's words, "A man is ethical only when life, as such,
is holy to him, that is, the lives of plants and animals as well
as the lives of men. Moreover, he is ethical also only when
he extends help to all life that is in need of it." [69] The celebration on the Sabbath of God's sanctification of this world (Gen.
2:2-3; Ex. 20:11) promotes this needed consciousness of the holiness of life and thus encourages the development of a much
needed ecological conscience.

This study of the Sabbath as service to our habitat has
shown how the day offers valuable theological incentives and
practical opportunities for the development of a responsible
stewardship of God's creation. The joyful celebration on the
Sabbath of God's creation, sanctification, redemption and restoration of all the natural order teaches the Christian to act not
as a *predator* but as a *curator* of the world. The distinctive
Sabbath lifestyle, characterized not by the *exploitation* but by
the *admiration* of the earth, not by the *devastation* of nature
but by the *exaltation* of its Creator, provides a valuable model
of responsible stewardship in an otherwise irresponsible society.

We asked at the outset of this chapter, What contribution
can the Sabbath make toward solving pressing human problems such as the sense of God's absence, the feeling of loneliness, the neglect of the needy and the ecological crisis? Our

study has shown that a rcovery of the Biblical values of the Sabbath contributes significantly to the solution of these problems. The Sabbath and its values offer to the believer an experience of the presence of God, a fresh revelation of His grace, a needed time for reflection and inner renewal, an opportunity to come close to loved ones and needy persons, and an exercise in responsible stewardship of God's creation. The celebration of the Sabbath represents indeed the *Good News of Service* to God, to oneself, to others and to our habitat.

CHAPTER
VII

the Sabbath

GOOD NEWS
of divine REST
for human
RESTLESSNESS

Our tension-filled and anguished, compressed lives long for rest. The heart specialist or the high-blood pressure physician often admonish us, saying, "You need to slow down and rest." Yet, how difficult it is to work off tension, to quiet restlessness! Some join athletic clubs, others meditation groups. Still others seek release from their tension by taking vacations, tranquillizers, drugs or alcohol. Experience tells us, however, that even fabulous vacations or magic pills provide at best only a temporary evasion but not a permanent quieting of inner tension and restlessness. How then can our restless lives experience perfect rest and peace? In the opening paragraph of his autobiography entitled *Confessions,* Augustine points to the real solution to the problem of human restlessness, when he says, "Thou hast made us for Thyself and our hearts are restless until they find rest in Thee."

True rest is to be found not in *places* or through *pills* but rather in a right relationship with a *Person,* the Person of the Savior who says: "Come to me, all you who are weary and burdened, and I will give you rest" (Matt. 11:28; NIV). Perfect rest and peace are not a human achievement but a divine gift. It is an experience that come to us when we allow Christ to harmonize our lives ("*I* will give you rest"—Matt. 11:28). Why is divine assistance needed to experience true rest and peace in our lives? The answer is to be found in the fact that perfect rest does not come about accidentally but is the result of an harmonious accord of the physical, mental and spiritual components of our being. Can we by ourselves harmonize these three, that is, our body, mind and soul? We can stretch our tired body on a bed but if our mind and soul are troubled, we have not rest but agitation, tension or even nightmares. As the various components of an orchestra need the direction of a skilful maestro to blend them into harmonious music, so the physical, mental and spiritual components of our being need the direction of our supreme Master in order for us to experience harmonious rest and peace.[1]

How can we enable Christ to harmonize and quiet our restless lives? Our study has shown that God gave mankind before and after the Fall a vital institution, the Sabbath day: a day specifically designed to free us from secular concerns in order to freely find rest in God (Heb. 4:9-10). It is to be regretted that this divine institution has often been neglected, disregarded or even perverted. This occurred in OT times and it is also happening in our materialistic-oriented society. Many people today view God's Holy Day as a time to seek for personal *profit* and *pleasure* rather than for divine *power* and *presence*. The story is told of a pastor calling upon a member who had missed church services for several weeks. The pastor asked him, "What keeps you away, friend?" To this the member replied: "I'd rather be in bed on Sunday morning thinking about the church than in the church thinking about my bed. At least my mind is in the right place." Indeed, for many the right place to be on their "Lord's Day" is not in God's sanctuary but rather in the sanctuary of a bed, a boat, a car, a restaurant, a football field, a cinema, a shopping mall, et cetera. Even those Christians who attend morning church services will often revert in the afternoon to places of business or entertainment. This is hardly reflective of what we have found to be the Biblical notion of Sabbathkeeping, namely, a day set apart to experience God's restful presence in our restless lives.

This prevailing trend raises a crucial question: Is the Sabbath institution a superseded religious tradition no longer relevant to space-age Christians? Or, Is this a divine ordinance still essential to Christian growth and survival? It is hard to believe that at the very time when the tyranny of things enslaves many lives, there should no longer be any need for the Sabbath day—the day whose very function is to free human beings from the bondage of materialism in order for them to experience divine peace and rest in their restless lives. Our investigation into the Good News of the Sabbath has shown that the Sabbath is indeed a vital divine institution that provides time and opportunities to develop a growing relationship with God and fellow beings. In a special sense the celebration of God's Holy Day enables the Lord of the Sabbath to bring His peace and rest to restless lives. To grasp more fully the latter important function of the Sabbath, we shall briefly review, by way of conclusion, seven of the significant Good News of the Sabbath that have emerged in the course of this study. It is to be hoped that this conclusive summary will help the reader to better appreciate how proper Sabbathkeeping enables the Savior to bring rest and peace to our restlessness.

1. *Rest of Creation*

A first way in which the Sabbath brings Christ's rest to our souls is by constantly reassuring us that our lives have meaning, value and hope because they are rooted in God from creation to eternity. This message of the Sabbath was seen especially in the first two chapters. We may call it "Christ's creation rest" for the human soul. It is the rest that Christ brings to those thinking persons who search for life's meaning and value in their ancestral roots; to those who wonder if their existence as well as that of the whole cosmos is the result of *chance* or of *choice*, that is, of a *merciless fate* or of a *merciful God*. To these persons through the Sabbath Christ offers His restful assurance that their ancestral roots are good because they are rooted in God Himself (Gen. 1:26-27); that their existence has value because it is not the product of chance but of a personal creation and redemption of a loving God.

We have found this reassuring message of the Sabbath in the creation story where the number seven, emphatic terms and the imagery of God's rest are used to proclaim the Good News that originally God created this world and all its creatures in a perfect and complete way. The believer who celebrates this Good News on the Sabbath by renewing his or her faith in the perfect Creator, and by delighting in the beauty of God's creation, experiences Christ's rest of creation. To experience this rest on the Sabbath means to rejoice in the divine assurance that human existence, in spite of its apparent futility and tragedy, has value because it proceeds from God and moves toward a glorious divine destiny. As eloquently expressed by Augustine, "Thy resting on the seventh day after the completion of Thy works foretells us through the voice of Thy Book, that we also, after completing our works through Thy generosity, in the Sabbath of eternal life shall rest in Thee."[2] To celebrate the Sabbath in this restless present means to experience a foretaste of the future rest and peace that awaits God's people; it means to rest in the assurance that "he who began a good work in you will bring it to completion at the day of Jesus Christ" (Phil. 1:6).

2. *Rest of Divine Presence*

A second way in which proper Sabbathkeeping brings Christ's rest to our lives is by enabling us to experience His divine presence. It is Christ's presence that brought stillness to the stormy lake of Galilee (Matt. 8:23-27) and it is also the assurance of His presence that can bring peace and stillness to troubled lives. This is basically the meaning of the holiness of the Sabbath which is frequently stated in the Bible. We have shown in chapter III that the holiness of the Sabbath consists in the special manifestation of God's presence through this day in the life of His people. The believer who on the Sabbath lays aside his secular concerns, turning off his receiver to the many distracting voices in order to tune in and listen to the voice of God, experiences in a real sense the spiritual presence of Christ. The heightened sense of the nearness of Christ's presence experienced on the Sabbath fills the soul with joy, peace and rest.

Relationship, if they are to survive, need to be cultivated. This is true both at a human and human-divine level. I vividly recall the A, B, C privilege-system that governed the social relationships among students of the opposite sex at Newbold College, in England, where I received my college training. A couple with an "A" status was entitled to a weekly encounter of about one hour in a designated lounge. However, those couples who qualified for a "B" or a "C" privilege could officially meet only biweekly or monthly. Frankly, I did my best to maintain the "A" status because I viewed those brief weekly encounters with my fiancée as indispensable for the survival of our relationship. The Sabbath is in a sense a special weekly encounter with our Creator-Redeemer. This encounter, however, lasts not merely *one hour* but *a whole day*. It is a sobering thought that to enter into the holy Sabbath day means, as we have seen, to enter in a special sense into the spiritual presence and communion of the Lord. Believers who cultivate Christ's presence during the Sabbath time and activities experience His rest and peace every day of their lives.

3. *Rest from Competition*

A third way in which true Sabbathkeeping brings Christ's rest to our lives is by releasing us from the pressure to produce and achieve. The pressure that our competitive society exerts on us can cause untold frustration. Competition can dishearten, dehumanize and demoralize a person. It can turn friends into foes. We noted in chapter III that in order to keep up with the Joneses, some Christians today, like the Israelites of old, choose to moonlight on the Sabbath. But the Scripture points to the senselessness of such greediness when it states with a point of irony, "They found none" (Ex. 16:27). The Sabbath teaches a greedy heart to be grateful, and a grateful heart is the abiding place of Christ's peace and rest.

By restricting temporarily our productivity, the Sabbath teaches us not to compete but to commune with one another. It teaches us to view fellow beings not quantitatively but qualitatively, that is, not in terms of their income but in terms of their human values.

By restricting temporarily our productivity, the Sabbath teaches us not to compete but to commune with one another. It teaches us to view fellow beings not *quantitatively* but *qualitatively*, that is, not in terms of their income but in terms of their human values. If Mr. Jones lives on social security, during the week we may be tempted to think of him in terms of his small income. On the Sabbath, however, as we worship and fellowship with Mr. Jones, we appreciate not the little that he makes but the much that he offers to the church and community through his Christian witness and example. Thus, by releasing us from the pressure of competition and production, the Sabbath enables us to appreciate more fully the human values of people and the beauty of things. This free and fuller appreciation of God, people and things brings joy, harmony and rest to our lives.

4. *Rest of Belonging*

A fourth way in which genuine Sabbathkeeping brings Christ's rest to our lives is by reassuring us of our belonging to Him. At the root of much human restlessness there is a sense of alienation, estrangement. The sense of not-belonging to anyone or anything will cause a person to feel bitter, insecure and restless. On the contrary, in a relationship of mutual belonging one experiences love, identity, security and rest. To enable human beings to conceptualize and experience a belonging relationship with Him, God has given helpful signs and symbols such as the rainbow, the circumcision, the Passover lamb and blood, the bread and wine. In chapter IV we found that the Sabbath occupies a unique place among these various God-given covenant signs or symbols, having functioned as the symbol *par excellence* of the divine election and mission of God's people. Being the symbol of divine ownership, the Sabbath constantly reminds the believer who keeps this day of his belonging to God. "The Sabbath,' aptly writes Chuck Scriven, "is the insignia of the man of faith, a sort of badge worn at God's request in order to recall God's loyalty to us and our loyalty to God. . . . It is a placard we carry to show the world what we stand for and whom we serve." [3]

During the week a person may feel frustrated by a sense of anonymity. "Who am I?" he asks, as he lives and moves among the crowd. The answer that often echoes back is, "You are a cog in a machine and a number in the computer." On the Sabbath the answer is different. The Christian who observes God's holy and chosen day hears the Lord saying, "You may know that I, the Lord, sanctify you" (Ex. 31:13). Being the symbol of divine ownership and sanctification, the Sabbath assures the Sabbath-keeper of his own divine election and sanctification. Moreover, as shown in chapter IV, the Sabbath offers not merely an assurance of belonging to God but also a concrete weekly opportunity to express such a commitment by re-enacting the baptismal covenant of self-renouncement and renewal. By renewing the sense of belonging to our Creator-Redeemer, the Sabbath restores a sense of human dignity, identity, peace and rest to our lives.

5. *Rest from Social Tensions*

A fifth way in which true Sabbathkeeping enables us to experience Christ's rest is by breaking down social, racial and cultural barriers. The inability or unwillingness to appreciate and accept another person's skin-color, culture, language or social status, is a major cause of much unrest, hate and tension in our contemporary society. After the Fall, as noted in chapter V, an important function of the Sabbath has been to teach equality and respect for every member of the human society. Every seven days, seven years (sabbatical year) and seven weeks of years (jubilee year), all persons, beasts and property were to become free before God. And genuine freedom leads to equality.

The uneven divisions of the Hebrew society leveled out as the Sabbath began. Samuel H. Dresner rightly complains that this equalizing function of the Sabbath has seldom been recognized. He goes on by saying, "Although one Jew may have peddled onions and another may have owned great forests of lumber, on the Sabbath all were equal, all were kings: all welcomed the Sabbath Queen, all chanted the *Kiddush*, all basked in the glory of the seventh day. . . . On the Sabbath there were neither banker nor clerk, neither farmer nor hired-hand, neither rich nor poor. There were only Jews hallowing the Sabbath." [4] It is noteworthy that Isaiah reassures the outcasts of Israel, specifically the eunuchs and the foreigners of whom the Assyrian and Babylonian wars had produced a great number, that by observing the Sabbath they would share in the blessings of God's covenant people, "for my house shall be called a house of prayer for all peoples" (Is. 56:1-7).

Many social injustices could have been avoided in the ancient and modern society if the concern for human rights expressed by the Sabbath (and its sister institutions) had always been understood and practiced. The Sabbath forces upon us the important issues of freedom and humanitarian concern for all, from our son to our servant (Ex. 20:10; 23:12; Deut. 5:14). By placing such issues before us at the moment of worship—the moment when we are truest to ourselves—, the Sabbath cannot leave us insensitive toward the suffering or social injustices experienced by others. It is impossible on the Sabbath to celebrate Creation and Redemption while hating those whom God has created and redeemed through His Son. True Sabbathkeeping demands that we acknowledge the Fatherhood of God by accepting and strengthening the brotherhood of mankind. The bond of brotherhood which the Sabbath establishes through its worship, fellowship and humanitarian services influences by reflex our social relationships during the week. To accept on the Sabbath those who belong to ethnic minorities or to a lower social status as brothers and sisters in Christ demands that we treat them as such during the weekdays as well. It would be a denial of the human values and experience of the Sabbath, if one were to exploit or detest during the week those whom the Sabbath teaches us to respect and love as God's creatures. By teaching us to accept and respect every person, whether rich or poor, black or white, as human beings created and redeemed by the Lord, the Sabbath breaks down and equalizes those social, racial, and cultural barriers which cause much tension and unrest in our society and consequently it makes it possible for the peace of Christ to dwell in our hearts.

6. *Rest of Redemption*

A sixth way in which Sabbathkeeping brings Christ's rest to our lives is by enabling us to experience through the physical rest the greater blessings of divine rest and peace of salvation. The relationship between the Sabbath rest and Christ's redemption-rest was examined in chapter V. There we saw that from the symbol of God's initial entrance into *human time,* the Sabbath became after the Fall the symbol of God's promise to enter *human flesh* to become "Emmanuel—God with us." The rest and liberation from the hardship of work, and from social inequalities which both the weekly and annual Sabbaths granted to all the members of the Hebrew society, was understood not merely as a commemoration of the past Exodus deliverance (Deut. 5:15), but also a prefiguration of the future redemption-rest to be brought by the Messiah. Christ fulfilled these OT Messianic expectations typified by the Sabbath (cf. Luke 4:21) by identifying His redemptive mission with the Good News of release and redemption of the Sabbath, thus making the day the fitting vehicle through which to experience His rest of salvation.

It was on a Sabbath day that, according to Luke (4:16-21), Christ inaugurated His public ministry in the synagogue of Nazareth by quoting a passage from Isaiah (61:1-2) and by claiming emphatically to be the fulfilment of the sabbatical liberation announced in that passage. In His subsequent ministry, we found that Christ substantiated this claim by revealing His redemptive mission especially through His Sabbath healing and teaching ministry (cf. Luke 13:16; Matt. 12:5-6; John 5:17; 7:22-23). Finally, it was on that historic holy Sabbath that Christ completed His redemptive mission ("It is finished"—John 19:30) by resting in the tomb (Luke 23:54-56). Christ's Sabbath rest in the tomb reveals the depth of God's love for His creatures. It tells us that in order to give them life, He was willing to experience not only the limitation of *human time* at creation but also the suffering, agony and death of *human flesh* during the incarnation. In the light of the cross, then, the Sabbath is a time to celebrate not only the Good News of God's perfect creation but also the Glad Tidings of Christ's complete redemption: it is the weekly celebration and jubilation of a liberated people; it is the day when we cease from our work to allow God to work in us, to bring to our lives His rest of forgiveness and salvation.

7. *Rest of Service*

A seventh way in which the Sabbath brings Christ's rest to our lives is by providing time and opportunities for service. Inner peace and rest are to be found not in *egocentric* (selfish) *relaxation* but rather in *heterocentric* (unselfish) *service*. The various types of service contemplated and made possible by the Sabbath have been considered in chapter VI. The study has shown that the Sabbath provides the time and the reasons for serving God, self, others and our habitat. We serve God on the Sabbath by resting to acknowledge His claim over our lives and by worshiping to celebrate His marvelous creation, redemption and ultimate restoration. This celebration of God's goodness offers us a fresh experience of divine rest and peace in our lives. We serve our personal needs on the Sabbath by taking time to reorder our lives, to sharpen our moral consciousness, to experience divine forgiveness, presence and rest.

We serve others on the Sabbath by coming closer to loved ones, friends and needy persons, sharing with them our friendship and concern. The service we render unto others on the Sabbath honors God and enriches our lives with a sense of restful satisfaction. We serve our habitat on the Sabbath by learning to act as *curators* rather than *predators* of this earth; by taking time to *admire* rather than to *exploit* God's creation; by experiencing rest and peace through the appreciation of God's creation.

Does the Sabbath bring divine rest to our human restlessness? This study has shown that the Sabbath does enable the Savior to bring perfect rest to our lives by offering us the opportunity to experience the rest of creation, the rest of divine presence, the rest of belonging, the rest from competition, the rest from social tensions, the rest of redemption and the rest of service. Is the Sabbath, then, Good News or bad news? A day of celebration or of frustration? We have found in the Scriptures that the Sabbath expresses God's Best News to the human family: the Good News that the Lord has created us perfectly, that He has redeemed us completely, that He loves us immensely and that He will restore us ultimately.

In this cosmic age, the Good News of the Sabbath provides the basis for a cosmic faith, a faith which embraces and unites creation, redemption and final restoration; the past, the present and the future; man, nature and God; this world and the world to come; a faith that recognizes God's dominion over the whole creation and human life by consecrating to Him the seventh day; a faith that fulfills the believer's true destiny in time and eternity; a faith that offers *Divine Rest for Human Restlessness*.

A FACSIMILE REPRODUCTION

OF THE COVER

A Historical Investigation
of the Rise of
Sunday Observance
in Early Christianity

SAMUELE BACCHIOCCHI

THE PONTIFICAL GREGORIAN
UNIVERSITY PRESS
ROME 1977

The following essay represents a brief summary of the writer's published dissertation. The facsimile reproduction of the cover is shown on the previous page. The book is distributed by the author. To purchase a copy mail your order (US $9.95, postage paid) to:

Dr. Samuele Bacchiocchi
230 Lisa Lane
Berrien Springs
Michigan 49103, USA

APPENDIX

FROM SABBATH TO SUNDAY

A Synopsis of the Published Dissertation [1]

The question of how and when the first day of the week—Sunday—came to be adopted by a majority of Christians as the day of rest and worship in place of the Biblically-ordained seventh-day Sabbath has long been debated. Especially in recent years, numerous studies, including several doctoral dissertations, have re-examined this question.[2] This renewed effort to ascertain the Biblical basis and historical genesis of Sunday observance may well reflect the desire to reassess its validity and relevance at a time when social and economic pressures are threatening its survival.

1. *Historical Views on the Origin of Sunday*

Traditionally the adoption of Sunday observance in place of the seventh-day Sabbath has been attributed to ecclesiastical authority rather than to Biblical precept or mandate. Thomas Aquinas (d. 1274), for example, states categorically: "In the New Law the observance of the Lord's day took the place of the observance of the Sabbath, not by virtue of the precept [Fourth Commandment] but by the institution of the Church."[3] The same view was reiterated three centuries later in the *Catechism of the Council of Trent* (1566), which states, "It pleased the Church of God that the religious celebration of the Sabbath day should be transferred to 'the Lord's day.'"[4] During the theological controversies of the sixteenth century, Catholic theologians often appealed to the ecclesiastical origin of Sunday in order to prove the power of their Church to introduce new laws and ceremonies.[5] The echo of such a controversy can be detected even in the historical Lutheran *Augsburg Confession* (1530), which states: "They [the Catholics] refer to the Sabbath-day as having been changed into the Lord's Day, contrary to the Decalogue, as it seems. Neither is there any example whereof they make more than concerning the changing of the Sabbath-day. Great, say they, is the power of the Church, since it has dispensed with one of the Ten Commandments!"[6]

The *Augsburg Confession* acknowledges the post-Biblical ecclesiastical origin of Sunday and accepts the right of the Church to introduce ordinances such as Sunday observance but refutes the Church's authority to make the keeping of any holy day into a thing "necessary to salvation." [7]   Similarly Calvin viewed Sunday as a human rather than divine institution. In his *Institutes of the Christian Religion*, Calvin explains: "It being expedient to overthrow superstition, the Jewish holiday was abolished; and as a thing necessary to retain decency, order, and peace in the Church ... the early Christians substituted what we call the Lord's day for the Sabbath." [8]   In the centuries following the Reformation two major and opposing views have been held and hotly debated regarding the origin and nature of Sunday. One view has maintained that Sunday originated by divine authority at the very inception of Christianity in order to commemorate the Lord's resurrection on the first day of the week. The supporters of this view have generally defended Sunday as the legitimate substitution of the seventh-day Sabbath, thus dependent like the latter upon the Fourth Commandment. Among the many theologians and confessional documents that have upheld this position, some of the most significant are: Erasmus (d. 1536),[9] Theodore Beza (d. 1605),[10] *Second Helvetic Confession* (1566),[11] Nicolas Bownde (d. 1607),[12] Antonius Walaeus (d. 1639),[13] Hamon L'Estrange (1641),[14] *Synod of Dort* (1619),[15] *Westminster Confession* (1647); [16] Gisbertus Voetius (d. 1676),[17] John Owen (d. 1683),[18] Henry Wilkinson (d. 1690),[19] Jonathan Edwards (d. 1758),[20] William Paley (d. 1805),[21] James Augustus Hessey (1860).[22]

A second view has regarded Sunday as an ecclesiastical institution independent of the Fourth Commandment. Some of the defenders of this view have placed the origin of Sunday within the apostolic age, others after it. The reason for its introduction supposedly was mainly pragmatic, namely to provide free time for public worship and rest to the workers. Generally this view has encouraged a more permissive type of Sunday observance, allowing work, sports and entertainments. Some of the significant exponents of this view have been: the Catholic Church,[23] Luther (d. 1546),[24] Calvin to some extent (d. 1564),[25] William Tyndale (d. 1536),[26] Thomas Cranmer (d. 1556),[27] John Prideaux (d. 1650),[28] Hugo Grotius (d. 1645),[29] Franciscus Gomarus (d. 1641),[30] Peter Heylyn (d. 1662),[31] John Cocceius (d. 1669),[32] John Milton (d. 1674),[33] John Samuel Stayk (d. 1710),[34] Edward Evanson (d. 1805),[35] Richard Whately (1830),[36] C. C. L. Franke (1826),[37] William Domville (1850),[38] and E. W. Hengstenberg (d. 1869).[39]

The debate over the origin and nature of Sunday is far from over. Major works have appeared recently on both sides of the Atlantic presenting two major explanations for the historical genesis and theological basis of Sunday observance. These explanations basically reflect the two historical positions mentioned above. One view, defended by scholars such as J. Francke, F. N. Lee, S. C. Mosna, Paul K. Jewett and the joint work of R. T. Beckwith and W. Stott,[40] argues that Sunday is a Biblical institution which originated with the Lord's resurrection on the first day of the week as the legitimate substitution of the seventh-day Sabbath. Consequently Sunday is regarded as the Christian Sabbath to be observed in accordance with the Fourth Commandment. The second view differs from the first in minimizing the Biblical basis for Sunday observance and in denying any link between Sunday and the Fourth Commandment. It holds that, unlike the Sabbath, Sunday originated not as a day of rest but as a brief time of worship which occurred before or after the hours of work. It was only in the fourth century that Sunday became a day of rest as a result of Constantine's decree in 321. The exponents of this view place the historical genesis of Sunday at different times. Willy Rordorf, for example, argues that Sunday worship began in conjunction with the appearances of the Risen Christ which supposedly set the pattern for a regular eucharistic celebration on every Sunday.[41]

The monumental symposium (about 700 pages) sponsored by the Tyndale Fellowship for Biblical Research in Cambridge, England and written by Professors D. A. Carson, Harold H. P. Dressler, C. Rowland, M. M. B. Turner, D. R. de Lacey, A. T. Lincoln, and R. J. Bauckham, concludes that "it is barely imaginable that first day Sabbath observance ... commenced before the Jerusalem council [A.D. 49]. Nor can we stop there. We must go on to maintain that first day Sabbath observance cannot easily be understood as a phenomenon of the apostolic age and of apostolic authority, at all." [42] A somewhat later date for the origin of Sunday is suggested by Hiley H. Ward in his book *Space-Age Sunday*. He argues that Sunday arose not as an "approximation" but "as an antithesis to the Sabbath" sometime between the first (A.D. 70) and the second (A.D. 135) Jewish war. A main factor in the rise of first-day worship was "convenience," that is, the practical necessity to dissociate from the Jews at a time when the Roman government adopted repressive measures against them on account of their frequent revolts.[43]

In the light of the ongoing debate, this study represents a renewed effort to hoping clarify the question of the time, place and causes of the origin of Sunday worship. Did this originate in Jerusalem during the lifetime of the apostles and by their authority to commemorate Christ's resurrection by means of the Lord's Supper celebration, or did it start sometime later, somewhere else and owing to differing factors? This clarification and verification of the historical genesis of Sundaykeeping is of great importance, since it may explicate not only the causes of its origin but also its applicability to Christians today.

2. *The Resurrection and the Origin of Sunday*

The resurrection and/or appearances of Christ which occurred on the first day of the week are generally regarded as the fundamental factor which determined the early abandonment of Sabbath-keeping and the institution of Sunday worship.[44] Do the earliest documentary sources support this popular claim? My own assessment of the sources indicates that this claim rests more on fantasies than on facts. No sayings can be found in the NT enjoining or suggesting to commemorate Christ's resurrection on the actual day on which it occurred. In fact, Sunday is called in the NT never "Day of the Resurrection," but consistently "first day of the week." Nowhere does the NT suggest that the Lord's Supper was celebrated on Sunday or that it commemorated Christ's resurrection. Paul, who claims to transmit what he "received from the Lord" (1 Cor. 11:23), repeatedly implies that the rite was celebrated at *indeterminate* time and days ("when you come together"—1 Cor. 11:18, 20, 33, 34)[45] and explicitly states that by partaking of the elements Christians "proclaim *the Lord's death* till he comes" (11:26). It is Christ's *sacrifice* and not His resurrection that Paul explicitly mentions.[46]

Does the fact that Christ was resurrected on Sunday presuppose that Christians should celebrate the event by resting and worshiping on the first day of the week? It would seem that the resurrection event per se presupposes work rather than rest. Why? At least for two reasons. First because it marks not the completion of Christ's earthly mission—which ended on Friday afternoon when the Savior said "It is finished" (John 19:30) and then rested on the Sabbath in the tomb—but rather the inauguration of Christ's new ministry. As the first day of creation so the first day of Christ's new ministration presupposes work rather than rest. Second, the very words spoken by the Risen Lord contain injunctions not to "come apart and celebrate my resurrection" but rather to "go and tell my brethren to go to Galilee" (Matt. 28:10; cf. Mark 16:7); "Go therefore and make disciples of all nations, baptizing them..." (Matt. 28:19; cf. Mark 16:15); "go to my brethren" (John 20:17); "Feed my sheep" (John 21:17). None of these utterances suggest a celebration of the resurrection by worshiping and/or resting on Sunday.

Was Christ's resurrection commemorated during NT times at the Passover celebration as many Christians do today? This hardly seems to be the case. Paul urges the Corinthians to "celebrate the [Passover] festival" in which "Christ, our paschal lamb, has been sacrificed" (1 Cor. 5:7-8). It is Christ's *sacrifice* rather than His *resurrection* that is explicitly associated with the Passover. The same meaning of the Passover is found in the earliest Eastern and Western documents which discuss the celebration of this festival. The apocryphal *Epistle of the Apostles* (about 150) urges to "celebrate the remembrance of my death, i.e. the passover." [47] The suffering and death of Jesus constitute also the recurring theme of Melito's *Sermon on the Passover* (about 170) where the very name "Passover" is mistakenly explained as a derivation from the verb "to suffer—*tou pathein.*" [48] Irenaeus (about 175) writes that Moses knew and "foretold ... the day of His [Christ] passion ... by the name given to the passover." [49]

In a Roman *Passover Homily*, most probably by Bishop Callistus (d. about 222), the Christian Passover is interpreted as the celebration of the sacrifice of the true Paschal lamb: "Here [Jewish Passover] a lamb is taken from the flock, there [Christian] a lamb that came from heaven; here the sign of blood . . . there the cup filled with blood and spirit." [50] In his analysis of these documents Marcel Richard expresses his surprise that the memory of the resurrection is even less evident in the Roman *Passover Homily* than in that of Melito.[51] Similar testimonies by Clement of Alexandria (d. about 220) and by Hippolytus (d. about 236) confirm that not only in Asia but also in Rome and Alexandria Passover was celebrated during the second century (whether on Nisan 14 or on Sunday) primarily as a memorial of Christ's suffering and sacrifice.[52]

The earliest explicit references to the Christian observance of Sunday are by Barnabas (about 135) and Justin Martyr (about 150). Both writers do mention the resurrection as a basis for Sunday observance but only as the second of two reasons, important but not predominant.[53] (This is not to deny the fact that in time the resurrection of Christ did become the primary theological motivation for Sunday worship.) [54] These and other indications discussed elsewhere discredit the contention that the origin of Sunday "is to be found solely in the fact of the Resurrection of Christ on the day after the Sabbath." [55]

3. *The Jerusalem Church and the Origin of Sunday*

Did the Jerusalem Church pioneer the adoption of Sunday observance in place of the seventh-day Sabbath? This popular thesis rests on several assumptions. It is assumed, for example, that since the resurrection and some of the appearances of Christ occurred on a Sunday in Jerusalem, Sunday worship presumably originated in the city itself by apostolic authority to commemorate these very events by a distinctive Christian day and worship. It is also presumed that since the change in the day of worship could be accomplished only by a church enjoying pre-eminent authority, the Jerusalem Church—the Mother Church of Christendom—is the only logical birthplace of such a change. Furthermore, the absence of any trace of a Sabbath-Sunday controversy between Paul and the Judaizing party is interpreted as indicating that first-day worship was early established by the apostolic authority residing in the Jerusalem Church and consequently Paul accepted the new day of worship as an accomplished fact.[56] Are these assumptions validated or invalidated by the earliest historical information on the Jerusalem Church? An objective evaluation of the evidences leaves us with no uncertain answer.

Ethnic composition and theological orientation. The book of Acts as well as several Judeo-Christians documents[57] persuasively demonstrate that both the ethnic composition and the theological orientation of the Jerusalem Church were profoundly Jewish. Throughout the book of Acts Luke reports again and again mass conversion of the Jews: 2:41; 4:4; 5:14; 6:1, 7; 9:42; 12:24; 13:43; 14:1; 17:10ff; 21:20. These converts included "devout" Jews (Acts 2:5, 41), "many of the priests" (Acts 6:7) and "many thousands" of Jews who had been and remained (note "are") "zealous for the law" (Acts 21:20). Jacob Jervell analyze., these references, interpreting them as showing that for Luke the mission to the Jews was indeed successful. The thousands of converted Jews are never viewed as a *new* Israel but as part of the *old* Israel who is *restored* in accordance with the promises God made in the OT (Acts 15:16-18; 1:6; 3:11-26).[58] "Because Jewish Christian are the restored Israel," Jervell maintains, "circumcision and the law become the very marks of their identity."[59]

Jervell's reconstruction of Luke's ecclesiology, according to which the converted Jews represent the restored Israel (Acts 15:16-18) through whom salvation is extended to the Gentiles, is somewhat too monolithic, failing to consider sufficiently the decisive impact of Christ's teaching and ministry.[60] Yet his claim that "Luke attaches importance to the Mosaic law and to the primitive church and Jewish Christians as being zealous for the law"[61] can hardly be disputed. Luke describes the Jerusalem Christians basically as pious Jewish believers who attend the temple (Acts 2:46; 3:1; 5:12), practice and promote the need for circumcision (Acts 11:2; 15:1, 5, 23; 16:3; 21:22; cf. Gal. 2:12; 3:1; 5:12; 6:12) and receive instruction from the Scriptures "every sabbath in the synagogues" (Acts 15:21; cf. 13:27). Christian attendance at the synagogue on the Sabbath extends beyond Jerusalem. Luke reports that Paul met regularly in the synagogue on the Sabbath with "Jews and Greeks" (Acts

18:4, 19; cf. 13:5, 14, 42, 44) and describes such an attendance as customary for Paul (Acts 17:2). Apollo, likewise, when he arrived at Ephesus, met with the believers in the synagogue (Acts 18:24-26).

The role of James. The profound attachment of the early Jerusalem Church to Jewish religious traditions and services is exemplified by the role of James as the defender of the law (Acts 15:1, 24; cf. Gal. 2:12). His election to the leadership of the Jerusalem Church was apparently supported by priestly and Pharisee converts (Acts 6:7; 15:5) who would naturally endorse James on account of his legendary adherence to the law. The latter is confirmed by several Judeo-Christian documents which stress also the "blood factor." [62] Being the "Lord's brother" (Gal. 1:19), James could claim blood relation to Christ and thus fulfill the role of a legitimate Christian "high-priest." [63] This reveals how Jewish-oriented the new Christian "priesthood" and leadership really were in the city. More relevant to our inquiry into the possible origin of Sunday observance in Jerusalem is the basic attitude of James and his party toward OT legal obligations.

At the first Christian council held (about 49-50) in the city of Jerusalem there was "much debate" (Acts 15:7) on whether or not Gentile Christians should be exempted from circumcision. Peter, Paul and Barnabas (vv. 7, 12) expressed their views on the matter, but the final word came from James, who endorsed the exemption from circumcision for the Gentiles but proposed that these should be notified "to abstain from pollution of idols and unchastity and from what is strangled and from blood. For from early generations Moses has had in every city those who preach him, for he is read every Sabbath in the synagogues" (vv. 20-21). The significance of James' proposal, which was adopted and implemented by the Council (Acts 15:20, 29; 21:25), lies in the fact that it contains several provisions which are clearly ceremonial (abstention from "pollution of idols and from what is strangled and from blood"—v. 20). The excessive concern of James and of the Apostles (Acts 15:22) that the Gentiles should respect the Jewish scruples regarding food laws and ritual defilment hardly allows for a unanimous abrogation of a weightier matter such as Sabbath observance. The very exemption from the circumcision was granted *only* "to the brethren who are of the Gentiles" (Acts 15:23). No concession was contemplated for the Jewish-Christians who continued to practice and to promote circumcision (Acts 21:24; Gal. 2:12; 5:12; 6:12).

It is noteworthy also that the authority of the apostolic decree stems from its being in harmony with the prophets (Acts 15:15-18) and Moses (v. 21). Several scholars have argued that the four provisions of the decree may well represent "what Leviticus 17-18 demands from the 'strangers' that sojourn among Israelites." [64] In that case the apostolic decree would represent not an abrogation but an application of the law to the Gentiles on the basis of the Mosaic provisions contemplated for the sojourner.[65] The statement made by James to support his proposal is also significant in this regard: "for from early generations Moses has had in every city those who preach him, for he is read every sabbath in the synagogues" (Acts 15:21). Though James' remark has been applied to different people (Gentiles, Christians, Jewish Christians, both, and the Christian Pharisaic party), most interpreters recognize that both in his proposal and in its justification, James reaffirms the binding nature of the Mosaic law which was customarily preached and read every Sabbath in the synagogues.

Paul's last visit to Jerusalem. The account of Paul's last visit to Jerusalem (Acts 21—A.D. 58-60), as well as Luke's mention that Paul "was hastening to be at Jerusalem, if possible, on the day of Pentecost" (Acts 20:16) and that they had spent the days of "Unleavened Bread" at Philippi (Acts 20:6), suggests that the Jewish liturgical calendar was still normative for Christians. What happened in Jerusalem itself is especially enlightening. James and the elders not only informed Paul that the many thousands of converted Jews were *"all zealous for the law"* (Acts 21:20), but they even pressured the apostle to prove that he himself "live[d] *in observance of the law"* (Acts 21:24), by undergoing a rite of purification at the temple. In the light of this deep commitment to the observance of the Law, it is hardly conceivable that the Jerusalem Church would have abrogated one of its chief precepts—Sabbathkeeping—and pioneered Sunday worship instead. As M. M. B. Turner rightly notes, "The lead given by James, whose Jewish piety was legendary, and by the conservative (priestly and Pharisee) element of the Jerusalem eldership, would have ensured Sabbath observation in Jerusalem and in the satellite churches." [66]

The Jerusalem Church after A.D. 70. The situation hardly changed after the Roman destruction of the temple in A.D. 70. The historians Eusebius (about 260-340) and Epiphanius (about 315-403) inform us that up to the seige of Hadrian (135), the Jerusalem Church was composed of and administered by converted Jews, characterized as "zealous to insist on the literal observance of the Law." [67] In fact, the orthodox Palestinian Jewish-Christian sect of the Nazarenes, who are generally regarded as "the very direct descendants of the primitive community" [68] of Jerusalem, according to Epiphanius, still observed in the fourth century OT practices such as "the circumcision, the Sabbath and others." [69] The implication is clear. The traditional custom of Sabbathkeeping survived among Palestinian Christians long after the destruction of the temple.

This conclusion is corroborated by the "Curse of the Christians"

(*Birkath-ha-Minim*), a prayer introduced by the Palestinian rabbinical authorities (about 80-90) to bar clandestine Jewish-Christian participation in Jewish synagogue services.[70] Participation by Palestinian Christians in synagogue services hardly suggests their pioneering a new day of worship. These historical data discredit any attempt to make Jerusalem the champion of liturgical innovations such as Sunday worship.[71] Of all the Christian Churches, this was both racially and theologically the most deeply rooted in Jewish religious traditions.

Hadrian's policy. Radical changes occurred in the Jewish world after A.D. 135. In that year the Roman Emperor Hadrian crushed the Second Jewish Revolt which had been unsuccessfully led by Barkokeba (132-135). Jerusalem became a Roman colony from which Jews and Jewish-Christians were excluded. Hadrian at this time prohibited the practice of the Jewish religion throughout the empire, condemning especially Sabbath observance.[72] These repressive anti-Jewish policies encouraged the production of a "Christian" *Against the Jews—Adversus Judaeos—*literature, advocating separation from and contempt for the Jews.[73] Characteristic Jewish customs such as circumcision and Sabbathkeeping were particularly condemned. These are circumstantial but impressive indications suggesting that Sunday observance was introduced at this time in conjunction with Easter-Sunday, as an attempt to clarify to the Roman authorities the Christian distinction from Judaism. To these indications we must now turn our attention.

4. *Rome and the Origin of Sunday*

New religious festivals such as Sunday observance could presumably be adopted and promoted only by a church that severed its ties with Judaism *early* and that enjoyed wide recognition. As we have seen, this excludes the Jerusalem Church prior to A.D. 135. After that time the Jerusalem Church lost its religious prestige and went almost into oblivion, thus it could hardly have pioneered such an important change. A most likely church appears to be that of the capital city of Rome, since significant social, religious and political conditions existed in the Roman Church which permitted and encouraged the abandonment of the Sabbath and the adoption of Sunday worship instead.

Characteristics of the Church of Rome. Contrary to most Eastern churches, the Church of Rome was composed predominantly of Gentiles converts. In his Epistle to this Church, Paul explicitly affirms: "I am speaking to you Gentiles: (Rom. 11:13).[74] The result was that in Rome, as well stated by Leonard Goppelt, "a chasm between the Church and the Synagogue is found everywhere, unknown in the Eastern Churches." [75]   The predominant Gentile membership apparently contributed to an early differentiation from the Jews in Rome. In A.D. 64, for instance, Nero clearly distinguished the Jews from the Christians when he placed the charge of arson exclusively on the latter.[76] The fact that the process of Christian differentiation from the Jews occurred earlier in Rome that in Palestine suggests the possibility that a new day of worship could have first been introduced in Rome as part of this process of differentiation from Judaism. To understand the possible causes for this development, it is necessary to consider briefly the relationship between the Empire and the Jews at this time.

Beginning with the First Jewish Revolt against Rome (66 to 70), various repressive measures—military, political and fiscal—were imposed by the Romans upon the Jews, on account of the Jewish resurgent nationalism which exploded in violent uprisings in places such as Mesopotamia, Cyrenaica, Palestine, Egypt and Cyprus. Militarily, according to contemporary historians, over a million Jews were slain in Palestine alone during the two major Jewish wars (70 and 135).[77] Politically, Vespasian (69-79) abolished the Sanhedrin and the office of the High Priest; later Hadrian (about 135) out-lawed the practice of Judaism altogether, *particularly Sabbathkeeping.*[78] Fiscally, the Jews were subjected to a discriminatory tax (the *fiscus judaicus*) which was introduced by Vespasian and increased first by Domitian (81-96) and later by Hadrian (117-138).[79]

That these repressive measures were intensively experienced in Rome is indicated by the contemptuous anti-Jewish literary comments of such writers as Seneca (d. 65), Persius (34-62), Petronius (about 66), Quintillian (about 35-100), Martial (40-104), Plutarch (46-119), Juvenal (about 125) and Tacitus (about 55-120), all of whom lived in Rome during most of their professional lives. They revile the Jews racially and culturally, deriding Sabbathkeeping and circumcision as examples of Judaism's degrading superstitions.[80]

The mounting hostility of the Roman populace against the Jews forced Titus, though "unwillingly" (*invitus*), to ask the Jewess Berenice, sister of Herod the Younger, whom he wanted to marry, to leave Rome.[81] The Jewish problem, as we noticed earlier, became particularly acute by Hadrian's time as a result of the Emperor's policy of radical suppression of the Jewish religion. These circumstances, as well as the conflict between Jews and Christians, encouraged the production of a whole body of anti-Jewish literature which developed a "Christian" theology of separation from and contempt for the Jews.[82] A practical outcome of this development was the substitution of characteristic Jewish festivities such as Passover and the Sabbath with Easter-Sunday and the weekly Sunday.

Rome and the Sabbath.   The epicenter of this development

appears to have been the Church of Rome where theological, social and liturgical measures were taken to wean Christians away from Sabbath veneration in order to enhance Sunday worship exclusively. *Theologically*, the Sabbath was reduced from a universal to a temporary Mosaic ordinance, which, as stated by Justin Martyr, God imposed exclusively on the Jews as "a mark to single them out for punishment they so well deserve for their infidelities." [83] *Socially*, the Sabbath was transformed from a traditional day of feasting and gladness into a day of fasting and gloom. The role of the Church of Rome in pioneering and promoting the Sabbath fast is well attested by the historical references from Bishop Callistus (217-222), Hippolytus (170-236), Bishop Sylvester (314-335), Pope Innocent I (401-417), Augustine (354-430) and John Cassian (360-435).[84] The Saturday fast served not only to express sorrow for Christ's death, but also, as emphatically stated by Bishop Sylvester, to show "contempt for the Jews—*exsecratione Judaeorum*" and for their Sabbath "feasting—*destructiones ciborum*." [85] The sadness and hunger resulting from the fast would enable Christians to avoid "appearing to observe the Sabbath with the Jews" [86] and would encourage them to enter more eagerly and joyfully into the observance of Sunday. *Liturgically*, the Sabbath was made into a non-religious day in which no eucharistic celebration was allowed since partaking of its elements would be regarded as breaking the fast.[87]

Most probably the weekly Sabbath fast developed as an extension or counterpart of the annual Holy Saturday of Easter season when all Christians fasted.[88] The latter, in fact, like the former, was designed to express not only sorrow for Christ's death but also contempt for its perpetrators, namely the Jews.[89] Moreover, since the weekly and the annual Saturday fasts as well as the weekly Sunday and Easter-Sunday are frequently presented by the Fathers as interrelated in their meaning and function,[90] presumably all these practices originated somewhat simultaneously as part of the Easter-Sunday celebration. It is important, therefore, to ascertain the time, place and causes of the origin of Easter-Sunday, since this could well mark the genesis of Sunday observance as well.

Rome and Easter-Sunday. The scarcity of documents and the controversial nature of their information make it very difficult to determine with absolute certainty where, when and by whom Easter-Sunday was first introduced. The historian Eusebius (about 260-340) provides the major account of the controversy that erupted in the second century between the Church of Rome which championed the Easter-Sunday date and the Asiatic Christians who defended the celebration of Passover on Nisan 14 (known as Quartodeciman tradition).[91] Being a strong supporter of the Easter-Sunday celebration made official by the Council of Nicaea (325), Eusebius does not hesitate to attribute to it an apostolic origin. In fact in introducing his report of the controversy, he explicitly affirms that Easter-Sunday "from apostolic tradition has prevailed to the present time" and again in concluding it, he ascribes to Palestinian synods (held about 198 at the request of Bishop Victor of Rome) the view that Easter-Sunday had come down "from the apostles." [92]

By these categorical affirmations, Eusebius has indeed succeeded in misleading some scholars credulously to accept the apostolic origin of Easter-Sunday.[93] A careful reading of Eusebius' account, however, leaves no doubt as to the bias and inaccuracy of his statements. As noted by Marcel Richard, "from the beginning of his account we observe that he [Eusebius] defines the Quartodeciman Passover as an ' old tradition ' while he reserves the 'apostolic tradition' for Easter-Sunday which he calls without hesitation 'the day of the resurrection of the Lord,' a very remarkable anachronism." [94] The anachronism is obvious, since Eusebius defines the Passover as "the mystery of the resurrection" [95] which, he implies, even the Quartodecimans celebrated, though on a different day. The latter is indicated by Eusebius' summary of the "ecclesiastical decree" promulgated by Synods summoned at the request of Bishop Victor (about 198). Supposedly the decree enjoined "that the mystery of the resurrection of the Lord should be celebrated *on no other* but the Lord's day." [96] The obvious implication is that "the mystery of the resurrection" had previously been celebrated on other days besides Sunday, an inference which is untrue. The earliest references from both the Easter-Sunday and the Quartodeciman tradition, as noted earlier, speak of the Passover as being primarily the celebration of Christ's *passion* rather than of His *resurrection*.[97] Tertullian (about 160-225), for example, refers to "*the passover of the Lord*, that is, the *passion of Christ*." [98] That this was the prevailing understanding is indicated also by Origen's attempt to refute the "passion" interpretation of the Passover by appealing to the etymological meaning of the Hebrew word *pesah*, which means "to pass over." [99]

The bias of Eusebius is even more glaring in his treatment of the origin of the Quartodeciman Passover. In introducing the two significant letters of Polycarp and Irenaeus, in each instance Eusebius presents the Quartodeciman tradition as an "old custom" and "ancient custom" but not as an "apostolic tradition." [100] The latter is reserved exclusively for Easter Sunday.[101] Yet the very documents cited by Eusebius twice proclaim emphatically the apostolic origin of the Quartodeciman Passover while they are silent over the alleged apostolicity of Easter-Sunday.[102] In the light of his concern to defend the apostolic origin of Easter-Sunday, Eusebius would not have missed the chance to substantiate such a claim by quoting a document supporting it, if only such a document had existed.[103] The portion of the letter of Irenaeus quoted by Eusebius rather suggests that Easter-Sunday originated in the early part of the second century. This is implied by Irenaeus' appeal to Bishop Victor of Rome (about 189-199) to emulate his predecessors, namely "Anicetus and Pius and Hyginus and Telephorus and Sixtus," [104] who, though they celebrated Easter on Sunday, nevertheless were at peace with those who observed it on Nisan 14. Irenaeus' mention of Bishop Sixtus (about 116-126) as the first non-observant of the Quartodeciman Passover suggests the possibility that Easter-sunday began to be celebrated in Rome on Sunday at about that time.[105]

This conclusion has been drawn by a good number of scholars. Henri Leclercq, for example, on the basis of Irenaeus' testimony places the origin of Easter-Sunday "toward the beginning of the second century, under the episcopate of Sixtus I in Rome, about the year 120." [106] Similarly Karl Baus writes: "It is no longer possible to determine when and by whom this Sunday Passover was introduced in Rome, but it must have become established there early in the second century, for Irenaeus plainly assumes the festival to have existed in the time of the Roman Bishop Xystus." [107] J. Jeremiah also remarks: "Irenaeus traces the Roman Sunday-Easter back to Xystus (c. 120), though he is not giving a time for the introduction of the paschal feast to Rome." [108]

The hypothesis of a Roman origin of Easter-Sunday at about the time of Sixtus is indirectly supported by Epiphanius' statement that the Easter-Controversy "arose after the time of the exodus of the bishops of the circumcision" from Jerusalem.[109] Such an exodus was ordered by Emperor Hadrian in A.D. 135 after crushing the Second Jewish Revolt. The Emperor, as noted earlier, adopted a policy of radical repression of Jewish rites and customs. To avoid such repressive measures Bishop Sixtus could well have taken steps to substitute characteristic Jewish festivals such as the weekly Sabbath and the annual Passover, with weekly Sunday and Easter-Sunday. The introduction of Easter-Sunday a few years later in Jerusalem by the new Greek bishops who replaced the Jewish-Christian leaders apparently met the resistance of those who were not prepared to accept such a change.

While the exact time of the origin of Easter-Sunday may be a subject of dispute, there seems to be a wide consensus of scholarly opinion regarding Rome as its birthplace. Some scholars, in fact, rightly label it as "Roman-Easter." [110] This is suggested not only by the role played by the Church of Rome in enforcing the new custom, but also by later historical sources. In two related documents, namely the conciliar letter of the Council of Nicaea (325) and Constantine's personal letter addressed to all the bishops, the

Church of Rome is presented as the first example to emulate on the matter of Easter-Sunday, undoubtedly because of her historical position and role in championing its observance.[111]

Widespread of Easter-Sunday. What caused many Christians to abandon the Quartodeciman Passover and to adopt Easter-Sunday instead? Was it a felt necessity, as in the case of the abandonment of the Sabbath, to dissociate from the Jews and their religious practices? Most scholars acknowledge anti-Judaism as an important factor. J. Jeremias, for example, sees "the inclination to break away from Judaism" as the major reason which led Rome and other churches to shift the celebration of the feast from the date of the Jewish Passover to the following Sunday.[112] Similarly J. B. Lightfoot holds, for example, that Rome and Alexandria adopted Easter-Sunday to avoid "even the semblance of Judaism."[113] Kenneth A. Strand rejects this explanation, arguing that "anti-Jewish sentiments are clear in the earliest second-century references to the weekly Sabbath and Sunday, but the opposite is the case regarding Quartodeciman-ism and the Easter Sunday. . . . Indeed, the very point in Irenaeus' letter to Victor is that the Roman bishops from Sixtus to Anicetus had *cordial relationships with the Quartodecimans.*"[114]

Strand's argument fails to recognize significant facts. In the first place, an apparent "cordial relationship" between Quartodeci-mans and Easter-Sunday observers does not preclude the existence of anti-Judaic sentiments. Justin Martyr, for example, speaking of those Christian Sabbathkeepers who did not compel others to keep the Sabbath, expressively states: "I hold that we ought to join our-selves to such, and associate with them in all things as kinsmen and brethren."[115] Yet we noticed earlier that Justin viewed the Sabbath as a trademark of Jewish depravity. This shows that "cordial relationships" and "anti-Jewish sentiments" were not neces-sarily mutually exclusive. Second, Strand's contention that "anti-Jewish sentiments" were present in the Sabbath/Sunday controversy but absent in the Quartodeciman and Sunday Passover, is hardly accurate. The very first *Paschal Homily* which has come down to us (by Melito of Sardis, about 170), interprets the Passover in the light of the "extraordinary murder" of Christ by the Jews:

> You killed this one at the time of the great feast.
> God has been murdered,
> the King of Israel has been destroyed
> by the right hand of Israel.
> O frightful murder!
> O unheard of injustice! [116]

A. T. Kraabel rightly expresses his surprise that a whole genera-tion of scholars could have read this Quartodeciman document without calling attention to the "prolonged, bitter, personal attack on 'Israel.' "[117] Similar "anti-Jewish sentiments" are expressed in the so-called *Teaching of the Twelve Apostles* (earlier half of third century) where Christians are enjoined to fast on Easter-Friday and Saturday "on account of the disobedience of our brethren [i.e., the Jews] . . . because thereon the People killed themselves in crucifying our Savior."[118] These and other documents[119] clearly show that anti-Judaic sentiments were present in the observance of both the Quartodeciman and Sunday Passover. In fact, initially no significant theological difference is detectable between the two traditions. In both instances the Passover observance basically consisted of a fast followed by a feast honoring Christ's passion. The controversy was not over the theological meaning of the Passover but rather over the length of the fast and the date of the feast.[120] In both traditions anti-Jewish sentiments were present and this fact helps to explain the existence of initial cordial relationships in spite of divergent practices. Obviously the Christians who observed Passover on the Sunday following the Jewish Passover could express dissociation from the Jews more effectively than the Quartodecimans who held to the Jewish date. This factor, as we shall now see, contributed significantly to the widespread acceptance of the Easter-Sunday practice.

A foreseeable development occurred in the latter half of the second century which brought to an end the cordial relationships between the two traditions. The Quartodecimans by maintaining the *Jewish date* could easily be led to accept also the *Jewish manner* of observing Passover. This is exactly what happened in the sixties, when some Quartodecimans, as reported by Apollinaris, Bishop of Hierapolis (about 170) "out of ignorance created dissensions . . . claiming that the Lord ate the paschal lamb with His disciples on Nisan 14 and that He suffered on the great day of unleavened bread (Nisan 15)."[121] These radical Quartodecimans maintained that Christians ought to celebrate the OT Passover at the *same time* and in the *same manner* as the Jews, eating the paschal lamb in a solemn feast on Nisan 14. Other Quartodecimans, however, held that Christians should celebrate not the Jewish paschal banquet but Christ's death.[122]

The controversy extended both in time and space well beyond the borders of Asia. Early in the third century, Clement in Alexandria and Hippolytus in Rome wrote against these radical Quartodecimans who had supporters in their communities.[123] In Rome the problem became acute when Blastus, a presbyter of the church, toward 180 became the leader of an independent church.[124] Tertullian reports that Blastus "wished to introduced Judaism in disguise; for he said that Easter ought not to be observed otherwise than according to the law of Moses on the fourteenth of the month." [125]   The Roman Bishop Victor (189-198) realized that the only way he could deal successfully with these Jewish-Quartodecimans in Rome was by attacking directly the whole Quartodeciman tradition, which had its strongest roots among the churches of Asia.

To accomplish this Victor urged the bishops not merely of Asia but of numerous provinces to press for a uniform adoption of Easter-Sunday in their dioceses by calling synods.   Victor's call was heeded and numerous synods were held which in most cases decided in favor of the Roman Easter.   Besides Victor's episcopal prestige, at least two other factors contributed to the wide acceptance of the Roman Easter at this time.[126]   First, there was that radical Quartodeciman faction which insisted on celebrating Passover not only on the *Jewish date* but also in a *Jewish manner*, eating the paschal lamb.   This faction seems to have caused considerable dissensions not only in Asia but also in Alexandria and in Rome itself.[127]   The transference of the Passover celebration from the Jewish date of Nisan 14 to the following Sunday was presumably viewed by many bishops as an effective measure to counteract the recrudescence of Judaizing tendencies in their churches.

Second, the growing theological importance being attached to Christ's resurrection [128] most probably encouraged the adoption of the Easter-Sunday practice, since the latter offered the possibility of celebrating both Christ's death and His resurrection on the actual days of the week on which these events occurred.   Third, the widening rift between the Church and the Synagogue—evidenced by the volume of "*Against the Jews*" literature produced at that time—spurred many Christians to dissociate from the Jews and their characteristic festivals such as the Sabbath and Passover.[129]   With regard to the Sabbath, we mentioned earlier some of the measures taken by the Church of Rome to wean Christians away from its observance and to encourage Sundaykeeping instead.   With regard to Passover, the Church of Rome introduced independent calendrical computations which were designed to ensure that the day of the full moon would always fall after the spring equinox (an event generally ignored by the Jews) and to guarantee that Easter-Sunday would never be celebrated at the same time as the Jewish Passover.[130]

The anti-Judaic motivation for the new computations is explicitly expressed in the treatise *On the Computation of Passover*, generally attributed to Cyprian and produced in the year 243, apparently to rectify an error which developed in the Roman Easter-tables produced by Hippolytus (about 222).   At the very outset the computist writes: "We desire to show to those who love and are eager for divine studies that Christians need at no time stray from the way of truth or *walk in blindness and stupidity behind the*

Jews as though they did not know what was the day of the Pas-sover." [131]   The same anti-Judaic motivation for the repudiation of the Quartodeciman Passover is forcefully expressed almost a century later in the Nicene conciliar letter of Constantine where the Emperor urges Christians to adopt unanimously the Easter-Sunday practice championed by the Church of Rome, in order to "have nothing in common with the detestable Jewish crowd. . . . All should unite in . . . avoiding all participation in the perjured conduct of the Jews." [132]

It is hoped that this brief excursus has sufficiently shown that anti-Jewish sentiments were indeed present in the theological inter-pretation of both the Quartodeciman and Sunday Passover and that they greatly contributed to the adoption and widespread observance of Easter-Sunday.   The close nexus existing between Easter-Sunday and weekly Sunday presupposes that the same anti-Judaic motivation contributed to the contemporaneous adoption of Sunday worship in place of Sabbathkeeping.   We have found support for this conclu-sion in the similarity of motives and measures taken by the Church of Rome to promote both weekly Sunday and Easter-Sunday in place of what was viewed as "Jewish" Sabbath and Passover.

The Primacy of the Church of Rome.   Did the Church of Rome enjoy in the second century sufficient authority to introduce and promote among Christian churches the observance of new festivities such as weekly Sunday and Easter-Sunday? [133]   The documents available leave no doubt as to the considerable authority and influence exerted at this time by the Roman Church.   A few examples will be cited to illustrate this fact.   Ignatius, in his prologue to the *Letter to the Romans,* greets the Roman Church with a profusion of honorific epithets which far surpass those found at the beginning of his letters to other churches. [134]   The Roman Church, writes Ignatius, "*presides* in the chief place of the Roman territory; a church worthy of God, worthy of honor, worthy of felicitation, worthy of praise, worthy of success, worthy of sanctification, and *presiding in love,* maintaining the law of Christ, and bearer of the Father's name." [135]

The phrase "presiding in love" has been the object of consider-able scholarly discussion.   The term "love"—*agape*—is repeatedly used by Ignatius as a personification of the Christian community where such love was manifested. [136]   To the Trallians, for example, Ignatius writes, "The love of the Smyrnaeans and the Ephesians sends you greetings" (13:1).   This suggests that Ignatius attributes to the Roman Church a presidency of love (not of law), that is, a leading concern for the welfare of other churches. [137]   It is unfor-tunate that what initially was a *presidency of love* in time became a *primacy of law,* that is, based on juridical claims. [138]   That Ignatius acknowledged the Roman presidency of love is indicated by his closing appeal to the same Church for his orphan Church: "Remember in your prayers the church of Syria, which has God for its pastor in my place. Jesus Christ alone will oversee it, *together with your love*" (9:1). Is it not remarkable that Ignatius should entrust his Church of Antioch into the loving care of the distant and (to him) unknown Church of Rome, rather than to one of the near and known churches of Asia? It is hard to escape the conclusion that Ignatius did attribute to the Roman Church an important role of pastoral leadership.[139]

Irenaeus, Bishop of Lyons, in his book *Against Heresies* (composed about 175-189), refutes heretics by appealing to the apostolic tradition preserved in a special way by the Church of Rome which he describes as "the greatest, the most ancient (*maxima et antiquissima*), and universally known Church founded and organized by the two most glorious apostles, Peter and Paul . . . For it is a matter of necessity that every Church should agree with this Church, on account of its preeminent authority (*potentior principalitas*), that is, the faithful everywhere, inasmuch as the apostolic tradition has been preserved continuously by those who exist everywhere." [140] The inaccuracies in this passage are significant. Obviously the Church of Rome was not "the most ancient" (*antiquissima*) since it was founded after that of Jerusalem. Nor was the Roman Church founded by Paul. In his letter to the Romans the Apostle explicitly acknowledges that he was not the founder of this Church (15:20-24). Yet these legendary claims reveal a method that was being developed to justify the *potentior principalitas* exerted by the Church of Rome.

A telling example of the authority of the Church of Rome is provided by the measures taken by Bishop Victor to enforce the adoption of Easter-Sunday. The Roman Bishop, as noted earlier, requested the convocation of councils in various provinces to implement the observance of Easter-Sunday (about 196). It is noteworthy that even those bishops who dissented from the Roman Easter complied with Victor's request. For example, Polycrates, Bishop of Ephesus, speaks of the "great multitude" of bishops whom he summoned at Victor's demand.[141] Was this just a matter of "courtesy to Victor" as argued by Kenneth A. Strand? [142] Polycrates' defiant tone ("I am not affrighted by terrifying word") rather indicates that Victor had pressured the bishops to endorse the Roman custom.[143] This is also supported by Victor's drastic action when notified of the Asian bishops' refusal to accept Easter-Sunday: "He [Victor] wrote letters and declared all the brethren there wholly excommunicated." [144] Jean Colson rightly remarks: "Note the *universal* power of excommunication claimed by the bishop of Rome. It is not merely a question of separating the Asian Churches from his own communion—as was commonly done by all bishops. Rather the separation from his own [Roman] communion resulted in the separation from all the other churches of the universe to which he notified by letters his sentence." [145]

The significance of Victor's policy is cogently analyzed by George La Piana in a penetrating essay published in *Harvard Theological Review*. La Piana explains that "When he [Victor] dared to ban a tradition which went back to apostolic times, but which had become a stumbling block to the unification and the peace of his community and to the triumph of the episcopal supremacy, Victor formulated implicitly the doctrine that tradition was not to be a millstone around the neck of a living institution. . . . This was the beginning of that historical process which in time led the Roman Church to identify Christian tradition with its own doctrine and its own organization." [146] The importance of the disciplinary measures taken by the Church of Rome to enjoin her practices on Christians at large has been grasped by few. Yet as La Piana persuasively shows, these measures have contributed to the increase and consolidation of the power of the Roman Church more than "theological debates and philosophical speculation." [147] The same author concludes that "it was under Victor that this process of expansion of Roman influence began to assume a definite form and to give rise to a tradition which was destined to play a part of capital importance in the history of Christianity." [148]

The sampling of historical evidences given above indicates that the Church of Rome enjoyed already in the second century sufficient authority to influence the greater part of Christendom to accept new customs such as Easter-Sunday and weekly Sunday.[149] The reasons for the adoption of these new festivities we have found to be, on the one hand, the social, military, political and literary anti-Judaic imperial policies which made it expedient for Christians to sever their ties with the Jews, and on the other hand, the very conflict existing between Jews and Christians. The Church of Rome, whose members experienced a break from the Jews earlier than in the East and whose authority was widely acknowledged (though challenged by some), appears to have played a leading role in inducing the adoption of the observance of Sunday and of Easter-Sunday. These new festivities appear to have been first introduced in the early part of the second century, at the time when Hadrian's (about 135) anti-Judaic repressive measures made it expedient for Christians to differentiate from the Jews by abandoning their characteristic festivals such as the Passover and the Sabbath. To wean Christians away from Sabbathkeeping we found that the Church of Rome employed both theological and practical measures. The Sabbath was re-interpreted to be a Mosaic institution imposed on the Jews as a sign of their unfaithfulness, and Christians were urged to fast and to abstain from religious assemblies on the Sabbath in order to show their dissociation from the Jews.

5. *Sun-Worship and the Origin of Sunday*

The social, political and religious conditions we have briefly surveyed explain why a new day of worship was substituted for the Sabbath, but they do not explain why Sunday was chosen rather than another day of the week (such as Friday, the day of Christ's passion). The diffusion of the Sun cults and the consequent advancement of "Sun-day" from the position of second to that of first day of the week provide a most plausible explanation.

The spread of Sun-worship. Recent studies have shown that "from the early part of the second century A.D. the cult of *Sol Invictus* was dominant in Rome and in other parts of the Empire." [150] Until toward the end of the first century A.D., the Romans worshiped their own "native Sun—*Sol indiges*," a name which appears in several ancient Roman texts.[151] But by the second century the Eastern cult of "*Sol Invictus*—Invincible Sun" penetrated into Rome in two different fashions: *privately* through *Sol Invictus Mithra* and *publicly* through that of *Sol Invictus Elagabal*.[152] Tertullian reports that in his own time (about 150-230) the Circus Maximus in Rome was "chiefly consecrated to the Sun, whose temple stands in the middle of it, and whose image shines forth from its temple summit; for they have not thought it proper to pay sacred honours underneath a roof to an object they have itself in open space." [153] The Emperor Hadrian (117-138) identified himself with the Sun in his coins [154] and dedicated to the Sun the famous *Colossus Neronis*, which Nero had erected representing himself as the Sun-god with seven long rays around his head.[155] Obviously Hadrian removed Nero's features from that colossal statue.

Various factors contributed to the spread of Sun-cults. An important one was the identification and worship of the Emperor as Sun-god, encouraged by the Easter theology of the "King-Sun" and by political considerations.[156] The Roman legionaries, who came in contact with the Easter *Sol Invictus Elagabal* and Mithraism, served also as the propagators of these Sun-cults in the West. Another significant factor was the syncretistic climate of the time. In a perceptive study Marcel Simon shows how the leading gods were assimilated with the solar deity.[157] An excellent example of this process of assimilation is provided by two inscriptions engraved on a column of the mithraeum of the thermae of Caracalla (211-217). The first proclaims: "Unique [is] Zeus, Serapis, Helios [i.e. Sun-god], the invincible master of the universe." [158] After the death of Caracalla, who had been a fervent supporter of Egyptian divinities, the name Serapis was chiseled out and that of "Mithra" was inserted instead.[159] The second inscription contains a dedication to "Zeus, Helios, the great Serapis, savior, who gives riches, who graciously hears, the invincible Mithra." [160] It is noteworthy that Mithra is not only associated with Serapis, Helius and Zeus, but is also mentioned last, apparently as the embodiment of them all.[161] Marcel Simon explains that the Sun-god (Helios) is "the essential and central element which ties together these divinities of different origin and absorbs them more than they absorb it." [162]

The spread and popularity of the Sun-cults caused a significant change in the sequence of the days of the week. The seven-day week was first adopted by the Roman Empire in the first century A.D. At that time the days of the week were named after the planets (as they still are). Saturn's day (Saturday) was originally the first day of the week and Sun's day (Sunday) was originally the second day of the week.[163] Under the influence of the prevailing Sun worship, however, a change occurred in the second century: The Sun's day (Sunday) was advanced from the position of second day of the week to that of first. (Each of the other days was advanced one day thus Saturday became the seventh day of the week).[164] It is difficult to determine the exact time when the primacy and prestige of the day of Saturn was transferred to that of the Sun. That this had occurred (or at least was in progress) already by the middle of the second century is clearly indicated by the famous astrologer Vettius Valens. In his *Anthology* composed between A.D. 154 and 174, he explicitly states: "And this is the sequence of the planetary stars in relation to the days of the week: Sun, Moon, Mars, Mercury, Jupiter, Venus, Saturn." [165] The same sequence occurs in a goblet found in 1633 at Wettingen near Baden, together with coins dating from Hadrian to Constantine II (died 340).[166] Additional confirmation of the dominant place occupied by the day of the Sun in the sequence of the days of the week is provided by statements from Justin Martyr and Tertullian, and several Mithraea, as well as the two constitutions of Constantine (March 3 and July 3, 321).[167]

Since the emergence of the day of the Sun over that of Saturn occurred presumably in the early part of the second century in concomitance with the Christian's adoption of Sunday observance in place of the Sabbath, one may ask, Did the advancement of the day of the Sun to the position of first day of the week possibly influence Christians who desired to differentiate themselves from the Sabbath of the Jews, to adopt and adapt this same day for their weekly worship?

Several indications, which we can only name in this essay, support this hypothesis. Indirectly, support is provided by the Fathers frequent condemnation of the Christian veneration of the Sun, by adoption of the symbology of the Sun in early Christian art and literature to represent Christ, by the change in orientation for prayer from Jerusalem to the East, and by the adoption as the Christian Christmas of the pagan feast of the *dies natalis Solis Invicti*.[168]

A more direct indication is provided by the frequent use of the symbology of the day of the Sun to justify Sunday observance. Justin Martyr (about 100-165) emphasizes that Christians assemble "on the day of the Sun . . . because it is the first day on which God, transforming the darkness and prime matter, created the world." [169] The nexus Justin establishes between the day of the Sun and the creation of light on the first day can hardly be regarded as a pure coincidence, since subsequently several Fathers reiterate the same connection. Eusebius (about 260-340), for instance, several times refers explicitly to the motifs of the light and of the day of the Sun to justify Sunday worship. In his *Commentary on Psalms* he writes: "*In this day of light*, first day and *true day of the sun*, when we gather after the interval of six days, we celebrate the holy and spiritual Sabbath. . . . In fact, it is on this day of the creation of the world that God said: '*Let there be light* and there was light.' It is also on this day that the *Sun of Justice* has risen for our souls." [170]

These and similar testimonies [171] indicate that the choice of the day of the Sun was motivated by the adequate time and effective symbology the day provided to commemorate two significant events of the history of salvation: *creation* and *resurrection*. Jerome (about 342-420) expresses well these dual reasons when he writes: "If it is called day of the Sun by the pagans, we most willingly acknowledge it as such, since it is on this day that the *light of the world* has appeared and on this day the *Sun of Justice* has risen." [172]

Conclusion

The conclusion that emerges from our investigation is that the adoption of Sunday observance in place of the Sabbath occurred, not in the Jerusalem Church by apostolic authority to commemorate Christ's resurrection, but rather in the Church of Rome during the early part of the second century, solicited by external circumstances. An interplay of political, social, pagan-religious and Christian factors—similar somewhat to those which gave rise to the December 25 observance of Christ's birth—made it expedient to adopt Sunday as a new day of worship. The fact that Sunday observance rests on questionable expediency rather than on a Biblical mandate makes it very difficult for religious leaders to articulate compelling theological reasons which are indispensable to promote the proper observance of God's Holy Day.

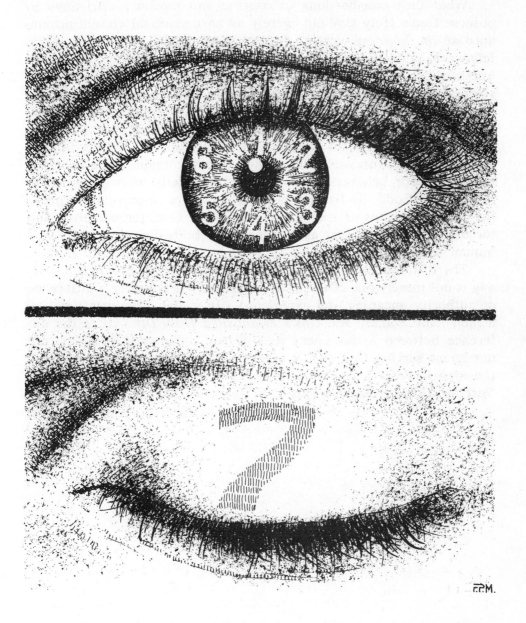

On the Sabbath the body can rest because the mind is at rest,
and the mind is at rest because it rests in God.

What then can be done to educate and motivate Christians to observe God's Holy Day not merely as an occasional church attendance at *the hour* of worship but as a *whole day* of rest, worship, fellowship and service? The proposal of our study is to lead people into a rediscovery and experience of the meaning, function and blessings of the Biblical seventh-day Sabbath: the day which originated not as an expedient *hour of worship* to show dissociation or contempt toward others, but as an express divine choice of a *24-hour day* in which to rest, to worship, to fellowship and to serve needy fellow beings. Our study has shown that the main concern of the Sabbath is for believers to rest from their daily work in order to find rest in God. By freeing us from our daily gainful employment, the Sabbath makes us free and available for God, for ourselves and for others, thus enabling us to experience both divine presence and human fellowship.

The difference then between the seventh-day Sabbath and Sunday is not merely one of names or numbers. It is rather a difference of authority, meaning and experience. It is the difference between a *man-made holiday* and *God's established Holy Day*. It is the difference between a day spent seeking for selfish gratifications and one spent serving God and humanity. It is the difference between the experience of a day of restlessness and that of a day of *Divine Rest for Human Restlessness*.

NOTES
ABBREVIATIONS
SELECTED BIBLIOGRAPHY
TABLE OF CONTENTS

ABBREVIATIONS

ANF   - *The Ante-Nicene Fathers.* 10 vols. Grand Rapids, Michigan 1973 reprint.

NPNF - *Nicene and Post-Nicene Fathers.* First and Second Series. Grand Rapids, Michigan, 1971, reprint.

CCL   - *Corpus Christianorum.* Series Latina. Turnholti, 1953ff.

CIL   - *Corpus Inscriptionum Latinorum.* Ed. A. Reimer. Berlin, 1863-1893.

CSEL - *Corpus Scriptorum Ecclesiasticorum Latinorum.* Vienne, 1866ff.

ET   - English Translation.

PL   - *Patrologie cursus completus, Series Latina.* Ed. J. P. Migne. Paris, 1844ff.

PG   - *Patrologie cursus completus, Series Graeca.* Ed. J. P. Migne. Paris, 1857ff.

INTRODUCTION

[1] From Clayton K. Harrop's private letter and evaluation of *From Sabbath to Sunday*, dated February 25, 1980. Permission to quote was granted.

[2] From Norman Vincent Peale's assessment of *From Sabbath to Sunday*, issued on June 6, 1979, with permission to quote from it. Prof. F. Sherwood Smith, Chairman, Bible Department, Cincinnati Christian Seminary, in his evaluation of my book, released for promotional use, on August 2, 1979, writes: "The book, with its historical facts and persuasive logic, will cause the Sunday observer to evaluate anew the ground for Sunday worship." Similarly, Prof. Eric W. Gritsch, Director of the *Institute for Luther Studies* at the Lutheran Theological Seminary, released on March 9, 1979 the following statement for public use: "This is a thorough study of the historical transition from Sabbath to Sunday celebrations. The study demonstrates that the Christian Sunday is a creation of the post-apostolic church rather than the result of a biblical mandate."

[3] See above note 2. Hoyt L. Hickman, Assistant General Secretary, Section on Worship, of the United Methodist Church, in his letter of May 19, 1978 writes to me: "I must admit that your point of view is one which most of us have simply not taken seriously enough. As you may know, there is increasing interest ecumenically in the whole matter of the observance of the Lord's Day and its relationship to the Sabbath, and I am sure that the points you raise will have to be given most careful consideration by all of us who are engaged in the re-evaluation that is taking place." Permission to quote was granted.

[4] Dr. James P. Wesberry, "A Renewed Program of Advance," *Sunday* 52 (Dec. 1975): 6.

CHAPTER I

THE SABBATH: GOOD NEWS OF HUMAN ROOTS

[1] Paul Tillich, *Systematic Theology*, 1957, I, p. 265. In his *Dynamics of Faith*, 1958, p. 42, Tillich uses the example of the flag to illustrate how a symbol participates in that reality "to which it points." He writes, "the flag participates in the power and dignity of the nation for which it stands. An attack on the flag is felt as an attack on the majesty of the group in which it is acknowledged. Such an attack is considered blasphemy." Similarly in the Scripture, the profanation of the Sabbath, the symbol of divine ownership and authority, is viewed as apostasy (Ezek. 20:13, 21). See discussion below, pp. 112-115.

[2] Tillich explains that a symbol "not only opens up dimensions and elements of reality which otherwise would remain unapproachable but also unlocks dimensions and elements of our soul which correspond to

the dimensions and elements of reality.... There are within us dimensions of which we cannot become aware except through symbols, as melodies and rhythms in music" (*Dynamics of Faith*, 1958, pp. 42, 43).

3 This connection is recognized by Solomon Goldman, who writes, "The whole purpose of the account of Creation was to emphasize the uniqueness and excellence of man and to impress him with the sanctity and blessedness of the seventh day or the Sabbath" (*In the Beginning*, 1949, p. 744).

4 Philo, *De opificio Mundi* 89; *De Vita Mosis* 1, 207; *De Specialibus Legibus* 2, 59.

5 R. W. Emerson, "The Divinity School Address," *Three Prophets of Religious Liberalism*, C. C. Wright, ed., 1961, p. 111.

6 Modern commentators generally divide Genesis 2:4 in two parts, attaching the first part of the verse (v. 4a) to the first creation story (so-called source P) and its second part (v. 4b) to the second creation story (source J). The reasons for such a division are convincingly refuted by U. Cassuto in *La Questione della Genesi*, 1934, pp. 268-272 and in *A Commentary on the Book of Genesis*, 1961, pp. 96-99.

7 For example, Nicola Negretti points out that "by means of Genesis 2:4a the author of the priestly story has linked together the creation week with the scheme of the *toledot* [generations] (cf. Gen. 5:1; 6:9; 10:1; 11:10-27; 25:12-19; 36:1-9; 37:2) and consequently he inserted it [i.e. the week] in th context of the history of salvation" (*Il Settimo Giorno*, Analecta Biblica 55, 1973, p. 93; cf. p. 165, n. 31). See also H. C. Leupold, *Exposition of Genesis*, 1950, p. 110; J. Scharbert, "Der Sinn der Toledot-Formel in der Priesterschrift," in *Wort-Gebot-Glaube, Alttestamentliche Abhandlungen zur Theologie des Alten und Neuen Testaments* 59 (1970) 45-56.

8 Genesis 2:4; 5:1; 6:9; 10:1; 11:10; 11:27; 25:12; 25:19; 36:1; 37:2.

9 The Kenite theory is traced back to Abraham Kuenen, *The Religion of Israel*, 1874, p. 274. It has been revived by Bernardus D. Eerdmans, "Der Sabbath," in *Vom Alten Testament: Festschrift Karl Marti*, No. 41 (1925), pp. 79-83; Karl Budde, "The Sabbath and the Week: Their Origin and their Nature," *The Journal of Theological Studies* 30 (1928): 1-15; H. H. Rowley, "Moses and the Decalogue," *Bulletin of the John Rylands Library*, 34 (1951-1952): 81-118; L. Koehler, "Der Dekalog," *Theologische Rundschau*, 1 (1929): 181.

10 The identification of Sakkuth and Kaiwan as names of Saturn has been challenged recently by Stanley Gervirtz, "A New Look at an Old Crux: Amos 5:26," *Journal of Biblical Literature* 87 (1968): 267-276; cf. William W. Hallo, "New Moons and Sabbaths: A Case-study in the Contrastive Approach," *Hebrew Union College Annual*, 48 (1977): 15. The rendering proposed by Gervirtz and Hallo is essentially similar to that of the New English Bible which reads, "No but now you shall take up the shrine of your idol king and the pedestals of your images (Heb. adds: the star of your gods), which you have made for yourselves" (Amos 5:26).

11 On the question of the origin of the planetarian week, see Samuele Bacchiocchi, *From Sabbath to Sunday*, 1977, pp. 241-247. Note that while Saturn day was initially the first day of the planetary wek, the OT Sabbath was always the seventh day of the week.

12 Joseph Z. Lauterbach points out that "when in later Jewish works an astrological connection between Saturn and the Jews is mentioned, it is emphasized that the Jews observe the Sabbath rather to demonstrate their independence of Saturn, that they need no help whatever from him, but rely on God alone" (*Rabbinic Essays*, 1951, p. 438). It is noteworthy

also that Jewish rabbis called Saturn *Shabbti* which means "the star of the Sabbath." This name represents, as noted by Hutton Webster, "not a naming of the day after the planet, but a naming of the planet after the day" (*Rest Days*, 1916, p. 244).

13 Cf. E. G. Kraeling, "The Present Status of the Sabbath Question," *The American Journal of Semitic Languages* 49 (1932-1933): 218-219; G. Fohrer, *Geschichte der israelischen Religion*, 1969, p. 108; J. J. Stamm, M. E. Andrew, *The Ten Commandments in Recent Research*, 1967, pp. 91-92; Roland de Vaux, *Ancient Israel*, Vol. II, 1965, p. 480.

14 George Smith, *Assyrian Discoveries*, 1883, p. 12.

15 Hutton Webster suggests that the original calendar possibly belonged to the age of Hammurabi (*Rest Days*, 1916, p. 223). William W. Hallo (n. 10) also argues that the Neo-Babylonian lunar festivals represents a survival of an older Sumerian tradition (p. 8).

16 The 19th day has been taken to represent the 49th day from the first of the preceding month, or seven evil days—*ûmê lemnûti*. However, since a lunar month lasts just over 29 days, the "weekly" cycle between the last evil day (28th day) and the first evil day (7th day) of the next month would be eight or nine days, depending on whether the last month was of 29 or 30 days.

17 R. W. Rogers, *Cuneiform Parallels to the Old Testament*, 1912, p. 189; C. H. W. Johns, *Assyrian Deeds and Documents*, II, 1901, pp. 40-41; George A. Barton, *Archeology and the Bible*, 1944, p. 308; Stephen Langdon, *Babylonian Menologies and the Semitic Calendars*, 1935, pp. 73 ff.

18 Each quarter of the moon represents 7 ¾ days, thus making it impossible to maintain an exact cycle of seven days.

19 Cf. Paul O. Bostrup, *Den israelitiske Sabbats Oprindelse og Karakter i Foreksilsk*, 1923, pp. 50-55.

20 Cf. Amos 8:5; Hosea 2:11; Isaiah 1:11-13; 2 Kings 4:23.

21 The period between two successive new moons (lunation) averages 29 days, 12 hours, 44 minutes and 2.8 seconds.

22 See note 23.

23 It is generally recognized that the Babylonian evil days had a religious but not a civil function. Hutton Webster (n. 15) points out that "Nothing in the cuneiform records indicates that the Babylonians ever employed them for civil purposes. These periods seem to have had solely a religious significance" (p. 230). Similarly Siegfried H. Horn remarks, "The cuneiform records do not say that anyone should rest on those five particular days of the month, or refrain from work, or worship the gods. They simply admonish certain persons—kings, physicians, et cetera—to avoid doing certain specified things on those five 'evil days' " ("Was the Sabbath Known in Ancient Babylonia? Archeology and the Sabbath," *The Sabbath Sentinel* [December 1979]: 21-22). In a Neo-Babylonian calendar and in its Kassite original published by René Labat, the majority of the days are unfavorable and multiples of seven can be either good or bad ("Un calendrier cassite de jours fastes et néfastes," *Sumer* 8 [1952]: 27); " Un almanach babylonien," *Review d'Assyrologie* 38 [1941]: 13-40.

24 Karl Budde (n. 9), p. 6.

25 E. A. Speiser, "The Creation Epic," in James B. Pritchard, *Ancient Near Eastern Texts*, 1950, p. 68. Cf. W. F. Lambert and A. R. Millard, *Atra-hasis: The Babylonian Story of the Flood*, 1969, pp. 56f; Theophilus G. Pinches, "Sapattu, the Babylonian Sabbath," *Proceedings of the Society of Biblical Archeology* 26 (1904): 51-56.

26 Certain cuneiform tablets refer to sacrifices made to the divine

kings of Ur on the new-moon and on the fifteenth day of the month. Cf. H. Radau, *Early Babylonian History*, 1900, p. 314.

[27] For example texts, see *Cuneiform Texts from Babylonian Tablets in the British Museum*, XVIII, 17c, d.

[28] M. Jastrow argues that *šabattu* was primarily a day of pacification of a deity's anger and the idea of rest applies to gods rather than to men (*Hebrew and Babylonian Traditions*, 1914, pp. 134-149).

[29] This theory was initially developed by Johannes Meinhold, *Sabbath und Woche im Alten Testament*, 1905, pp. 3ff. In an early study (*Sabbat und Sonntag*, 1909, pp. 9, 34), Meinhold attributed the change from monthly full-moon day to the weekly Sabbath to Ezekiel. In a later essay, however ("Zur Sabbatfrage," *Zeitschrift für die Alttestamentliche Wissenschaft* 48 [1930]: 128-32), he places the process in postexilic times, in conjunction with Nehemiah's reforms. This theory has been adopted with some modifications by several scholars. Cf. Samuel H. Hooke, *The Origin of the Early Semitic Ritual*, 1938, pp. 58-59; Adolphe Lods, *Israel: From its Beginning to the Middle of the Eighth Century*, 1932, p. 438; Sigmund Mowinckel, *Le Décalogue*, 1927, p. 90; Robert H. Pfeiffer, *Religion in the Old Testament: The History of a Spiritual Triumph*, 1961, pp. 92-93.

[30] Karl Budde (n. 9), p. 9. Cf. E. G. Kraeling (n. 13), p. 222; J. H. Meesters, *Op zoek naar de oorsprong van de Sabbat*, 1966, pp. 28-34.

[31] 2 Kings 4:23 alludes to the celebration of the Sabbath in the company of the prophet Elisha (about 852-798 B.C.) and 2 Kings 11:4-12 describes the changing of guards on the Sabbath at the time when Athaliah, queen of Judah, was overthrown, about 835 B.C.

[32] N. H. Tur-Sinai, "Sabbath und Woche," *Bibliotheca Orientalis* 8 (1951): 14. Tur-Sinai points out that since the Jewish month-names do not follow the Babylonian ones, the latter could hardly have influenced the month-names of the former.

[33] George A. Barton, *The Royal Inscriptions of Sumer and Akkad*, 1929, pp. 187, 229, 253.

[34] James B. Pitchard, *Ancient Near Eastern Texts Relating to the Old Testament*, 1955, pp. 44, 94.

[35] These are a Neo-Babylonian syllabary which lists only the first seven days of the month, apparently viewing them as a unit, and a letter admonishing to "complete the day of the new moon, the seventh day and the day of full moon." A. L. Oppenheim, "Assyriological Gleanings II," *Bulletin of the American Schools of Oriental Research*, 93 (1944): 16-17; Alfred Jeremias, *Das Alte Testament im Lichte des Alten Orients*, 1930, p. 75. For an examination of the texts, see Horn (n. 23), pp. 20-22.

[36] Friedrich Delitzsch, *Babel und Bible*, 1903, p. 38. Cf. J. Hehn, *Siebenzahl und Sabbat bei den Babyloniern und im Alten Testament*, 1907, pp. 4-44, 77-90; A. S. Kapelrud, "The Number Seven in Ugaritic Texts," *Vetus Testamentum* 18 (1968): 494-499; H. J. Kraus, *Worship in Israel*, 1966, pp. 85-87; Nicola Negretti, *Il Settimo Giorno*, 1973, pp. 31-109; S. E. Loewenstein, "The Seven Day-Unit in Ugaritic Epic Literature," *Israel Exploration Journal* 15 (1965): 121-133.

[37] Siegfried H. Horn (n. 23), p. 21.

[38] Ibid., p. 21.

[39] See below p. 36.

[40] For a report on 41 Flood stories from different parts of the world, see B. C. Nelson, *The Deluge Story in Stone*, 1949.

[41] A five-day period, known as *hamuštum*, appears to have been familiar to the ancient Assyro-Babylonians. A. H. Sayce was the first to argue that the term *hamuštum*, occurring in cuneiform tablets of the

age of Hammurabi, represented five-day periods or a sixth of a month ("Assyriological Notes—No. 3," *Proceedings of the Society of Biblical Archeology,* 19 (1897): 288. However, Julius and Hildegard Lewy interpret *hamuštum* as a fifty-day period ("The Origin of the Week and the Oldest West Asiatic Calendar," *Hebrew Union College Annual* 17 (1942-43): 1-152. Another differing identification of the word, namely a six-day period or a fifth of a month has been proposed by N. H. Tur-Sinai (n. 32), pp. 14-24. Recently the five-day period identification has been defended again by Kemal Balkan, "The Old Assyrian Week," *Studies in Honor of Benno Landsberger on His Seventy-fifth Birthday April 12, 1965,* (Chicago, 1965), pp. 159-174. Cuneiform texts also contain traces of five-day periods associated with lunar phases. For references, see A. Jeremias, *The Old Testament in the Light of the Ancient East,* 1911, p. 65

[42] For example, J. Morgenstern confidently asserts, "All available evidence indicates unmistakably that the sabbath can have originated only in an agricultural environment. Actually the Hebrews became acquainted with the sabbath only after they had established themselves in Palestine and had settled down there alongside their Canaanite predecessors in the land, whom in some measure they displaced, and had borrowed from them the techniques of tilling the soil, and with this various institutions of agricultural civilization, of which the sabbath was one" (*The Interpreter's Dictionary of the Bible,* 1962, s.v. "Sabbath").

[43] Willy Rordorf articulates this view emphatically but not convincingly. He maintains that "in the oldest stratum of the Pentateuch the sabbath is, therefore, to be understood as a *social institution.* After every six days of work a day of rest is inserted for the sake of the cattle and of the slaves and employees.... The observance of the sabbath does, therefore, point us to the period after the occupation of Canaan" (*Sunday: The History of the Day of Rest and Worship in the Earliest Centuries of the Christian Church,* 1968, p. 12).

[44] The reason Rordorf gives for this transformation is "the fact that from the time when the Jews were no longer in their own country they no longer had any slaves, and so they scarcely knew what to make of the motivation of sabbath observance on the ground of social ethics" (n. 43, p. 18).

[45] Rordorf (n. 43), p. 11, *"We are certainly justified in regarding Ex. 23:12 and 34:21 as our earliest versions of the sabbath commandment"* (italics his).

[46] On the basis of this criterion the Sabbath commandment found in Exodus 20:8-11, as well as other references to the Sabbath (such as Gen. 2:2-3; Ex. 16:4-5, 22-30; 31:12-17; Lev. 23:3; Num. 15:32-36; 28:9-10) are attributed to the so-called Priestly Document. The latter, according to the modern critical view, represents the last of the four major sources of the Pentateuch and was allegedly produced around the time of Ezra 500 to 450 B.C. All the Sabbath texts of the Priestly documents are examined by Niels-Erik A. Andreasen, *The Old Testament Sabbath, A Tradition-Historical Investigation,* 1972, pp. 62-89. It is noteworthy that, as admitted by Gerhard von Rad, an eminent OT scholar, "a particularly important factor for the dating of the Priestly Document is the prominence which it gives to the Sabbath and to circumcision" (*Old Testament Theology I,* 1962, p. 79). The assumption is, as von Rad readily admit, that the Sabbath had no cultic significance before the exile and that "it was in the Exile that the Sabbath and circumcision won a *status confessionis,*" that is, confessional importance (p. 79). The weakness of this whole argument for the lateness of the Sabbath as a religious

institution, and thus for the Priestly Document, is that it rests on the gratuitous assumption that socio-economic concerns preceded theological motivations for the Sabbath. But, is such a dichotomy really justifiable? In our view this hardly seems to be the case. See the discussion that follows. It is unfortunate that a misunderstanding of the "wholly unparalleled institution of the Sabbath has also contributed toward the rejection of the Mosaic authorship of the Decalogue" (Solomon Goldman, *The Ten Commandments*, 1956, p. 64).

[47] Saul J. Berman points out that one of the functions of the legislation of the sabbatical year was to severely "limit the institution of slavery. The critical reversal of values evident in the Torah, as opposed to what we find in general ancient Near Eastern society, is perhaps nowhere more evident than in this area. While the contemporaries of the ancient Israelites saw no evil in slavery and used their legal system to preserve the institution, the Torah manifests a clear preference for freedom and uses the legal structure to limit the evil, as well as the incidence, of slavery. Thus, Hammurabi's Code (# 282) provides that an escaped slave who denies his status, when recaptured, is to have his ear cut off as a penalty for his crime. The Torah uses a similar though less painful penalty, the piercing of the ear, but for exactly the opposite crime, the refusal to go free after six years and insisting on remaining a slave (Ex. 21:6). The shift in values, from affirmation of slavery to its negation, could not be more obvious to people familiar with the penal system of the ancient Near East" ("The Extended Notion of the Sabbath," *Judaism* 22 [1973]: 350).

[48] The liberating function of the Sabbath years is discussed in chapter V, part I.

[49] In this regard Ernst Jenni has observed that the social function of the Sabbath is not separated from Israel's redemptive experience (*Die theologische Begründung des Sabbatgebotes im Alten Testament*, 1956, pp. 15-19). Note also that in Deuteronomy no less than five times appeal is made to "remember" divine deliverance in order to be compassionate toward the defenseless in society (Deut. 5:15; 15:15; 16:12; 24:18, 22).

[50] Abram Herbert Lewis, *Spiritual Sabbatism*, 1910, p. 67.

[51] Eduard Lohse disagrees with such an assumption. He writes, "Absolute rest from work is enjoined by the Sabbath commandment. This order does not necessarily presuppose agricultural conditions such as obtained in Israel only after the conquest. It could well have been observed by nomads. Hence the keeping of the Sabbath goes back to the very beginning of Yahweh religion" ("*Sabbaton*," *Theological Dictionary of the New Testament*, VII, 1971, p. 3). Cf. H. H. Rowley (n. 9), p. 117.

[52] Cf. William Foxwell Albright, *Yahweh and the Gods of Canaan: A Historical Analysis of Two Contrasting Faiths*, 1968, pp. 64-73; John Bright, *A History of Israel*, 1959, pp. 72-73; H. H. Rowley, *From Joseph to Joshua: Biblical Traditions in the Light of Archeology*, 1950, pp. 157ff.

[53] Similarly Solomon Goldman points out, "Did not Roger Williams see more than most New Englanders of his day? Did he not found Rhode Island in the hope that it might serve in time to come as 'a shelter to persons distressed for conscience'? Did not Jefferson anticipate in so many ways the America of our day? And did not Lincoln urge his generation so to formulate the law of the land as to make provision for the teeming millions that were some day to inhabit it? Why, then, is such foresight denied to Moses?" (n. 46, p. 64).

[54] Cf. Friedrich Delitzsch, *Babel und Bibel*, 5th ed., 1905, p. 65. Other supporters of this view are mentioned by Karl Budde (n. 9), p. 5.

[55] Karl Budde notes that "Nehemiah (Neh. 13:17-21) has to take proceedings against the Canaanite tradesmen who bring their goods into Jerusalem on the Sabbath. And even though we have little information available as to the *ancient* Canaanites, yet we have abundance from the contemporary Phoenicians, their kinsmen, over the whole of the Mediterranean as far as Carthage, Gaul, and Spain: nowhere is there the slightest trace of the Sabbath; on the contrary Israel feels conscious that no parallel for it is to be found in the whole of her environment" (n. 9, p. 5). Similarly Eduard Lohse remarks, "The idea that they might have taken over the Sabbath from the Canaanites is ruled out by the fact that no trace of the Sabbath has been found among the latter" (n. 51, p. 3).

[56] Cf. E. G. Kraeling (n. 13), pp. 226-228; Martin P. Nilsson, *Primitive Time-Reckoning*, 1920, pp. 324-346; H. Webster, *Rest Days: A Study in Early Law and Morality*, 1911, pp. 101-123; Ernst Jenni (n. 49), p. 13.

[57] See above n. 36. Cf. also James B. Pritchard (n. 34), pp. 143, 144, 150, 94. Also E. G. Kraeling (n. 13), p. 228.

[58] Cf. Hans-Joachim Kraus (n. 36), pp. 81-87; C. W. Kiker, "The Sabbath in the Old Testament Cult," Th.D. dissertation, Southern Baptist Theological Seminary, 1968, pp. 76-111.

[59] The hypothesis is weakened also by the fact that the earliest regulations regarding the annual festivals (Ex. 23:14-17; 34:18-23) do not enjoin cessation of work nor are these festivals mentioned in any way in the various references to the observance of the seventh day.

[60] See above nn. 29, 30.

[61] Hans-Joachim Kraus (n. 36), p. 87; J. Morgenstern (n. 42), p. 139; M. Jastrow, "The Original Character of the Hebrew Sabbath," *American Journal of Theology* 2 (1898): 324; Georg Beer, *Exodus*, 1939, p. 103; Hans Schmidt, "Mose und der Dekalog," *Eucharisterion: H. Gunkel zum 60. Geburtstage*, FRLANT 19 (1923): 105; Martin P. Nilsson (n. 56), p. 331.

[62] See above n. 44. Cf. Eduard Lohse (n. 51), p. 5: "In the postexilic community the Sabbath commandment is indeed the most important part of the divine law." Harold H. P. Dressler similarly maintains that "pre-exilic Israel did not keep the Sabbath as a *religious institution* until the Babylonian Exile" ("The Sabbath in the Old Testament," in *From Sabbath to Lord's Day: A Biblical, Historical and Theological Investigation*, D. A. Carson, ed. [to be published in 1980], p. 28 manuscript).

[63] See above n. 30.

[64] That Ezekiel is not transforming the Sabbath from a social to a religious institution is indicated also by the fact that he associates the profanation of the Sabbath with the disregard for social obligations toward parents, strangers and the underprivileged (Ezek. 22:7-8). The social and religious aspects of the Sabbath are viewed by the prophet as mutually dependent.

[65] Niels-Erik Andreasen, *Rest and Redemption*, 1978, p. 29, underscores this point, writing, "To be sure, the prophet Ezekiel who lived in captivity during this period mentions the sabbath repeatedly, but he nearly always speaks of it in connection with the Jerusalem temple and its holy things (Ezek. 22:8, 26; 23:38), or in connection with the future temple for which he fervently hoped (Ezek. 44:24; 45:17; 46:1-4, 12)."

[66] See below, pp. 35, 44.

[67] See, for example, the tractate *Shabbath*, 7, 2, in H. Danby, *The Mishnah*, 1933, pp. 100-136; George Foot Moore, *Judaism in the First Centuries of the Christian Era*, 1946, pp. 19-39; S. T. Kimborough, "The

Concept of Sabbath at Qumran," *Revue de Qumran* 5 (1962): 483-502;
1 Macc. 2:29-41; 1:15, 60; 2 Macc. 6:10; Jub. 50:8.

[68] See below, pp. 163-165.

[69] Cf. also Jub. 2:20-22. Such an exclusive interpretation of the Sabbath led some Rabbis to teach that non-Jews were actually forbidden to observe the Sabbath. For example, Simeon b. Lagish said: "A Gentile who keeps the Sabbath deserves death" (*Sanhedrin* 586). Earlier, "R Jose b. Hanina said: A non-Jew who observe the Sabbath whilst he is uncircumcised incurs liability for the punishment of death. Why? Because non-Jews were not commanded concerning it" (*Deuteronomy Rabbah* 1:21).

[70] *Genesis Rabbah* 11:7; 64:4; 79:6.

[71] See below, p. 43.

[72] Cf. *Genesis Rabbah* 11:2, 6, 8; 16:8; 79:7; 92:4; *Pirke de Rabbi Eliezer* 18, 19, 20; *The Books of Adam and Eve* 51:1-2; *Apocalypse of Moses* 43:1-3; *Yoma* 28b. In these references, however, one can at times detect a tension between the universalistic creation-Sabbath and the exclusivistic Mosaic-Sabbath. The *Book of Jubilees* (second century B.C.) offers an example. While on the one hand it says that God "kept Sabbath on the seventh day and hallowed it for all ages, and appointed it as a sign for all His works" (Jub. 2:1), on the other it holds that God "allowed no other people or peoples to keep the Sabbath on this day, except Israel only" (Jub. 2:31). For a discussion of the question, see Robert M. Johnston, "Patriarchs, Rabbis, and Sabbath," *Andrews University Seminary Studies* 12 (1974): 94-102.

[73] The argument appears for the first time in the writings of Justin Martyr, *Dialogue with Trypho* 19, 6; 23, 3; 27, 5; 29, 3; 46, 2-3. Cf. Irenaeus, *Adversus haereses* 4, 16, 2; Tertullian, *Adversus Judaeos* 2; Eusebius, *Historia Ecclesiastica* 1, 4, 8; *Demonstratio evangelica* 1, 6; *Commentaria in Psalmos* 91. The argument is also found in the *Syriac Didascalia* 26, "If God willed that we should be idle one day for six, first of all the patriarchs and the righteous men and all that were before Moses would have remained idle (upon it)" (Connolly, p. 236). For an analysis of Justin Martyr, see S. Bacchiocchi (n. 11), pp. 223-233.

[74] For example, John Gill, *The Body of Divinity*, 1951, 965. The view is expressed emphatically by Robert A. Morey, "Is Sunday the Christian Sabbath?," *Baptist Reformation Review* 8 (1979): 6: "But isn't the Sabbath creation ordinance found in Gen. 2:1-3? No, the word 'Sabbath' does not appear in the text. A biblical-theological approach would show that Gen. 2:1-3 is *Moses'* comment looking back to the creation period within the context of his own understanding of the Ten Commandments, and not a reference to Adam's understanding in the beginning of history." Similarly Harold H. P. Dressler (n. 62) p. 22 manuscript, "Genesis 2 does not mention the word 'Sabbath.' It speaks about the 'seventh day.' Unless the reader equates 'seventh day' and 'Sabbath,' there is no reference to the Sabbath here." But, isn't the equation between the "seventh day" and the "Sabbath" explicitly made in Ex. 20:8-11?

[75] U. Cassuto, *A Commentary on the Book of Genesis*, 1961, p. 63.

[76] U. Cassuto (n. 75), p. 68, explains: "The Torah, it seems to me, purports to say this: Israel's Sabbath day shall not be as the Sabbath of the heathen nations; it shall not be the day of the full moon, or any other day connected with the phases of the moon, but it shall be the *seventh day* (this enables us to understand why this particular name, *the seventh day*, is emphasized here), the seventh in *perpetual* order, independent and free from any association with the signs of the heavens

and any astrological concept." Cf. N. M. Sarna, *Understanding Genesis,* 1923, p. 23. The reason for the use of the "seventh day" instead of the Sabbath must be seen in the light of the whole purpose of the creation story, which is to challenge, as Herold Weiss point out, "a mythological understanding of the world where brooks, mountains, animals, stars or trees have 'powers' of their own. Here we have a secular world. God is clearly outside it, but He left His mark in it when He trusted man with His image" ("Genesis, Chapter One: A Theological Statement," *Spectrum* 9, 1979: 61). The same observation is made by Harvey Cox, *The Secular City,* 1965, pp. 22-23.

77 Harold H. P. Dressler, for example, writes: "There is no command of God that the seventh day should be kept in any way. In retrospect we are told that God 'rested' (Ex. 20:11) and was 'refreshed' (Ex. 31:17)" (n. 62, p. 22 manuscript). Cf. Gerhard von Rad, *The Problem of the Hexateuch and other Essays,* 1966, p. 101, n. 9; Robert A. Morey (n. 74), p. 6; C. H. MacKintosh, *Genesis to Deuteronomy,* 1965, p. 23).

78 John Murray, *Principles of Conduct,* 1957, p. 32.

79 The universal implications of the creation Sabbath are recognized by numerous scholars. U. Cassuto (n. 75), p. 64, for example, comments: "Every seventh day, without intermission since the days of creation, serves as a memorial to the idea of the creation of the world by the word of God, and we must refrain from work thereon so that we may follow the Creator's example and cleave to His ways. Scripture wishes to emphasize that the sanctity of the Sabbath is older than Israel, and rests upon all mankind." *The Interpreter's Bible* I, p. 489: "The fact that P thus connects the origin of the sabbath not with some event in the life of the patriarchs—as he connected circumcision in ch. 17—or in the history of Israel, but with Creation itself, is of significance. For the implication of this passage is that observance of the day... is really binding upon all mankind." Cf. W. H. Griffith Thomas, *Genesis,* 1960, p. 33; Joseph Breuer, *Commentary on the Torah,* 1948, pp. 17-18; Frank Michaeli, *Le Livre de la Genèse,* 19, pp. 30-31; Julian Morgenstern, *The Book of Genesis,* 1965, p. 38; C. Westermann, *Genesis,* 1974, p. 236; Niels-Erik Andreasen (n. 65), p. 75).

80 This argument is presented by Roger D. Congdon in his doctoral dissertation. He writes: "There is absolutely no mention of the sabbath before the Lord said to Moses... These words indicate that the event was bound to the Decalogue of Sinai. The quoted words are recorded in Exodus 16:4. The first mention of the sabbath in the Bible and the first known chronological use of the word in all history is in Exodus 16:23" ("Sabbatic Theology," [Th.D. dissertation, Dallas Theoogical Seminary, 1949], pp. 122-12). Cf. Robert A. Morey (n. 74), p. 6.

81 This does not imply that the ethical principles of the Ten Commandments were unknown. Is not Cain condemned for murdering his brother (Gen. 4:9-11) and Abraham commended for keeping God's commandments?

82 Cf. Ex. 7:25; 12:15, 16, 19; 13:6, 7.

83 This is not to deny that the Sabbath may have been viewed by some Israelites as a relatively new institution, especially because of its inevitable neglect during the Egyptian oppression.

84 Note the emphasis on the home celebration of the Sabbath in Lev. 23:3: "The seventh day is a Sabbath of solemn rest, a holy convocation; you shall do no work; it is *a sabbath to the Lord in all your dwellings.*" Cf. Ex. 16:29. Jacob Z. Lauterbach (n. 12), p. 440, points out that "the main center of the Sabbath observance is in the family

circle at the home and many of its ceremonies are calculated to strengthen the bonds of love and affection between the members of the family, to emphasize the parental care and duties, and to increase the filial respect and reverence for parents."

[85] It was primarily this concern over legalistic Sabbatarianism that led Luther and other radicals to view the Sabbath as a superseded Mosaic institution. See below p. 47. In our time this view is popular among dispensationalists and antinomian Christians.

[86] J. Calvin, *Institutes of the Christian Religion*, 1972, II, p. 339. Cf. K. Barth, *Church Dogmatics*, 1958, III, part 2, p. 50.

[87] For a survey of creationistic theories, see Frank Lewis Marsh, *Studies in Creationism*, 1950, pp. 22-40.

[88] Herold Weiss (n. 76), p. 59.

[89] See below chapter V.

[90] Note that the construction in Greek is *dia* followed by an accusative which denotes the reason for the making of the Sabbath, namely "on account of man," or as expressed by H. E. Dana, *"For the sake of, for, Mark 2:27"* (*A Manual Grammar of the Greek New Testament*, 1962, p. 102).

[91] For an examination of Mark 2:27, see S. Bacchiocchi (n. 11), pp. 55-61. That Christ's saying alludes to the original (creation) function of the Sabbath is recognized by numerous scholars. See, among others, Charles E. Erdman, *The Gospel of Mark*, 1945, p. 56; H. B. Swete, *The Gospel According to St. Mark*, 1902, p. 49; J. A. Schep, "Lord's Day Keeping from the Practical and Pastoral Point of View," in *The Sabbath-Sunday Problem*, 1968, pp. 142-143; Roger T. Beckwith and W. Stott, *This is the Day*, 1978, p. 11; Francis Nigel Lee, *The Covenantal Sabbath*, 1966, p. 29.

[92] D. A. Carson argues that the verb *ginomai* should not be taken as "a technical expression for 'created,' since its meaning varies according to the context" ("Jesus and the Sabbath in the Four Gospels," in *From Sabbath to Lord's Day: A Biblical, Historical, and Theological Investigation*, to be published in 1980, p. 123 manuscript). The observation is correct, but the context does suggest that the verb refers to the original "making" of the Sabbath, for at least two reasons. First, because the statement (2:27) concludes Christ's argument on the humanitarian function of the Sabbath (2:23-26) by pointing to its original and thus ultimate purpose. Second, because Christ's claim of Lordship over the Sabbath (2:28) depends upon the fact that He *made* the day for man's benefit (2:27). For further discussion, see S. Bacchiocchi (n. 11), pp. 59-61.

[93] D. A. Carson objects to drawing a parallel between Matt. 19:8 and Mark 2:27, because in the latter the phrase "from the beginning" is absent. Thus, Carson argues, Jesus is appealing "not to a determinate time, but to a determinate purpose" (n. 92, p. 125). But, can time and purpose be really separated? Did not Christ establish the *purpose* of marriage by referring back to the *time* of its origin? Similarly, is not the human *purpose* of the Sabbath established with reference to the *time* the day was made?

[94] See S. Bacchiocchi (n. 11), pp. 38-48; idem, "John 5:17: Negation or Clarification of the Sabbath," Paper Presented at the Annual Meeting of the Society of Biblical Literature, New Orleans, Louisiana, November 11, 1978; cf. below pp. 155-158.

[95] The passage is examined at length below in chapter V.

[96] The author suggests at least three different levels of meaning. See below, p. 136.

97 The statement is reported by Eusebius in *Praeparatio evangelica* 13, 12.

98 Philo, *De Opificio Mundi* 89; *De Vita Mosis* 1, 207; *De Specialibus Legibus* 2, 59.

99 Philo, *De Decalogo* 97.

100 Philo, *De Opificio Mundi* 89.

101 *Syriac Didascalia* 26, ed. Connolly, p. 233.

102 Athanasius, *De sabbatis et circumcisione* 4, *PG* 28, 138 BC. For additional examples and discussion, see S. Bacchiocchi (n. 11), pp. 273-278.

103 *Constitution of the Holy Apostles* VII, 23, *Ante-Nicene Fathers* VII, 469.

104 Ibid., VII, 36, p. 474; cf. II, 36.

105 Jean Daniélou, *The Bible and Liturgy*, 1966, p. 276.

106 Augustine, *The City of God*, XXII, 30, trans. Henry Bettenson, 1972, p. 1090.

107 The fact that in the creation story there is no mention of "evening... morning" for the seventh day is interpreted by Augustine as signifying the eternal nature of the Sabbath rest both in mystical and in eschatological sense.

108 Augustine, *Confessions* XIII, 35-36. Cf. *Sermon* 38, *PL* 270, 1242; *De Genesis ad litteram* 4, 13, *PL* 34, 305. The "already" and the "not yet" dimensions of the Sabbath rest are concisely presented by Augustine in his *Commentary on Psalm* 91, 2: "One whose conscience is good, is tranquil, and this peace is the Sabbath of the heart. For indeed it is directed toward the hope of Him Who promises, and although one suffers at the present time, he looks forward toward the hope of Him Who is to come, and then all the clouds of sorrow will be dispersed. This present joy, in the peace of our hope, is our Sabbath" (*PL* 27, 1172).

109 In his *Epistula 55 ad Ianuarium* 22, Augustine explains: "Therefore of the ten commandments the only one we are to observe spiritually is that of the sabbath, because we recognize it to be symbolic and not to be celebrated through physical inactivity" (*CSEL* 34, 194). One wonders, How is it possible to retain the Sabbath as the symbol of mystical and eschatological rest in God, while denying the basis of such a symbol, namely, its literal Sabbath rest experience? For a discussion of this contradiction, see below pp. 55-56 and 167-168.

110 Eugippius (about 455-535), for example, quotes *verbatim* from Augustine, *Adversus Faustum* 16, 29 (*Thesaurus 66*, *PL* 62, 685). Cf. Bede (about 673-735), *In Genesim* 2, 3, *CCL* 118A, 35; Rabanus Maurus (about 784-856), *Commentaria in Genesim* 1, 9, *PL* 107, 465; Peter Lombard (about 1100-1160), *Sententiarum libri quatuor* 3, 37, 2, *PL* 192, 831.

111 Chrysostom, *Homilia* 10, 7 *In Genesim*, *PG* 53, 89. Ephraem Syrus (about 306-373) appeals to the Sabbath "law" to urge that "rest be granted to servants and animals" (*S. Ephraem Syri hymni et sermones*, ed. T. J. Lamy, I, 1882, p. 542). For a brief survey of the application of the Sabbath law to Sunday observance, see L. L. McReavy, "'Servile Work': The Evolution of the Present Sunday Law," *Clergy Review* 9 (1935): 273-276. For a sampling of texts, see Willy Rordorf, *Sabbat et dimanche dans l'Eglise ancienne*, 1972, nos. 140, 143. H. Huber describes the development until the late Middle Ages (*Geist und Buchstabe der Sonntagsruhe*, 1958, pp. 117ff.

112 Peter Comestor, *Historia scholastica: liber Genesis* 10, *PL* 198, 1065. On the development of the principle of "one day in seven," see discussion in Wilhelm Thomas, "Sabbatarianism," *Encyclopedia of the Lutheran Church*, 1965, III, p. 2090.

[113] The distinction was explicitly made, for example, by Albertus Magnus (about 1200-1280). See Wilhelm Thomas (n. 112), p. 2278.

[114] Thomas Aquinas, *Summa Theologica*, Part I-II, Q. 100, 3, 1947, p. 1039. The distinction between the moral and ceremonial aspects of the Sabath is clearly stated also in Pt. II-II, Q. 122, 4: "It is a moral precept in the point of commanding man to set aside a certain time to be given to Divine things. For there is in man a natural inclination to set aside a certain time for each necessary thing... Hence according to the dictate of reason, man sets aside a certain time for spiritual refreshment, by which man's mind is refreshed in God. And thus to have a certain time set aside for occupying oneself with Divine things is the matter of a moral precept. But, in so far as this precept specializes the time as a sign representing the Creation of the world, it is a ceremonial precept. Again, it is a ceremonial precept in its allegorical signification, as representative of Christ's rest in the tomb on the seventh day: as also in its moral signification, as representing cessation from all sinful acts, and the mind's rest in God, in which sense, too, it is a general precept. Again, it is a ceremonial precept in its analogical signification, as foreshadowing the enjoyment of God in heaven" (n. 114, p. 1701).

[115] Aquinas subdivided the Mosaic law into moral, ceremonial and judicial precepts. The moral precepts of the decalogue are viewed as precepts also of the Natural Law, that is to say, they are precepts binding upon all men because they are discoverable by all through human reason without the aid of special revelation. Cf. Aquinas (n. 114), Part I-II, Q. 100, 1 and Q. 100, 3, pp. 1037, 1039.

[116] Thomas Aquinas (n. 114), Part I-II, Q. 100, 5, p. 1042. See also above n. 114.

[117] See n. 116. Note also that Aquinas attributes a similar symbolic function to Sunday: "As to the sabbath, which was a sign recalling the first creation, its place is taken by the *Lord's Day*, which recalls the beginning of the new creature in the Resurrection of Christ" (n. 114, Part I-II, Q. 103, 3, p. 1085).

[118] Thomas Aquinas (n. 114), Part I-II, Q. 107, 3, p. 1111.

[119] See L. L. McReavy (n. 111), pp. 279f. A brief survey of the development of Sunday laws and casuistry is provided by Paul K. Jewett, *The Lord's Day*, 1972, pp. 128-169. A good example of the adoption of Aquinas' moral-ceremonial distinction can be found in the *Catechism of the Council of Trent*. See below n. 142.

[120] Karlstadt's concept of the Sabbath rest contains a strange combination of mystical and legalistic elements. Basically he viewed the day as a time to abstain from work in order to be contrite over one's sins. For a clear analysis of his views, see Gordon Rupp, *Patterns of Reformation*, 1969, pp. 123-130; idem, "Andrew Karlstadt and Reformation Puritanism," *Journal of Theological Studies* 10 (1959): 308-326; cf. Daniel Augsburger, "Calvin and the Mosaic Law," Doctoral dissertation, Strasbourg University, 1976, pp. 248-249; J. N. Andrews and L. R. Conradi, *History of the Sabbath and First Day of the Week*, 1912, pp. 652-655.

[121] Luther, *Against the Heavenly Prophets*, *Luther's Works*, 1958, 40: 93. A valuable study of Luther's views regarding the Sabbath is to be found in Richard Muller, *Adventisten-Sabbat-Reformation*, Studia Theologica Lundensia, 1979, pp. 32-60.

[122] *Concordia or Book of Concord, The Symbols of the Evangelical Lutheran Church*, 1957, pp. 174.

[123] *Augsburg Confession* (n. 122), p. 25; cf. Philip Schaff, *The Creeds of Christendom*, 1919, III. p. 69.

[124] *The Large Catechism* (n. 122), p. 175.

[125] *Erlanger* ed., 33:67, cited in Andrews and Conradi (n. 120), p. 627.

[126] Melanchthon, *On Christian Doctrine, Loci Communes 1555*, Clyde L. Manschreck, ed. and trans., 1965, p. 96.

[127] Melanchthon (n. 126), p. 98. In his first edition of the *Loci Communes* (1521) Melanchthon acknowledges his indebtedness to Luther's *Treatise on Good Works* (1520) for his understanding of the Fourth Commandment.

[128] The concept of the Sabbath as "renouncement and renewal" is discussed below, pp. 120-123. I do not share, however, Melanchthon's understanding of Sabbathkeeping as self-mortification, since the Sabbath is not a day of gloom but of gladness. Cf. *Loci Communes Theologici* (1521), in *Melanchthon and Bucer*, L. J. Satre and W. Pauck, trans., 1969, p. 55.

[129] See note 127. This aspect of the Sabbath is considered in several places below; see chapters III, IV, VI and VII.

[130] Luther (n. 121), p. 93; cf. p. 97.

[131] Melanchthon (n. 126), pp. 96-97.

[132] Melanchthon (n. 126), p. 97.

[133] It should be noted, however, that the theological orientation of the Sabbath rest "to the Lord your God" (Ex. 20:11; 31:17; Deut. 5:14) could imply a call to cease from all work in order to worship God in a public assembly. This is suggested by the fact that in the annual feasts, the prohibition of work and the list of persons who were to rest (strikingly similar to that of the Sabbath commandment) are given to ensure the participation of all in the "holy assembly" (Num. 28:18; 25, 26; 29:1, 7, 12, 35; Lev. 23:7, 21, 23-25, 28-32, 35; Deut. 16:8, 11). While acknowledging this possibility, the fact remains that the emphasis of the Fourth Commandment is not on "the office of preaching" but on rest from work. The act of making oneself available for God on the Sabbath does represent a meaningful worship response to God. See below, pp. 174-180.

[134] An incisive criticism of the Natural Law theory is offered by D. J. O'Connor, *Aquinas and Natural Law*, 1967.

[135] Melanchthon (n. 126), p. 96, labels this antinomian position as "childish contention." He them refutes it by appealing to the distinction between the *specific* and the *general* aspects of the Sabbath. Calvin also in 1562 wrote a pamphlet to refute a book written by a Dutchman who advocated that Christ abolished all ceremonies, including the observance of a day of rest (*Response à un Holandois, Corpus Reformatorum* 1863, 9:583-628). In a letter against antinomians ("Wider die Antinomer," 1539), Luther wrote: "I wonder exceedingly how it came to be imputed to me that I should reject the law of ten commandments... Can it be imaginable that there should be any sin where there is no law? Whoever abrogates the law, must of necessity abrogate sin also" (*Erlanger* ed. 32:4, cited in Andrews and Conradi [n. 120], p. 626).

[136] *Augsburg Confession* (n. 122), p. 25. The *Confession* arraigns especially the Catholic Church for requiring the observance of holy days as a condition to salvation: "For those who judge that by the authority of the Church the observance of the Lord's Day instead of the Sabbathday was ordained as a thing necessary, do greatly err" (loc. cit.). Luther recognized that his harsh statements against the Decalogue were necessitated by prevailing perversions. In response to an antinomian, Luther wrote in 1541: "If heretofore I in my discourses spoke and wrote so harshly against the law, it was because the Christian church was over-

whelmed with superstitions under which Christ was altogether hidden and buried; ... but as to the law itself, I never rejected it" (cited in Robert Cox, *The Literature of the Sabbath Question*, 1865, I, p. 388).

[137] *Augsburg Confession* (n. 122), p. 25.

[138] See below, pp. 120-122, 169.

[139] Luther, *Treatise on Good Works* (1520), *Selected Writings of Martin Luther*, 1967, 1:154b.

[140] Luther (n. 122), p. 174.

[141] Winton V. Solberg, *Redeem the Time*, 1977, pp. 15-19; A. G. Dickens, *The English Reformation*, 1964, p. 34; George H. Williams, *The Radical Reformation*, 1962, pp. 38-58, 81-84, 815-865.

[142] *Catechism of the Council of Trent*, J. Donovan, trans., 1908, p. 342.

[143] Ibid., p. 343.

[144] The Catholic deletion of the second commandment is compensated by advancing the position of the remaining eight and by treating as two distinct precepts the tenth commandment. This arbitrary re-arrangement shows its inconsistency, for example, in the *Catechism of the Council of Trent* where all the ten commandments are examined individually with the exception of the ninth and tenth which are treated as one (see n. 142, p. 401).

[145] For example, the *Catechism of the Council of Trent*, part III, chapter 4, questions 18 and 19 (n. 142), p. 347. In his address before the Council of Trent, Caspar della Fossa stated: "The Sabbath, the most glorious day in the law, has been changed into the Lord's day ... This and similar matters have not ceased by virtue of Christ's teaching (for he says he came to fulfill the law, not to destroy it), but they have been changed by virtue of the authority of the church. Should this authority cease (which would surely please the heretics), who would then witness for truth and confound the obstinacy of the heretics?" (Mansi 33:533, cited in Andrews and Conradi [n. 120], p. 589). On the use of this argument by Catholic authorities in French Switzerland, see Daniel Augsburger, "Sunday in the Pre-Reformation Disputations in French Switzerland," *Andrews University Seminary Studies* 14 (1976): 265-277.

[146] Johann Eck, *Enchiridion locorum communium adversus Lutherum et alias hostes ecclesiae*, 1533, p. 79.

[147] Ibid.

[148] *Catechism of the Council of Trent* (n. 142), pp. 344-345.

[149] Ibid., p. 346.

[150] Ibid., p. 347.

[151] See below ns. 154, 155.

[152] A valuable survey of the ideas and influence of these Sabbatarians is provided by G. F. Hasel, "Sabbatarian Anabaptists," *Andrews University Seminary Studies* 5 (1967): 101-121; 6 (1968): 19-28. On the existence of Sabbathkeepers in various countries, see Andrews and Conradi (n. 120), pp. 633-716. Cf. Richard Muller (n. 121), pp. 110-129.

[153] In a list of eleven sects by Stredovsky of Bohemia, "Sabbatarians" are listed in the third place after Lutherans and Calvinists. The list is reprinted by Josef Beck, ed., *Die Geschichts-Bücher der Widertäufer in Österreich-Ungarn* ("Fontes Rerum Austriacarum," Wien, 1883), 43:74. For an analysis of this and three other lists, see Hasel (n. 152), pp. 101-106, who concludes: "These early enumerations seem to indicate that Sabbatarian Anabaptists were considered to be an important and strong group" (p. 106). Cf. Henry A. DeWind, "A Sixteenth Century Description of Religious Sects in Austerlitz, Moravia," *Mennonite Quarterly Review* (1955): 51; George H. Williams (n. 141), p. 676, 726, 732, 848, 408-410, 229, 257, 512.

[154] Desiderius Erasmus, "Amabili ecclesiae concordia," *Opera Omnia* V: 505-506; translation by Hasel (n. 152), p. 107.

[155] Luther reports: "In our time there is a foolish group of people who call themselves Sabbatarians [Sabbather] and say one should keep the Sabbath according to Jewish manner and custom" (*D. Martin Luthers Werke*, Weimer ed. 42:520). In his *Lectures on Genesis* (4:46) Luther furnishes similar information: "I hear that even now in Austria and Moravia certain Judaizers urge both the Sabbath and circumcision; if they should boldly go on, not being admonished by the work of God, they certainly might do much harm" (cited in Andrews and Conradi [n. 120], p. 640.

[156] J. G. Walch, ed., *Dr. Martin Luthers sämmtliche Schriften*, 1910, 20: 1828ff. Cf. D. Zscharnack, "Sabbatharier," *Die Religion in Geschichte und Gegenwart*, 1931, 5: 8.

[157] On Oswald Glait, see the recent study of Richard Muller (n. 121), pp. 117-125. Cf. Hasel (n. 152), pp. 107-121.

[158] On Andreas Fisher see the treatment by Richard Muller (n. 121), pp. 125-130; Petr Ratkoš, "Die Anfänge des Wiedertäufertums in der Slowakei," *Aus 500 Jahren deutsch-tschechoslowakischer Geschichte*, Karl Obermann, ed., 1958, pp. 41-59.

[159] Caspar Schewenckfeld's refutation of Glait's book is found in S. D. Hartranft and E. E. Johnson, eds., *Corpus Schwenckfeldianorum*, 1907, 4: 451ff.

[160] Ibid., p. 458. The translation is by Hasel (n. 152), p. 119.

[161] Ibid., p. 491.

[162] Ibid., pp. 457-458.

[163] An Anabaptist (Hutterian) Chronicle provides this moving account of Glait's final days: "In 1545 Brother Oswald Glait lay in prison in Vienna for the sake of his faith... Two brethren also came to him, Antoni Keim and Hans Standach, who comforted him. To them he commended his wife and child in Jamnitz. After he had been in prison a year and six weeks, they took him out of the city at midnight, that the people might not see or hear him, and drowned him in the Danube" (A. J. F. Zieglschmid, ed., *Die älteste Chronik der Hutterischen Brüder*, 1943, pp. 259, 260, 266, trans. by Hasel [n. 152], pp. 114-115).

[164] A brief historical survey of seventh-day Sabbathkeepers from the fifteenth to the seventeenth century is found in Andrews and Conradi (n. 120), pp. 632-759. A more comprehensive and critical study of Sabbathkeeping through the ages is scheduled for early publication (1980?) by the Review and Herald under the title *The Sabbath in the Scriptures and History*. About 20 scholars have contributed chapters to this new study.

[165] R. J. Bauckham, "Sabbath and Sunday in the Protestant Tradition," (n. 62), p. 526 manuscript. In 1618, for example, John Traske began preaching that Christians are bound by the Fourth Commandment to keep Saturday scrupulously. Under pressure, however, he later recanted in *A Treatise of Liberty from Judaism* (1620). Theophilus Brabourne, also an Anglican minister, published in 1628 *A Discourse upon the Sabbath Day* where he defended the observance of Saturday instead of Sunday. The High Commission induced him to renounce his views and to conform to the established church. Cf. Robert Cox, *The Literature of the Sabbath Question*, 1865, 1:157-158.

[166] Cf. W. Y. Whitley, *A History of British Baptists*, 1932, pp. 83-86; A. C. Underwood, *A History of the English Baptists*, 1947, chaps. 2-5.

[167] Seventh Day Baptist General Conference, *Seventh Day Baptists in*

Europe and America, 1910, I, pp. 127, 133, 153. Cf. Winton U. Solberg (n. 141), p. 278.

[168] Raymond F. Cottrell notes: "The extent to which pioneer Seventh-day Adventists were indebted to Seventh Day Baptists for their understanding of the Sabbath is reflected in the fact that throughout the first volume [of *Advent Review and Sabbath Herald*] over half of the material was reprinted from Seventh Day Baptist publications" ("Seventh Day Baptists and Adventists: A Common Heritage, *Spectrum* 9 [1977]: 4).

[169] The Church of God Seventh Day traces their origin back to the Millerite movement. Mr. Gilbert Cranmer, a follower of Miller's views, who for a time associated himself with the Seventh Day Adventists, in 1860 was elected as the first president of a group known first as Church of Christ and later Church of God Seventh Day. Their 1977 report gives an estimated membership of 25,000 persons ("Synopsis of the History of the Church of God Seventh Day," compiled in manuscript form by their headquarters in Denver, Colorado).

[170] The 1974 *Directory of Sabbath-Observing Groups*, published by *The Bible Sabbath Association*, lists over 120 different denominations or groups observing the seventh-day Sabbath.

[171] A comprehensive study of Calvin's understanding of the Fourth Commandment is provided by Daniel Augsburger (n. 120), pp. 248, 284.

[172] John Calvin, *Commentaries on the First Book of Moses Called Genesis*, trans. John King, 1948, p. 106. The same view is repeated a few lines below: "Inasmuch as it was commanded to men from the beginning that they might employ themselves in the worship of God, it is right that it should continue to the end of the world" (p. 107).

[173] John Calvin, *Commentaries on the Four Last Books of Moses Arranged in the Form of a Harmony*, trans. Charles William Bingham, 1950, p. 437.

[174] Ibid., p. 439.

[175] Ibid., p. 440. Zwingli also accepted the Sabbath as a creation institution, designed to serve as a type of the eternal Sabbath and to provide time to "consider God's kind deeds with thankfulness, hear His law and Word, praise Him, serve Him and finally care for the neighbor" (*H. Zwinglis Sämtliche Werke.* Corpus Reformatorum, 1905-1953, 13:16, 395). Cf. Edwin Kunzli, "Zwingli als Ausleger von Genesis und Exodus," Th.D. dissertation, Zurich, 1951, p. 123.

[176] John Calvin, *Institutes of the Christian Religion*, trans. Henry Beveridge, 1972, I, p. 341.

[177] John Calvin (n. 172), p. 106.

[178] Ibid.

[179] John Calvin (n. 176), p. 343.

[180] Ibid. Calvin summarizes the distinction between the ceremonial and moral aspects of the Sabbath, saying: "The whole may be thus summed up: As the truth was delivered typically to the Jews, so it is imparted to us without figure; first, that during our whole lives we may aim at a constant rest from our own works, in order that the Lord may work in us by his Spirit; secondly, that every individual, as he has opportunity, may diligently exercise himself in private, in pious meditation on the works of God, and at the same time, that all may observe the legitimate order appointed by the Church, for the hearing of the word, the administration of the sacraments, and public prayer: and, thirdly, that we may avoid oppressing those who are subject to us" (ibid.).

[181] John Calvin (n. 173), pp. 435-436.

[182] Zacharias Ursinus, *The Summe of Christian Religion*, Oxford, 1587, p. 955.

[183] On the enormous influence of Nicolas Bownde's book, *The Doctrine of the Sabbath*, see Winton U. Solberg (n. 141), pp. 55-58. The book was enlarged and revised in 1606. Bownde insists that the Sabbath originated in Eden and consequently the Fourth Commandment is a moral precept binding on both Jews and Christians. The latter are urged to observe Sunday as carefully as the Jews did their Sabbath.

[184] In the 163rd session of the Synod of Dort (1619) a commission of Dutch theologians approved a six-point document where the traditional ceremonial/moral distinctions are made. The first four points read as follows:

"1. In the *Fourth Commandment* of the Law of God, there is something *ceremonial* and something *moral*.

2. The resting upon the *seventh day* after the creation, and the strict observance of it, which was particularly imposed upon the *Jewish* people, was the *ceremonial* part of that law.

3. But the *moral* part is, that a certain day be fixed and appropriated to the service of God, and as much rest as is necessary to that service and the holy meditation upon Him.

4. The *Jewish Sabbath* being abolished, Christians are obliged solemnly to keep holy the Lord's *Day*" (Gerard Brandt, *The History of the Reformation and Other Ecclesiastical Transactions in and about the Low Countries*, London, 1722, 3: 320; cf. pp. 28-29, 289-290).

[185] *The Westminster Confession*, chapter 21, article 7, reads: "As it is of the law of nature, that in general, a due proportion of time be set apart for the worship of God; so, in his Word, by a positive, moral, and perpetual commandment, binding all men in all ages, he hath particularly appointed one day in seven for a Sabbath, to be kept holy unto him: which, from the beginning of the world to the resurrection of Christ, was the last day of the week; and, from the resurrection of Christ was changed into the first day of the week" (Philip Schaff, *The Creeds of Christendom*, 1919, 3:648-649).

[186] R. J. Bauckham, "Sabbath and Sunday in the Protestant Tradition," (n. 62), p. 510 manuscript.

[187] Willem Teellinck, *De Rusttijdt: Ofte Tractaet van d'onderhoudinge des Christelijken Rust Dachs* (*The Rest Time: Or a Treatise on the Observance of the Christian Sabbath*), Rotterdam, 1622. William Ames, *Medulla Theologica*, Amsterdam, 1623, trans. John D. Eusden, *The Marrow of Theology*, 1968, pp. 287-300, provides a theoretical basis for Sunday observance. Antonius Walaeus, *Dissertatio de Sabbatho, seu Vero Sensu atque Usu Quarti Praecepti* (*Dissertationon the Sabbath, Or the True Meaning and Use of the Fourth Commandment*), Leiden, 1628. Walaeus' work represents a major literary defence of the Edenic origin of the Sabbath and of its application to Sunday observance.

[188] An earlier treatise against Sabbatarianism was produced by Jacobus Burs, *Threnos, or Lamentation Showing the Causes of the Pitiful Condition of the Country and the Desecration of the Sabbath*, Tholen, 1627. Andreas Rivetus refuted Gomarus' contention that the Sabbath was a Mosaic ceremony abrogated by Christ in his *Praelectiones* (*Lectures*), 1632. Gomarus replied with a voluminous *Defensio Investigationis Originis Sabbati* (*A Defense of the Investigation into the Origin of the Sabbath*), Gronigen, 1632. To this Rivetus countered with *Dissertatio de Origine Sabbathi* (*Dissertation on the Origin of the Sabbath*), Leyden, 1633.

[189] The controversy flared up again in Holland in the 1650's. Gisbertus Voetius and Johannes Cocceius were the two opposing leaders in the new round. For a brief account see Winton U. Solberg (n. 141),

p. 200. Solberg provides an excellent survey of the controversy over the Sabbath in seventeen-century England (pp. 27-85) and especially in the early American colonies (pp. 85-282).

[190] Willy Rordorf's book (n. 43) was first published in 1962 in German. Since then it has been translated into French, English and Spanish. Its influence is evidenced by the many and different responses it has generated.

[191] Roger T. Beckwith and Wilfrid Stott, *This is the Day. The Biblical Doctrine of the Christian Sunday*, London, 1978.

[192] Rordorf's denial of any connection between Sunday and the Fourth Commandment can be traced historically in the writing of numerous anti-Sabbatarian theologians, such as Luther (n. 122, 123); William Tyndale, *An Answer to Sir Thomas More's Dialogue* (1531), ed. Henry Walter, Cambridge, 1850, pp. 97-98; the formulary of faith of the Church of England known as *The Institution of a Christian Man* (1537); Franciscus Gomarus (n. 188); Francis White, *A Treatise of the Sabbath-Day: Concerning a Defence of the Orthodox Doctrine of the Church of England against Sabbatarian Novelty* (London, 1635); Peter Heylyn, *The History of the Sabbath* (London, 1636); James A. Hessey, *Sunday: Its Origin, History, and Present Obligation* (London 1866); Wilhelm Thomas, *Der Sonntag im frühen Mittelalter* (Göttingen, 1929); C. S. Mosna, *Storia della Domenica dalle Origini fino agli Inizi del V Secolo* (Rome, 1969); D. A. Carson, ed., *From Sabbath to Lord's Day: A Biblical, Historical and Theological Investigation* (to be published in 1980).

[193] This concern is expressed, for example, by P. Falsioni, in *Rivista Pastorale Liturgica* (1967): 311, 229, 97, 98; (1966): 549-551. Similarly Beckwith and Stott point out: "Whether the Christian Sunday could have survived to the present day if this sort of attitude [Rordorf's view] had prevailed among Christians in the past is extremely doubtful, and whether it will survive for future generations if this sort of attitude now becomes prevalent is equally uncertain" (n. 191, p. ix).

[194] Beckwith points out, for example, that "if Jesus regarded the sabbath as *purely* ceremonial and *purely* temporary, it is remarkable that he gives so much attention to it in his teaching, and also that in all he teaches about it he never mentions its temporary character. This is even more remarkable when one remembers that he emphasizes the temporary character of other parts of the Old Testament ceremonial—the laws of purity in Mark 7:14-23 and Luke 11:39-41, and the temple (with its sacrifices) in Mark 13:2 and John 4:21. By contrast, we have already seen, he seems in Mark 2:27 to speak of the Sabbath as one of the unchanging ordinances for all mankind" (n. 191), p. 26; cf. pp. 2-12.

[195] Beckwith (n. 191), pp. 45-46. Beckwith and Stott's view of the Sabbath as an unchanging creation ordinance upon which the observance of Sunday rests, can be traced historically in the writings of theologians such as Aquinas (partly—n. 114, 115, 116); Calvin (partly—n. 172-180); Richard Hooker, *Laws of Ecclesiastical Polity* (1597), V: 70, 3; Nicholas Bownde (n. 183); William Teellinck, William Ames and Antonius Walaeus (n. 187); formularies of faith such as the *Westminster Confession* (n. 185) and the Synod of Dort (n. 184); E. W. Hengstenberg, *Über den Tag des Herrn* (1852); recently by J. Francke, *Van Sabbat naar Zondag* (Amsterdam, 1973); Karl Barth, *Church Dogmatics*, 1956, III, pp. 47-72; Paul K. Jewett (partly), *The Lord's Day: A Theological Guide to the Day of Worship* (1971); Francis Nigel Lee, *The Covenantal Sabbath* (1966). Lee's study, though sponsored by the British *Lord's Day Observance Society*, can hardly be taken seriously on account of its eccentric nature. He

speculates, for example on "The Sabbath and the time of the fall" (pp. 79-81).

[196] Beckwith and Stott (n. 191), pp. 141, 143.

[197] See especially the first four chapters of my book *From Sabbath to Sunday*, where the alleged Biblical evidences for an apostolic origin of Sunday are examined.

[198] Nahum M. Sarna (n. 76), p. 21, points out that "The seventh day is what it is because God chose to 'bless it and declare it holy.' Its blessed and sacred character is part of the divinely ordained cosmic order. It cannot, therefore, be abrogated by man and its sanctity is a reality irrespective of human activity."

[199] Elizabeth E. Platt, "The Lord Rested, The Lord Blessed the Sabbath Day," *Sunday* 66 (1979): 4.

[200] This aspect of the message of the Sabbath is examined in the following chapter and in chapter VI, part 4, under the heading of "The Sabbath and the Ecological Crisis."

CHAPTER II

THE SABBATH: GOOD NEWS OF PERFECT CREATION

[1] The meaning of the Sabbath in Hebrews 4 is examined at length in chapter V.

[2] Gen. 1:4, 10, 12, 18, 21, 24, 31.

[3] U. Cassuto, *A Commentary on the Book of Genesis*, 1961, pp. 14-15. Cassuto provides an illuminating analysis of the use of the number seven in the creation story. See also his essay "La creazione del mondo nella Genesis," in *Annuario di Studi Ebraici* 1 (1934): 47-49.

[4] Nicola Negretti, *Il Settimo Giorno*, Pontifical Biblical Institute Press, 1973, pp. 149-152.

[5] Ibid., p. 152.

[6] See above chapter I, n. 36, 57.

[7] See above p. 26.

[8] Nicola Negretti (n. 4), pp. 31-62 offers a sampling of ancient Near Eastern texts where the septenary structure occurs in various literary forms.

[9] James B. Pritchard, ed. *Ancient Near Eastern Texts*, 1950, (UT krt A 206-211), p. 145. A similar example is found in the *Gilgamesh Epic*: "One day, a second day, Mount Nisir held the ship fast, Allowing no motion. A third day, a fourth day, Mount Nisir held the ship fast, Allowing no motion. A fifth, a sixth (day), Mount Nisir held the ship fast, Allowing no motion. When the seventh day arrived, I sent forth and set free a dove." (Pritchard [n. 9], tablet XI, p. 94).

[10] For example, Gen. 4:15, 24; 29:18-20; 41:2-54; Lev. 12:2; 13:5, 21, 26; 26:18-21; Ruth 4:15; 1 Sam. 2:5; 2 Kings 5:10; Prov. 24:16; Dan. 3:19; Ps. 12:6; Is. 30:26; Rev. 1:4; 5:1.

[11] R. Pettazzoni, "Myths of Beginning and Creation-Myths," in *Essays on the History of Religion*, trans. H. T. Rose, 1954, pp. 24-36. A brief but informative treatment is found in Niels-Erik A. Andreasen, *The Old Testament Sabbath*, SBL Dissertation Series 7, 1972, pp. 174-182. For examples of texts, see Pritchard (n. 9), pp. 5, 61, 69, 140.

[12] Pritchard (n. 9), p. 68.

[13] Andreasen (n. 11), p. 196. Similarly, Gerhard von Rad explains, "Rest ... testifies negatively first of all, but that is important enough, that the world is no longer in process of being created. It was not and is not incomplete, but it has been 'completed' by God" (*Genesis: A Commentary*, 1961, p. 60). Elsewhere von Rad says, "the completion of God's creation was the resting on the seventh day" (*Old Testament Theology*, 1962, p. 147).

[14] Karl Barth, *Church Dogmatics*, ET 1956, III, part 2, p. 51.

[15] Ibid., part 1, p. 213.

[16] Dietrich Bonhoeffer, *Creation and Fall. A Theological Interpretation of Genesis 1-3*, 1964, p. 40. Cf. Cassuto (n. 3), p. 62.

[17] Quoted in Abraham Joshua Heschel, *The Sabbath: Its Meaning for Modern Man*, 1952, p. 32.

[18] Pacifico Massi, *La Domenica*, 1967, p. 368.

[19] A good treatment of the historical development of the Apostles' Creed is found in Philip Schaff, *History of the Christian Church*, 1959, II, pp. 528-537; idem, *Creeds of Christendom*, 1884, I, pp. 3-42; II, pp. 10-73.

[20] George Elliot, *The Abiding Sabbath*, 1884, pp. 17-18.

[21] Karl Barth (n. 14), III, part 1, p. 22.

[22] Ellen White, *The Great Controversy Between Christ and Satan*, 1950, p. 438.

[23] Harvey Cox, *Turning East*, 1977, p. 65.

[24] For a description of the positive celebration of the Sabbath in the Jewish home, see Nathan Barack, *A History of the Sabbath*, 1965, pp. 89-105; Jacob Z. Lauterbach, *Rabbinic Essays*, 1951, pp. 454-470; Abraham E. Millgram, *The Sabbath: The Day of Delight*, 1944, pp. 23-333, 395-437.

[25] The question of feasting or fasting on the Sabbath in early Christianity is discussed in Samuele Bacchiocchi, *From Sabbath to Sunday*, 1977, pp. 185-198.

[26] Ellen White, *Testimonies for the Church*, 1948, VI, p. 359.

[27] Abraham Joshua Heschel (n. 17), p. 21.

CHAPTER III

THE SABBATH: GOOD NEWS OF GOD'S CARE

[1] A penetrating analysis of some of the causes for the prevailing skepticism about God's concern for human affairs is offered by Herbert W. Richardson, *Toward an American Theology*, 1967, pp. 1-21.

[2] George Elliot, *The Abiding Sabbath*, 1884, p. 27, comments, "God blessed the seventh day, and sanctified it. God can bless the seventh day only by making it a blessing to man. Insensate time cannot feel the benedictions of Deity. Man's blessing is a prayer, but God's blessing is an act. He alone can give the blessing he pronounces. The Sabbath serves man's whole nature, and thus it is to him a blessing." Similarly Joseph Breuer, *Introduction to Rabbi Samson Raphael Hirsch's Commentary on the Torah*, 1948, interprets the blessing of the Sabbath as meaning that "God bestowed on the seventh day the power to succeed in its Divine destination and 'sanctified it,' i.e. raised it above any attempt to remove it from its appointed position.... This seventh day and all that it means to mankind will succeed in its task to educate and win back an estranged mankind." H. C. Leupold, *Exposition of Genesis*, 1950,

p. 103, remarks, "those blessings of the Sabbath that are later to flow forth for the good of man are potentially bestowed on it."

3 Nicola Negretti, *Il Settimo Giorno*, Pontifical Biblical Institute, 1973, p. 170. Negretti sees the "unsealing" of the sanctity and blessedness of the Sabbath in the narrative of the manna and of Sinai; see pp. 171-251.

4 Gerhard von Rad, *Genesis: A Commentary*, 1961, p. 60.

5 H. C. Leupold. (n. 2), p. 103, explains that "on the one hand, the verb 'he sanctified it' (*qiddesh*), being a *Piel* stem, has the connotation of a causative... and on the other hand, it has at the same time a declarative sense: 'He declared holy or consecrated.' "

6 Nicola Negretti (n. 3), p. 228.

7 Ellen White, *The Story of Patriarchs and Prophets*, 1958, p. 313.

8 Samuel Terrien, *The Elusive Presence*, 1978, p. 392.

9 It is noteworthy that the Romans used the term *Sabbateion* to describe the Jewish *meeting place* (synagogue), obviously because such gatherings occurred on the Sabbath. Cf. Flavius Josephus, *Antiquities of the Jews*, 16, 6.

10 I. Grunfeld relates a touching episode where the Sabbath helped tormented Jews to forget their misery: "The train dragged on with human freight. Pressed together like cattle in the crowded trucks, the unfortunate occupants were unable even to move. The atmosphere was stifling. As the Friday afternoon wore on, the Jews and Jewesses in the Nazi transport sank deeper and deeper into their misery. Suddenly an old Jewish woman managed with a great effort to move and open a bundle. Laboriously she drew out—two candlesticks and two *challot*. She had just prepared them for the Sabbath when she was dragged from her home that morning. They were the only things she had thought worth while taking with her. Soon the Sabbath candles lit up the faces of the tortured Jews and the song of 'Lekhah Dodi' transformed the scene. Sabbath with its atmosphere of peace had descended upon them all" (*The Sabbath: A Guide to its Understanding and Observance*, 1972, p. 1).

11 Herbert W. Richardson (n. 1), p. 130.

12 Ibid.

13 Karl Barth, *Church Dogmatics*, ET 1956, III, part 2, p. 62. Luther emphasizes in his *Large Catechism* that to rest on the holy day does not simply mean to "sit behind the stove and do no rough work, or deck ourselves with a wreath and put on our best clothes, but that we occupy ourselves with God's Word, and exercise ourselves therein" (*Concordia or Book of Concord. The Symbols of the Evangelical Lutheran Church*, 1957, p. 175).

14 Thomas Aquinas, *Summa Theologica*, Part II-II, Q. 122, 4, 1.

15 John Murray, *Principles of Conduct*, 1957, pp. 33-34 writes: "The reason for the cycle of labour and rest is that God himself followed this sequence. The governing principle of this ethic is not merely the will of God but conformity to the pattern of divine procedure. In this particular Adam was to be a son of the Father in heaven." Nicola Negretti (n. 3), p. 168, similarly remarks: "The origin, the meaning and the dynamic of the human work-rest are found in the creative divine work-rest. Not only, but the human work-rest expresses, continues and actualizes the creative divine work-rest." Also Rousas John Rushdoony, *The Institutes of Biblical Law*, 1973, p. 146, notes, "The Sabbath gives purpose to man's life, in that it makes labor meaningful and purposive: it links it to a joyful consummation."

16 Karl Barth (n. 13), pp. 50-51.

17 Hiley H. Ward, *Space-Age Sunday*, 1960, p. 146. A similar proposal

is advanced by Christopher Kiesling, *The Future of the Christian Sunday*, 1970, pp. 81-102.

[18] Hiley H. Ward (n. 17), p. 147.

[19] George Elliot (n. 2), p. 83, writes: "The command, 'Pray without ceasing,' does not make stated worship less valuable or even less necessary. Quite the contrary; it is the hour of prayer alone that gives that spirit of prayer which abides with us during the whole day. So it is only a hallowed Sabbath that can lend a Sabbath's blessing to the entire week."

[20] Ibid., p. 82.

[21] H. H. Rowley aptly remarks, "It is significant that in our day impatience with the sabbath as a day of rest is the accompaniment of the widespread abandonment of the sabbath as a day of worship" (*Worship in Ancient Israel: Its Form and Meaning*, 1967, p. 241).

CHAPTER IV

THE SABBATH: GOOD NEWS OF BELONGING

[1] A major study of the OT covenant has been done by D. J. McCarthy, *Treaty and Covenant*, Analecta Biblica, 1963, 2nd edition 1972. See also his survey, *Old Testament Covenant: A Survey of Current Opinions*, Oxford, 1972. Cf. G. E. Mendenhall, *Law and Covenant in Israel and the Ancient Near east*, 1955. Also his article in *The Interpreter's Dictionary of the Bible*, 1962, s.v. "Covenant"; K. Baltzer, *The Covenant Formulary in Old Testament, Jewish, and Early Christian Writings*, trans. by D. E. Green. Oxford, 1971.

[2] J. J. Stamm and M. E. Andrew, *The Ten Commandments in Recent Research*, 1967, p. 70. A little further the two authors remark, "Neither grace nor the demand made on us can be regarded as more important or more primary than the other. In fact, this very statement is misleading in as far as it gives the impression that they are necessarily two different things. They always belong together. God's grace can only be given to us in the demand made upon us, and in receiving the gift, we are freed from the slavery of that performance in our own strength which can only lead to proud and self-satisfied legalism" (p. 72).

[3] For example, the sacrifice of divided animals (Gen. 15:7-16); the passover lamb and blood (Ex. 12:12-14); the tabernacle (Ex. 25:8).

[4] The language in these references is clearly that of the covenant. Note, for example, the expression "between me and you" (Ex. 31:13, 16; Ezek. 20:12, 20). Ernst Jenni explains that the Sabbath is wholly a covenant institution (*Die theologische Begründung des Sabbatgebotes in Alten Testament*, 1956, pp. 13-15).

[5] Quoted in Karl Barth, *Church Dogmatics*, ET, 1956, III, part 2, p. 51, emphasis supplied.

[6] Ibid., III, part 1, p. 98. Karl Barth emphasizes that "It is the covenant of the grace of God which in this event, at the supreme and final point of the first creation story, is revealed as the starting-point for all that follows. Everything that precedes is the road to this supreme point" (p. 98).

[7] Ibid., III, part 1, pp. 216, 217.

[8] Emperor Hadrian's prohibition of Sabbathkeeping is discussed in Samuele Bacchiocchi, *From Sabbath to Sunday*, 1977, pp. 159-161.

9 W. E. H. Lecky notes that "of all the failures of the French Revolution, none was more complete than the substitution of a tenth for a seventh day of rest, which they established and tried to enforce by law. The innovation passed away without protest or regret" (*Democracy and Liberty*, 1930, II, p. 109). Cf. Charles Huestis, *Sunday in the Making*, 1929, p. 134.

10 Dennis J. McCarthy, *Old Testament Covenant*, 1972, p. 88.

11 Quoted by Augusto Segre, in "Il Sabato nella storia Ebraica," in the symposium *L'uomo nella Bibbia e nelle culture ad essa contemporanee*, 1975, p. 116. Herbert W. Richardson expresses a similar view, saying: "I believe that the power of Judaism to survive in the face of constant enmity and disadvantage arises from its firm sense of being a 'holy people,' i.e., from its recurring celebration of the Sabbath sacrament" (*Toward an American Theology*, 1967, p. 132).

12 Quoted by R. H. Martin, *The Day: A Manual on the Christian Sabbath*, 1933, p. 184. Cf. *Sunday* 65 (1978): 22.

13 M. G. Kline, *Treaty of the Great King. The Covenant Structure of Deuteronomy*, 1963, p. 18. Gerhard von Rad recognizes the "right of ownership" expressed by the Sabbath and says, "it is the day which really belongs to God and sets a standard undefiled by any kind of human business.... the celebration of the sabbath, at least in Israel's earlier period, was discharged by abstaining demonstratively from productive labour, and symbolically handing the day back to God" (*Deuteronomy. A Commentary*, 1966, p. 58).

14 A. T. Lincoln brings out this function of the Sabbath, saying, "By bringing all routine work to a halt for twenty-four hours the people were acting out their allegiance and confessing that the covenant Lord was specifically Lord of their time. This is why the Sabbath could serve as a sign of the whole covenant relationship. By demonstrably laying down her work and allowing the seventh day to, as it were, 'lie fallow,' Israel was acknowledging her complete dependence on her Suzerain" ("From the Sabbath to the Lord's Day: A Biblical and Theological Perspective," in *From Sabbath to the Lord's Day: A Biblical, Historical and Theological Investigation*, D. A. Carson, ed. [to be published in 1980], p. 563 manuscript).

15 John Calvin acknowledges this function of the Sabbath, writing, "under the rest of the seventh day, the divine Lawgiver meant to furnish the people of Israel with a type of the spiritual rest by which believers were to cease from their works, and allow God to work in them" (*Institutes of the Christian Religion*, 1972, I, p. 339).

16 See *The Interpreter's Dictionary of the Bible*, 1962, s.v. "Holiness." Johannes Pedersen explains that holiness as the experience of divine power through places or times functions as a regulating principle of the whole life (*Israel: Its Life and Culture* 1940, III-IV, p. 287).

17 A. Martin points out that the divine choice of the Sabbath fulfills a double function. "In the first place it is a time which man, object of divine election, sets apart for the service of God. Secondly, the exercise of setting aside time reminds the Christian that he himself has been set apart" ("Notes sur le Sabbat," *Foi et Vie* 5 [1975]: 18).

18 Ibid., p. 17.

19 Abraham Joshua Heschel writes: "The Hebrew word *le-kadesh*, to sanctify, means, in the language of the Talmud, to consecrate a woman, to betroth. Thus the meaning of that word on Sinai was to impress upon Israel the fact that their destiny is to be the groom of the sacred day" (*The Sabbath: Its Meaning for Modern Man*, 1951, pp. 51-52).

[20] Nathan A. Barack remarks that the celebration of the Sabbath "from sundown to sundown enables the observer to welcome it, and usher it out, by means of appropriate rituals. The day is complete and distinctive. The religious experience of welcoming, and taking leave from, the holy day makes the life of the observer also distinctive" (*A History of the Sabbath*. 1965, p. 32).

[21] M. L. Andreasen, *The Sabbath: Which Day and Why?*, 1942, p. 243.

[22] The influence of the Roman legislation against secret societies and gatherings (*hetaeriae*) on Christian's worship habits, is discussed in *From Sabbath to Sunday* (n. 8), pp. 95-99.

[23] This view is expressed by G. E. Mendenhall. He writes: "The surprising infrequency of references to covenant in the NT raises great difficulties, even though it is understandable. The covenant for Judaism meant the Mosaic law and for the Roman Empire a covenant meant an illegal secret society. This two-sided conflict made it nearly impossible for early Christianity to use the term meaningfully" (*The Interpreter's Dictionary of the Bible*, 1962, s.v. "Covenant," p. 722). Note that even the covenant meaning of the Lord's Supper ("new covenant in my blood"— I Cor. 11:25) is not found in the post-NT literature (such as *Didache*, 9, 10, 14), presumably because of the same Roman *hetaeriae* (n. 22) legislation.

[24] Louis Tamminga, "Review of *Promise and Deliverance* by S. G. De Graaf," *Baptist Reformation Review* 3 (1979): 31.

[25] Philip Melanchthon, *On Christian Doctrine. Loci Communes 1555*, trans. by Clyde L. Manschreck, 1965, p. 98. Emphasis supplied.

[26] A. Martin (n. 17), p. 20.

[27] Karl Barth (n. 5), p. 54.

[28] Ibid.

[29] George Foot Moore correctly points out that Sabbathkeeping was "even more significant than circumcision. The latter sign of the covenant was imposed on an infant by his parents without his understanding or will, solely by virtue of his descent; whereas the keeping of the sabbath in the face of wordly interest was a standing evidence of the intelligent and self-determined fidelity of the man to the religion in which he was brought up from a child" (*Judaism in the First Centuries of the Christian Era*, 1927, p. 24).

[30] Sakae Kubo comments that the Sabbath "recalls to his [Christian] mind the time when his re-creation took place, his baptism which memorializes the once-and-for-all event. The Sabbath weekly reminds us of the once-and-for-all completed Creation event, our redemption by Christ, and our new creation" (*God Meets Man*, 1978, p. 49).

[31] Abraham Joshua Heschel (n. 19), p. 99.

[32] Fritz Guy, "Holiness in Time: A Preliminary Study of the Sabbath as Spiritual Experience," a paper presented at Andrews University, 1961, p. 5.

[33] For example, Hiley H. Ward writes: "The day [Sabbath] is intangible, not something made with hands, according to Jewish rabbis. But is it really intangible? When it is defined, with regulations attached to keeping the day, a way of life imposed, it becomes as tangible as a millstone upon the neck of a person" (*Space-Age Sunday*, 1960, p. 146).

[34] A. Martin (n. 17), pp. 24-25.

[35] Karl Barth (n. 5), p. 54. Cf. idem, III, part 1, p. 226.

[36] Ibid., p. 227.

[37] Karl Barth expresses eloquently this function of the Sabbath, saying: "The aim of the Sabbath commandment is that man shall give

and allow the omnipotent grace of God to have the first and last word at every point; ... that he shall place himself, with his knowing, willing and doing, unconditionally at its disposal" (n. 5, p. 54).

CHAPTER V

THE SABBATH: GOOD NEWS OF REDEMPTION

[1] Karl Barth has recognized and emphasized the redemptive meaning and function of the Sabbath. James Brown summarizes Barth's view, saying: "The fundamental meaning of the Sabbath is thus that it is a sign of salvation altogether, first and last, of God, in His covenant relation with His creature" ("The Doctrine of the Sabbath in Karl Barth's *Church Dogmatics,*" *Scottish Journal of Theology,* 20 (1967): 7.

[2] See Gerhard von Rad, "Das theologische Problem des alttestament-lichen Schöpfungsglaubens," in *Gesammelte Studien zum Alten Testament,* 1958, pp. 136-147.

[3] A. T. Lincoln notes this double function of the Sabbath. He writes: "As regards the work of creation God's rest was final, but as that rest was meant for humanity to enjoy, when it was disturbed by sin, God worked in history to accomplish his original purpose" ("Sabbath, Rest and Eschatology in the New Testament," in *From Sabbath to Lord's Day: A Biblical, Historical and Theological Investigation,* D. A. Carson, ed., to be published in 1980, p. 319 manuscript; cf. p. 310).

[4] Herbert W. Richardson rightly emphasizes the connection between the sanctification of the creation Sabbath and the incarnation of Christ. He writes, for example, "God created the world so that the Sabbath guest, Jesus Christ, might come and dwell therein. That is, the world was created for the sake of 'Emmanuel, God with us.' The incarnation is, therefore, not a rescue operation, decided upon only after sin had entered into the world. Rather, the coming of Christ fulfills the purpose of God in creating the world. Sanctification, not redemption, is the chief work of Jesus Christ—'God with us' rather than 'God for us'" (*Toward an American Theology,* 1967, p. 139). Richardson is right in emphasizing the sanctification function of the Sabbath but wrong in doing so at the expense of redemption. To be a symbol of a divine-human relationship the Sabbath does not have to cease being a symbol of redemption. Sanctification and redemption are not mutually exclusive but equally included, both in the meaning of the Sabbath and in the work of Christ. A valuable critique to Richardson's book is offered by Roy Branson, Fritz Guy and Earle Hilgert, "*Toward an American Theology:* A Symposium on an Important Book," *Andrews University Seminary Studies* 7 (1969): 1-16.

[5] See C. K. Barrett, in "The Eschatology of the Epistle to the Hebrews," in *The Background of the New Testament and its Eschatology,* D. Daube and W. D. Davies, eds., 1956, p. 365. The tension can be seen, for example, in the description of the church as living "at the end of the age" (9:26; 1:2) and yet "eagerly waiting for him [Christ]" (9:28; 2:10).

[6] Note that the term *katapausis* is used in the Septuagint to designate the rest of the Sabbath. Cf. Ex. 35:2; II Macc. 15:1.

[7] Plutarch, *De Superstitione* 3 and *Moralia* 166a; Justin Martyr, *Dialogue with Trypho* 23, 3; Epiphanius, *Adversus haereses* 30, 2, 2; *Martyrium Petri et Pauli* 1; *Constitutions of the Holy Apostles* 2, 36, 2. For

a treatment of the question, see O. Hofius, *Katapausis*, Tübingen, 1970, pp. 103-105.

8 W. Rordorf emphasizes the Christological implication of "Today": "We shall misunderstand the burden of the passage if we do not hear in it the decisive significance of the 'Today.' The new day of the 'Today' has dawn in Christ (v. 7). On this new day it is possible to enter into the rest, and yet more: on this new day this rest has become a reality for those who believe" (*Sunday*, 1968, p. 112). Note also the similarity with the "Today" of Luke 4:21 and John 9:4.

9 Gerhard von Rad, "There Remains Still a Rest for the People of God," in *The Problem of the Hexateuch and Other Essays*, 1965, p. 102. A similar view is expressed by Karl Barth: "From creation—preceding and superseding every human decision of obedience or disobedience—there remains (*apoleipetai*) for the people of God the Sabbath rest (*sabbatismos*), the divinely willed and ordered fellowship, relationship and agreement between His own and human freedom as the goal and determination of the way to which this people continually have to be recalled, to which God never wearies to recall them, and to which, at the end and climax of that intercourse, He has definitively recalled them in His Son (Heb. 4:9)" (*Church Dogmatics* ET, 1958, III, part 1, p. 227).

10 Abraham Joshua Heschel, *The Sabbath: Its Meaning for Modern Man*, 1952, p. 23.

11 Gerhard von Rad traces the development of the theme of "rest" in the OT from national-political to personal-spiritual experience (see n. 9, pp. 94-102). Ernst Jenni maintains that the Sabbath contributed to the development of the theme of Israel's rest (*Die theologische Begründung des Sabbatgebotes im Alten Testament*, 1956, p. 282).

12 Theodore Friedman, "The Sabbath: Anticipation of Redemption," *Judaism* 16 (1967): 445. Friedman notes that "at the end of the Mishnah *Tamid* (*Rosh Hashanah* 31a) we read: 'A Psalm, a song for the Sabbath day—a song for the time-to-come, for the day that is all Sabbath rest in the eternal life.' The Sabbath, the Gemara asserts, is one-sixtieth of the world to come" (ibid., p. 443).

13 For examples, see Theodore Friedman (n. 12): cf. *Rosh Hashanah* 31a; *Mekilta Ex.* 31:13; *Pirke de Rabbi Eliezer* 19; *Aboth de R. Nathan* 1.

14 *Sanhedrin* 97a.

15 *Vita Adae et Evae* 51:1, 2, in *The Apocrypha and Pseudepigrapha of the Old Testament*, R. H. Charles, ed., 1913, II, p. 153. Cf. *Apocalypsis of Mosis* 43:3. A similar view is found in *Genesis Rabbah* 17:5: "There are three antitypes: the antitype of death is sleep, the antitype of prophecy is dream, the antitype of the age to come is the Sabbath." Cf. *Genesis Rabbah* 44:17.

16 R. Longenecker points out that in the OT "greater emphasis is given to a description of the Age itself than to God's anointed instrument who will usher in that Age. While sections and chapters are devoted to the former (e.g., Is. 26-29; 40ff.; Ezek. 40-48; Dan. 12; Joel 2:28-3:21), definite references to the latter are confined, in the main, to a few specific verses (e.g., Is. 9:6f; Micah 5:2; Zech. 9:9)" (*The Christology of Early Jewish Christianity*, 1970, pp. 63-64).

17 II Baruch 29:3, in Charles (n. 15), p. 497, emphasis supplied. Similarly in IV Ezra 8:52, the seer is assured: "For you is opened Paradise, planted the Tree of life; the future Age prepared, plenteousness made ready; a City builded, a *Rest* appointed" in Charles (n. 15), p. 598, emphasis supplied. See also references above, n. 13.

18 *Mishna Tamid* 7:4. The viewing of the Sabbath as the symbol

and anticipation of the Messianic age gave to the celebration of the weekly Sabbath a note of gladness and hope for the future. Cf. *Genesis Rabbat* 17; 44; *Baba Berakot* 57f. Theodore Friedman shows how certain Sabbath regulations established by the school of Shammai were designed to offer a foretaste of the Messianic age (n. 12, pp. 447-452).

[19] Harold H. P. Dressler aptly remarks: "Trained by the regular recurrence of this gracious gift, Israel was able to stand in freedom, responsibility, trust and gratitude before her Creator on the Sabbath day, worshipping him, the Lord of the Sabbath, and looking forward with joy and anticipation to the coming of the final rest" ("The Sabbath in the Old Testament," [n. 3], p. 32).

[20] Niels-Erik Andreasen argues that the "remembrance clause" ("you shall remember that you were a servant in the land of Egypt"—Deut. 5:15a) does not constitute the real reason for Sabbathkeeping since structurally the sentence is not preceded by the preposition "for" (as in Ex. 20:11a) but is placed in parallelism with the previous sentence of vv. 13-14 (*Rest and Redemption*, 1978), pp. 49-50). Nicola Negretti, though he recognizes the "parallelistic arrangement," shows in his structural analysis that the "conclusion 'therefore'—'al ken' does represent "the conscious effort to link the Sabbath to the theme of the exodus" (*Il Settimo Giorno*, Pontifical Biblical Institute, 1973, p. 132). Negretti's conclusion is supported by the fact that the same "remembrance clause" is explicitly given in Deuteronomy as the reason for emancipating slaves in the sabbatical year (15:15), for celebrating the feast of weeks (16:12), and for doing justice to the underprivileged (24:17-18, 21-22).

[21] Hans Walter Wolff, "The Day of Rest in the Old Testament," *Concordia Theological Monthly*, 43 (1972): 500.

[22] Niels-Erik Andreasen (n. 20), p. 52.

[23] Ibid.

[24] In a passage of the Talmud, the seventh day, the seventh year and the seventh millennium are interrelated as follows: "R. Kattina said: Six thousand years shall the world exist, and one [thousand, the seventh], it shall be desolate, as it is written, *And the Lord* alone *shall be exalted in that day*... Just as the seventh year is one year of release in seven, so is the world: one thousand years out of seven shall be fallow, as it is written, *A Psalm and a song for the Sabbath day* [Ps. 92:1], meaning the day that is altogether Sabbath" (*Sanhedrin* 976, trans. by H. Freedman, 1935, II, p. 657).

[25] II Chronicles 36:21 mentions the non-observance of the sabbatical years. There are, however, some historical allusions to the keeping of the annual sabbaths (Josephus, *Antiquities* 11, 86; 14, 10, 6; 15, 1, 2; I Macc. 6:49-53; Tacitus, *Histories* 5, 2, 4). Cf. Jer. 34; Neh. 10:32; 2 King 19:29; Is. 37:30. S. W. Baron argues in favor of the existence and influence of the Sabbath and jubilee legislation (*A Social and Religious History of the Jews*, 1952, I, pp. 332-333). Similarly, Edward Neufeld, "Socio-economic background of *Yobel* and *šemitta*," *Rivista degli Studi Orientali* 38 (1958): 119-124; J. H. Yoder, *The Politics of Jesus*, 1972, pp. 69-70. We concur with Robert B. Sloan's statement: "The popular clamor, prophetic remonstrances, and eschatological appeal surrounding this ordinance serve to illustrate both its continuing fecundity throughout the history of Israel and its apparently simultaneous lack of regular, consistent enforcement" (*The Favorable Year of the Lord. A Study of Jubilary Theology in the Gospel of Luke*, 1977, p. 27).

[26] Robert B. Sloan (n. 25), p. 37 notes that "of the approximately fifty instances of *aphesis* in the LXX, 22 are found in Lev. 25 and 27

where it translates in most cases the Hebrew *yobel* 'year of jubilee' and in other cases, most notably Lev. 25:10, it is used to translate *deror* 'release.' "

27 See, Rudolf Bultmann, *"aphesis,"* *Theological Dictionary of the New Testament,* 1974, I, p. 511: "The noun *aphesis* almost always means 'forgiveness.' "

28 Julian Morgenstern maintains that "In all likelihood the 'great trumpet' (Is. 27:13), a blast from which would inaugurate a new and happier era for conquered and dispersed Israel, was a *yobel.* All this suggests cogently that the ram's-horn trumpet was of unusual character, used only upon extraordinary occasions and for some particular purpose (cf. Ex. 19:136).... This year acquired its name just because this unique, fiftieth year was ushered in by this blast upon the *yobel* whereas the commencement of ordinary years was signalized by a blast upon only a *šophar* (II Sam. 15:10; cf. Lev. 23:24)" (*The Interpreter's Dictionary of the Bible,* 1962, s.v. "Jubilee, Year of," II, p. 1001).

29 C. D. Ginsburg notes the connection between the Day of Atonement and the inauguration of the jubilee year. In his comment on Leviticus 25:9, he writes: "On the close of the great Day of Atonement, when the Hebrews realized that they had peace of mind, that their heavenly Father had annulled their sins, and that they had become re-united to Him through His forgiving mercy, every Israelite was called upon to proclaim throughout the land, by nine blasts of the cornet, that he too had given to soil rest, that he had freed every encumbered family estate, and that he had given liberty to every slave, who was now to rejoin his kindred. Inasmuch as God has forgiven his debts, he also is to forgive others" (*Leviticus,* in *Ellicott's Commentary on the Whole Bible,* I, p. 454). Cf. Robert B. Sloan (n. 25), p. 15.

30 Rousas John Rushdoony, *The Institutes of Biblical Law,* 1973, p. 141.

31 Even if one takes the "seven weeks" of Daniel 9:25 as an independent unit, it would still consist of one jubilee. It is more feasible, however, to take v. 24 as a summary of the whole time period. See André Lacocque, *The Book of Daniel,* 1979, p. 191.

32 For an excellent exegetical analysis of Daniel 9:24-27, bringing out the Messianic eschatology of the passage, see Jacques Doukhan, "The Seventy Weeks of Daniel 9: An Exegetical Study," *Andrews University Seminary Studies* 17 (1979): 1-22.

33 On the rabbinic and Qumranic eschatological interpretation of Isaiah 61:1-3, see James A. Sanders, "From Isaiah 61 to Luke 4," in *Christianity, Judaism and Other Greco-Roman Cults,* Jacob Neusner, ed., 1975, pp. 82-92. Further examples and discussions are provided by I. Howard Marshall, *The Gospel of Luke,* 1978, p. 182.

34 The text is translated and analyzed by Joseph A. Fitzmyer, in "Further Light on Melchizedek from Qumran Cave 11," *Journal of Biblical Literature* 86 (1967): 25-41. See also M. Miller, "The Function of Isa. 61:1-2 in 11Q Melchizedek," *Journal of Biblical Literature* 88 (1969): 467-469.

35 The translation is by Fitzmyer (n. 34), p. 28. The dependency upon Daniel 9:25 is explicit in line 18 which reads "and the herald i[s] [th]at [An]ointed One (about) whom Dan[iel] said ..."

36 *Sanhedrin* 97b. For other references and discussion, see George Wesley Buchanan, "Sabbatical Eschatology," *Christian News From Israel,* 18 (December 1967): 51-54.

37 Abraham Joshua Heschel (n. 10), p. 68. Similarly Jacob Fichman writes: "When the hour of the Sabbath-welcome arrives, there is felt a kind of foretaste of the promised Redemption, even as with every out-

going of the Sabbath there is a feeling of the renewal of the enslave-
ment, of the gloom ahead," (quoted by Abraham E. Millgram, *Sabbath.
The Day of Delight*, 1944, p. 391).

[38] The fundamental role of the passage has been recognized by many
scholars. Hans Conzelmann affirms: "Luke 4:18 is one of the programmatic passages which describe the ministry of Jesus in the words of
the Septuagint" (*The Theology of St. Luke*, 1960, p. 221). Similarly Gunther
Bornkamm says: "The evangelist Luke has expressly set down the relevant word of the prophet as the governing text of all Jesus' works"
(*Jesus of Nazareth*, 1940, p. 75).

[39] Most scholars view Luke's account of the Nazareth address as
being a Lucan redaction of Mark 6:1-6. For examples, see I. Howard
Marshall (n. 33), p. 179. Thus Christ's speech would have been delivered
not at the beginning but sometime later in His ministry. W. Lane, *The
Gospel According to Mark*, 1974, p. 201, n. 2, however, argues in favor
of two different visits to Nazareth. The latter appears plausible espe-
ially since the Sabbath healings of the demon-possessed in the synagogue
of Capernaum and of Simon's mother-in-law, which in Luke follow the
Nazareth visit, are placed by Mark at the outset of Christ's ministry
(Mark 1:21-31).

[40a], [40b] M. M. B. Turner, "The Sabbath, Sunday and the Law in Luke-
Acts," (n. 3), p. 147 manuscript. Cf. I. H. Marshall (n. 33), p. 181.

[41] See W. Grundmann, *Das Evangelium nach Lukas*, 1961, p. 120; K. H.
Rengstorf, *Das Evangelium nach Lukas*, 1969, p. 67.

[42] On the influence of the synagogue upon the Christian divine service,
see C. W. Dugmore, *The Influence of the Synagogue upon the Divine Office*,
1964; A. Allan McArthur, *The Evolution of the Christian Year*, 1953; Dom
Benedict Steuart, *The Development of Christian Worship*, 1953.

[43] Luke 4:16, 31; 6:1, 2, 5, 6, 7, 9; 13:10, 14, 15, 16; 14:1, 3, 5; 23:54, 56;
Acts 1:12; 13:14, 27, 42, 44; 15:21; 16:13; 17:2; 18:4.

[44] A number of scholars recognize in this text Luke's concern to show
that the community observed the Sabbath. Cf. I. H. Marshall (n. 33),
p. 883; F. Godet, *A Commentary on the Gospel of Saint Luke*, 1870, II,
p. 343; A. R. Leaney, *A Commentary on the Gospel According to Saint
Luke*, 1966, p. 288. The same view is implied by the translators of the
New International Version: "Then they went home and prepared spices
and perfumes. But they rested on the Sabbath in obedience to the commandment" (Luke 23:56).

[45] See above n. 39.

[46] The two crucial terms of the passage are "to proclaim" and
"release." Both of these terms, which recur twice, are technical terms
for the Sabbath years. For an informative treatment of this question,
see Robert B. Sloan (n. 25), pp. 32-42. P. Miller rightly notes: "The tie
that binds Isaiah 61:1-2 and 58:6 together in Luke 4 is the small word
aphesis, the word translated "release" for the captives and "liberty" for
the oppressed.... it is the catchword binding the two quotations together. Out of the four sentences in Isaiah 58:6 that all say essentially
the same thing, the one chosen here in the gospel quotation is the one
that in the Greek translation uses *aphesis*" ("Luke 4:16-21," *Interpretation*
29 [October, 1975]: 419).

[47] H. Conzelmann (n. 38), p. 180. See also n. 38; Robert B. Sloan
(n. 25), p. 49. Similarly G. B. Caird points out that Luke "places the
incident at the beginning of his story of the Galilean ministry, because
it announces the *pattern* which the ministry is to follow" (*Saint Luke*,
1963, p. 86). Robert C. Tannehill also writes: "These words and acts

[Luke 4:16-30] have typical programmatic significance for the whole of Jesus' ministry as Lukes understands it.... Luke chose to make this quotation [Luke 4:18-19] the title under which the whole ministry of Jesus is placed. He did so because it expresses clearly certain important aspects of his own understanding of Jesus and his ministry" ("The Mission of Jesus according to Luke 4:16-30," in *Jesus in Nazareth*, 1972, pp. 51, 72).

48 A. Strobel argues that behind Christ's quotation lay an actual historical jubilee year which is dated in A.D. 26-27 (*Kerygma und Apokalyptik*, 1967, p. 105-111). If this were the case, then Christ's speech would have added significance since it would have been delivered in the context of an actual jubilee year.

49 P. K. Jewett, *The Lord's Day*, 1072, p. 27. W. Rordorf similarly comments: "By means of this quotation from the prophet, Luke's Gospel does therefore describe the effect of Jesus' coming as the inauguration of the sabbath year" (*Sunday*, 1968, p. 110). Cf. W. J. Harrington, *A Commentary, The Gospel according to St. Luke*, 1967, p. 134.

50 R. J. Banks maintains that "the theme of his Gospel, that is announced at Nazareth in Luke 4:16f. and is reiterated during the Resurrection appearances in 24:44ff.,... fashions the material related to the Law. In these passages the saving ministry of Jesus is presented as the 'fulfilment' of all that was promised to Israel and this is the thrust of the legal material in Luke as well" (*Jesus and the Law in the Synoptic Tradition*, 1975, p. 248).

51 Roger T. Beckwith correctly points out that "if Jesus regarded the sabbath as *purely* ceremonial and purely temporary, it is remarkable that in all he teaches about it he never mentions its temporary character. This is even more remarkable when one remembers that he emphasizes the temporary character of other parts of the Old Testament ceremonial—the laws of purity in Mark 7:14-23 and Luke 11:39-41, and the temple (with its sacrifices) in Mark 13:2 and John 4:21. By contrast, as we have already seen, he seems in Mark 2:27 to speak of the sabbath as one of the unchanging ordinances for all mankind" (*This is the Day*, 1978, p. 26).

52 M. M. B. Turner (n. 40), p. 147-148 manuscript.

53 Ibid., p. 148.

54 I. H. Marshall (n. 33), p. 185. P. K. Jewett also remarks, "Jesus commented on this Scripture, which speaks of the age of the Messiah in the language of the Sabbatical Year, telling the people that *on that day* the prophet's words were fulfilled in their ears (Luke 4:17-21)" (n. 49, p. 27, emphasis supplied).

55 P. Miller, see quotation in n. 46.

56 D. A. Carson, "Jesus and the Sabbath in the Four Gospels," (n. 3), p. 97 manuscript.

57 Matt. 12:1-8, 9-14; 24:20; Mark 1:21-28; 2:23-28; 3:1-6; Luke 4:16-30, 31-37, 38-39; 6:1-5, 6-11; 13:10-17; 14:1-6; John 5:2-18; 7:21-24; 9:1-41.

58 In *From Sabbath to Sunday*, 1977, p. 35, I wrote: " This work of clarifying the intent behind the commandments was a dire necessity, since with the accumulation of traditions in many cases their original function had been obscured. As Christ put it, 'You have a fine way of rejecting the commandment of God in order to keep your tradition!' (Mark 7:9). The fifth commandment, for instance, which enjoins to 'honor your father and your mother,' according to Christ, had been made void through the tradition of the *Corban* (Mark 7:12-13). This apparently consisted of translating a service or obligation to be rendered to one's parents, into a gift to be given to the temple. The Sabbath command-

ment was no exception and, unless liberated from many senseless casuistic restrictions, would have remained a system for self-righteousness rather than a time for loving the Creator-Redeemer and one's fellow beings."

[59] Harald Riesenfeld, *The Gospel Tradition*, 1970, p. 118.

[60] G. B. Caird, *Saint Luke*, 1963, p. 171. Cf. also W. Grundmann, *Das Evangelium nach Lukas*, 1961, pp. 278-281.

[61] P. K. Jewett (n. 49), p. 42.

[62] C. F. Evans, "Sabbath," *A Theological Word Book of the Bible*, 1959, p. 205.

[63] This view is expressed, for example, by M. M. B. Turner who writes: "There is no question here of the Sabbath being particularly appropriate for such healing, any more than it is particularly appropriate on that day to loose oxen and donkey from their crib and to water them. The argument, in other words, is not that the Sabbath *is* a special day, in this respect, but precisely that it is *not*. The inbreaking kingdom, the loosing of Satan's captives, is no respecter of days" (n. 40, p. 155 manuscript). The same view is held by D. A. Carson (n. 56), p. 94 manuscript. Carson's argument that Jesus healed the woman not because it was appropriate to the Sabbath, but because of "His concern to be getting on with His mission" creates an unjustifiable tension between Christ's mission and the meaning of the Sabbath. Luke gives no hint that Christ is impatient to get on with His ministry in spite of the Sabbath but rather that He acted intentionally ("ought not"—v. 16) because it was Sabbath. Note that Christ postponed "mass" healings until after the Sabbath (Luke 4:40-41; Mark 1:32). He healed some specific chronic individuals to challenge prevailing misconceptions and thus to clarify the meaning of the Sabbath and of His mission.

[64] Nathan A. Barack correctly affirms: "The Sabbath inspires its beneficiaries to feel that the universe is the work of a purposeful Creator, that human life has meaning and sanctity, that all life must be preserved, and that even animals must be provided with their necessary rest" (*A History of the Sabbath*, 1965, p. XII).

[65] Robert Banks (n. 50), p. 131 comments in this regard: "Luke desires to highlight those works of Jesus which bring salvation and healing to men, which as v. 16 makes clear, especially occur on that day." Similarly I. H. Marshall (n. 33), p. 559, writes: "Hence it was necessary for her to be released immediately, even though it was Sabbath, perhaps indeed all the more fitting on the Sabbath," Cf. also above ns. 60, 61, 62.

[66] Samuele Bacchiocchi, "John 5:17: Negation or Clarification of the Sabbath?," paper presented at the annual meeting of the Society of Biblical Literature, New Orleans, Louisiana, November 21, 1978. See also my treatment in *From Sabbath to Sunday*, 1967, pp. 38-48.

[67] See, for example, George Allen Turner, Julius R. Mantey, O. Cullmann, E. C. Hoskyns, and F. Godet *in loco*.

[68] Emphasis supplied.

[69] A. T. Lincoln, "Sabbath, Rest and Eschatology in the New Testament," (n. 3), p. 319 manuscript.

[70] A. Corell emphasizes the connection between the nature of the divine works and the meaning of the Sabbath, saying: "Indeed, it was by an appeal to the nature of his works that Jesus refuted the Jews when they accused him of breaking the Sabbath—'My Father worketh even until now and I work' (v. 17). Thus he pointed out that, while the Law of Moses forbade that men should do their own work on the Sabbath, it could in no wise forbid or prevent the accomplishment of God's work on that day. He, himself, had come to do the works of

God ... which, being of eschatological significance, belonged to the Sabbath in a very special way ... Indeed, his very doing of these things was a sure sign that the real Sabbath of fulfilment had come" (*Consummatum Est*, 1957, p. 63). Cf. John Murray, *Principles of Conduct*, 1957, p. 33.

[71] D. A. Carson fails to recognize the redemptive function of the Sabbath brought out by Christ in this (John 7:23) and similar statements (Matt. 12:5-6; Luke 13:16), and consequently, he disclaims any link between the Sabbath and Jesus' redemptive mission (n. 56, p. 109 manuscript). He further concludes that "John, by taking the discussion into Christological and eschatological realms, does not deal explicitly with the question of whether or not Christians are to observe the weekly Sabbath" (ibid.). Such a conclusion fails to note that the discussion of "Christological and eschatological realms" takes place not without but within the intended meaning of the Sabbath. Moreover, is not Jesus' example of Sabbathkeeping paradigmatic for Christians? O. Cullmann ably shows that "John reveals a tendency in accounts of all events of Christ's life to trace the line from the Jesus of history to the Christ of the community and his chief interest is in connection with early Christian worship" (*Early Christian Worship*, 1966, p. 91; cf. p. 59). This suggests that the sabbatical sayings of 5:17 and 9:4 were reported by John to justify the understanding and practice of the Sabbath rest of the community: a day to experience God's redemptive working by ministering to the needs of others. This conclusion is indirectly supported by a number of recent studies which argue convincingly for a Palestinian provenance of John's Gospel. The numerous linguistic and conceptual similarities which have been established between John's interpretation of Christ and the Old Testament portrayal of Moses are taken as evidence of John's effort to present Christ to Palestinian Jewish communities, in terms of their expectations of the Messiah as a "Prophet-like-Moses." (A valuable survey of studies is provided by F. Lamar Cribbs, in "The 'Prophet-like-Moses' Import of the Johannine *'Ego Eimi'* Sayings," a paper presented at the annual meeting of the Society of Biblical Literature, New Orleans, Louisiana, November 21, 1978). If John utilizes the accepted figure and authority of Moses to prove Christ's true Messiahship to Palestinian Jews, then he could hardly have intended to negate Mosaic instructions regarding the Sabbath when he reported what Jesus said and did on such a day. This is further borne out by the fact that to justify the Sabbath works and words of Christ, appeal is made in John 5 specifically to the authority of the "Scriptures" (v. 39) and of Moses himself: "It is Moses who accuses you,... If you believed Moses, you would believe me, for he wrote of me" (vv. 45-46). For a treatment on the Palestinian Christians' attachment to Sabbathkeeping, see my study *From Sabbath to Sunday*, pp. 132-164.

[72] Ellen White expresses this view, saying: "Upon one Sabbath day, as the Savior and His disciples returned from the place of worship, they passed through a field of ripening grain" (*The Desire of Ages*, 1940, p. 284). D. A. Carson interprets the episode as "a leisurely Sabbath afternoon stroll" (n. 56, p. 75 manuscript). This interpretation reflects contemporary customs but hardly harmonizes with the travel restrictions (Sabbath day's journey of 2/3 of a mile) existing at that time.

[73] This argument is well stated by Ellen White: "If it was right for David to satisfy his hunger by eating of the bread that had been set apart to a holy use then it was right for the disciples to supply their need by plucking the grain upon the sacred hours of the Sabbath" (n. 72, p. 285).

[74] M. M. B. Turner (n. 40), p. 150. Cf. Robert Banks (n. 50), pp. 115-116; M. D. Hooker, *The Son of Man in Mark*, 1967, p. 97, similarly argues on the basis of the "special position" enjoyed by David and Christ.

[75] See Willy Rordorf (n. 8), p. 61. My response to Rordorf's argument is given in *From Sabbath to Sunday*, pp. 50-61.

[76] Note that later the Church of Rome did turn the Sabbath from a day of feasting into a day of fasting in order to put an end to its festive and religious significance. The question is treated at length in my study (n. 75), pp. 185-198.

[77] D. A. Carson (n. 56), pp. 84-85 manuscript.

[78] Willy Rordorf frankly admits: "Subsequent reflection leads us to notice that all the scriptural passages which the Church adduced in order to justify Jesus' infringements of the sabbath refer to priestly functions which have precedence over the sabbath. In the story of David eating the shewbread (in I Sam 21:1-7) it is, in fact, the priest who, above all, does something forbidden when, in answer to David's request, he gives him the shewbread to eat" (n. 8, p. 114).

[79] Rousas John Rushdoony observes that "*forgiveness* is a basic aspect of the sabbath." He argues that the petition of the Lord's Prayer "forgive our debts" derives from the cancellation of debts of the Sabbath years (n. 30, pp. 140-141). Several scholars share the same view. See, for example, Robert B. Sloan (n. 26), pp. 139-140; Ernst Lohmeyer, *Das Vater-unser*, 1946, p. 112 f.; F. Charles Fensham, "The Legal Background of Mt. VI: 12," *Novum Testamentum* 4 (1960): 1-2.

[80] Ellen White (n. 72), p. 285.

[81] See, for example, D. M. Cohn-Sherbok, "An Analysis of Jesus' Arguments Concerning the Plucking of Grain on the Sabbath," *Journal for the Study of the New Testament* 2 (1979): 31-41 Cf. D. A. Carson (n. 56), p. 126 manuscript.

[82] Robert Banks (n. 50), p. 117. Cf. Morna D. Hooker, *The Son of Man in Mark*, 1967, p. 98; P. K. Jewett (n. 49), p. 37; Niels-Erik Andreasen (n. 20), p. 99.

[83] D. A. Carson (n. 56), p. 85 manuscript.

[84] Ibid., p. 83. Cf. W. Rordorf (n. 8), pp. 70, 296.

[85] David Hill stresses this function of Christ's question reported in Matthew 12:5: "The verse provides a precedent for the action of the disciples *within the Law itself*, and therefore places Jesus securely within the Law" (*The Gospel of Matthew*, 1972, p. 211).

[86] This view is emphatically stated by Etan Levine: "The Pharisees are not being told that the Sabbath injunctions should be abrogated; rather, within their own realm of discourse they are being reminded that plucking grain on the Sabbath is legitimate for sacred purposes. Thus, Jesus does not abrogate the *Torah*, but exercises his prerogative to interpret it, in this case defining the 'sacred' in term other than the Temple ritual, as the text explicitly states" ("The Sabbath Controversy According to Matthew," *New Testament Studies* 22 [1976]: 482). Similarly William L. Lane writes: "The divine intention was in no way infringed by the plucking of heads of grain on the part of Jesus' disciples" (*The Gospel according to Mark*, 1974, p. 120).

[87] The connection is recognized by W. Rordorf (n. 8), p. 109; J. Daniélou, *Bible and Liturgy*, 1956, p. 226; David Hill (n. 85), pp. 209-210.

[88] D. A. Carson (n. 56), p. 98 manuscript.

[89] J. C. Fenton links Christ's rest with the Sabbath rest of the expected Messianic age: "By those who labour and are heavy-laden is probably meant those who find the Law, as it was expounded by the

Scribes and Pharisees, too difficult to keep. *I will give you rest*: The weekly Sabbath rest was thought of as an anticipation of the final rest of the messianic age" (*The Gospel of Matthew*, 1963, p. 187).

90 M. Maher provides examples and a helpful treatment in "Take My Yoke Upon You—Matt. 11:29," *New Testament Studies* 22 (1976): 97-103.

91 *Pirke Aboth* 3:5; cf. 6:2; *Sirach* 51:26.

92 Cf. Galatians 5:1: "yoke of slavery." Later Christians used the term "yoke" to refer to Christ's new Law, grace or word. See, for example, *Epistles of Barnabas* 2, 6; *I Clement* 16, 17; Justin Martyr's, *Dialogue with Trypho* 53, 1.

93 M. Maher (n. 90), p. 99.

94 Jacob Jervell convincingly shows that Luke's references to the mass conversions which are distributed "carefully throughout his account" are intended to show that the Christian mission to the Jews was successful (*Luke and the People of God. A New Look at Luke-Acts*, 1972, pp. 41-69).

95 Hans Walter Wolff notes the connection between the divine rest of creation and of redemption. Commenting on God's creation rest, Wolff writes: "We are able to comprehend this fully only in the light of Jesus Christ's exhaustion in His work of redemption, as it is expressed in His cry: 'It is finished.' In offering up Himself, God gave us everything" (n. 21, p. 501).

96 D. A. Carson keenly notes that "Matthew does not introduce any Sabbath controversy until almost half way through his Gospel; but when he suddenly inserts two Sabbath pericopae (Matt. 12:1-14), he places them immediately after Jesus' invitation to the burdened and weary to find rest in his easy yoke. As if such a justaposition were not enough, Matthew then carefully points out that the Sabbath conflicts occurred 'at that time'—presumably at or near the time when Jesus had spoken of his rest. This is as much as to say that the rest he offers infinitely surpasses the rest which the Pharisees wanted the people to observe" (n. 56).

97 A. T. Lincoln rightly explains, "The linking of *katapausis* [rest] in LXX Ps. 94:11 with the divine rest at creation is facilitated by the fact that the cognate verb is used in the LXX of Gen. 2:2 (and God rested—*katepausen*...) and that *katapausis* itself is used of Sabbath rest in Ex. 35:2; II Macc. 15:1" (n. 69, p. 327 manuscript).

98 Among the commentators who view the fulfilment of the Sabbath rest to be exclusively future are: E. Käsemann, O. Michel, H. Windisch, W. Manson, F. F. Bruce, F. Delitzsch, R. C. H. Lenski, *in loco*; cf. also G. von Rad (n. 9), pp. 101f.

99 See, A. T. Lincoln (n. 69), p. 334 manuscript.

100 The question of whether the recipients of Hebrews were Gentile or Jewish Christians is still debated. For a discussion of this problem see W. G. Kummel, *Introduction to the New Testament*, 1975, pp. 398-401.

101 H. C. Kee, F. W. Young and K. Froehlich note: "The entire doctrinal part of the Letter (chapter 1:1-10:18) could be seen as arguing against Christian tendencies to make the Jewish sacrificial cult respectable again as a tool to gain access to God in the wake of the new interest in cult, liturgy, sacrament, and effective forms of worship" (*Understanding the New Testament*, 1973, p. 300). Similarly Bruce M. Metzger remarks: "Many of them felt themselves drawn to Jewish liturgy, and were on the point of renouncing Christianity and returning to their ancestral Jewish faith" (*The New Testament. Its Background, Growth, and Content*, 1965, p. 249).

102 George Wesley Buchanan, *To the Hebrews*, 1972, pp. 72-75.

[103] The pre-eminent study is by E. Käsemann, *Das wandernde Gottesvolk*, 1938. For a recent treatment of this question, see W. G. Johnsson, "The Pilgrimage Motif in the Book of Hebrews." *Journal of Biblical Literature* 97 (1978): 239-251. In my view, A. T. Lincoln offers a valid criticism of the application of the pilgrimage motif to the "rest" of Hebrews. He writes: "The model of the church as a company of wanderers on a journey to a distant heavenly resting place, reflected in the title of Käsemann's study of Hebrews, *Das wandernde Gottesvolk*, when it has been applied to this passage, has misled too many commenta ors into supposing the rest is entirely future. Whatever truth there may be to this model, it does not reflect accurately the situation of the people of God depicted in our passage. As 3:16-19 make clear, the setting which the writer has in mind for Israel in the wilderness is that recorded in Num. 14 and the Numbers passage influences his interpretation throughout. In Num. 14 the wilderness generation are not in the midst of their wandering but stand right on the verge of entry into the promised land, having arrived at the goal of their pilgrimage. It is this which provides the comparison with the NT people of God. Both groups stand directly before the fulfilment of God's promise" (n. 69, pp. 329, 330, manuscript).

[104] S. Kistemaker emphasizes the significance of the use of the present tense, saying: "The author does not employ the future tense, nor does he say, 'we are sure to enter.' By placing *eiserkometha* ['we enter'] emphatically first in the sentence, he wishes to affirm that God's promise has become reality in accordance with His plan and purpose" (*The Psalm Citations in the Epistle to the Hebrews*, 1961, p. 109). Hugh Montefiore offers a similar comment: "The Greek text means neither that they are certain to enter, nor that they will enter, but that they are already in the process of entering" (*The Epistle to the Hebrews*, 1964, p. 83). Cf. C. K. Barret (n. 5), p. 372. This interpretation clarifies, as noted by W. Rordorf, "the decisive significance of 'Today.' The new day of the 'Today' has dawned in Christ (v. 7). On this new day it is possible to enter into the rest, and yet more: on this new day this rest has become a reality for those who believe" (n. 8, p. 112). Note the similarity with the "today" of Luke 4:19 and John 9:4.

[105] A. T. Lincoln (n. 69), p. 332 manuscript.

[106] Harald Riesenfeld expresses this view. Speaking of the Sabbath, he writes: "Jesus made it appear that that same law had completed its function and belonged to the past—to be succeeded by a higher and better reality" (*The Gospel Tradition*, 1970, p. 121).

[107] This argument is developed especially by A. T. Lincoln (n. 69), pp. 333-334 manuscript.

[108] Translation by E. J. Goodspeed, *The Apostolic Fathers*, 1950, pp. 40-41.

[109] Justin Martyr, *Dialogue with Trypho* 80, 81; Tertullian, *Against Marcion* 3, 24; Hippolytus, *Commentary on Daniel* IV, 23, 4-6; Cyprian, *Ad Fortunatum* 2; Augustine, *Sermons* 259, 2 and *City of God* 20, 7, 1; Victorinus, *On the Creation of the World* 6; Lactantius, *Divine Institutions* 7.

[110] V Ezra 2:24, 34; Origen, *Against Celsus* 6, 61; also *Sermon on Numbers* 23, 4; Eusebius, *Commentary on Psalms* 91; Jerome, *Commentary on Ezekiel* VI (on 20:10); Chrysostom, *Sermons on Hebrews* 6, 1 (on ch. 4); Augustine, *Epistle* 55; *City of God* 22, 30; *Sermons* 9. 3; Bede, *Commentary on Genesis* 2:3 (*CCL* 118A, 35); Rabanus Maurus, *Commentary on Genesis* 1:9 (*PL* 107, 465); Peter Lombard, *Sentences*

3, 37, 2 (*PL* 192, 831); a similar eschatological interpretation is found in Otto of Lucca, *Sentences* 4, 3 (*PL* 176, 122); Martin of Leon, *Sermons* 15 (*PL* 208, 782). Cf. John Calvin, *Commentary on Hebrews* 4:10 and *Institutes of Christian Religion* 2, 8, 30. P. K. Jewett (n. 49, p. 83: "The fulfilment of the Sabbath rest which we have in Christ is not only a present reality, but also a future hope.... The principle of the Sabbath, then, is both an Old Testament ceremonialism which has been fulfilled and done away in Christ and at the same time a permanent interpretive category of redemptive history, having definite eschatological implications"; cf. Harald Riesenfeld (n. 59), p. 133; O. Cullmann, "Sabbat und Sonntag nach dem Johannes-Evangelium," *In Memoriam Ernst Lohmeyer*, 1951, pp. 127-131; especially J. Daniélou, "La typologie millénariste de la semain dans le christianisme primitif," *Vigiliae Christianae* 2 (1948): 1-16; recently, R. T. Beckwith (n. 51), p. 12.

111 For examples and discussion of the spiritual interpretation of the Sabbath Commandment, see W. Rordorf (n. 8), pp. 100-108; Franz X. Pettirsch also notes: "The early fathers of the Church applied the law of Sabbath rest only allegorically to abstention from sin; a literal application to work was foreign to their thinking" ("A Theology of Sunday Rest," *Theology Digest* 6 [1958]: 116). The author explains how during the Middle Ages the formula "servile work" was interpreted in a literal sense as meaning "field work, any heavy work" (p. 117). The spiritual interpretation of the Sabbath rest as "self-renunciation" is advocated also by John Calvin, in *Commentaries on the Four Last Books of Moses*, C. W. Bingham, trans. 1950, p. 436.

112 A. T. Lincoln, for example, argues that "the new covenant people of God discharge their duty of Sabbath observance, according to this writer [Hebrews], by exercising faith. Thereby they participate in God's gift of eschatological salvation and cease from their own works which now have not a physical reference but as elsewhere in the NT a salvation connotation, that which this writer in 6:1 ('repentance from dead works') and 9:14 ('from dead works') calls dead works" (n. 69, p. 333 manuscript).

113 John Calvin, *Institutes of Christian Religion*, 1972, II, p. 339.

114 By resting on the Sabbath after the similitude of God (Heb. 4:10), the believer, as Karl Barth puts it, "participates consciously in the salvation provided by him [God]" (*Church Dogmatics*, ET 1958, III, part 2, p. 50).

115 F. F. Bruce acknowledges that the redemptive meaning of the Sabbath rest found in Hebrews 4 "is implied by our Lord's words in John 5:17" (*The Epistle to the Hebrews*, 1974, p. 74).

116 Augustine, *City of God* XXII, 30.

CHAPTER VI

THE SABBATH: GOOD NEWS OF SERVICE

1 Franz X. Pettirsch, "A Theology of Sunday Rest," *Theology Digest* 6 (1958): 115.

2 Pacifico Massi rightly observes that "for the Jews rest is an act of worship, a kind of liturgy. This enables us to understand how a series of ritualistic prescriptions were imposed on the liturgy of rest" (*La Domenica*, 1967, p. 366).

3 The Reformers' view of work as "a divine calling" apparently has contributed in subsequent centuries to idealize work as the object of

living. Max Weber proposed that Protestant work ethics became responsible for the rise of capitalism (*The Protestant Ethic and the Spirit of Capitalism*, 1958). Weber's thesis is rather unilateral and has been strongly criticized. For a brief discussion, see Niels-Erik Andreasen, *The Christian Use of Time*, 1978, pp. 32-34.

4 The first statement is by Rabbi Solomo Alkabez and the second is from "The Evening Service for the Sabbath." Both are cited by Abraham Joshua Heschel, in *The Sabbath: Its Meaning for Modern Man*, 1952, p. 14.

5 A. Martin, "Notes sur le Sabbath," *Foi et Vie* 5 (1975): 50. The same author wisely remarks, "We do not need leisure to have a Sabbath: we need the Sabbath to experience leisure" (ibid., p. 48).

6 Alfred Barry, *The Christian Sunday*, 1905, p. 69.

7 Christopher Kiesling, *The Future of the Christian Sunday*, 1970, p. 16. This view is ably defended by W. Rordorf who writes: "Right down to the fourth century the idea of rest played absolutely no part in the Christian Sunday. Christians like everyone else worked on that day: it would not have occurred to them to do otherwise. It was only when the Emperor Constantine the Great elevated Sunday to be the statutory day of rest in the Roman Empire that Christians tried to give a theological basis to the rest from work on Sunday which was now demanded by the State: to this end they fell back on the sabbath commandment" (*Sunday*, 1968, pp. 296-297; cf. pp. 167-168). W. Scott has challenged Rordorf's thesis, but, in my view, Stott's analysis of sources leaves much to be desired (*This is the Day. The Biblical Doctrine of the Christian Sunday*, 1978, pp. 50-103).

8 Christopher Kiesling (n. 7), p. 16.

9 Ibid., p. 23.

10a Ibid., p. 23. Kiesling notes that "Some suggest that Canon 1248 of the Code of Canon Law, which obliges Catholics to observe Sunday worship and rest, should be changed so that the obligation of weekly worship could be fulfilled on some other day of the week" (p. 32). Kiesling views this proposal as "individualistic" and suggests a compromise solution, namely the retention of Sunday on one hand and the development, on the other hand, of a Christian lifestyle which is "less dependent upon it; consequently if the Christian Sunday is overwhelmed in the culture of the future, there will be something to take its place" (ibid. p. 34). The least that can be said of this proposal is that it ignores the vital function of the Biblical Sabbath for the Christian life and that it conditions the relevance and survival of a divine institution (seventh-day Sabbath) to cultural trends. To this Kiesling might reply that since Sunday is an ecclesiastical and not a Biblical institution, the Church has the right to annul it, if she deems it necessary. Obviously such an explanation is unacceptable to those Christians who maintain the *sola Scriptura* principle.

10b Ibid., p. 23.

11 Ibid., p. 32.

12 The *Directory of Sabbath-Observing Groups* published by The Bible Sabbath Association (1974) lists no less than 120 different churches or groups observing the seventh-day Sabbath.

13 W. J. Harrelson, *From Fertility Cult to Worship*, 1969, p. 19.

14 On the question of the origin of the synagogue, see H. H. Rowley, *Worship in Ancient Israel: Its Form and Meaning*, 1967, pp. 87, 224-241; J. Morgensten, "Sabbath," *Interpreter's Dictionary of the Bible*, 1962, IV, pp. 135-141; R. de Vaux, *Ancient Israel II: Religious Institutions*, 1961, pp. 343f.

[15] This is suggested also by the fact that the Sabbath is frequently associated with the annual feasts which are explicitly designated as "solemn assembly" (Lev. 23:7, 8, 21, 23, 27, 35). If the feasts dedicated "to the Lord your God" were celebrated by a "solemn assembly," we would expect the same to be true in the case of the Sabbath. This nexus is clearly established in Leviticus 23 where the Sabbath opens the list of "the appointed feasts of the Lord" and is designated as "a holy convocation": "Six days shall work be done; but on the seventh day is a sabbath of solemn rest, a holy convocation; you shall do no work; it is a sabbath to the Lord in all your dwellings" (Lev. 23:2). Note also that the Sabbath shares the same theological direction ("to the Lord") and prohibition of work of the annual feasts (Num. 28:18, 25, 26; 29:1, 7, 12, 35; cf. Deut. 16:8). These elements, shared in common by the Sabbath and the annual feasts, were apparently designed to ensure the participation of all in the holy assembly. For a discussion of this question, see Niels-Erik Andreasen, *Rest and Redemption*, 1978, pp. 64-68.

[16] On the influence of the synagogue upon Christian divine service, see note 42 of chapter V.

[17] It is noteworthy that the Jews through the centuries have expressed the joyful celebration of the Sabbath through the ritual of the kindling of lights. As Abraham E. Millgram explains, "The kindling of the Sabbath lights is one of the most impressive home ceremonies, symbolizing the essential characteristic of the Sabbath—light, joy and good cheer" (*Sabbath. The Day of Delight*, 1944, p. 10).

[18] In a terrible indictment, Paul denounces the universal sin of those who serve and worship "the creature rather than the Creator" (Rom. 1:25).

[19] A. Martin eloquently explains that to observe the Sabbath "means to silence our questioning in order to make place for the Word of God which is true silence and true peace. Because it is in the silence of the Sabbath that one can hear the whispering of the Word. To live the Sabbath covenant means not to say that 'God is dead' under the pretense that He does not say anything: it is not God who is dead; it is we who must die to our babbling. The Sabbath alliance means to be still and experience the grand silence of the Word of God. Because it is in the silence that God speaks" (n. 5, p. 31).

[20] George Elliott, *The Abiding Sabbath: An Argument for the Perpetual Obligation of the Lord's Day*, 1884, p. 81.

[21] Ibid.

[22] William Hodgkins, *Sunday: Christian and Social Significance*, 1960, p. 219. Hodgkins rightly observes that in the congregational worship "the individual shares in the strength of the spiritual influence produced by a company of people, and when this is carried out under the skilful guidance of a minister achieves a sense of purpose that is impossible to anyone sat in an armchair listening to a service from a radio set or watching it on television, or reading a devotional book or taking a two minute sermon from a newspaper. This is the great advantage of the Church, that for this communal act of devotion there is really no substitute" (ibid.).

[23] Gabriel Marcel views the lack of reflection as a major cause of the dehumanizing conditions prevailing in today's world (*The Mystery of Being*, vol. I, *Reflection and Mystery*, 1960, pp. 44-47). On the significance of reflection in Christian worship, see James White, *The Worldliness of Worship*, 1967, pp. 48-78. John Bosco perceptively wrote: "Modern man is only satisfied with himself when he has not a moment left for himself; the more he does the more he believes he can do. But the

speed one takes neutralizes in reality personality and life. The internal reality of man is destroyed by the swirl of external life. Man loses the ability to accomplish his acts, that is, to engage himself totally in a reflective action" ("Juste place dans notre vie personnelle," in *Le Semeur*, 1947, p. 262).

[24] Harvey Gallagher Cox, *Turning East. The Promise and Peril of the New Orientalism*, 1977, p. 65.

[25] Ibid.

[26] Ibid., p. 66.

[27] Ibid., p. 68.

[28] Ibid., p. 72.

[29] Herbert Saunders, "Reaching a Pluralistic Society With the Sabbath Truth," *The Sabbath Sentinel* 30 (1978): 5.

[30] Achad Haam, *Il Birio*, 1927, p. 54.

[31] Samuel H. Dresner, *The Sabbath*, 1970, p. 63. Earlier Dresner writes: "Man is half-animal, half-angel, and for six days there is a struggle between the two. One day a week, however, we learn to make peace between body and soul, between spirit and flesh" (ibid., p. 52).

[32] "The Christianity Today Gallup Poll: An Overview," *Christianity Today* 23 (Dec. 21, 1979): 14.

[33] Ibid.

[34] A. H. Lewis, "The Divine Element in the Weekly Rest Day," in *The World's Parliament of Religions*, John Henry, ed., 1893, p. 740.

[35] Cf. R. J. Banks, *Jesus and the Law in the Synoptic Tradition*, 1975, p. 124.

[36] David Hill points out that "the argument has the effect of placing Jesus firmly within the Law, rightly understood: he does good on the Sabbath, and so fulfils the will of God, who desires merciful action rather than ritualistic legalism" (*The Gospel of Matthew*, 1972, p. 213).

[37] G. B. Caird rightly asks: "Which is keeping the spirit of the sabbath better he [Christ] with his deed of mercy or they with their malicious designs? The question needs no answer: it is always right to do good, and what better day than the sabbath could there be for doing the works of God!" (*Saint Luke*, 1963, p. 99).

[38] Ellen White, *The Desire of Ages*, 1940, p. 287.

[39] W. Manson, *The Gospel of Luke*, 1930, p. 60.

[40] W. Rordorf (n. 7), p. 68. My response to Rordorf's arguments is found in *From Sabbath to Sunday*, 1977, pp. 31-34.

[41] It is noteworthy that the Sabbath is related to social concern also in Isaiah 58. A study of the structure of the whole chapter indicates that the Sabbath is viewed "as the means by which Israel should manifest true fasting, i.e. social concern for the oppressed" (Sakae Kubo, *God Meets Man*, 1978, p. 47). James Muilenburg also argues for the unity of the chapter and thus the connection between the social concern of true fasting and proper Sabbathkeeping ("Isaiah 40-66," *Interpreter's Bible*, 1956, V, p. 677). Cf. C. Westermann, *Isaiah 40-66: A Commentary*, 1969, p. 340.

[42] Richard S. McConnell, *Law and Prophecy in Matthew's Gospel*, Dissertation, University of Basel, 1969, p. 72. My extensive treatment of Christ's pronouncement is found in *From Sabbath to Sunday*, 1977, pp. 56-61.

[43] Ellen White, *Testimonies for the Church*, 1948, VI, p. 359.

[44] George Elliott remarks: "In France, during the Revolution, the substitution of the tenth for the seventh day was accompanied by a divorce law, under whose provision within three months there was

recorded one divorce for every three marriages in Paris alone" (*The Abiding Sabbath: An Argument for the Perpetual Obligation of the Lord's Day*, 1884, p. 61).

[45] Samuel M. Segal explains that "according to Jewish law, every man should have marital relations at least once a week, preferably on Friday night. Since the Song of Songs speaks of the love between man and woman, the man reads it at the ushering in of the Sabbath in order to create an atmosphere of love and affection. It is for this reason, too, that on Friday night, during the meal, the man recites the last chapter of Proverbs, in which the woman is idealized" (*The Sabbath Book*, 1942, p. 17).

[46] See above n. 41.

[47] Cf. *Jewish Encyclopedia*, 1962, s.v. "Sabbath."

[48] Henlee H. Barnette, *The Church and the Ecological Crisis*, 1972, p. 65.

[49] The importance of theological convictions for solving the ecological crisis is stressed in the report issued by the Anglican commission which was appointed to study this problem. "Society as a whole," the report says, "will only adopt a different style of living if it has come under the impulse of a popular and imaginative way of seeing things in their wholeness. Such a vision needs more than a secular ideology. We believe that it can come about only through the agency of a theology, that is to say, through man's understanding of himself as a creature who finds his true being in a relationship of love with God and in cooperation with God in his purpose for the world" (*Man and Nature*, Hugh Montefiore, ed., 1975, p. 77). Later the report emphasizes again that "theological convictions can change and eventually affect policies" (ibid., p. 80).

[50] Ibid., p. 180.

[51] "Our scientific atmosphere," ably writes Eric C. Rust, "has nullified the desire to rejoice and celebrate and reduced nature and all its constituent creatures to 'Its.' We do not see them as 'Thous' but as objects which science and technology can use and control. They have become means to our economic ends rather than ends in themselves. We have forgotten that our God rejoiced in his creation and declared it to be good because it contained potentially the possibilities for the realization of his purpose" (*Nature: Garden or Desert*, 1971, p. 133).

[52] The trend has been, especially in Western Christianity, to view redemption more as an *ethical* than a *physical* or *natural* process. Much has been said about the redemption of the individual from sin and from this sinful world, but little has been said about God's plan for the ultimate restoration of Planet Earth to its original purpose and beauty. "It is as though the central element of a story has been isolated from its beginning and its end, and so has lost its essential meaning and interest" (*Man and Nature* [n. 49], p. 39). Eastern theology apparently has maintained a more cosmic view of redemption. For a brief but excellent treatment of this question, see A. M. Allchin, "The Theology of Nature in the Eastern Fathers and among Anglican Theologicans," in *Man and Nature* (n. 49), pp. 143-154.

[53] J. R. Zurcher provides a perceptive analysis of the influence of Platonic anthropology on the development of the Christian dualistic concept of human nature (*The Nature and Destiny of Man. Essay on the Problem of the Union of the Soul and the Body in Relation to the Christian Views of Man*, 1969, pp. 1-22). Paul Verghese traces back to Augustine the unbalanced emphasis on human depravity and the con-

sequent disparagement of the material world. He writes: "Regard the flesh, the body, matter as evil, or even inferior, and one has already began the deviation from Christian faith" (*Freedom of Man*, 1972, p. 55).

54 A Biblical theology of redemption must start not from mankind's Fall but from its perfect creation. It should acknowledge that despite the reality of sin, human beings and this world essentially still are the good creation of God. Thus mankind's creation, redemption and restoration must be viewed as part of God's cosmological—not merely anthropological—redemptive activity. Jacob Needleman argues that it is the lack of a Christian cosmology that encourages some people to turn to Eastern religions such as Buddhism, Hinduism and Islam in order to find a universal and a personal salvation (*The New Religions*, 1972).

55 Cf. Psalms 104; 8; 19:1-6.

56 Some argue that the Judeo-Christian tradition is largely responsible for the prevailing irresponsible exploitation of nature. The proof-text often cited to defend this view is Genesis 1:28: "God said to them, 'Be fruitful and multiply, and fill the earth and subdue it; and have dominion over the fish of the sea and over the birds of the air and over every living thing that moves upon the earth." The emphasis in this passage on man's *dominion* and subjugation of nature is held responsible for mankind's unrestrained exploitation of nature. This view is defended, for example, by Lynn White, "The Historical Roots of the Ecological Crisis," *Science* (March 10, 1967): 1205f.; Ian McHarg, *Design with Nature*, 1969. Any attempt to explain the ecological crisis on the basis of *one cause* is shortsighted to say the least. Moreover Genesis 1:28 can hardly be interpreted as a divine charter for unrestricted human exploitation of this world. Man's dominion is patterned after God's dominion since God created man in His image (Gen. 1:26-27). Gerhard von Rad emphasizes that human "dominion" must be understood in the light of man's creation in the image of god (*Genesis: A Commentary*, 1963, p. 56). This means that human dominion must be informed by love and must be exercised responsibly. It involves tilling and keeping the earth (Gen. 2:15; Lev. 25:1-5), caring for animals and wild life (Deut. 25:4; 22:6-7). Henlee H. Barnette rightly comments: "Made in the *imago Dei*, man possesses both dignity and dominion, by which he shares in the sovereignty of God in relation to the world. But man in his pride and selfish desires to be wholly sovereign, tends to ignore the fact that his dominion is under and limited by the dominion of God" (n. 48, p. 80).

57 Eric C. Rust rightly says: "Despite all that the Bible says about sin and the need for redemption, man is not so radically lost that his Creator does not continue to trust him with the stewardship of his world!" (n. 51, p. 27).

58 Cf. Ps. 107:33, 34; Zeph. 2:9; Jer. 49:20, 33; Job 38:26-29; Jer. 2:7.

59 Similar OT descriptions are found in Is. 35; 65:17; 66:22; 2:4; Hos. 2:18; Ez. 47:1-2; 34:25-27; Zech. 14:4.

60 Rudolf Bultmann notes that creation "has a history which it shares with man" (*Theology of the New Testament*, 1951, I, p. 30).

61 Henlee H. Barnette cogently remarks: "In one respect, the biblical and scientific views of the eschaton are similar: the planet earth will be consumed with fire. In the scientific view there is no hope for the cosmos; it will be left void and cold. In the biblical perspective there is a future hope for nature and God's people in a radically transformed world, a new heaven and a new earth" (n. 48, pp. 76-77).

62 Samuel Raphael Hirsch, "The Sabbath," *Judaism Eternal*, Israel Grunfeld, ed., 1956, p. 37.

63 Robert and Leona Rienow, *Moment in the Sun*, 1967, pp. 141f.
64 See Martin Noth, *Exodus*, J. H. Marks, trans., 1962, p. 189.
65 A. Martin (n. 5), p. 41.
66 Albert Camus, *The Rebel*, 1962, p. 299.
67 Abraham Joshua Heschel (n. 4), p. 28.
68 Ibid., pp. 28, 29.
69 Albert Schweitzer, *Out of My Life and Thought*, C. T. Campion, ed., 1953, p. 126.

CHAPTER VII

GOOD NEWS OF DIVINE REST FOR HUMAN RESTLESSNESS

1 For further treatment of this concept, see above chapter VI, "A remedy for leisure-worship."
2 Augustine, *Confessions* XIII, 36.
3 Chuck Scriven, "Beyond Arithmetic: A Look at the Meaning of the Sabbath," *Insight* (Sept. 6, 1971): 17.
4 Samuel H. Dresner, *The Sabbath*, 1970, p. 43.

APPENDIX

FROM SABBATH TO SUNDAY

1 This essay represents a brief summary of the writer's published dissertation, *From Sabbath to Sunday: A Historical Investigation of the Rise of Sunday Observance in Early Christianity* (Rome: The Pontifical Gregorian University Press, 1977). The book is sold directly by the author ($10.00 postage paid), 230 Lisa Lane, Berrien Springs, Michigan, 49103, USA. The reader will be frequently referred to this study for a more extensive treatment of various issues. Space limitation has necessitated the total omission of significant aspects of the problem such as the NT references to the first day of the week (1 Cor. 16:1-3; Acts 20:7-12) and to the Lord's day (Rev. 1:10); Paul's attitude toward the Sabbath (Col. 2:14-17; Rom. 14:5-6; Gal. 4:10); the earliest patristic references to Sunday by Ignatius, Barnabas and Justin Martyr; the development of the theology of Sunday in the early Church. All of these issues are discussed extensively in *From Sabbath to Sunday*, to which the reader is referred in order better to assess the validity of the conclusions of this essay.
2 For a bibliography of significant studies dealing with the historical genesis of Sunday observance, see *From Sabbath to Sunday*, pp. 333-338.
3 Thomas Aquinas, *Summa Theologica*, 1947, Q. 122, Art. 4, II, p. 1702.
4 J. Donovan, ed. *Catechism of the Council of Trent*, 1908, chapter IV, question 18, p. 347.
5 On the use of this argument in the disputations between Catholics and Protestants in French Switzerland, see Daniel Augsburger, "Sunday in the Pre-Reformation Disputations in French Switzerland," *Andrews University Seminary Studies* 14 (1976): 265-277. For a survey of the use of this argument in the disputations between Catholic and Lutheran theologians, see J. N. Andrews and L. R. Conradi, *History of the Sabbath*, 1912, pp. 586-595.

6 *Augsburg Confession*, Art. 28, in *Concordia or Book of Concord, the Symbols of the Evangelivcal Lutheran Church*, 1957, p. 24. Luther explicitly stated that Sunday is not "celebrated in Christendom by God's command.... Yet it is a necessity and is ordained by the church for the sake of the imperfect laity and the working class" (*D. Martin Luthers Werke*, Weimer, 1888, 6:243, 1. 31).

7 *Augsburg Confession* (n. 6), p. 25.

8 John Calvin, *Institutes of the Christian Religion*, 1972, I, p. 343.

9 In his *Symbolum*, Erasmus writes: "By His rest in the tomb, Christ abrogated the Jewish Sabbath and by His resurrection on the eighth day he commended to us the evangelical Sabbath" (*D. Erasmi opera omnia*, 1962, 5:1190E).

10 Theodore Beza infers from 1 Cor. 16:2 and Acts 20:7 that "the religious assemblies of the Lord's day are of apostolical and truly divine tradition" (*Novum Testamentum. Ejusdem T. Bezae annotaziones*, 1642, cited by Robert Cox, *The Literature of the Sabbath Question*, 1865, I, p. 134). The two volumes by Robert Cox provide a most comprehensive and handy collection of documents on the Sabbath question. Most of the quotations and references below are drawn from this fine collection, which henceforth will be cited as "Cox."

11 *The Second Helvetic Confession* (1566), chapter 24, states: "From the very times of the Apostles, not merely were certain days in each week appointed for religious assemblies, but the Lord's Day itself was consecrated to that purpose and to holy rest" (Philip Schaff, *The Creeds of Christendom*, 1919, p. 298).

12 Nicolas Bownde in his popular book *The True Doctrine of the Sabbath* (1595) argues that the Fourth Commandment is moral and perpetual. The actual day was changed from Saturday to Sunday by apostolic authority (Cox I, pp. 145-151).

13 Antonius Walaeus, professor of Theology at Leyden, wrote *Dissertatio de Sabbato* (1628) in which he distinguishes between the ceremonial and moral aspects of the Sabbath. The latter is applicable to Sunday, which he views as an apostolic institution (Cox I, pp. 441-442).

14 Hamon L'Estrange, in his book *God's Sabbath before the Law, under the Law, and under the Gospel* (1641) dedicated to the Long Parliament, maintains that the Sabbath-day was changed by Christ at His resurrection: "No sooner was the old Sabbath abolished, than the new established and installed" (p. 71; cited by Cox I, p. 202).

15 Articles 4 and 5 of the *Synod of Dort* read: "4. The Sabbath of the Jews having been abrogated, the Lord's Day must be solemnly sanctified by Christians. 5. From the time of the apostles this day was always observed in the ancient Catholic Church" (cited by Cox I, p. 218).

16 *The Westminster Confession of Faith*, chapter 21, article 7, states: "He hath particularly appointed one day in seven for a Sabbath, to be kept holy unto him: which, from the beginning of the world to the resurrection of Christ, was the last day of the week; and, from the resurrection of Christ, was changed into the first day of the week, which in the Scripture is called the Lord's day, and is to be continued to the end of the world as the Christian Sabbath" (Philip Schaff [n. 11], pp. 648-649).

17 Gisbertus Voetius, a leading Dutch theologian, in his book *Lachrymae Crocodili Abstersae* (1627) defends the notion that the primitive Sabbath was transferred to Sunday by apostolic authority.

18 John Owen, an eminent English theologian, in his treatise *Exercitations concerning the Name, Original Nature, Use, and Continuance, of a*

Day of Sacred Rest (1671), advocates strongly the divine authority and moral nature of Sundaykeeping (Cox II, pp. 22-28).

[19] Henry Wilkinson, Principal of Magdalen Hall, Oxford, wrote a 94-page treatise *On the Divine Authority of the Lord's Day*, where he presents the name "Lord's Day" as a proof that Sunday was instituted by the Lord Himself (Cox I, p. 265).

[20] Jonathan Edwards, President of the College of New Jersey, preached a series of sermons *On the Perpetuity and the Change of the Sabbath* (1804), arguing that the first day of the week is the Christian Sabbath which was established by apostolic authority (Cox II, pp. 176-183).

[21] William Paley, Archdeacon of Carlisle, discusses at length the institution of the Sabbath in his treatise *The Principles of Moral and Political Philosophy* (1785). In chapter VII, Paley argues that Sunday worship "originated from some precept of Christ, or of His Apostles" (cited by Cox II, p. 255).

[22] James Augustus Hessey, in his famous Bampton Lectures delivered at the University of Oxford in 1860 and published under the title *Sunday: Its Origin, History, and Present Obligation* (1866), maintains that Sunday is a "Divine institution" because it was "observed by the Apostles and their immediate followers" (p. 39).

[23] See above notes 3, 4, 5.

[24] See above note 6.

[25] See above note 8.

[26] William Tyndale, the famous translator of the Scriptures in modern English, accepted the ecclesiastical origin of Sunday, but rejected its obligations. He wrote: "As for the Sabbath, we be lords over the Sabbath, and yet change it into Monday, or into any other day as we see need... Neither was there any cause to change it from the Saturday to Sunday, but to put a difference between ourselves and the Jews" (cited by Hessey [n. 22], p. 198).

[27] Thomas Cranmer, Archbishop of Canterbury (burned at Oxford, 1555), argues in his *Confutation of Unwritten Verities* that "since the Church has without challenge shifted the Sabbath from Saturday to Sunday, thus altering the law of God, much more has it authority to make *new* laws for things necessary to salvation" (cited by Cox I, p. 135).

[28] John Prideaux, Bishop of Worcester, in his discourse on *The Doctrine of the Sabbath* (published in 1634), reasons that the Lord's day is founded not on the Fourth Commandment but only on the authority of the Church (Cox I, p. 165).

[29] Hugo Grotius, an eminent Dutch jurist, deals at length with the Sabbath question in his *Opera Omnia Theologica*, refuting "those who think that the Lord's Day was substituted for the Sabbath—a thing nowhere mentioned either by Christ or his apostles" (cited by Cox I, p. 223).

[30] Franciscus Gomarus, professor of theology at Leyden, wrote the famous treatise *Investigatio Sententiae et Originis Sabbati* (1628), in which he holds that the Fourth Commandment is not binding upon Christians and that there is no proof that the apostles appointed the Lord's Day as a new day of worship (Cox I, p. 442).

[31] Peter Heylyn, sub-dean of Westminster and chaplain to Charles I, wrote a two-volume treatise on *The History of the Sabbath* (1636). In the first chapter of the second volume, Heylyn argues that Christ prepared the ground for the "dissolution" of the Sabbath and that "The Lord's Day was not enjoined by him or his apostles in its place, but was instituted by the authority of the church" (cited by Cox I, p. 177).

[32] John Cocceius, professor of theology at the University of Leyden, wrote a major study entitled *Indagatio Naturae Sabbati et Quietis Novi Testamenti* (1658). His position is that the Lord's Day arose among early Christians not without "divine providence" but without an express divine command (p. 35; Cox II, p. 1, 2).

[33] John Milton, the famous English poet and theologian, examines the question of the Sabbath in his work, *A Treatise on Christian Doctrine*. His view is that "the original Sabbath is abrogated, and since we are nowhere told that it has been transferred from one day to another, nor is any reason given why it should be so transferred, the Church, when she sanctioned a change in this matter, evidenced, not her obedience to God's command (inasmuch as the command existed no longer), but her own rightful liberty" (cited by Cox II, p. 52).

[34] John Samuel Stryk, a German jurist, examines the juridical basis of Sunday observance in his work *Commentatio de Jure Sabbathi* (1756). His position is that "the Sunday of Christians does not stand on any common ground with the Sabbath of the Jews. It has not been introduced by a direct Divine command; for it cannot be proved that the observance originated with the apostles; ... The observance of the Sunday rests entirely upon a simple arrangement of the Church" (cited from Hengstenberg's review of Stryk's book by Cox II, p. 135).

[35] Edward Evanson, rector of Tewkesbury, in England, in his work *Arguments against and for the Sabbatical Observance of Sunday*, "denies that we have any proof of the Lord's Day having been observed by the Apostles or other primitive Christians as a Sabbath" (Cox II, p. 292).

[36] Richard Whately, Archbishop of Dublin, in his *Thoughts on the Sabbath* (published in 1830), maintains that there is no connection between Sabbath and Sunday and that the Lord's Day was instituted not by the apostles but by the Church that succeeded them (Cox II, p. 333).

[37] C. C. L. Franke, a German theologian, strongly emphasizes in his treatise *De Diei Dominici apud Veteres Christianos Celebratione* (1826) that Sunday is a purely ecclesiastical institution since there is no trace of apostolic or divine support for it (Cox II, p. 438).

[38] William Domville, according to Robert Cox, made "the most valuable contribution in this century [19th century] to the literature of the Sabbath Question" (Cox II, p. 357). In his treatise *The Sabbath, or, an Examination of the Six Texts Commonly Adduced from the New Testament in Proof of a Christian Sabbath*, he emphatically states: "there is not a single instance recorded in Scripture of the observance of Sunday by the Apostles themselves ... consequently there are no just grounds for presuming that a precept from Christ or his Apostles did once exist ... the observance of Sunday ... is *not* an institution of *Divine* appointment" (p. 2151, cited by Cox II, p. 185).

[39] E. W. Hengstenberg, professor of theology at the University of Berlin, wrote a major study on *The Lord's Day* (translated into English by James Martin, 1853), in which he treats the Sabbath as a purely Jewish institution and Sunday as an ecclesiastical creation (Cox II, p. 439).

[40] J. Francke, *Van Sabbat naar Zondag*, 1973. F. N. Lee, *The Covenantal Sabbath*, 1969. C. S. Mosna, *Storia della domenica dalle origini fino agli inizi del V secolo*, Analecta Gregoriana 170, 1969. Paul K. Jewett, *The Lord's Day: A Theological Guide to the Christian Day of Worship*, 1971. R. T. Beckwith and W. Stott, *This is the Day: The Biblical Doctrine of the Christian Sunday in its Jewish and Early Christian Setting*, 1978.

[41] Willy Rordorf, *Sunday: The History of the Day of Rest and Worship in the Earliest Centuries of the Christian Church*, 1968, especially pp. 215-237.

[42] M. M. B. Turner, "The Sabbath, Sunday and the Law in Luke-Acts," in *From Sabbath to Lord's Day: A Biblical, Historical and Theological Investigation*, D. A. Carson, ed., soon to be published, p. 198, manuscript.

[43] Hiley H. Ward, *Space-Age Sunday*, 1960, pp. 70-71. The conclusion of my own investigation is to a large extent similar to Ward's position. I hope that my analysis of the political, social and pagan-religious situation of the time explains sufficiently the underlying causes for the change from Saturday to Sunday observance in the early part of the second century (see *From Sabbath to Sunday*, pp. 165-300).

[44] C. S. Mosna, for example, concludes his investigation into the origin of Sunday worship, stating categorically: "Therefore we can conclude with certainty that the event of the resurrection has determined the choice of Sunday as the day of worship of the first Christian community" (n 40, pp. 44, 53). See *From Sabbath to Sunday*, pp. 74-89 for a bibliography on the supporters of the resurrection/appearance origin of Sunday.

[45] The fact that Paul employs the adjective "Lord's" to describe only the nature of the Supper and not of Sunday (the latter he calls by the Jewish designation "first day of the week"—1 Cor. 16:2), specially when the mentioning of the sacredness of the time could have strengthened the apostle's plea for a more worshipful attitude during the partaking of the Lord's Supper, hardly suggests that Sunday was already known as "Lord's Day" or that the Lord's Supper was celebrated exclusively on Sunday. Possibly the Lord's Supper was celebrated on different days and in different homes to avoid the suspicion of the hetaeriae. See my discussion in *From Sabbath to Sunday*, 95-102.

[46] It is notworthy that in the *Didache*, regarded as the most ancient source of ecclesiastical legislation (dated between 70-150), in the instructions given regarding the thanksgiving prayer to be offered over the cup and bread, mention is made of life, knowledge, church unity, faith, immortality, creation and food (chs. 9, 10), but no allusion is made to Christ's resurrection.

[47] E. Hennecke, ed., *New Testament Apocrypha*, 1963, I, p. 199.

[48] Gerald F. Hawthorne, "A new English Translation of Melito's Paschal Homily," in *Current Issues in Biblical and Patristic Interpretation*, ed., Gerald F. Hawthorne, 1975, p. 160. "Passover" in Hebrew means "passing over" and not "to suffer." The erroneous definition obviously represents the prevailing interpretation of the feast, namely, the commemoration of Christ's suffering. Se also below notes 49 to 52 and 98.

[49] Irenaeus, *Against Haresies* 4, 10, 1, *ANF* 1, 473. See also Tertullian, *On Baptism* 19; Justin Martyr, *Dialogue with Tdypho* 72.

[50] M. P. Nautin, ed., *Une homélie inspirée du traité sur la Pâque d'Hippolyte*, Sources Chrétiennes 27, 1960, p. 35.

[51] Marcel Richard, "La question pascale au IIe siècle," *L'Orient Syrien* 6 (1961): 182.

[52] Clement of Alexandria in a fragment of his work *Treatise on the Passover* preserved in the *Chronicon Paschale*, says: "Christ always ate the paschal lamb with His disciples in His earlier years, but not in the last year of His life, in which He was Himself the lamb immolated upon the cross" (*Chronicon Paschale, PG* 92, 81). Hippolytus, in a fragment of his treatise *On the Passover*, explains that "Christ did not eat the passover but suffered it, because it was not time for Him to eat" (*Chronicon Paschale, PG* 92, 79). These and similar testimonies discredit Eusebius' claim that by Victor's time (about 195) practically all Christians viewed the Passover as the celebration of "the mystery of the resurrection"

(*Eccl. Hist.* V, 23, 2). Eusebius' bias in favor of the antiquity and popularity of Easter-Sunday are examined further below, see pp. 248-249.

[53] Barnabas' first theological reason for Sunday observance is the eschatological significance of the "eighth day" which, he claims, represents "the beginning of another world" (*Epistle of Barnabas* 15,8). Justin's first reason for the Christians' Sunday assembly is the commemoration of the inauguration of creation: "because it is the first day on which God, transforming the darkness and prime matter created the world" (*I Apology* 67). Both texts are examined in *From Sabbath to Sunday*, pp. 218-233 and in my other study, *Anti-Judaism and the Origin of Sunday*, 1975, pp. 94-116.

[54] Several liturgical practices such as the prohibition to fast and to kneel on Sunday, as well as the celebration of a Sunday morning Lord's Supper, were introduced to honor specifically the memory of the resurrection. Augustine explicitly explains, for instance, that on Sunday "fasting is interrupted and we pray standing, because it is a sign of the resurrection" (*Epistola* 55, 28, *CSEL* 34, 202); cf. Basil, *De Spiritu Sanctu* 27, 66; *Apostolic Constitutions* 2, 59; Cyprian, *Epistola* 63, 15, *CSEL* 3, 2 714.

[55] J. Daniélou, *Bible and Liturgy*, 1956, p. 243; cf. pp. 242, 222.

[56] For an analysis of these arguments see chapter V, "Jerusalem and the Origin of Sunday," in *From Sabbath to Sunday*, pp. 132-164.

[57] For a brief survey of Jewish-Christian literature, see *From Sabbath to Sunday*, pp. 143-144.

[58] Jacob Jervell, *Luke and the People of God*, 1972, pp. 50-59. Several of the chapters of Jervell's book first appeared as essays in several journals, and were delivered as lectures at a seminar held at Yale University.

[59] Ibid., pp. 142-143.

[60] M. M. B. Turner examines Jervell's arguments at length and criticizes them as being somewhat too radical. Yet he concludes by acknowledging that "for the sake of the mission to the Jews, the law was necessary for Jewish Christians, and Gentile Christians were to fulfill their part (the decrees) so that association with them would be no hindrance to the Jewish mission" (n. 42, p. 179, manuscript).

[61] Jacob Jervell (n. 58), p. 142.

[62] A concise survey of the exaltation of James in Judeo-Christian literature is provided by B. Bagatti, *The Church from the Circumcision*, 1971, pp. 70-78. My brief treatment of this question is found in *From Sabbath to Sunday*, pp. 142-145.

[63] The conversion of "a great many of the priests" (Acts 6:7) presumably contributed to maintaining a Jewish-oriented ministry, since most probably they ministered to the "many thousands" of Jewish converts (Acts 21:20).

[64] Jacob Jervell (n. 58), p. 144. Cf. H. Waitz, "Das problem des sogenannten Aposteldekrets," *Zeitschrift für Kirchengeschichte* 55 (1936): 277.

[65] M. M. B. Turner's argument that "the council's final court of appeal is not Moses and the law—they are not so much mentioned in the letter—but the Spirit (15:28)" (n. 42, p. 170, manuscript), fails to recognize that the decision is reached by appealing to the prophets (Amos 9:11; cf. Jer. 12:15) and to Moses (Acts 15:16-21). Thus the Holy spirit guides in the application of the OT to the new situation rather than in the abrogation of the Mosaic law.

[66] M. M. B. Turner (n. 42), p. 183, manuscript. In the same symposium A. T. Lincoln writes: " By its silence in regard to any Sabbath controversy the Acts account strongly suggests that Jewish christians

must have continued to keep th Sabbath. The Sabbath was an institution too central to Judaism for it to have been tampered with without provoking extremely hostile reaction and persecution, and yet there is no record in Acts of the early Christians being persecuted on this account. Instead they appear to have taken advantage of their observance to preach Jesus as the Messiah at the same time (cf. Acts 5:42)" (n. 42, pp. 580-581, manuscript). Christ's admonition, "Pray that your flight may not be in winter or on a Sabbath" (Matt. 24:20), provides, as stated by E. Lohse, another " example of the keeping of the Sabbath by Jewish-Christians" ("sabbaton," Theological Dictionary of the New Testament 7 [1968], p. 29). For my analysis of the text see From Sabbath to Sunday, pp. 69-71, 150-151.

[67] Eusebius, Ecclesiastical History 3, 27, 3; cf. 4, 5, 2-11; Epiphanius, Adversus haereses 70, 10, PG 42, 355-356. On the liberal wing of the Ebionites who observed Sunday in addition to the Sabbath, see my discussion in From Sabbath to Sunday, pp. 153-156.

[68] M. Simon, "La migration à Pella. Légende ou réalité," in Judéo-Christianisme, ed., Joseph Moingt, 1972, p. 48. For a similar assessment, see J. Daniélou, The Theology of Jewish Christianity, 1964, p. 56; B. Bagatti (n. 62), pp. 31-35.

[69] Epiphanius, Adversus haereses 29, 7, PG 42, 407.

[70] For the text of the malediction and its significance, see From Sabbath to Sunday, pp. 157-159.

[71] M. M. B. Turner admits that "it is all but impossible to believe that Sunday was established as the Lord's Day, as a holy convocation and as a christian response to a creation ordinance, in Palestine shortly after the resurrection. The arguments against this position are virtually conclusive: ... The earliest Jewish Christians, almost without exception, kept the whole law and were theologically committed to it. There is no indication of their sensing the inner freedom that would be required to allow for so fundamental a manipulation" (n. 42, p. 195).

[72] The following quotation is a sample of statements often occurring in the Talmud regarding Hadrian's anti-Jews policies: "The Government of Rome had issued a decree that they should not study the Torah and that they should not circumcise their sons and that they should profane the Sabbath" (Ros. Has. 19a in The Babylonian Talmud, trans. I. Epstein, 1938, vol. 13, p. 78. B. Bat. 60b similarly states: "a Government has come to power which issues cruel decrees against us and forbids to us the observance of the torah and the precepts...." (Babylonian Talmud, vol. 25, p. 246); see also Sanh. 11a, 14a; Abod. Zar. 8b. In the Midrash Rabbah (eds. H. Freedman, M. Simon, 1939) also occur frequent references to Hadrian's decree. In commenting on Exodus 15, 7, it states for instance: "For even if an enemy decrees that they should desecrate the Sabbath, abolish circumcision or serve idols, they [i.e., the Jews] suffer martyrdom rather than be assimilated" (3:170; cf. also the comment under Ecclesiastes 2, 17).

[73] An excellent survey of the Christian anti-Jewish literature of the second century is provided by F. Blanchetière, "Aux sources de l'anti-judaïsme chrétien," Revue d'histoire et de Philosophie Religieuse 53 (1973) 353-398; cf. my brief analysis of this literature in From Sabbath to Sunday, 178-185.

[74] Cf. also Rom. 1:13-15 where Paul says: "I am eager to preach the gospel to you also who are in Rome ... in order that I may reap some harvest among you as well as among the rest of the Gentiles" (emphasis supplied).

[75] Leonard Goppelt, Les Origines de l'Eglise, 1961, p. 203.

[76] According to Tacitus, Nero "fastened the guilt [of arson] and inflicted the most exquisite tortures on ... Christians" (*Annales* 15, 44).

[77] Tacitus gives an estimate of 600,000 Jewish fatalities for the A.D. 70 war (*Historiae* 5, 13. Josephus referring to the same war, speaks of 1,000,000 Jews who were either killed or perished during the siege (*War of the Jews* 6, 9, 3). In the Barkokeba war, according to Dio Cassius (about 150-235), 580,000 Jews were killed in action, besides the numberless who died of hunger and disease" (*Historia* 69, 13).

[78] See n. 72 above.

[79] According to Suetonius (about 70-122) the *fiscus judaicus* was exacted for the temple of *Jupiter Capitolinus* even from those "who without publicly acknowledging that faith yet lived as Jews" (*Domitianus* 12). Under Hadrian (117-138), according to Appian, a contemporary historian, the Jews were subjected at that time to a "poll-tax ... heavier than that imposed upon the surrounding people" (*Roman History, The Syrian Wars* 50). To evidence their severance from Judaism and thereby avoid the payment of a discriminatory tax, the leaders of the Church of Rome could well have introduced at this time Sunday worship in place of "Jewish" Sabbath-keeping.

[80] The texts of these and of other Roman authors are cited in *From Sabbath to Sunday*, pp. 173-177.

[81] Suetonius' expressive *invitus invitam* (*Titus* 7, 1, 2) indicates that the separation was difficult for both of them.

[82] See n. 73 above.

[83] Justin Martyr, *Dialogue with Trypho* 23, 3; cf. 29, 3; 16, 1; 21, 1. Justin's texts are quoted and discussed in *From Sabbath to Sunday*, pp. 223-233 and in *Anti-Judaism and the Origin of Sunday*, pp. 101-114.

[84] The references are given and discussed in *From Sabbath to Sunday*, pp. 189-192.

[85] S. R. E. Humbert, *Adversus Graecorum calumnias* 6, PL 143, 933.

[86] Victorinus (about 304), *De fabrica mundi* 5, CSEL 49, 5.

[87] Pope Innocent I (402-417), in his famous decretal establishes that "as the tradition of the Church maintains, in these two days [i.e., Friday and Saturday] one should not absolutely celebrate the sacraments" (*Ad Decentium*, Epist. 25, 4, 7, PL 20, 555); Socrates (about 439) confirms Innocent I's decretal when he reports that "although almost all churches throughout the world celebrate the sacred mysteries on the Sabbath of every week, yet the Christians of Alexandria and at Rome, on account of some ancient tradition, have ceased to do this" (*Historia ecclesiastica* 5, 22, NPNF 2nd, II, 132); Sozomen (about 440) refers exclusively to religious assemblies, saying that while "the people of Constantinople, and almost everywhere, assemble together on the Sabbath, as well as on the first day of the week," such a "custom is never observed at Rome or at Alexandria" (*Historia ecclesiastica* 7, 19, NPNF 2nd, II, 390).

[88] Tertullian (*On Fasting* 14) and Augustine (*Epistle to Casulanus* 36) associate the two, though approving of the annual paschal Sabbath fast and condemning the weekly Sabbath fast which Rome and a few Western Churches practiced. A similar connection is found in the *Apostolic Constitutions* 5, 15, 20 and in the *Apostolic Canons* 64. Willy Rordorf observes that since "the whole of Western Christendom by this time [i.e. Tertullian's time] fasted on Holy Saturday, it would have been easy to have come up with the idea of fasting on every Saturday (just as every Sunday was a little Easter)" (n. 41, p. 143).

[89] The *Didascalia Apostolorum* (about 250), for example, enjoins Christians to fast on Eastery-Friday and Saturday "on account of the

disobedience of our brethren [i.e., the Jews] . . . because thereon the People killed themselves in crucifying our Savior" (14, 19, trans. H. Connolly, 1929, p. 190). In the *Apostolic Constitutions*, a related document, in a similar vein Christians are enjoined to fast on Easter-Friday and Saturday "because in these days . . . He was taken from us by the Jews, falsely so named, and fastened to the cross" (5, 18, *ANF* VII, 447; cf. 5, 15, p. 445). Epiphanius also refers to an alleged apostolic ordinance which established: "when they [i.e., the Jews] feast, we should mourn for them with fasting, because in the feast they fastened Christ on the Cross" (*Adversus haereses* 70, 11, *PG* 42, 359-360).

[90] Tertullian, for example, shows how close a relation existed between the annual Easter-Sunday and the weekly Sunday by prohibiting kneeling and fasting during both festivities: "On Sunday it is unlawful to fast or to kneel while worshipping. We enjoy the same liberty from Easter to Pentecost" (*De Corona* 3, 4; cf. *On Idolatry* 14). Similar testimonies are found in *Fragments from the Lost Writings of Irenaeus* 7, *ANF* I, pp. 569-570; Origen, *Homilia in Isaiam* 5, 2, *GCS* 8, 265, 1; Eusebius, *De solemnitate paschali* 7, 12, *PG* 24, 710A; Innocent I, *Ad Decentium*, Epistola 25, 4, 7, *PL* 20, 555. These and other references are cited in *From Sabbath to Sunday*, pp. 204-205.

[91] Eusebius' account of the Easter controversy is found in his *Ecclesiastical History* 5, 23-25.

[92] Eusebius, *Ecclesiastical History* 5, 23, 1 and 5, 25, 1.

[93] For example, W. Rordorf, "Zum Ursprung des Osterfestes am Sonntag," *Theologische Zeitschrift* 18 (1962): 167-189. Similarly Kenneth A. Strand argues on the basis of Eusebius' and Sozomen's accounts that "Rome and other places where Peter and Paul labored did indeed receive from these apostles a Sunday-Easter tradition, whereas Asia received from John a Quartodeciman observance" (*Three Essays on Early Church History with Emphasis on the Roman Province of Asia*, 1967, p. 36). For my analysis of Strand's arguments, see *From Sabbath to Sunday*, pp. 202-205.

[94] Marcel Richard (n. 51), p. 211.

[95] Eusebius, *Ecclesiastical History* 5, 23, 1, 2; 5, 24, 11.

[96] Ibid., 5, 23, 2.

[97] See above notes 46 to 52.

[98] Tertullian, *An Answer to the Jews* 10, *ANF* 1, 167. Similarly Justin Martyr writes: "For the passover was Christ who was afterwards sacrificed . . . And it is written, that on the day of the passover you seized Him, and that also during the passover you crucified Him" (*Dialogue with Trypho* III, *ANF* 1, 254). Hippolytus argues that the month of the Passover has been since the beginning the first month because it "is honored by His holy sacrifice" (*Homélies Pascales* I, ed., P. Nautin, *Sources Chrétiennes* 27, 1950, p. 149). It is noteworthy that a century later Eusebius gives a different explanation for the primacy of the month of the passover, namely, because it is the time when "the Lord of the whole world celebrated the mystery of His own feast [i.e. resurrection]" (*De solemnitate paschali*, *PG* 24, 697A). This difference between Hippolytus and Eusebius shows that the resurrection interpretation of the Passover represents a later development which discredits Eusebius' attempt to make the Passover, already in Victor's time, the universal festival of the resurrection.

[99] Origen, *Homelies Paschales* II, ed., P. Nautin, *Sources Chrétiennes* 36, p. 35 n. 1.

[100] Eusebius, *Ecclesiastical History* 5, 24, 1 and 11; cf. 5, 23, 1.

101 Ibid., 5, 23, 1 and 5, 25, 1.

102 Both Polycrates (5, 24, 3) and Irenaeus (5, 24, 16) explicitly trace back the Quartodeciman Passover to "John the disciple of the Lord."

103 Marcel Richard makes the same observation when he points out that "if Eusebius had found in that letter [of the Palestinian synod] a clear affirmation of the apostolic origin of the Easter-Sunday celebration, he would not have missed the chance to mention it" (n. 51, p. 210).

104 Eusebius, *Ecclesiastical History*, 5, 24, 14.

105 Kenneth A. Strand rejects this conclusion, because, he argues, Irenaeus' list of Roman bishops serves to illustrate "peaceful relationship, not the origin of practices" ("Bacchiocchi on Sabbath and Sunday," *Andrews University Seminary Studies* 17 [1979]: 92). Strand's assessment is hardly accurate, since Irenaeus discusses cordial relationship in the context of the origin of divergent practices: "This variety in its observance has not *originated* in our time; but long before in that of our ancestors" (Eusebius, *Eccl. Hist.* 5, 24, 13; emphasis supplied). Then Irenaeus gives the name of some of the "ancestors" (back to Sixtus) who lived peaceably in spite of divergent practices. Thus "origin of practices" and "peaceful relationship" are not at all divorced in Irenaeus' letter.

106 Henry Leclercq, "Pâques," in *Dictionnaire D'Archéologie Chrétienne et de Liturgie*, 1938, XIII, p. 1524.

107 Karl Baus, *From the Apostolic Community to Constantine*, Handbook of Church History, 1965, I, p. 270. The same view is expressed by B. Lohse, *Das Passafest der Quartadecimaner*, 1953, p. 117.

108 J. Jeremias, "Pascha," *Theological Dictionary of the New Testament*, 1973, V, p. 903, n. 66. A similar view is expressed by Millard Scherich, "Paschal Controversies," *The New International Dictionary of the Christian Church*, 1974, p. 750.

109 Epiphanius, *Adversus haereses* 70, 10 *PG* 42, 355-356. The Bishop makes specific reference to the fifteen Judeo-Christian bishops who until A.D. 135 practiced the Quartodeciman Passover, since they based themselves on a document known as the *Apostolic Constitution* where the following rule is given: "you shall not change the calculation of time, but you shall celebrate it at the same time as your brethren who came out from the circumcision. With them observe the Passover" (ibid., *PG* 42, 357-358). A similar injunction is found in the *Didascalia Apostolorum* 21, 17. For a discussion of Epiphanius' text see *From Sabbath to Sunday*, pp. 161-162 and *Anti-Judaism and the Origin of Sunday*, pp. 45-52.

110 The expression "Roman Easter" is frequently used as a designation for Easter-Sunday by C. S. Mosna (n. 40), pp. 117, 119, 333; cf. also Mario Righetti, *L'Anno liturgico, manuale di storia liturgica*, 1969, II, pp. 245-246.

111 The conciliar decree of the Council of Nicaea specifically enjoins: "All the brethren in the East who formerly celebrated Easter with the Jews, will henceforth keep it at the same time as the Romans . . ." (Socrates, *Ecclesiastical History* 1, 9). Constantine, in his personal letter, exhorts all bishops to embrace "the practice which is observed at once in the city of Rome, in Africa, in all Italy, Egypt . . ." (Eusebius, *Life of Constantine* 3, 19). The *Chronicon Paschale* similarly reports that Constantine urged all Christians to follow the custom of "the ancient church of Rome and Alexandria" (*PG* 92, 83).

112 J. Jeremias (n. 108), p. 903, n. 64.

113 J. B. Lightfoot, *The Apostolic Fathers*, 1885, II, part 1, p. 88.

114 Kenneth A. Strand (n. 105), p. 93. Strand's position is that Easter-Sunday stemmed from the sectarian solar calendar used by Qumranites

and similar groups, where the annual omer day and the day of Pentecost always fell on Sunday (n. 93, pp. 34-40; n. 105, p. 95). Thus both the Quartodeciman and the Easter-Sunday practice would reach back to apostolic time, having risen contemporaneously as a result of differences existing in Jewish modes of reckoning. This hypothesis was proposed over twenty years ago by J. van Goudoever (*Biblical Calendars*, 1959, pp. 161-162, 19-20), but it has been practically ignored in recent studies dealing with the influence of Qumran on early Christianity. The reason is that while right after the Dead Sea Scrolls discoveries, the tendency was to make early Christianity dependent upon Qumran's religious ideologies and practices, today after three decades of mature reflection, scholars generally agree that the differences between primitive Christianity and Qumran are more impressive than the apparent similarities. William S. LaSor, for example, concludes his twenty years' investigation of the Scrolls saying: "It seems reasonable to conclude that the two movements [Qumran and Christianity] were independent beyond the initial origin in Judaism. . . . The differences are such that they seem to require independent development of the two movements" (*The Dead Sea Scrolls and the New Testament*, 1972, p. 254. See also pp. 201-205 where LaSor presents cogent reasons which discredit the suggestion that the Synoptics used the Qumran calendar). There are no indications of the use of a sectarian solar calendar in the book of Acts, where the Jerusalem Church is presented as following closely the normative calendar of the temple (see *From Sabbath to Sunday*, pp. 142-150). As far as later Christianity is concerned, in all the documents discussing the Passover question, I have not found a single passing reference to the solar calendar of Qumran ("jubilees calendar") being mentioned to justify the Sunday celebration of the Passover or the method used for such a calendrical calculation. J. van Goudover (*Biblical Calendars*, 1959, pp. 161-162) argues for the possible influence of the old calendar of Enoch and Jubilees upon early Christians by referring to Anatolius (d. 282), Bishop of Laodicea. In his *Paschal Canons*, Anatolius insists that "it is altogether necessary to keep the passover and the feast of unleavened bread after the equinox" because this has been taught by such Jewish authorities as Philo, Josephus, Aristobulus and by "the teaching of the Book of Enoch" (cited by Eusebius, *Eccl. Hist.* 7, 32, 16-19). This reference however has no probative value for Easter-Sunday because Anatolius is mentioning the Book of Enoch not to defend Easter-Sunday but the celebration of the Quartodeciman Passover after the vernal equinox. Moreover the Bishop views the post-equinox Passover celebration not as a peculiarity of sectarian Judaism but as the general practice of all "the Jews of old." To prove it, Anatolius mentions a number of Jewish authorities, all of whom, with the exception of the Book of Enoch, do not represent sectarian Judaism. Thus the hypothesis of a Jewish sectarian solar calendar influence on the origin of Easter-Sunday (and presumably of weekly Sunday) represents a gratuitous speculation devoid of any historical support.

[115] Justin Martyr, *Dialogue with Trypho* 47, *ANF* I, 218.

[116] Translation by Gerald F. Hawthorne (n. 48), pp. 171-172.

[117] A. T. Kraabel, "Melito the Bishop and the Synagogue at Sardis: Text and Context," in *Studies Presented to George M. A. Hanfmann*, 1971, p. 81.

[118] *Didascalia Apostolorum* 14, 19, trans. H. Connolly, 1929, pp. 184 and 190.

[119] Epiphanius, for example, writes: "when they [i.e., the Jews] feast, we should mourn for them with fasting, because in that feast they

fastened Christ on the Cross" (*Adversus haereses* 70, 11, *PG* 42, 359-360);
cf. *Apostolic Constitutions* 5, 18. In a *Paschal Homily* delivered in A.D.
387, the author explains the origin of various divergent Passover practices.
Speaking of the Montanists (originated about 170) he says that "they are
careful to dissociate themselves from the practice of the Jews" by celebrating Passover on the Sunday following the 14th day of the month. Nevertheless, the author notes, the Montanists are mistaken in determining
their Easter-Sunday because they reckon the latter from the 14th day of
the solar rather than of the lunar month (*Homelies Paschales* III: *Une
homélie anatolienne sur la date de Pâques en l'an 387*, eds. F. Floeri and
P. Nautin, Source Chrétienne 48, 1957, p. 118). In the same document the
author explains that Christians by celebrating Passover on the Friday-
Sabbath-Sunday after the 14th, "reject the sillness of the Jews and at
the same time the folly of the heretics" (ibid., p. 162). The anti-Judaic
motivation for the Easter-Sunday dating could hardly have been expressed
more emphatically.

120 It is noteworthy that Irenaeus specifies that "the controversy is
not only concerning the day but also concerning the very manner of the
fast" (Eusebius, *Eccl. hist.* 5, 24, 12). This text as well as other documents
make no mention of an *initial* theological controversy over the actual
significance attributed to the Passover. This fact discredits the popular
contention that the Quartodecimans celebrated Christ's *passion* while the
Easter-Sunday observers emphasized His *resurrection* (cf. Henri Leclercq
[n. 105], p. 1524; Charles Joseph Hefele, *A History of the Christian
Councils*, 1883, I, pp. 300-302). On the *passion* significance of the Passover
see above notes 46 to 52 and 97, 98.

121 *Chronicon Paschale*, *PG* 92, 79D. According to Apollinaris, the
radical Quartodecimans appealed to Matthew's chronology of the passion-
week ("they pretend that Matthew teaches it") to defend their dating
and their manner of observing Passover. A fragment of Melito's treatise
On the Passover, reported by Eusebius, confirms the existence of such
a controversy: "While Servilius Paulus was proconsul of Asia, at the time
when Sagaris suffered martyrdom, there arose in Laodicea a great strife
concerning the Passover" (Eusebius, *Eccl. Hist.* 4, 26, 3).

122 Apollinaris belonged to the latter group ("orthodox" Quartodecimans). He refutes those who ate the paschal lamb at the same time
and manner as the Jews, saying: "The 14th of Nisan is the true Passover
of the Lord, the great Sacrifice; instead of the lamb we have the Son of
God" (*Chronicon Paschale* 92, 82). The two Quartodeciman groups dif-
fered not only on the dating of Christ's passion (14th versus 15th of
Nisan) but also on their attitude toward the Jewish Passover. Apollinaris,
who wrote two books *Against the Jews* (Eusebius, *Eccl. Hist.* 4, 27, 1)
insisted on dissociating from the Jewish paschal banquet. Like Melito
and Polycrates, Apollinaris was a Johannine Quartodeciman who held
that Christ on the last year of His life did not eat but suffered as Passover
on Nisan 14th. Thus the Jewish paschal feast was abolished by the
death of Christ which took place on the day of the Passover (John 19:14).
Christians were therefore urged to fast on the 14th to commemorate
the death of Christ and the crime committed by the Jews ("When they
[the Jews] feast, we should mourn for them with fasting"—Epiphanius,
n. 119). The fast was broken at dawn of Nisan 15th with the celebration of the Lord's Supper. For a concise treatment of the controversy
among Quartodecimans, see Charles Joseph Hefele (n. 120), pp. 301-313.

123 Clement of Alexandria wrote a *Treatise on the Passover* to refute
radical Quartodecimans. A fragment, which has been preserved, is quoted

above, n. 52. Hippolytus attacked the same group in Rome. In a preserved fragment of his treatise *Against all Heresies*, he writes: "The controversy still lasts, for some erroneously maintain that Christ ate the Passover before His death and *that consequently we ought to do so also.* But, at the time when Christ suffered, He did not eat the legal Passover, for He was Himself the Passover that had been previously announced and that was on that day fulfilled in Him" (*Chronicon Paschale PG* 92, 79).

[124] See Eusebius, *Ecclesiastical History* 5, 15, 1.

[125] Tertullian, *De Praescriptione, CSEL* 27, p. 225.

[126] Wide acceptance of the Roman Easter does not mean, as held by Kenneth A. Strand, that the Quartodeciman practice was "utterly restricted to Asia or Asian Christians" (n. 93, p. 36). In addition to the many reasons already given in *From Sabbath to Sunday*, p. 198, n. 97, it should be pointed out that Eusebius' restriction of the Quartodeciman practice to "the dioceses of Asia" (*Eccl. Hist.* 5, 23, 1) is discredited by the following facts: (1) Eusebius himself reports that Victor attempted to excommunicate "the parishes of all Asia and *the neighboring (paroikias) provinces*" (ibid., 5, 24, 1). The last statement clearly implies that the Quartodeciman practice extended beyond *Asia Proconsularis.* (2) The testimonies of Hippolytus of Rome and of Clement of Alexandria (see above n. 123) indicate, as noted by Henri Leclercq, that "the Asiatics were not isolated and their practice is found very far from the borders of Asia Minor" (n. 106, p. 1527). (3) Firmilian, bishop of Caesarea in Cappadocia, in his letter to Cyprian (dated 256) speaks of "diversities" among Roman Christians "concerning the celebration of Easter" (*The Epistles of Cyprian* 74, 6, *ANF* V, 391). This suggests, as pointed out by James F. McCue, "that the uniformity which had been sought by Victor sixty years earlier had not been achieved and that it was still somewhat bitterly resisted" ("The Roman Primacy in the Patristic Era," in *Papal Primacy and the Universal Church*, 1974, p. 67). Consequently Eusebius' statement that all bishops consulted by Victor expressed a "unanimous decision" (*Eccl. Hist.* 5, 23, 3) against the Quartodeciman practice cannot be taken at face value but rather as an extravagant and exaggerated assessment. This is further indicated not only by the "*lengthy discussion*" that preceded the decision but also by the admonition to send copies of the conciliar letter to "every church" (*Eccl. Hist.* 5, 25, 1). Such an effort was hardly necessary if Quartodecimans were restricted to the province of Asia.

[127] See above n. 123.

[128] Several liturgical practices were introduced to honor the resurrection. Cyprian (died 258), for example, explains that though Christ partook of the Lord's Supper in the evening, "we celebrate it in the morning on account of the resurrection of the Lord" (*Epistola* 63, 15 *CSEL* 3, 2, 714). For the same reason Tertullian (died 225) regards as "unlawful . . . fasting and kneeling in worship on the Lord's day" (*De corona* 3, 4, *ANF* III, p. 94). See also above n. 54.

[129] For a brief survey of "Christian" literature produced at that time to defame the Jews, see *From Sabbath to Sunday*, pp. 179-184.

[130] The earliest Roman computation that has come down to us is by Hippolytus. His treatise *On Easter* which explains the system has not survived, but his table listing the Easter full-moons, calculated for the years 222 to 333, is still visible (in the Vatican Museum) on the left side of the marble throne and statue of Hippolytus which was found in 1551.

[131] Pseudo-Cyprian, *De Pascha computus*, trans. G. Ogg, 1955, p. 1.

[132] Eusebius, *Life of Constantine* 3, 18-19 *NPNF* 2nd, I, pp. 524-525.

[133] The question is examined at greater length in *From Sabbath to Sunday*, pp. 207-211.

[134] On the significant difference between Ignatius' praise for the Church of Rome and his commendation for the other churches, see the comparative analysis done by Jean Colson, *L'Épiscopat Catholique*, 1963, pp. 43-47.

[135] Ignatius, *To the Romans*, prologue, trans. James A. Kleist, *Ancient Christian Writers*, 1946, p. 80.

[136] See, for example, *To the Philadelphians* 11, 2; *To the Smyrnaeans* 12, 1; *To the Romans* 9, 3.

[137] An example of the concern of the Church of Rome for the welfare of other churches is provided by Clement's letter to the Corinthians. Another example is the letter of Dionysius of Corinth to Bishop Soter of Rome (about 180) which says: "For from the beginning it has been your practice to do good to all the brethren in various ways and to send contributions to the many churches in every city. Thus relieving the want of the needy . . . encouraging the brethren from abroad with blessed words, as a loving father his children" (Eusebius, *Eccl. Hist.* 4, 23, 10).

[138] The Pseudo-Isidorian Decretals offer an example of (interpolated) legal documents used to defend papal supremacy.

[139] The leadership role of the Church of Rome is also indicated by Ignatius' remark: "You have never envied any one; you have taught others. What I desire is that what you counsel and ordain may always be practiced" (*To the Romans* 3, 1). Kenneth A. Strand's argument that Ignatius *"does not so much as greet or even mention a bishop of Rome"* (n. 105, p. 96) fails to recognize that the lack of any reference to a single bishop may show that initially the prestige and influence of the Roman Church was dependent not upon exceptionally gifted leaders but rather upon other factors such as her geographical-political location, the cosmopolitan representation of her membership, her concern for other churches and her association with the ministry and martyrdom of Peter and Paul (cf. Ignatius, *To the Romans* 4, 3; Clement, *To the Corinthians* 5, 4-5).

[140] Irenaeus, *Against Heresies* 3, 3, 1 ANF I, p. 415. Kenneth A. Strand argues on the basis of a different rendering of Irenaeus' text (suggested by the translators of *ANF* in their comments to the text—*ANF* I, p. 461) that for Irenaeus the "preeminent authority" of the Church of Rome rests not on the authority of her bishop but rather upon the cosmopolitan representation within her church ("the faithful from all parts, representing every Church, are obliged to resort to Rome"—*ANF* I, p. 461; cf. Strand n. 105, p. 98). Strand's argument deserves consideration because it suggests, as noted by George La Piana, that "the many problems which concerned so many churches were at the same time problems of the Roman community" since so many various groups were represented in Rome ("The Roman Church at the End of the Second Century," *Harvard Theological Review* 18 [1925]: 252). On account of this fact, La Piana rightly states: "It is not an exaggeration to say that the Church of Rome became very early the great laboratory of Christian and ecclesiastical polity" (ibid., p. 203). This valid observation, however, does not minimize but rather maximizes the authority of the Church of Rome by pointing to a significant contributary factor, namely, her wide ethnic cosmopolitan representation which fostered her "preeminent authority."

[141] Eusebius, *Ecclesiastical History* 5, 23, 8.

[142] Kenneth A. Strand (n. 105), p. 97.

[143] Eusebius, *Ecclesiastical History* 5, 23, 7. James F. McCue rightly points out that "from the defensive and at points defiant tone of Poly-

crates' response, it is reasonable to infer that he is aware of a certain pressure to conform to the Roman custom. . . . we clearly have to do, in the Roman request-demand for an account of the Asian custom, with a noteworthy instance of far-reaching Roman activity" (n. 126, p. 67).

144 Eusebius, *Ecclesiastical History*, 5, 23, 9. The fact that Victor may not have carried out his excommunication on account of Irenaeus' intervention does not detract from the bishop's consciousness of his authority to separate the Asian Christians from the communion of the rest of the churches, if necessary. It is noteworthy that Irenaeus does not challenge Victor's right to excommunicate but "exhorts him respectfully and with great consideration—*prosekontos*" (trans. by Giuseppe del Ton, *Eusebio di Cesarea. Storia Ecclesiastica*, 1964, p. 414).

145 Jean Colson (n. 134), p. 50.

146 George La Piana (n. 140), p. 235.

147 Ibid., p. 204. The Roman Catholic Church's effort to assert her supremacy by imposing her liturgical practices continued for centuries. As examples could be cited her promotion of the Christmas date of December 25 in the fourth century and of the Roman Easter (in England—seventh century) and Sabbath fasting in later centuries (see *From Sabbath to Sunday*, p. 194, n. 84, and pp. 257-260).

148 Ibid., p. 252.

149 Additional indications are provided in *From Sabbath to Sunday*, pp. 207-211. It is significant to note that in his *Prescription Against Heretics* 36 (written about 200 before becoming a Montanist) Tertullian refutes the heretics by appealing to "Rome, from which there comes even into our own hands the very authority (of apostles themselves). How happy is its church, on which apostles poured forth all their doctrine along with their blood! where Peter endures a passion like his Lord's! where Paul wins his crown in a death like John's!" (*ANF* III, p. 260). On becoming a Montanist, however, Tertullian radically changed his attitude toward the Roman Church. In his treatise *On Modesty* 1, written after 208, Tertullian ridicules the claim of the Roman Bishop (possibly Victor—*ANF* IV, p. 74, n. 7) to have power to remit grievous sins, saying: "*The Pontifex Maximus*—that is, the bishop of bishops—issues an edict: 'I remit, to such as have discharged (the requirements of) repentance, the sins both of adultery and of fornication.' O edict, on which cannot be inscribed 'Good deed!'" (*ANF* IV, p. 74; cf. also *On Modesty* 21). Tertullian's sarcastic challenge of the names and claims of the Roman Bishop (possibly Victor himself) only serves to substantiate the unusual authority asserted by the Bishop of Rome by the end of the second century.

150 Gaston H. Halsberghe, *The Cult of Sol Invictus*, 1972, p. 44. Marcel Simon notes that recent archeological discoveries have shown that the geographical distribution of Mithraism was greater than previously thought ("Mithra, Rival du Christ?" in *Acta Iranica 17. Actes du 2e Congrès International Téhéran, du 1er au 8 septembre 1975*, [Leiden: E. J. Brill, 1978], pp. 459-460).

151 *Fasti of Philocalus, Corpus Inscriptionum Latinorum* I:2, 324, 4192. For texts and discussion see *From Sabbath to Sunday*, pp. 239-241.

152 The differentiation between the two cults is persuasively demonstrated by Gaston H. Halsberghe (n. 150), p. 35.

153 Tertullian, *The Shows* 8, *ANF* III, p. 83. Tacitus confirms the existence of the temple in the Circus dedicated to the Sun in his *Annales* 15, 74, 1.

154 See Harold Mattingly, *The Roman Imperial Coinage* 1962, II, p. 360, plate XII, n. 244.

[155] Elius Spartianus, *Hadrianus* 19.

[156] This factor is noted especially by Franz Cumont, *The Mysteries of Mithra*, 1956, p. 101.

[157] Marcel Simon (n. 150), pp. 466-477.

[158] M. J. Vermaseren, *Corpus Inscriptionum et Monumentorum Religionis Mithriacae*, 1956, I, p. 190, n. 463.

[159] F. Cumont, *Les Religions orientales dans le Paganism romain*, 1929, p. 79, illust. 5 and p. 236, n. 37.

[160] See above n. 158. For epigraphic texts of the first century B.C., identifying Mithras with Mercury or with Apollo and Helios, see R. Turcan, *Les Religions de l'Asie dans la vallée du Rhone*, 1972, pp. 34f. Also by the same author, *Mithras Platonicus*, 1975, p. 19. Additional texts are given by Vivien J. Walters, who writes: "The classic example comes from Merida, a marble statue of a naked Mercury, sitting on a large boulder, with an inscription dated by the year of the *colonia* to A.D. 155 and dedicated to Mithras" (*The Cult of Mithras in the Roman Provinces of Gaul*, 1974, p. 118).

[161] "Obviously," writes Marcel Simon, "in a sanctuary dedicated to Mithras, his name being last, indicates his privileged position and the adjectives which precede his name are related precisely to him" (n. 150, p. 469).

[162] Ibid. In his *Saturnales* I, 17-23, Macrobius (about 400) endeavors to demonstrate that all the gods are a manifestation of the Sun-god—*ad solemn referunt*.

[163] See, for example, the mural inscriptions and pictures of the seven planetary gods which have been uncovered in Pompeii and Herculaneum. These and other indications are discussed in *From Sabbath to Sunday*, pp. 241-247.

[164] This change did not affect the sequence of the days of the week but only their numbering. Moreover the change did not affect the week of the Jews for whom the Sabbath (Saturday for the Romans) had always been the seventh day.

[165] Vettius Valens, *Anthologiarum* 5, 10, ed. G. Kroll, p. 26. See the informative study by Robert L. Odom, "Vettius Valens and the Planetary Week," *Andrews University Seminary Studies* 3 (1965): 110-137.

[166] This information has been graciously supplied to me by Willy Rordorf, who examines the significance of the planetary gods appearing on the Wettingen's goblet, in a paper presented at an International Congress on Mithraism in 1978. The title of the paper is "Le christianisme et la semaine planétaire: à propos d'un gobelet trouvé à Wettingen en Suisse."

[167] For texts and discussion see *From Sabbath to Sunday*, pp. 247-251. Kenneth A. Strand objects to the influence of the pagan day of the Sun on the Christian adoption of Sunday for two reasons. First, because Mithraism, "one cult that did show honor to Sunday" was mainly "a soldier's religion" and thus had a limited influence on Christianity (n. 105, p. 90). Second, Strand maintains that Christians who were willing to sacrifice their lives rather than adopt pagan practices would hardly have been influenced by the pagan day of the sun in choosing their new day of worship (ibid.). Strand's arguments ignore several significant facts. First, recent studies have shown that Mithraism was more widespread and influential than earlier thought (see, for example, the two volumes [*Corpus*] by M. J. Vermaseren [n. 158] which list the many Mithraic inscriptions and monuments according to the respective Roman provinces where they have been found. Note that all the provinces are well

represented. Cf. n. 150 and Vivien J. Walters, n. 160, pp. 1-49). Second, the advancement of the day of the Sun from second to first day of the week was influenced not merely by Mithraism but rather by the syncretistic solar-worship of which Mithraism was a component (see notes 157 to 162). In his apology *To the Pagans* (written in 197), Tertullian replies to the taunt that Christians were Sun-worshipers by underscoring: "It is you [pagans], at all events, who have admitted the sun into the calendar of the week; and you have selected its day [Sunday] in preference of the preceding day [Saturday] as the most suitable in the week for either an entire abstinence from bath . . . or for taking rest and for banqueting" (1, 13, *ANF* III, p. 123). Note that Tertullian attributes to the pagans in general (and not specifically to the Mithraists) the responsibility for the advancement and preference of the day of the Sun over that of Saturn. Third, while it is true that Christians "were ready to give up life itself rather than adopt known pagan practices" (Strand, n. 105, p. 90), yet as Jacquetta Hawkes well puts it: "with the malicious irony so often apparent in history, even while they fought heroically on one front, their position was infiltrated from another" (*Man and the Sun*, 1967, p. 199). Tertullian, for example, strongly refutes the pagan charge that Christians were Sun-worshipers (*Apology* 16, 1; *To the Pagans* 1, 13, 1-5), yet at the same time he chides the Christians at length for celebrating pagan festivals within their own communities (*On Idolatry* 14). On the influence of Sun-worship on Christian art, on literature, on the eastward orientation for prayer and on the adoption of the date of Christmas, see *From Sabbath to Sunday*, pp. 253-261.

[168] A concise survey of the influence of astrological beliefs on early Christianity is provided by Jack Lindsay, *Origin of Astrology*, 1972, pp. 373-400. For references and discussion on the influence of Sun-cults on Christian art and liturgy, see *From Sabbath to Sunday*, pp. 253-261.

[169] Justin Martyr, *I Apology* 67.

[170] Eusebius, *Commentaria in Psalmos* 91 *PG* 23, 1169-1172 (emphasis supplied). Similarly in his *Life of Constantine*, Eusebius states that "the Savior's day . . . derives its name from light and from the sun" (4, 18, *NPNF* 2nd, I, p. 544).

[171] Maximus of Turin (about 400-423) views the designation of the "day of the Sun" as a proleptic announcement of the resurrection of Christ: "We hold the day of the Lord to be venerable and solemn, because on it the Savior, like the rising sun, conquered the darkness of the underworld and gleamed in the glory of the resurrection. This is why the same day was called day of the sun by the pagans, because the Sun of Justice once risen would have illuminated it" (*Homilia* 61, *PL* 57, 371). Gaudentius, Bishop of Brescia (about 400), (*Sermo* 9, *De evangelica lectione* 2, *PL* 20, 916 and *De Exodo Sermo* 1, *PL* 20, 845), explains that the Lord's day became first in relationship to the Sabbath, because on that day the Sun of righteousness has appeared, dispelling the darkness of the Jews, melting the ice of the pagans and restoring the world to its primordial order; cf. Hilary of *Poitiers, Tractatus in Psalmos* 67, 6, *CSEL* 27, 280; Athanasius, *Expositio in Psalmos* 67, 34, *PG* 27, 303; Ambrose, *Hexaemeron* 4, 2, 7; and *Epistula* 44, *PL* 16, 1138.

[172] Jerome, *In die dominica Paschae homilia CCL* 78, 550, 1, 52 (emphasis supplied). The same explanation is given by Augustine, in *Contra Faustum* 18, 5 and in *Sermo* 226, *PL* 38, 1099.

SELECTED BIBLIOGRAPHY

Andreasen, M. L., *The Sabbath: Which Day and Why?* Washington D.C., 1942.

Andreasen, N. E., *The Christian Use of Time.* Nashville, 1978.

—, *The Old Testament Sabbath.* Society of Biblical Literature Dissertation Series, 7. Missoula, Montana, 1972.

—, "Festival and Freedom: A Study of an Old Testament Theme," *Interpretation* 28 (1974): 281-297.

—, *Rest and Redemption.* Berrien Springs, Michigan, 1978.

Andrews, J. N., *History of the Sabbath and First Day of the Week.* Washington D.C., 1912.

Augsburger, D., "Sunday in the Pre-Reformations Disputations in French Switzerland," *Andrews University Seminary Studies* 14 (1976): 265-278.

Bacchiocchi, S., *Anti-Judaism and the Origin of Sunday.* Fifth chapter of Italian dissertation. Rome, 1975.

—, *From Sabbath to Sunday: A Historical Investigation of the Rise of Sunday Observance in Early Christianity.* Rome, 1977.

—, *Rest for Modern Man.* Nashville, 1966.

—, "Rome and the Origin of Sunday," *Encounter* 40 (1979): 359-375.

—, "How it Came About. From Saturday to Sunday," *Biblical Archeological Review* IV, 3 (1978): 32-40.

Barack, Nathan A., *A History of the Sabbath.* New York, 1965.

Barclay, W., *The Ten Commandments for Today.* New York, 1973.

Barry, A., *The Chistian Sunday.* London, 1905.

Barth, K., *Church Dogmatics* III, 1 and III, 4. Edinburgh 1958 and 1961.

Beare, F. W., "The Sabbath Was Made for Man?" *Journal of Biblical Literature* 79 (1960): 130-136.

Beckwith, Roger T. and Stott W., *This is the Day: The Biblical Doctrine of the Christian Sunday.* London, 1978.

Bettinger, J. Q., *A Plea for the Sabbath and for Man.* Chicago, 1892.

Berman, S. J., "The Extended Notion of the Sabbath," *Judaism* 22 (1973): 342-353.

Branson, R. and Scriven, Ch., eds., *Festival of the Sabbath.* Spectrum 9 (1977). Contributions by N. E. Andreasen, S. Bacchiocchi, R. Branson, F. Guy, S. Kubo, G. Winslow, et al.

Brown, J., "Karl Barth's Doctrine of the Sabbath," *Scottish Journal of Theology* 19 (1966): 409-425.

Buchanam, G. W., "Sabbatical Eschatology," *Christian News From Israel* 18 (Dec. 1967): 49-55.

Budde, K., "The Sabbath and the Week: Their Origin and their Nature," *Journal of Theological Studies* 30 (1929): 1-15.

Cadet, J., "Repos dominical et loisir humain," *La Maison-Dieu* 83 (1965): 71-97.

Colson, F. H., *The Week.* Cambridg, 1926.

Cotton, P., *From Sabbath to Sunday.* Bethlehem, Pa., 1933.

Cox, H., *Turning East.* New York, 1977.

Cox, R., *The Literature of the Sabbath Question.* 2 vols. Edinburgh, 1865.

Crafts, W. F., *The Sabbath for Man*. New York, 1885.

Cullmann, O., *Early Christian Worship*. London, 1966.

—, "Sabbath und Sonntag nach dem Johannesevangelium," in W. Schmauch, ed., *In Memoriam E. Lohmeyer*. Stuttgart, 1951, pp. 127-131.

Daniélou, J., *The Bible and Liturgy*. South Bend, Indiana, 1965.

Dix, G., *The Shape of Liturgy*. London, 1945.

Domville, W., *The Sabbath*. London, 1855.

Dresner, S. H., *The Sabbath*. New York, 1970.

Dubarle, A. M., "La signification religieuse du sabbat dans la Bible," in *Le Dimanche, Lex Orandi 39*. Paris, 1965, pp. 43-59.

Duchesne, L., *Origines du culte chrétien*. Paris, 1920.

Dugmore, C. W., *The Influence of the Synagogue upon the Divine Office*. London, 1944.

Dumaine, H., "Dimanche," in *Dictionnaire d'archéologie chrétienne et de liturgie*. Paris, 1921, IV: 858, 994.

Elliott, G., *The Abiding Sabbath: An Argument for the Perpetual Obligation of the Lord's Day*. New York, 1884.

Féret, H. M., "Le source bibliques," in *Le jour de Seigneur*. Congress National de Pastorale Liturgique, Lyon 1947. Paris, 1948, pp. 39-104.

Friedman, T., "The Sabbath: Anticipation of Redemption," *Judaism* 16 (1967): 443-457.

Froger, J., "Histoire du dimanche," in *Vie Spirituelle* 76 (1947): 502-522.

Gaillard, J., "Le dimanche, jour sacré," in *Vie Spirituelle* 76 (1947): 520ff.

Gaster, Th. H., "Le jour de repos," *Evidences* 43 (1954): 43-48.

Goldman, S., *The Ten Commandments*. Chicago, 1956.

Goudoever, J. van., *Biblical Calendars*. Leiden, 1959.

Grunfeld, D. I., *The Sabbath: A Guide to its Understanding and Observance*. New York, 1972.

Grelot, P., "Du sabbat juif au dimanche chrétien," *La Maison Dieu* 123, 124 (1975): 79-107 and 14-54.

Guy, F., *Holiness in Time: A Preliminary Study of the Sabbath as Spiritual Experience*. Unpublished thesis, Andrews University, 1961.

Hahn, F., *The Worship of the Early Church*. Philadelphia, 1973.

Hallo, W. W., "New Moons and Sabbaths: A Case-study in Contrastive Approach," *Hebrew Union College Annual*, 48 (1977): 15ff.

Heschel, A. J., *The Sabbath, Its Meaning for Modern Man*. New York, 1951.

Hessey, J. A., *Sunday, Its Origin, History and Present Obligation*. London, 1860.

Hodgkins, W., *Sunday: Christian and Social Significance*. London, 1960.

Horn, S. H., "Was the Sabbath Known in Ancient Babylonia? Archeology and the Sabbath," *The Sabbath Sentinel* (Dec. 1979): 20-22.

Hruby, K., "La célébration du sabbat d'après les sources juives," *Orient Syrien* 7 (1962): 435-463; continuation in *Orient Syrien* 8 (1963): 55-79.

Jay, B., "Jésus et le sabbat," *Etudes Théologiques et Religieuses* 50 (1975): 65-68.

Jenni, D., *Die theologische Begründung des Sabbatgebotes im Alten Testament*. Zurich, 1956.

Jervell, J., *Luke and the People of God*. Minneapolis, 1972.

Jewett, P. K., *The Lord's Day: A Theological Guide to the Christian Day of Worship*. Grand Rapids, 1971.

Jones J. R., *A Theological Study of the Sabbath in Relation to the New Testament Understanding of Redemptive History*. Unpublished thesis, Andrews University, 1965.

Johnston, R., "Patriarchs, Rabbis, and the Sabbath," *Andrews University Seminary Studies* 12 (1974): 94-102.

Jungmann, J. A., *The Early Liturgy: To the Time of Gregory the Great.* South Bend, Indiana, 1962.

Kimbrough Jr. S. ., "The Concept of the Sabbath at Qumran," *Revue de Qumran* 5 (1966): 483-502.

Kiesling, C., *The Future of the Christian Sunday.* New York, 1970.

Kraeling, E. G., "The Present Status of the Sabbath Question," *American Journal of Semitic Languages and Literatures* 49 (1932-33): 218-228.

Kubo, S., *God Meets Man: A Theology of the Sabbath and the Second Advent.* Nashville, 1978.

Langdon, S., *Babylonian Menologies and the Semitic Calendars.* London, 1935.

Lauterbach, J. Z., *Rabbinical Essays.* Cincinnati, 1951.

Lee, F. N., *The Covenantal Sabbath.* London, 1969.

Leitch, J. W., "Lord also of the Sabbath," *Scottish Journal of Theology* 19 (1966): 426-433.

Levine, E., "The Sabbath Controversy According to Matthew," *New Testament Studies* 22 (1976): 480-483.

Lewis, A. H., *Spiritual Sabbatism.* Plainfield, New Jersey, 1910.

Lewy, J. and H., "The Origin of the Week and the Oldest West Asiatic Calendar," *Hebrew Union College Annual* 17 (1942-43): 1-152.

Lohse, E., "Sabbaton" in *Theological Dictionary of the New Testament,* ed. G. Kittel, vol. 7, Grand Rapids, 1968, pp. 1-35.

Lotz, W., *Questionum de Historia Sabbati.* Leipzig, 1883.

Martin, A. G., "Notes sur le sabbat," *Foi et Vie* 74 (1975): 13-51.

Martin, R. H., *The Day: A Manual on the Christian Sabbath.* Pittsburgh, 1933.

Martin, R. P., *Worship in the Early Church.* Grand Rapids, 1974.

Massi, P., *La domenica nella storia della salvezza.* Naples, 1967.

McArthur, A. A., *The Evolution of the Christian Year.* London, 1953.

Meek, Th. J., "The Sabbath in the Old Testament: Its Origin and Development," *Journal of Biblical Literature* 33 (1914): 201-212.

Miller, P., "Luke 4:16-21," *Interpretation* 29 (Oct. 1975): 417-421.

Millgram, A. E., *The Sabbath: The Day of Delight.* Philadelphia, 1047.

Moore, G. F., *Judaism in the First Centuries of the Christian Era.* Cambridge, 1946.

Morgenstern, J., "Sabbath," *Interpreter's Dictionary of the Bible.* Ed. G. A. Buttrick, New York, 1962, vol. 2, pp. 135-141.

Morey, R. A., "Is Sunday the Christian Sabbath?," *Baptist Reformation Review* 8 (1979): 3-19.

Mosna, S. C., *Storia della domenica dalle origini fino agli inizi del v secolo.* Rome, 1969.

Moule, C. F. D., *Worship in the New Testament.* London, 1961.

Muller, R., *Adventisten - Sabbat - Reformation.* Lund, 1979.

Murray, J., *Principles of Conduct,* London, 1957.

Negretti, N., *Il settimo giorno: Indagine critico-teologica delle tradizioni presacerdotali e sacerdotali circa il sabato biblico.* Analecta Biblica 55. Rome, 1973.

Nielsen, E., *The Ten Commandments in New Perspective.* London, 1968.

North, R., "The Derivation of the Sabbath," *Biblica* 36 (1955): 182-201.

Olsen, V. N., "Theological Aspects of the Seventh-day Sabbath," *Spectrum* 4 (1972): 5-18.

Petterisch, F. X., "A Theology of Sunday Rest," *Theology Digest* 6 (1958): 91-94.

Pinches, T. G., "Sappatu, the Babylonian Sabbath," *Proceedings of the Society of Biblical Archeology* 26 (1904): 51-56.

Quervain, A. de, *Die Heiligung: Ethik*. Zurich, 1946.

Rad, G. von, "There Remains Still a Rest for the People of God: An Investigation of a Biblical Conception," in *The Problem of the Hexateuch and Other Essays*. Trans. by E. W. Trueman Dickens. New York, 1966, pp. 94-102.

Richardson, A. W., *Toward an American Theology*. New York, 1967.

Riesenfeld, H., "The Sabbath and the Lord's Day," in *The Gospel Tradition*. Oxford, 1970, pp. 111-137.

Rordorf, W., *Sunday: The History of the Day of Rest and Worship in the Earliest Centuries of the Christian Church*. Philadelphia, 1968.

Rowley, H. H., "Moses and the Decalogue," *Bulletin of the John Rylands Library* 34 (1951-1952): 81-118.

Rushdoony, J. R., *The Institutes of Biblical Law*. The Craig Press, 1973.

Sarna, N. M., "The Psalm for the Sabbath Day (Ps. 92)," *Journal of Biblical Literature* 81 (1962): 155-168.

Saunders, E. H., *The Sabbath: Symbol of Creation and Re-Creation*. Plainfield, New Jersey, 1970.

Segal, S., *The Sabbath Book*. New York, 1957.

Segre, A., "Il sabato nella storia Ebraica," in the symposium *L'uomo nella Bibbia e nelle culture ad esse contemporanee*. Rome, 1975.

Sloan, Robert B., *The Favorable Year of the Lord. A Study of Jubilary Theology in the Gospel of Luke*. Austin, Texas, 1977.

Steuart, Don B., *The Development of Christian Worship*. New York, 1953.

Solberg, W. V., *Redeem the Time: The Puritan Sabbath in Early America*. Cambridge, Massachusetts, 1977.

Strand, K. H., *Essays on the Sabbath in Early Christianity, with a Source Collection on the Sabbath Fast*. Ann Arbor, 1972.

Stamm, J. J. and Andrews, M. E., *The Ten Commandments in Recent Research*. Naperville, 1967.

Terrien, S., *The Elusive Presence*. New York, 1978.

Tsevat, M., "The Basic Meaning of the Biblical Sabbath," *Zeitschrift für die alttestamentliche Wissenschaft* 84 (1972): 447-459.

Unger, M. F., "The Significance of the Sabbath," *Bibliotheca Sacra* 123 (1966): 53-59.

Ward, Hiley H., *Space Age Sunday*. New York, 1960.

Webster, H., *Rest Days: A Study in Early Law and Morality*. New York, 1916.

Wolff, H. W., "The Day of Rest in the Old Testament," *Concordia Theological Monthly* 43 (1972): 498-506.

Yamashiro, G., *A Study of the Hebrew Word Sabbath in Biblical and Talmudic Literatures*. Unpublished thesis, Harvard University, 1955.

TABLE OF CONTENTS